THE GUINNESS RUGBY UNION FACT BOOK

Cover photographs, from top: Peter Winterbottom, Harlequins v Bath, 1992 (*Allsport*); JPR Williams (*Allsport*); Wales v Scotland, 1981 (*Bob Thomas Sports Photography*); Will Carling, England v Australia, World Cup Final 1991 (*Allsport*)

THE GUINNESS RUGBY UNION FACT BOOK

Chris Rhys

GUINNESS PUBLISHING

Published in Great Britain by Guinness Publishing Ltd, 33 London Road, Enfield, Middlesex

All illustrations courtesy of Allsport UK Ltd.

Cover design by Ad Vantage Studios
Text design and layout by Steve Leaning

Typeset by Ace Filmsetting Ltd, Frome, Somerset

Printed and bound in Great Britain by The Bath Press, Bath

'Guinness' is a registered trademark of Guinness Publishing Ltd

A catalogue record for this book is available from the British Library

ISBN 0-85112-539-5

CONTENTS

INTRODUCTION

In 1981, research for the first edition of the Guinness Book of Rugby Facts and Feats revealed that, far from the widely held official belief that rugby union was played in 'around 30 countries', the sport featured in sixth place in the list of the world's most popular sporting activities. It was confirmed that 106 countries were playing the game, with only football (146), basketball (143), athletics (140), volleyball (120) and swimming (110) having a wider playing fraternity.

Far from being a game which was the exclusive property of the British, Irish and the colonial countries with a little help from the French and their dependencies, rugby was found to be played from Andorra to Zimbabwe. Not only that, but many emerging nations had already structured their game to include innovations such as league and cup competitions long before some of their senior partners.

At the end of the first edition of the Guinness book, and as a result of discovering over 70 more countries playing the game than originally thought, the final chapter was entitled 'Anatomy of a World Cup'. The feasibility study listed the prime considerations of venues, finance, administration and participants. Issues such as sponsorship and qualifying tournaments were suggested. It was also noted that the very nature of rugby, its camaraderie and its sound values, would make it better equipped than most sports to dismantle any potential barriers.

As to how many countries are now playing the game, it is a little difficult to assess exactly, though a figure in the region of 120 would probably be accurate. There have been casualties, countries where expatriates have finished their contracts and where political obstacles have defeated even the most dedicated organisers. But there have been additions, notably Namibia, to the fold, while the situation in Eastern Europe may provide a number of separate unions.

In the years since the 1981 edition, rugby has undergone changes that no one would have envisaged. There have been two highly successful World Cup competitions, league rugby has been accepted throughout Britain and Ireland, Western Samoa – with a population of 167 000 – beat Wales at Cardiff, the USA met the Soviet Union on a rugby field, and South Africa's isolation is at an end. Standards are narrowing – Italy lost 70–6 to New Zealand in the 1987 World Cup and 31–21 four years later, Namibia beat three World Cup qualifiers, while Canada and Western Samoa reached the 1991 World Cup quarter-finals. Women's rugby had its own World Cup.

The Guinness Rugby Union Fact Book encompasses this growth and development of the game through a mix of results, statistics, milestones, anecdotes and records. Rugby football is undisputedly the world's number one growth sport . . .

LANDMARKS

While the various rugby union books from Guinness were being compiled, some doubts (none authenticated) led to queries as to whether William Webb Ellis was in fact the instigator of modern rugby; the Chinese are said to have played a form of rugby in the years BC, the Italians claim that Roman legions had played a form of football, while several mentions of football and handball were to be read in British archives. Indeed, a Mr T Harris in a speech to the Old Rugbeian Society said, 'I remember William Webb Ellis perfectly. He was an admirable cricketer, but was generally inclined to take unfair advantages at football. I should not quote him in any way as an authority . . .'

But whatever went before Ellis, it is known that he picked up the ball and ran with it. The earlier 'references' above remain unproven. It is therefore appropriate, as this chapter traces the development of the game from Rugby School throughout the world in a very short space of time,that William Webb Ellis is the first name mentioned.

'Landmarks' pinpoint some of the first happenings in rugby – a sport that has developed from barely legalised mayhem in the early days through to the almost professional, worldwide approach of today. Some of the details more relevant to each particular country will be contained in 'Milestones' sections under that country later in the book.

The aim is to include the 'firsts' – first clubs, first internationals, first rules, changes in scoring, tactical changes, and other achievements. Some dates are still disputed, and where this is so, the decision has been made to include the date supplied by the country in question.

LANDMARKS

1823 William Webb Ellis 'picked up the ball and ran with it' at Rugby School.

1839 Arthur Pell, an old boy of Rugby School, introduced the game at Cambridge University, which lays claim to be the first club.

The Dowager Queen Adelaide watched a game at Rugby School.

1842 Rugby School awarded caps for football.

1843 Guy's Hospital Rugby Club formed – the first official rugby club.

1845 Rugby School drew up its rules for football.

Laws: Goalposts became H shaped – with scoring depending on kicking the ball over the bar.

1848 Cambridge rules drawn up – it became the basis for the rules of Association Football.

1851 The first rugby ball, made by William Gilbert, an oval shaped ball inflated by a pig's bladder, was on show at the International Exhibition at London. It was called a 'Rugby School Football'.

1854 Trinity College Dublin RFC founded.

1857 Liverpool and Edinburgh Academicals RFC founded – the first open clubs.

1858 Edinburgh Academy first met Merchiston Castle in the oldest school match in the world. The fixture is still played today.

1862 Blackheath (founded 1858) drew up its own rules – throttling in scrum prohibited!

First recorded match in South Africa – Civilians v Military at Cape Town – in which A Van Der Byl, the Merchiston captain in 1858, played.

1863 First Richmond v Blackheath match, the game's longest surviving regular top class fixture.

The Football Association founded – soccer then went its own way with its own set of rules. Rugby clubs met to formulate and standardise their rules, after Blackheath withdrew from FA following the controversial outlawing of 'hacking'.

1864 Sydney University founded, the first club outside Britain and Ireland. A match played in Montreal, Canada.

1870 First match in New Zealand between Nelson FC and Nelson College on May 14.

1871 First international match at Raeburn Place, Edinburgh. Scotland beat England by a goal and a try to a goal on Monday March 27. The teams played 20 a side. On January 26, the Rugby Football Union was formed by 32 members representing 20 clubs.

Nelson RFC formed as New Zealand's first club.

Neath RFC formed as Wales' first senior club.

1872 William Webb Ellis died on January 24.

First University match – Oxford beat Cambridge.

England's first home international v Scotland at Kennington Oval, London – now the Oval cricket ground.

Calcutta and Bombay RFCs formed in India – first clubs in India.

Le Havre RFC formed in France by English students – first French club.

1873 First game in Argentina between Banks and City in Buenos Aires. First official game in Canada between Canadians and English at Toronto.

Scottish Rugby Union founded.

1874 First game in the USA – at Cambridge, Mass., between McGill University of Montreal and Harvard University.

Formation of Irish Rugby Union (for first time – without Ulster) and Southern RU in Australia (forerunner of New South Wales RU).

Laws: Captains are the sole arbiters of disputes. Winning team is decided on goals kicked, then tries.

1875 Hospitals' Cup instituted – first English Cup competition.
Hamilton Football Club (and possibly Villager FC) are first South African clubs to be founded.
Laws: Teams reduced from 20 to 15 players a side.
1876 First record of the feat of William Webb Ellis appeared in the Meteor.
Laws: Tries are recognised as part of the scoring of points.
1877 Calcutta Cup struck and awarded.
First rugby club in Paris – the English Taylors RFC.
Laws: Points scoring system amended and teams reduced to 15 players in internationals.
Tactics: HH Johnston (Scotland) became first to play as a single full-back.
1878 First 'floodlight' match by 'electricity' – Broughton v Swinton in Lancashire on October 22. Reports also of 'floodlight' games at Coltbridge, near Murrayfield.
Ceylon RFU formed.
1879 Irish Rugby Union formed again with the inclusion of Ulster.
First game played in Holland.
1880 Welsh Rugby Union formed.
Travelling expenses first paid for internationals by Rugby Football Union!
Internationals played on a Saturday.
1881 Neutral referees first allowed to be appointed for internationals.
First England v Wales match won by England by the equivalent of 69–0 on modern scoring values – England then dropped Wales from fixtures.
First game played in Uruguay between sides at Montevideo Cricket Club.
Tactics: Scotland played with three threequarters for the first time v Ireland in Belfast – passing half-backs developed.
1882 American Football – gridiron – played in USA following adoption of different rules to rugby.
First major overseas international tour – New South Wales to New Zealand. The boat journey took five days.
Blues awarded for rugby at Oxford – athletics, cricket and rowing had already awarded blues.
Laws: Free kick by way of penalty introduced.
First neutral referee for Scotland v England.
1883 Coventry introduced four threequarters in a match against Stratford-on-Avon.
Ned Haig, the local butcher, organised the first sevens game at Melrose, Scotland.
Laws: Proposal that referees be provided with whistles.
1884 A dispute over the legality of Scotland's winning try against England led to the cancellation of fixtures and the eventual formation of the International Rugby Board to preside over decisions.
First rugby match in Fiji at Ba between soldiers representing Fiji and the Europeans.
Laws: One referee and two umpires control matches.
1885 Irish Rugby Union proposes the idea of an International Board.
Blues awarded at Cambridge University.
Laws: Referee allowed to use whistle, but only when an umpire agrees with the decision.
1886 International Rugby Board formed.
The referee and two umpires should be the arbiters of matches, not the captains as previously.
Wales play four threequarters against Scotland at Cardiff – the first time in internationals this has happened.
Laws: The Rugby Union introduces a points scoring system,which no one else accepts.
1887 The Prince of Wales became Patron of the Rugby Football Union.
GC Lindsay scored a record five tries for Scotland v Wales – the record still stands (though equalled) in major internationals.
1888 First British tourists – RL Seddon's team to Australia.
The New Zealand Maoris (plus four white players) started their tour in the reverse direction in what is still the longest tour of all – 74 matches in 18 months (107 if matches at home are included!)
1889 English County Championship began.
South African Rugby Football Board formed. South African Provincial championship began – Lord Currie donated the Currie Cup for competition in 1891.
Touch judges took over from umpires.
Rugby Football Association decreed that there should be a close season from May 1 to August 31 in Northern Hemisphere.
1890 International Rugby Board firmly established – England had six seats on the Board as they had most clubs (480) – Wales, Scotland and Ireland each had two places.
Uniform scoring decreed by International Board.
Barbarian RFC founded.
1891 First British tourists – English and Scottish players – on major overseas tour. They visit South Africa, who play their first international against the tourists at Port Elizabeth on July 30. The British team compile the best record of all with 19 consecutive wins and 224 points to one – conceding just a solitary try.
Laws: Dead-ball line introduced after Bristol player ran for 300 metres beyond goal line trying to touchdown against Newport!
1892 New Zealand Rugby Football Union founded.
Laws: RFU decree that all matches, without exception, shall be 15 players a side.
First French Championship final – Racing Club beat Stade Francais 4–3 in a match refereed by the founder of the modern Olympic movement, Baron Pierre de Coubertin.
Laws: Balls to be of standard weight; mauls in the goal area abolished.
1893 Broken-time argument raged – clubs in Cheshire, Lancashire and Yorkshire began to withdraw and form the Northern Union, later the Rugby League.
Laws: Advantage law came into being.
1894 Try worth three points after being valued at two points in restructuring in 1891.
1895 Rugby took further roots in Europe with clubs at Geneva, Switzerland and in what is now Czechoslovakia, at the Prague Yacht Club.
Plaque to commemorate William Webb Ellis erected at Rugby School.
Last international at Raeburn Place, where the first international took place.
Laws: Referees given sole charge of matches – no appeal allowed
1896 South Africa wear green for the first time.
Arthur Gould controversy begins – Welsh RU donate house to mark Gould's retirement, other nations think the move is 'professional', and break off fixtures.
1897 Rugby introduced into Japan.

Teams are numbered for the first time.
Rugby League's Challenge Cup inaugurated.
1899 Argentinian RFU formed.
Inverleith international ground opened.
1900 Rugby played at the Olympic Games in Paris.
Scotland choose Inverleith as their permanent home, after Raeburn Place, Anniesland, and Powderhall.
1901 First Barbarian RFC tour of Wales.
1902 Canada tour the British Isles for the first time.
Ranfurly Shield inaugurated in New Zealand, with Auckland as first winners.
1903 South Africa adopt green jerseys for first time against Great Britain on September 12 at Newlands, Cape Town.
Tactics: New Zealand adopt 2–3–2 formation in scrum.
1904 Mr P Cole becomes the first paid secretary of the Rugby Football Union.
Fiji begins its club competition.
1905 New Zealand tour Britain, USA and Canada, losing only to Wales. Billy Wallace scored 230 points on tour – still a record for any touring team.
Tactics: New Zealand's 1905 tourists had first and second five eighths, a 2–4–2 scrum, hookers throwing ball in.
Laws: Field goal abolished. Modern scoring adopted.
1906 January 1 – France play their first international, losing 38-6 to New Zealand at the Parc des Princes. England play France later the same year.
First Inter Services match – Army v Royal Navy.
Northern Union (Rugby League) reduced players from 15 to 13 a side.
1907 The RFU purchased the site at Twickenham.
Rugby League takes hold in NSW and Queensland, Australia.
French Sports Association (forerunner of French Rugby Federation) applies for recognition.
1908 Llanelli first to beat the inaugural Australian tourists – the verse 'Who beat the Wallabies' being added to the song Sospan Fach.
Australian team choose Wallabies as nickname in preference to Wolves.
Australia win Olympic gold in London – beat Cornwall in final 32-3.
Rugby introduced to Portugal.
1909 First recorded match in Kenya, when Settlers play Officials at Mombasa.
1910 First international at Twickenham, England beat Wales.
France enter Championship for first time, bringing it to Five Nations.
First match played in Italy.
1911 France gain first international win beating Scotland 16–15 at Stade Colombes, Paris.
Rugby becomes organised in Thailand with HMS Hampshire donating the Hampshire Cup to the Royal Bangkok Sports Club.
1913 Foundation of Fijian RU and Romanian RU.
1914 Romanian Championship began.
Scottish Rugby Union re-constituted.
1914-18 World War 1 – no fewer than 111 rugby internationals lost their lives; Scotland 30, England 26, France 23, Wales 10, Ireland 9, New Zealand 9, South Africa 4.
Delft Students Rugby Club, Holland's first club, founded in 1918.
1919 Rugby ceases in Queensland until 1929, the players preferring the advantages of Rugby League.
1920 FFR (Federation France de Rugby) founded, moving away from a body which controlled all athletics sports in the country, the first Ministry for Sport.
Rugby played at the Olympics at Antwerp, confusion when both USA and France claim the gold three months apart!
Rugby introduced to the Caribbean countries by visiting Royal Navy ships.
1921 France move to the Stade Colombes permanently.
Kenya RFU founded.
Jubilee year of Rugby Football Union.
1922 Death of GAJ Rothney, originator of the Calcutta Cup.
In Wales v England match, numbers worn by both teams for the first time – some clubs (Bristol and Leicester even today) prefer letters.
The Northern Union becomes The Rugby League.
First matches in both Malawi and Singapore.
1923 November 1 – England and Wales beat Scotland and Ireland by 21–16 at the Close, Rugby School, to commemorate rugby's centenary.
First official match in Uganda – Secretary's XV v Uganda Railways.
Rugby Football Unions founded in Tonga and Spain.
1924 New Zealand's Invincibles tour Britain, winning all 30 games.
USA became Olympic Games gold medallists – event not contested since.
First official tour by British Lions – team was selected as opposed to previous tours which were by invitation.
Bermuda RFU founded.
First matches in Mauritius at the Football and Hockey Club.
1925 Cyril Brownlie becomes the first to be sent off in an international when dismissed by Albert Freethy at Twickenham playing for New Zealand against England.
Murrayfield stages first match as new headquarters of Scottish RU.
Rugby first played in Mexico.
Laws: Matches to be of 40 minutes each half, with five minutes interval – referees to be sole judge of time.
1926 First Middlesex Sevens event, won by Harlequins.
Australia, New Zealand and South Africa gain full representation on International Board.
Rugby Football Unions founded in Japan and the Caribbean, first clubs formed in Czechoslovakia.
1927 G Rowland Hill knighted for services to Rugby.
Lord Wakefield proposes that lineouts be abolished and players allowed to throw the ball to anyone, as in soccer.
First Portuguese Championship.
Broadcasting site erected at Twickenham.
1928 Death of Sir Rowland Hill.
Italian Rugby Federation founded, also Czechoslovakian RFU.
1929 Queensland RFU reformed after ceasing in 1919.
Canadian and Belgian RFUs founded.
1930 Laws: International Board assume control for framing the Laws of the Game.
1931 Lord Bledisloe donates the Bledisloe Cup for competition between New Zealand and Australia.
France expelled by four Home Unions.
Swedish RFU founded.
1932 Dutch RFU founded.
Tactics: New Zealand adopt three man front row.
1933 First match in the Soviet Union – Moscow Dynamo v

Moscow PE College, and first inter city match – Moscow beat Minsk 6–0.
1934 Federation of Amateur Rugby (FIRA) founded with France, Italy, West Germany, Portugal, Romania, Sweden, Catalonia (Spain), Holland, and Czechoslovakia as founder members. Belgium joined two months later, in March.
Moscow Dynamo win first Soviet Union Championship.
1936 King Edward VIII became Patron of the Rugby Football Union, later succeeded by George VI.
1937 New Zealand section of Barbarians RFC founded.
Calcutta Cup match broadcast on radio.
Laws: Penalty try always awarded under the posts.
1938 First televised international – England v Scotland at Twickenham.
Mexico and Thailand RFUs formed.
1939 Australia tour Britain but return home without playing due to onset of World War II.
France re-admitted to International Championship.
1939-45 World War II.
1946 Rugby begins to pick up threads after War.
Concession that allowed rugby league and union players to play together while in the Armed Services during wartime extended to peacetime.
1947 International matches resumed – France play in International Championship again.
1948 Barbarians play a touring side (Australia) for the first time, after a request for an extra match – January 31.
Australian RFU founded – previously the game governed by NSW and Queensland Rugby Unions.
Laws: Dropped Goal reduced in value from 4 to 3 points.
1949 Ireland win the Grand Slam for the only time (to date).
1950 Danish RFU founded.
Michel Pomathios becomes first Frenchman to be selected for Barbarians.
1951 Ravenhill, Belfast, ceases to be an international ground.
Lansdowne Road becomes Ireland's permanent headquarters.
South Africa beat Scotland 44–0 at Murrayfield, heaviest defeat in a major international until 1991.
Shanghai RFC disbanded and offered funds of £400 to RFU, who furnished the Royal Retiring Room at Twickenham.
Uruguay RFU formed.
1952 French Federation abolishes Championship but clubs refuse to co-operate.
Hong Kong RFU formed, Spain starts league competition.
1953 Wales beat New Zealand 13–8, the last time they have done so to date.
East African RFU formed by Kenya, Tanganyika and Uganda.
Queen Elizabeth II becomes Patron of Rugby Football Union.
Laws: Lineout and scrums tidied to encourage open play.
1954 Yugoslavian RU founded.
1955 First 100 000 crowd at Ellis Park to watch British Isles beat South Africa 23–22.
Laws: International touch judges must be qualified referees.
1956 Newly formed Moroccan and East German RFUs join FIRA.
1957 Portuguese Rugby Federation formed – starts club championship.
Poland joins FIRA.
95 000 watched Romania lose 18–15 to France in Bucharest.
Llanelli became first British club to tour Soviet Union.
1958 Sweden joins FIRA.
1959 France win International Championship outright for the first time.
Rugby's first major sponsorship when Murrayfield allows under-soil heating.
Jamaica RFU founded, Bermuda RFU re-formed.
William Webb Ellis' grave found at Menton in France, when searching for grave of Percy Carpmael, founder of the Barbarians.
1960 South African section of Barbarians RFC founded.
1961 FIRA started European Cup for clubs, along similar lines to its soccer namesake.
1962 Beziers win first European Cup, beating Grivitza Rosie of Romania 11–6.
1963 Unions in Brazil and Barbados founded.
1964 Grivitza Rosie win second European Cup, beating Mont de Marsan of France (Benoit Dauga's club) 10–0.
Competition discontinued because of costs and visa problems; no sponsorship as today.
South American Championship staged for first time.
1965 Canadian RFU re-formed.
1966 Soviet Union RFU founded.
First Caribbean Championship staged.
Laws: International Board proposes standard numbering.
1967 New Zealand cancel tour to South Africa because of refusal by South Africa to allow Maoris to tour.
Cricketer Basil D'Oliveira not allowed to tour South Africa – decision to affect rugby world as well.
Switzerland's first clubs formed, Bulgaria joins FIRA.
1968 Replacements allowed in international matches.
Asian RFU founded, Paraguay RFU formed.
1969 IG McCrae becomes the first replacement in international rugby when he comes on for Scotland against France for GC Connell.
Fiji set world record with 457 points in eight days – including two scores of 113 points in the Pacific Games.
Soviet Union begins league with 10 clubs from Moscow, Kiev and Tbilisi.
1970 Johnny Johnson replaced Frenchman Robert Calmat (injured) as referee during England v Wales game at Twickenham.
Commemorative plaque placed at 1 Cockspur Street, on site of old Pall Mall Restaurant, where Rugby Football Union was founded.
Laws: Touch kicking on the full only from within own 22 metres line, makes significant move in opening up the game.
1971 Centenary of The Rugby Football Union.
First win in series in New Zealand for British Lions under captain John Dawes.
Laws: Try revalued from three to four points.
RFU's formed in Israel, Gulf, Gibraltar and Switzerland.
1972 First English club knock-out competition.
Centenary match at Menton, France, to commemorate death of William Webb Ellis.
First Asian Championships held in Hong Kong.
Last international match at old Colombes Stadium; France beat England 37–12.
1973 Scottish RU centenary – first season of league competition in Scotland, the first home nation to run official national leagues.
First FIRA Championship won by France.
First international at the new Parc des Princes – France 16 Scotland 13.
1974 Willie John McBride's British Lions win 21 of 22

matches, held to a draw in the last match, 13–13 v South Africa Irish.
Irish RU centenary (Part I).
1975 Mike Burton becomes first Englishman to be sent off (v Australia).
Norman Sanson (Scotland) becomes the first neutral international referee when he handles both Tests between South Africa and France.
Scotland v Wales at Murrayfield attracts a crowd believed to be in the region of 104 000 – a new world record – but police dispute the figure.
Soviet Union joins FIRA and makes debut in FIRA Championship.
1976 First Hong Kong Sevens tournament – the world's top sevens event.
FIRA spreads wings as small RFUs in Madgascar, Mauritius, and Martinique join.
1977 First sendings off in history of International Championship with Norman Sanson dismissing Willie Duggan (Ireland) and Geoff Wheel (Wales) at Cardiff.
Soviet Union stage international festival.
1978 New Zealand achieve first Grand Slam over four Home Nations.
1979 New French senior scoring record – Racing Club de Paris 140 St Medard 0, including 27 tries. Also Michel Fabre breaks senior try scoring record with 11 tries in Beziers 100–0 win over Montchanin.
USA begins national club championship.
Irish RU Centenary (Part II)
1980 Welsh RU centenary.
1981 Errol Tobias is first black player to represent South Africa (versus Ireland).
1984 Jean-Patrick Lescarboura (France) drops a goal in all four Five Nations matches.
1986 Cavaliers banned by New Zealand for going to South Africa to play four Tests.
1987 Inaugural World Cup competition won by New Zealand.
1989 Centenary of South African Rugby Board.
1991 Second World Cup won by Australia.
Wales lose by a record 63–6 to Australia, after losing 71–8 to NSW a week earlier.
Wales beaten by Western Samoa in World Cup.
1992 England win first back to back Grand Slam since their other successes in 1914 and 1924.
Major rule changes include the awarding of five points for a try. Last four-point try scored by David Sole (Scotland v Australia). First five-point try by Va'aiga Tuigamale (New Zealand v Australia).

INTERNATIONAL RECORDS

Due to the rapid expansion of the game, there is still some confusion as to what constitutes a world record. In earlier days, the eight member nations of the International Rugby Board (IRB) – comprising France, New Zealand, Australia, South Africa and the four Home Nations – ruled world rugby, with records kept only for matches between those countries. Then with the arrival of Romania and Argentina on the world scene, some countries, notably France, awarded caps and kept international records to include these newer nations.

The first World Cup in 1987 saw the IRB member nations also include *those* results in their records. Countries such as Wales confused the issue still further by awarding caps against Western Samoa (then unknown!) in 1986 and against the Barbarians in 1990, even though the Barbarians, being a club side, were not strictly international opposition. South Africa included results against the 1986 New Zealand Cavaliers, who were banned in New Zealand!

The following list of match records are therefore in tiers, listed for the major IRB members and World Cup matches, followed by the Associate members of the IRB (the emerging nations), and finally, should it be necessary, for any credible 'internationals' between the smaller nations.

The standard ruling (for want of any decision from the IRB) is that the *Guinness Rugby Union Fact Book* follows each country's choice to award caps to opposition considered worthy of international status. Records are as on 1 July 1992.

MATCH RECORDS

HIGHEST SCORE

The highest score is **74** points by **New Zealand** in their 74–13 win against Fiji in the 1987 World Cup at Christchurch. New Zealand scored 12 tries, with four each from winger Craig Green and fullback John Gallagher. The match also represents the **most points scored (87)** in a major international.

The highest score between two IRB member nations is **63** points by **Australia** in their 63–6 win against Wales in Brisbane in 1991. Australia scored 12 tries from nine different players. A week earlier New South Wales had beaten a Welsh XV 71–8 at Sydney, scoring 13 tries, with five tries for David Campese.

The highest score in another international is **111** points by **Zimbabwe** in their 111–12 win against Nigeria in 1987 at Nairobi, Kenya. The 113 points scored by Fiji against the Solomon Islands and against New Caledonia in 1969 are not recognised due to the standard of the opposition.

BIGGEST WINNING MARGIN

The biggest winning margin in an international is **64** points by **New Zealand** in their 70–6 win against Italy in the 1987 World Cup at Auckland. Twelve tries were scored.

The biggest winning margin in an international between two IRB member nations is **57** points by **Australia** in their 63–6 win against Wales at Brisbane in 1991.

The biggest winning margin in another international is **99** points by **Zimbabwe** in their 111–12 win against Nigeria in 1987 at Nairobi, Kenya.

Right *Grant Fox kicks for goal during New Zealand's record 74–13 win over Fiji. Fox kicked 10 conversions in the match, another record.*

MOST DROPPED GOALS

No player has scored more than **3** dropped goals in an international. The following have done so in major internationals:

Pierre Albaladejo (France)	v Ireland	1960	Paris
Phil Hawthorne (Australia)	v England	1967	Twickenham
Naas Botha (South Africa)	v South America	1980	Durban
Naas Botha (South Africa)	v Ireland	1981	Durban
Jean-Patrick Lescarboura (France)	v England	1985	Twickenham
Jean-Patrick Lescarboura (France)	v New Zealand	1986	Christchurch
Didier Camberabero (France)	v Australia	1990	Sydney

Hugo Porta (Argentina) kicked three dropped goals against Australia in 1979 and New Zealand in 1985 – both at Buenos Aires.

MOST TRIES

Two countries have scored **13** tries in a major international – England scored 13 against Wales in 1881 at Blackheath before uniform scoring was adopted, the forwards George Burton (4) and Henry Vassall (3) scoring most tries. When **France** beat Zimbabwe 70–12 in the 1987 World Cup at Auckland, they also scored 13 tries in a match where Didier Camberabero collected a world record 30 points.

The most tries scored in another international is **20** by Zimbabwe in their 111–12 win against Nigeria in 1987 at Nairobi, Kenya. Richard Tsimba and Mark Neill each scored five tries.

MOST PENALTIES

The most penalties kicked in an international between IRB member nations is **7** by **Simon Hodgkinson** (England) against Wales at Cardiff in 1991. England won 25–6, their first win at Cardiff since 1963.

The most penalties kicked in another international is **8** by **Mark Wyatt** (Canada) against a Scotland XV at St John, New Brunswick in 1991. The Scotland XV did not award caps.

Hugo Porta kicked seven penalties in Argentina's 31–27 defeat by France in Buenos Aires in 1974.

MOST CONVERSIONS

The most conversions kicked in an international is **10** by **Grant Fox** (New Zealand) in the 74–13 win against Fiji in the 1987 World Cup at Christchurch.

The most conversions kicked in an international betwen IRB member nations is **8** by **Jack Bancroft** (Wales) against France at Swansea in 1910. Wales scored 10 tries and won 49–14.

The most conversions kicked in another international is **14** by **Martin Grobler** (Zimbabwe) against Nigeria at Nairobi in 1987 in Zimbabwe's 111–12 win. Zimbabwe scored 20 tries.

MOST TRIES – INDIVIDUAL

5 G Lindsay (Scotland) v Wales, 1887
D Lambert (England) v France, 1907
R Underwood (England) v Fiji, 1989

MOST POINTS – INDIVIDUAL

30 Didier Camberabero (France): 3 tries, 9 con v Zimbabwe, 1987 (France won 70–12)
27 Gavin Hastings (Scotland): 2 tries, 8 con, 1 pen v Romania, 1987 (Scotland won 55–28)
26 Grant Fox (New Zealand): 10 con, 2 pen v Fiji, 1987 (New Zealand won 74–13)
26 Alan Hewson (New Zealand): 5 pen, 2 con, 1 try, 1 drop v Australia, 1982 (New Zealand won 33–18)
25 Philippe Berot (France): 6 con, 1 try, 3 pen v Romania, 1987 (France won 49–3)
24 Sebastian Viars (France): 2 tries, 5 con, 2 pen v Ireland, 1992 (France won 44–12)
24 Michael Lynagh (Australia): 2 tries, 8 con v USA, 1990 (Australia won 67–4)
24 Michael Lynagh (Australia): 4 pen, 6 con v France, 1990 (Australia won 48–31)
24 Fergie McCormick (New Zealand): 5 pen, 3 con, 1 drop v Wales, 1969 (New Zealand won 33–12)

TOUR RECORDS

BEST POINTS MARGIN ON TOUR

976 for, **59** against – New Zealand in 1905–6 in Great Britain, France and Canada (830 points in Great Britain alone, 868 in Great Britain and France)

BIGGEST VICTORY BY TOURING TEAM

112 pts (117–6) New Zealand v South Australia, 1974
103 pts (103–0) New Zealand v Northern New South Wales, 1962
102 pts (106–4) New Zeland v Japan XV, 1987
99 pts (99–0) New Zealand v South Australia, 1984

MOST POINTS IN TOUR MATCH – INDIVIDUAL

43 Robbie Deans (New Zealand) v South Australia, 1984: 14 con, 3 tries, 1 pen
41 Joe Karam (New Zealand) v South Australia, 1974: 15 con, 2 tries, 1 pen
38 Bob Jarden (New Zealand) v Mid-Western Australia, 1951: 6 tries, 10 con
37 Alan Old (British Lions) v South West Districts, 1974: 15 con, 1 try, 1 pen
36 Neil Bennett (England) v Western Australia, 1975: 2 tries, 8 con, 3 pen, 1 drop
35 De Wet Ras (South Africa) v Uruguay XV, 1980: 12 con, 2 tries, 1 pen

MOST TRIES IN TOUR MATCH – INDIVIDUAL

8 Rod Heeps (New Zealand) v Northern New South Wales, 1962
7 Patrice Lagisquet (France) v Paraguay, 1988
6 Roy Dryburgh (South Africa) v Queensland, 1956
Stuart Boyce (Australia) v Wairapa, 1962
David Duckham (British Lions) v West Coast Buller, 1971
John J Williams (British Lions) v South West Districts, 1974

MOST TRIES ON TOUR – TEAM

215 New Zealand in 1905–6 in 33 matches in Great Britain and France

MOST TRIES IN TOUR MATCH – TEAM

22 New Zealand against Northern New South Wales, 1962

INDIVIDUAL CAREER RECORDS

Though the world records of leading points scorers and leading try scorers in international rugby are well chronicled, there are increasing enquiries as to who holds the world record for points and tries in international rugby in each position.

Because of early descrepancies, positions refer, for example, simply to wings, not left and right (and similarly for other positions on the field where the same occurs).

MOST TRIES IN INTERNATIONALS

48 David Campese (Australia)
38 Serge Blanco (France)
35 Rory Underwood (England)
32 John Kirwan (New Zealand)
25 Philippe Sella (France)
24 Ian Smith (Scotland)
23 Christian Darrouy (France)
23 Gerald Davies (20 for Wales, 3 for British Isles)
20 Gareth Edwards (Wales)
20 Patrice Lagisquet (France)
20 Terry Wright (New Zealand)

THE RECORD HOLDER

David Campese (Australia)
Born 21 October 1962 at Queanbeyan, Australian Capital Territory, Campese played for the local club and state, before moving to Randwick and New South Wales. Gained his first cap against New Zealand in 1982. In the Australian winters he plays in Italy for Milan. He currently works in Public Relations. On 1 July 1992 his international record stood at 48 tries, 8 conversions, seven penalty goals and two drop goals for a total of 235 points from an Australian record 66 caps. Campese was equal top try scorer in the 1991 World Cup with six tries.

Below *Campese breaks for the line to score for Australia against New Zealand in the 1991 World Cup semi-final.*

MOST POINTS IN INTERNATIONALS

721 Michael Lynagh (Australia)
533 Grant Fox (New Zealand)
420 Gavin Hastings (Scotland)
332 Didier Camberabero (France)
308 Michael Kiernan (Ireland)
301 Andy Irvine (273 for Scotland, 28 for British Isles)
301 Paul Thorburn (Wales)

THE RECORD HOLDER

Michael Lynagh (Australia)
Michael Patrick Lynagh took over from Andy Irvine as world rugby's most prolific points scorer. He was born on 25 October 1963 in Brisbane and plays for Queensland University and Queensland. He made his first appearance for Australia in 1984 with the 1991 World Cup final being his 53rd cap, a total which includes 45 games at fly half, seven in the centre, and one as replacement full back. He has scored 24 points in a game against the USA and France, and has scored 23 points on four occasions.

Michael Lynagh of Australia, the most prolific points scorer in the history of international rugby.

MOST CONVERSIONS IN INTERNATIONALS

121 Michael Lynagh (Australia)
104 Grant Fox (New Zealand)
57 Gavin Hastings (Scotland and British Isles)
46 Didier Camberabero (France)
45 Michel Vannier (France)
43 Paul Thorburn (Wales)
43 Naas Botha (South Africa)
40 Michael Kiernan (Ireland)

MOST PENALTY GOALS IN INTERNATIONALS

132 Michael Lynagh (Australia)
101 Grant Fox (New Zealand)
82 Gavin Hastings (Scotland and British Isles)
69 Paul Thorburn (Wales)
67 Andy Irvine (Scotland and British Isles)
67 Dusty Hare (England)
62 Paul McLean (Australia)
61 Ollie Campbell (Ireland)

MOST DROPPED GOALS IN INTERNATIONALS

15 Rob Andrew (England and British Isles)
15 Jean-Patrick Lescarboura (France)
15 Naas Botha (South Africa)
13 Jonathan Davies (Wales)
12 Pierre Albaladejo (France)
12 John Rutherford (Scotland and British Isles)
11 Guy Camberabero (France)
10 Barry John (Wales and British Isles)
10 Didier Camberabero (France)

MOST POINTS IN INTERNATIONALS BY POSITION

FULL BACK

420 Gavin Hastings (Scotland)
Gavin Hastings began his career with 18 points – six penalties – on his international debut against France in 1986. To date he has scored 392 points for Scotland, plus a further 28 for the British Isles.

WING

172 David Campese (Australia)
Campese's tally includes 36 of his 48 tries, 5 conversions, 5 penalties and 1 dropped goal.

CENTRE

152 Steve Fenwick (Wales)
Fenwick scored 152 points for Wales in his 30 internationals from 1975–80, playing in the Grand Slam teams of 1976 and 1978. He equalled the then International Championship record of 38 points in 1979. Fenwick scored four tries, 11 conversions, 35 penalty goals and three dropped goals. He joined Cardiff rugby league club in 1981.

OUTSIDE HALF

648 Michael Lynagh
Lynagh's total excludes 73 points scored in seven matches as centre and one at full back.

SCRUM HALF

91 Gareth Edwards (Wales)
Edwards, the world record try scorer for a scrum half, scored 20 tries in international rugby – all for Wales, none for the British Isles. He scored eight three point tries, 12 four point tries, a penalty goal and two conversions for Wales, plus four drop goals – three for Wales and one for the British Isles.

FORWARDS

Kicking forwards are a much rarer breed these days, while those who were kickers had a habit of playing in more than one position in the scrum – usually lock and no. 8.
The leading kickers in the forwards are:
68 Peter Brown (Scotland) – three tries (two three point tries and one at four points), six conversions, and 15 penalty goals from 1964–73.
48 Okey Geffen (South Africa) – nine conversions and 10 penalties. He kicked five penalties on his debut v New Zealand in 1949, and seven conversions in the then record 44–0 win v Scotland in 1951.
47 Jakobus Pieter 'Tiny' Naude (South Africa) – two tries, four conversions and 11 penalties from 1963–1969

MOST APPEARANCES IN INTERNATIONALS

93 Serge Blanco (France)
84 Philippe Sella (France)
81 Mike Gibson (Ireland/Lions)
80 Willie John McBride (Ireland/Lions)
69 Roland Bertranne (France)
66 David Campese (Australia)
65 Fergus Slattery (Ireland/Lions)
63 Gareth Edwards (Wales/Lions)
63 JPR Williams (Wales/Lions)
63 Michel Crauste (France)
63 Benoit Dauga (France)
61 Jean Condom (France)
60 Andy Irvine (Scotland/Lions)

THE RECORD HOLDERS

Rob Andrew (England and British Isles)
Scored his record-equalling drop goal in the 1991 World Cup semi-final against Scotland. He has scored 14 for England and one for the British Isles v Australia in 1989.

Naas Botha (South Africa)
South Africa's proposed readmission to international rugby offered Botha a new opportunity to break the record. He scored 268 points in 23 Tests from 1980–89.

Jean-Patrick Lescarboura (France)
His total includes drop goals against all four opponents in the 1984 Five Nations Championship. He scored 200 points in 28 internationals for France from 1982–90.

MOST TRIES IN INTERNATIONALS BY POSITION

FULL BACK
34 Serge Blanco (France)
Blanco made a world record 93 appearances for France from 1980-91 scoring 38 tries. His appearances include 34 tries in 81 internationals at full back and four tries in 12 internationals on the wing.

WING
36 David Campese (Australia)
Campese overtook Rory Underwood's record of 35 tries from the wing in the series against Scotland in 1992.

CENTRE
22 Philippe Sella (France)
Sella had 83 caps at the end of the 1992 International Championship which included six caps on the wing, and one at full back.
Sella's total tries for the centre does not include his three tries scored while playing on the wing for France.

OUTSIDE HALF
9 Michael Lynagh (Australia)
Lynagh's tries from outside (fly half) are part of his world record number of points. He has scored three tries from centre.

SCRUM HALF
20 Gareth Edwards (Wales)
Made his 53 appearances for Wales in consecutive internationals from 1967–78. He also played 10 internationals for the British Isles 1968–74 but did not score any tries.

PROP FORWARD
8 Robert Paparemborde (France), **Amedee Domenech** (France)
Paparemborde made 55 appearances for France from 1975–1983 while Domenech made 52 appearances against all countries from 1952–63.

HOOKER
6 Phil Kearns (Australia)
Phil Kearns made his international debut in 1990 and has already amassed more tries than any other hooker. He is the regular hooker for Australia, and was in their 1991 World Cup winning team. He is certain to continue to improve this record in the future

FLANKER
15 Ian Kirkpatrick (New Zealand)
Kirkpatrick made 36 appearances as flanker, and a further three as no. 8, where he scored another international try; his career tally of 16 tries is a former New Zealand record.

LOCK FORWARD
7 'Ferdie' Bergh (South Africa)
Willem Ferdinand Bergh played in 17 Tests from 1931-1938. He played for Stellenbosch University and Western Province, and would have scored more international tries, but for the curtailing of his career by the outbreak of war in 1939.

NO. 8
9 Derek White (Scotland)
White holds the Scottish record of 11 tries by a forward with John Jeffrey. He has also played at no. 8 and flanker and scored two further tries.

Serge Blanco (dark shirt) at the end of his world record 93rd and last international – France v England in Paris, 1991.

INTERNATIONAL RESULTS

This chapter contains all the results and scorers from the major internationals in rugby history. It has always been a point of debate as to what constitutes a full international, whether it should be a match against one of the major countries, whether this definition should be extended to include the World Cup competing nations, or whether it should simply be left up to each individual country to decide to class a match as an international or not.

The Guinness Rugby Union Fact Book takes the view that each country makes its own decision as to whether to award caps, but because of a lack of any definite ruling from the International Board, the World Cup is treated separately. It is an issue that is crying out for an official decision as to what constitutes a full international.

The section sets out the complete results of matches between International Board countries, and includes points scorers at each international.

POINTS SCORING SYSTEM

1875 Three touchdowns equalled one try; three tries equalled one goal.

1886 Ireland, Scotland and Wales introduced points scoring but points values varied until England joined the other countries and adopted the International Board's uniform system.

1887 Try = one point, Goal = three points.

1890–1992

	T	C	PG	DG	GM
1890–1	1	2	2	3	3
1891–3	2	3	3	4	4
1893–1905	3	2	3	4	4
1905–48	3	2	3	4	3
1948–71	3	2	3	3	3
1971–92	4	2	3	3	3
1992–	5	2	3	3	3

Abbreviations used

T = try *C* = conversion *PG* = penalty goal *DG* = dropped goal *GM* = goal from mark

Sebastian Viars (France) converts another try on his way to an international championship record 24 points against Ireland at Parc des Princes in 1992.

MATCHES BETWEEN INTERNATIONAL BOARD COUNTRIES

		Matches	E	A	F	I	N	S	SA	W	Drawn
England	v Australia	17	5	12	–	–	–	–	–	–	–
	v France	68	37	–	24	–	–	–	–	–	7
	v Ireland	105	61	–	–	36	–	–	–	–	8
	v New Zealand	16	3	–	–	–	13	–	–	–	–
	v Scotland	109	53	–	–	–	–	39	–	–	17
	v South Africa	9	2	–	–	–	–	–	6	–	1
	v Wales	98	39	–	–	–	–	–	–	47	12
Australia	v France	23	–	9	12	–	–	–	–	–	2
	v Ireland	13	–	7	–	6	–	–	–	–	–
	v New Zealand	93	–	24	–	–	64	–	–	–	5
	v Scotland	14	–	7	–	–	–	7	–	–	–
	v South Africa	28	–	7	–	–	–	–	21	–	–
	v Wales	15	–	7	–	–	–	–	–	8	–
France	v Ireland	65	–	–	35	25	–	–	–	–	5
	v New Zealand	28	–	–	5	–	23	–	–	–	–
	v Scotland	63	–	–	30	–	–	30	–	–	3
	v South Africa	19	–	–	3	–	–	–	12	–	4
	v Wales	66	–	–	27	–	–	–	–	36	3
Ireland	v New Zealand	12	–	–	–	0	11	–	–	–	1
	v Scotland	104	–	–	–	45	–	54	–	–	5
	v South Africa	10	–	–	–	1	–	–	8	–	1
	v Wales	95	–	–	–	32	–	–	–	57	6
New Zealand	v Scotland	16	–	–	–	–	14	0	–	–	2
	v South Africa	37	–	–	–	–	15	–	20	–	2
	v Wales	15	–	–	–	–	12	–	–	3	–
Scotland	v South Africa	8	–	–	–	–	–	3	5	–	–
	v Wales	96	–	–	–	–	–	41	–	53	2
South Africa	v Wales	7	–	–	–	–	–	–	6	–	1

NATIONAL SUMMARY

	Matches	Won	Lost	Drawn
England	422	200	177	45
Australia	203	73	123	7
France	332	136	172	24
Ireland	404	145	233	26
New Zealand	217	152	55	10
Scotland	410	174	207	29
South Africa	118	78	31	9
Wales	392	204	164	24

THE INTERNATIONAL CHAMPIONSHIP

Historians searching for the exact starting date of the International Championship will probably agree only on one fact – that there was never an official recognition of the Championship in the first place! The four Home Nations at no stage sat around the table and discussed the future structure of the game. There was no sanctioning of Triple Crowns and Grand Slams while Wooden Spoons and subsequent jargon have been allowed to develop through the decades. It seems that the newspapers of the day used those terms as catchphrases and they just caught on; first mention of anything as controversial as a Championship table only appeared in *The Times* in 1896, some 25 years after rugby's first acknowledged international.

So if there is a date which could describe the first 'official' International Championship, the most likely is that of the 1882–83 season – it was the first time that England had played three other nations, Scotland, Ireland and Wales. Though England had first played Scotland at Raeburn Place, Edinburgh, on 27 March 1871, Ireland had not joined the fray until 1875 and Wales played their first international in 1881. Welsh participation now allowed a full cycle of internationals to be played.

England won all three matches in 1883, beating Scotland in the decider, with the weaker Wales and Ireland each losing to both countries. The Wales v Ireland 'Wooden Spoon' match did not happen because of travel difficulties.

In 1884 the pattern continued with England winning the crucial match with Scotland, and Wales gaining their first points against the Irish at Cardiff. The 'table' had a uniform look with all countries playing three matches.

But just when some form of consistency and organisation had become apparent, confusion and chaos became the order of the day. In that 1884 match at Blackheath, Scotland had protested that England's winning try was unfair; the problem was that there was no one in officialdom to protest to. England and Scotland cancelled fixtures and dialogue, whereupon Wales and Ireland came up with a suggestion to form a Board to discuss future disputes. The International Board was the result, though England – who had agreed to it in principle – failed to show up at the first meeting, feeling that their hold on rugby decisions would be eroded.

Order was not fully restored until 1890 when England resumed fixtures in the Championship. In the meantime Wales and Ireland had fallen out for a season, and the International Board had made significant strides in decision-making, though six of the 14 Championships were disrupted for various reasons.

The final link in the chain involved France. Their entry into what became the Five Nations Championship was completed in 1910 after having played 'friendlies' against England from 1906, Wales since 1908 and Ireland from a year later. But the Five Nations became Four again for 16 years from 1931 to 1947 when France failed to heed several warnings concerning professionalism in the club ranks and were excluded from participation. They were admitted back into the fold for 1940 but war prevented their return for another seven years.

It would be unwise then to write of the very basis of rugby's winter showpiece as a figment of the imagination. But the stark truth is that the Five Nations Championship was never organised – it just happened. And it explains why there are no Cups or Trophies for the Triple Crown, the Grand Slam and the International Championship. Over to you, sponsors . . .

CHAMPIONSHIP MATCH RECORDS – INDIVIDUAL

Tries: **5** GC Lindsay (Scotland) v Wales 1887
5 D Lambert (England) v France 1907
Conversions: **8** J Bancroft (Wales) v France 1910
Penalties: **7** SD Hodgkinson (England) v Wales 1991
Drop Goals: **3** P Albaladejo (France) v Ireland 1960
3 JP Lescarboura (France) v England 1985
Points: **24** S Viars (France) v Ireland 1992

CHAMPIONSHIP RECORDS IN A SEASON – INDIVIDUAL

Tries: **8** CN Lowe (England) 1914
8 IS Smith (Scotland) 1925
Conversions: **12** JM Webb (England) 1992
Penalties: **18** SD Hodgkinson (England) 1991
Drop Goals: **5** G Camberabero (France) 1967
Points: **67** JM Webb (England) 1992

TRIES IN ALL FOUR GAMES

HC Catchside (England) 1924
AC Wallace (Scotland) 1925
P Esteve (France) 1983
P Sella (France) 1986

DROP GOALS IN ALL FOUR GAMES

JP Lescarboura (France) 1984

TEAM RECORDS

Highest score: Wales 49 France 14 1910
Most tries in a match: **12** Scotland v Wales 1887, Wales v France 1910, England v France 1914

CHAMPIONSHIP SEASON RECORDS – TEAM

Most points scored: **118** England 1992
Most points conceded: **116** Ireland 1992
Most tries scored: **21** Wales 1910
Most tries conceded: **22** France 1910
Most tries (aggregate): **55** 1911
Least tries (aggregate): **12** 1959

SEQUENCES

Best unbeaten run: **13** England (1922–25), including record 10 consecutive wins
Most games without win: **17** France (1911–25) – all defeats

GRAND SLAM WINNERS

England 10 times: 1913, 1914, 1921, 1923, 1924, 1928, 1957, 1980, 1991, 1992.
Wales 8 times: 1908, 1909, 1911, 1950, 1952, 1971, 1976, 1978.
France 4 times: 1968, 1977, 1981, 1987.
Scotland 3 times: 1925, 1984, 1990.
Ireland once: 1948.

TRIPLE CROWN WINNERS

Wales 17 times: 1893, 1900, 1902, 1905, 1908, 1909, 1911, 1950, 1952, 1965, 1969, 1971, 1976, 1977, 1978, 1979, 1988.
England 17 times: 1883, 1884, 1892, 1913, 1914, 1921, 1923, 1924, 1928, 1934, 1937, 1954, 1957, 1960, 1980, 1991, 1992.
Scotland 10 times: 1891, 1895, 1901, 1903, 1907, 1925, 1933, 1938, 1984, 1990.
Ireland 6 times: 1894, 1899, 1948, 1949, 1982, 1985.

WINNERS

1882	England
1884	England
1885*	–
1886	Scotland/England
1887	Scotland
1888*	–
1889*	–
1890	England/Scotland
1891	Scotland
1892	England
1893	Wales
1894	Ireland
1895	Scotland
1896	Ireland
1897*	–
1898*	–
1899	Ireland
1900	Wales
1901	Scotland
1902	Wales
1903	Scotland
1904	Scotland
1905	Wales
1906	Ireland/Wales
1907	Scotland
1908	Wales
1909	Wales
1910	England
1911	Wales
1912	England/Ireland
1913	England
1914	England
1920	England/Scotland/Wales
1921	England
1922	Wales
1923	England
1924	England
1925	Scotland
1926	Scotland/Ireland
1927	Scotland/Ireland
1928	England
1929	Scotland
1930	England
1931	Wales
1932	England/Wales/Ireland
1933	Scotland
1934	England
1935	Ireland
1936	Wales
1937	England
1938	Scotland
1939	England/Wales/Ireland
1947	Wales/England
1948	Ireland
1949	Ireland
1950	Wales
1951	Ireland
1952	Wales
1953	England
1954	England/France/Wales
1955	France/Wales
1956	Wales
1957	England
1958	England
1959	France
1960	France/England
1961	France
1962	France
1963	England
1964	Scotland/Wales
1965	Wales
1966	Wales
1967	France
1968	France
1969	Wales
1970	France/Wales
1971	Wales
1972*	–
1973	Quintiuple tie
1974	Ireland
1975	Wales
1976	Wales
1977	France
1978	Wales
1979	Wales
1980	England
1981	France
1982	Ireland
1983	France/Ireland
1984	Scotland
1985	Ireland
1986	France/Scotland
1987	France
1988	Wales/France
1989	France
1990	Scotland
1991	England
1992	England

* Matches not completed

Wales have won the title outright most times: 21; England have won it 20 times, Scotland 13, Ireland 10, and France 9.

ENGLAND v IRELAND

5 Feb 1883
Whalley Range, Manchester
ENGLAND 1g 3t
T: Bolton, Tatham, Twynam, Wade
C: Evanson
IRELAND 1t
T: Forrest

4 Feb 1884
Lansdowne Road, Dublin
IRELAND 0
ENGLAND 1g
T: Bolton *C:* Sample

7 Feb 1885
Whalley Range, Manchester
ENGLAND 2t
T: Bolton, Hawcridge
IRELAND 1t
T: Greene

6 Feb 1886
Lansdowne Road, Dublin
IRELAND 0
ENGLAND 1t
T: Wilkinson

5 Feb 1887
Lansdowne Road, Dublin
IRELAND 2g
T: Montgomery, Tillie *C:* Rambaut (2)
ENGLAND 0

15 Mar 1890
Rectory Field, Blackheath
ENGLAND 3t
T: Rogers, Morrison, Stoddart
IRELAND 0

7 Feb **1891**
Lansdowne Road, Dublin
IRELAND 0
ENGLAND 9
T: Lockwood (2), Wilson (2), Toothill
C: Lockwood

6 Feb 1892
Whalley Range, Manchester
ENGLAND 7
T: Evershed, Percival *C:* Woods
IRELAND 0

4 Feb 1893
Lansdowne Road, Dublin
IRELAND 0
ENGLAND 4
T: Bradshaw, Taylor

3 Feb 1894
Rectory Field, Blackheath
ENGLAND 5
T: Lockwood *C:* Taylor
IRELAND 7
T: John Lytle *DG:* Forrest

2 Feb 1895
Lansdowne Road, Dublin
IRELAND 3
T: L Magee
ENGLAND 6
T: Fegan, Thomas

1 Feb 1896
Meanwood Road, Leeds
ENGLAND 4
DG: Byrne
IRELAND 10
T: Sealy, Stevenson *C:* Bulger

6 Feb 1897
Lansdowne Road, Dublin
IRELAND 13
T: Gardiner (2), Bulger *GM:* Bulger
ENGLAND 9
T: Robinson *PG:* Byrne (2)

5 Feb 1898
Athletic Ground, Richmond
ENGLAND 6
T: Robinson *PG:* Byrne
IRELAND 9
T: Lindsay, Magee *PG:* Bulger

4 Feb 1899
Lansdowne Road, Dublin
IRELAND 6
T: Allen *PG:* Magee
ENGLAND 0

3 Feb 1900
Athletic Ground, Richmond
ENGLAND 15
T: Robinson (2), Gordon-Smith
C: Alexander *DG:* Gordon-Smith
IRELAND 4
DG: Allison

9 Feb 1901
Lansdowne Road, Dublin
IRELAND 10
T: Davidson, Gardiner *C:* Irwin (2)
ENGLAND 6
T: Robinson *PG:* Alexander

8 Feb 1902
Welford Road, Leicester
ENGLAND 6
T: Cooper, Williams
IRELAND 3
T: F Gardiner

14 Feb 1903
Lansdowne Road, Dublin
IRELAND 6
T: Ryan *PG:* Corley
ENGLAND 0

13 Feb 1904
Rectory Field, Blackheath
ENGLAND 19
T: Moore (2), Vivyan (2), Simpson
C: Vivyan (2)
IRELAND 0

11 Feb 1905
Mardyke, Cork
IRELAND 17
T: Moffatt (2), Allen, Maclear, Wallace
C: Maclear
ENGLAND 3
T: Cooper

10 Feb 1906
Welford Road, Leicester
ENGLAND 6
T: Jago, Mills
IRELAND 16
T: Tedford (2), Maclear, Purdon
C: Gardiner, Maclear

9 Feb 1907
Lansdowne Road, Dublin
IRELAND 17
T: Caddell (2), Tedford, Thrift *C:* Parke
GM: Parke
ENGLAND 9
T: Imrie, Slocock *PG:* Pickering

8 Feb 1908
Athletic Ground, Richmond
ENGLAND 13
T: Hudson (2), Williamson *C:* Wood (2)
IRELAND 3
PG: Parke

13 Feb 1909
Lansdowne Road, Dublin
IRELAND 5
T: Parke *C:* Pinion
ENGLAND 11
T: Palmer (2), Mobbs *C:* Palmer

12 Feb 1910
Twickenham
ENGLAND 0
IRELAND 0

11 Feb 1911
Lansdowne Road, Dublin
IRELAND 3
T: Tom Smyth
ENGLAND 0

10 Feb 1912
Twickenham
ENGLAND 15
T: Roberts (2), Birkett, Brougham, Poulton
IRELAND 0

8 Feb 1913
Lansdowne Road, Dublin
IRELAND 4
DG: Lloyd
ENGLAND 15
T: Coates (2), Pillman, Ritson
PG: Greenwood

14 Feb 1914
Twickenham
ENGLAND 17
T: Lowe (2), Davies, Pillman, Roberts
C: Chapman
IRELAND 12
T: Jackson, Quinn *C:* Lloyd *DG:* Lloyd

14 Feb 1920
Lansdowne Road, Dublin
IRELAND 11
T: Dickson, Lloyd *C:* Lloyd *PG:* Lloyd
ENGLAND 14
T: Lowe, Mellish, Myers, Wakefield
C: Greenwood

12 Feb 1921
Twickenham
ENGLAND 15
T: Blakiston, Brown, Lowe
C: Cumberlege
IRELAND 0

11 Feb 1922
Lansdowne Road, Dublin
IRELAND 3
T: Wallis
ENGLAND 12
T: Lowe, Gardner, Maxwell-Hyslop, Smallwood

10 Feb 1923
Welford Road, Leicester
ENGLAND 23
T: Lowe, Corbett, Price, Smallwood, Voyce *C:* Conway (2) *DG:* Davies
IRELAND 5
T: McClelland *C:* Crawford

9 Feb 1924
Ravenhill, Belfast
IRELAND 3
T: Douglas
ENGLAND 14
T: Catcheside (2), Corbett, Hamilton-Wickes *C:* Conway

14 Feb 1925
Twickenham
ENGLAND 6
T: Smallwood (2)
IRELAND 6
T: T Hewitt, H Stephenson

13 Feb 1926
Lansdowne Road, Dublin
IRELAND 19
T: Cussen (2), F Hewitt, G Stephenson
C: G Stephenson (2) *PG:* G Stephenson (2)
ENGLAND 15
T: Haslett, Periton, Young *C:* Francis (3)

12 Feb 1927
Twickenham
ENGLAND 8
T: Gibbs, Laird *C:* Stanbury
IRELAND 6
T: H McVicker *PG:* G Stephenson

11 Feb 1928
Lansdowne Road, Dublin
IRELAND 6
T: Arigho, Sugden
ENGLAND 7
T: Richardson *DG:* Richardson

9 Feb 1929
Twickenham
ENGLAND 5
T: Smeddle *C:* Wilson
IRELAND 6
T: Davy, Sugden

8 Feb 1930
Lansdowne Road, Dublin
IRELAND 4
DG: Murray
ENGLAND 3
T: Novis

14 Feb 1931
Twickenham
ENGLAND 5
T: Black *C:* Black
IRELAND 6
T: McMahon *PG:* Murray

13 Feb 1932
Lansdowne Road, Dublin
IRELAND 8
T: Waide *C:* Murray *PG:* Murray
ENGLAND 11
T: Burland *C:* Burland *PG:* Burland (2)

11 Feb 1933
Twickenham
ENGLAND 17
T: Novis (2), Booth, Gadney, Sadler
C: Kendrew
IRELAND 6
T: Hunt *PG:* Murray

10 Feb 1934
Lansdowne Road, Dublin
IRELAND 3
T: Morgan
ENGLAND 13
T: Fry (2), Meikle *C:* Gregory (2)

9 Feb 1935
Twickenham
ENGLAND 14
T: Giles *C:* Boughton *PG:* Boughton (3)
IRELAND 3
T: O'Connor

8 Feb 1936
Lansdowne Road, Dublin
IRELAND 6
T: Bailey, Boyle
ENGLAND 3
T: Sever

13 Feb 1937
Twickenham
ENGLAND 9
T: Butler, Sever *PG:* Cranmer
IRELAND 8
T: Morgan (2) *C:* Bailey

12 Feb 1938
Lansdowne Road, Dublin
IRELAND 14
T: Bailey, Cromey, Daly, Mayne
C: Crowe
ENGLAND 36
T: Giles, Bolton, Marshall, Nicholson, Prescott, Reynolds, Unwin *C:* Parker (6)
PG: Parker

11 Feb 1939
Twickenham
ENGLAND 0
IRELAND 5
T: Irwin *C:* McKibbin

8 Feb 1947
Lansdowne Road, Dublin
IRELAND 22
T: O'Hanlon (2), Mullan (2), McKay
ENGLAND 0

14 Feb 1948
Twickenham
ENGLAND 10
T: Guest (2) *C:* Uren (2)
IRELAND 11
T: Kyle, McKay, McKee *C:* Mullan

12 Feb 1949
Lansdowne Road, Dublin
IRELAND 14
T: O'Hanlon, McKee *C:* Norton
PG: Norton (2)
ENGLAND 5
T: van Ryneveld *C:* Holmes

11 Feb 1950
Twickenham
ENGLAND 3
T: Roberts
IRELAND 0

10 Feb 1951
Lansdowne Road, Dublin
IRELAND 3
PG: McKibbin
ENGLAND 0

29 Mar 1952
Twickenham
ENGLAND 3
T: Boobyer
IRELAND 0

14 Feb 1953
Lansdowne Road, Dublin
IRELAND 9
T: Mortell *PG:* Henderson (2)
ENGLAND 9
T: Evans *PG:* Hall (2)

13 Feb 1954
Twickenham
ENGLAND 14
T: Butterfield, Regan, Wilson *C:* King
PG: King
IRELAND 3
PG: Murphy-O'Connor

12 Feb 1955
Lansdowne Road, Dublin
IRELAND 6
T: O'Reilly *PG:* Henderson
ENGLAND 6
T: Butterfield, Hastings

11 Feb 1956
Twickenham
ENGLAND 20
T: Butterfield, Evans, Jackson *C:* Currie
PG: Currie (2), Allison
IRELAND 0

9 Feb 1957
Lansdowne Road, Dublin
IRELAND 0
ENGLAND 6
T: Jackson *PG:* Challis

8 Feb 1958
Twickenham
ENGLAND 6
T: Ashcroft *PG:* Hetherington
IRELAND 0

14 Feb 1959
Lansdowne Road, Dublin
IRELAND 0
ENGLAND 3
PG: Risman

13 Feb 1960
Twickenham
ENGLAND 8
T: Marques *C:* Rutherford *DG:* Sharp
IRELAND 5
T: Culliton *C:* Kiernan

11 Feb 1961
Lansdowne Road, Dublin
IRELAND 11
T: Kavanagh *C:* Moffett *PG:* Moffett (2)
ENGLAND 8
T: Roberts, Rogers *C:* Risman

10 Feb 1962
Twickenham
ENGLAND 16
T: Roberts, Sharp, Wade *C:* Sharp (2)
PG: Sharp
IRELAND 0

9 Feb 1963
Lansdowne Road, Dublin
IRELAND 0
ENGLAND 0

8 Feb 1964
Twickenham
ENGLAND 5
T: Rogers *C:* Willcox
IRELAND 18
T: Flynn (2), Casey, Murphy *C:* Kiernan (3)

13 Feb 1965
Lansdowne Road, Dublin
IRELAND 5
T: Lamont *C:* Kiernan
ENGLAND 0

12 Feb 1966
Twickenham
ENGLAND 6
T: Greenwood *PG:* Rutherford
IRELAND 6
T: McGrath *PG:* Kiernan

11 Feb 1967
Lansdowne Road, Dublin
IRELAND 3
PG: Kiernan
ENGLAND 8
T: McFadyean *C:* Hosen *PG:* Hosen

10 Feb 1968
Twickenham
ENGLAND 9
DG: Finlan *PG:* Hiller (2)
IRELAND 9
PG: Kiernan (3)

8 Feb 1969
Lansdowne Road, Dublin
IRELAND 17
T: Bresnihan, Murphy *C:* Kiernan (2)
DG: McGann *PG:* Kiernan
ENGLAND 15
T: Duckham *PG:* Hiller (4)

14 Feb 1970
Twickenham
ENGLAND 9
T: Shackleton *DG:* Hiller (2)
IRELAND 3 *PG:* Kiernan

13 Feb 1971
Lansdowne Road, Dublin
IRELAND 6
T: Duggan, Grant
ENGLAND 9
PG: Hiller (3)

12 Feb 1972
Twickenham
ENGLAND 12
T: Ralston *C:* Hiller *PG:* Hiller (2)
IRELAND 16
T: Flynn, Grace *C:* Kiernan
DG: McGann *PG:* Kiernan

10 Feb 1973
Lansdowne Road, Dublin
IRELAND 18
T: Grace, Milliken *C:* McGann (2)
DG: McGann *PG:* McGann
ENGLAND 9
T: Neary *C:* Jorden *PG:* Jorden

Ralph Keyes breaks through to score for Ireland at Twickenham in 1992 but England won comfortably, 38–9.

16 Feb 1974
Twickenham
ENGLAND 21
T: Squires *C:* Old *PG:* Old (5)
IRELAND 26
T: Gibson (2), Moloney, Moore
C: Gibson (2) *DG:* Quinn *PG:* Ensor

18 Jan 1975
Lansdowne Road, Dublin
IRELAND 12
T: Gibson, McCombe *C:* McCombe (2)
ENGLAND 9
T: Stevens *C:* Old *DG:* Old

6 Mar 1976
Twickenham
ENGLAND 12
PG: Old (4)
IRELAND 13
T: Grace *DG:* McGann *PG:* McGann (2)

5 Feb 1977
Lansdowne Road, Dublin
IRELAND 0
ENGLAND 4
T: Cooper

18 Mar 1978
Twickenham
ENGLAND 15
T: Dixon, Slemen *C:* Young *PG:* Young
IRELAND 9
DG: Ward *PG:* Ward (2)

17 Feb 1979
Lansdowne Road, Dublin
IRELAND 12
T: MacLennan *C:* Ward *DG:* Ward
PG: Ward
ENGLAND 7
T: Bennett *PG:* Bennett

19 Jan 1980
Twickenham
ENGLAND 24
T: Scott, Slemen, Smith *C:* Hare (3)
PG: Hare (2)
IRELAND 9
PG: Campbell (3)

7 Mar 1981
Lansdowne Road, Dublin
IRELAND 6
DG: Campbell, MacNeill
ENGLAND 10
T: Dodge, Rose *C:* Rose

6 Feb 1982
Twickenham
ENGLAND 15
T: Slemen *C:* Rose *PG:* Rose (3)
IRELAND 16
T: MacNeill, McLoughlin *C:* Campbell
PG: Campbell (2)

19 Mar 1983
Lansdowne Road, Dublin
IRELAND 25
T: Slattery, Campbell *C:* Campbell
PG: Campbell (5)
ENGLAND 15
PG: Hare (5)

18 Feb 1984
Twickenham
ENGLAND 12
PG: Hare (3) *DG:* Cusworth
IRELAND 9
PG: Ward (3)

30 Mar 1985
Lansdowne Road, Dublin
IRELAND 13
T: Mullin *PG:* Kiernan (3) *DG:* Kiernan
ENGLAND 10
T: Underwood *PG:* Andrew (2)

1 Mar 1986
Twickenham
ENGLAND 25
T: Richards (2) *Penalty try:* Davies
C: Andrew (3) *PG:* Andrew
IRELAND 20
T: Ringland, Mullin, McCall *C:* Kiernan
PG: Kiernan

7 Feb 1987
Lansdowne Road, Dublin
IRELAND 17
T: Kiernan, Matthews, Crossan
C: Kiernan *PG:* Kiernan
ENGLAND 0

19 Mar 1988
Twickenham
ENGLAND 35
T: Oti (3), Underwood (2), Rees
C: Webb, Andrew (3) *PG:* Webb
IRELAND 3
DG: Kiernan

18 Feb 1989
Lansdowne Road, Dublin
IRELAND 3
PG: Kiernan
ENGLAND 16
T: Moore, Richards *C:* Andrew
PG: Andrew (2)

20 Jan 1990
Twickenham
ENGLAND 23
T: Underwood, Probyn, Egerton, Guscott *C:* Hodgkinson (2)
PG: Hodgkinson
IRELAND 0

2 Mar 1991
Lansdowne Road, Dublin
IRELAND 7
T: Geoghegan *PG:* BA Smith
ENGLAND 16
T: Underwood, Teague *C:* Hodgkinson
PG: Hodgkinson (2)

1 Feb 1992
Twickenham
ENGLAND 38
T: Webb (2), Morris, Guscott, Underwood, Halliday *C:* Webb (4)
PG: Webb (2)
IRELAND 9
T: Keyes *C:* Keyes *PG:* Keyes

OTHER MATCH

The Dublin Millennium Challenge
23 Apr 1988
Lansdowne Road, Dublin
IRELAND 10
T: Smith, MacNeill *C:* Kiernan
ENGLAND 21
T: Underwood, Harding *C:* Webb (2)
PG: Webb (3)

Not for the International Championship

ENGLAND v SCOTLAND

THE CALCUTTA CUP

3 Mar 1883
Raeburn Place, Edinburgh
SCOTLAND 1t
T: Reid
ENGLAND 2t
T: Rotherham, Bolton

1 Mar 1884
Rectory Field, Blackheath
ENGLAND 1g
T: Kindersley *C:* Bolton
SCOTLAND 1t
T: Jamieson

13 Mar 1886
Raeburn Place, Edinburgh
SCOTLAND 0
ENGLAND 0

5 Mar 1887
Whalley Range, Manchester
ENGLAND 1t
T: Jeffery
SCOTLAND 1t
T: Morton

1 Mar 1890
Raeburn Place, Edinburgh
SCOTLAND 0
ENGLAND 1g 1t
T: Evershed, Dyson *C:* Jowett

7 Mar 1891
Athletic Ground, Richmond
ENGLAND 3
T: Lockwood *C:* Alderson
SCOTLAND 9
T: W Neilson, JE Orr *C:* MacGregor (2)
DG: Clauss

5 Mar 1892
Raeburn Place, Edinburgh
SCOTLAND 0
ENGLAND 5
T: Bromet *C:* Lockwood

4 Mar 1893
Headingley, Leeds
ENGLAND 0
SCOTLAND 8
DG: Boswell, Campbell

17 Mar 1894
Raeburn Place, Edinburgh
SCOTLAND 6
T: Boswell (2)
ENGLAND 0

9 Mar 1895
Athletic Ground, Richmond
ENGLAND 3
PG: Byrne
SCOTLAND 6
*T:*GT Neilson *PG:* GT Neilson

14 Mar 1896
Old Hampden Park, Glasgow
SCOTLAND 11
T: Fleming, Gedge, Gowans *C:* Scott
ENGLAND 0

13 Mar 1897
Fallowfield, Manchester
ENGLAND 12
T: Fookes, Robinson *C:* Byrne
DG: Byrne
SCOTLAND 3
T: Bucher

12 Mar 1898
Powderhall, Edinburgh
SCOTLAND 3
T: McEwan
ENGLAND 3
T: Royds

11 Mar 1899
Rectory Field, Blackheath
ENGLAND 0
SCOTLAND 5
T: Gillespie *C:* Thomson

10 Mar 1900
Inverleith, Edinburgh
SCOTLAND 0
ENGLAND 0

9 Mar 1901
Rectory Field, Blackheath
ENGLAND 3
T: Robinson
SCOTLAND 18
T: Gillespie, Welsh, Timms, Fell
C: Gillespie (3)

15 Mar 1902
Inverleith, Edinburgh
SCOTLAND 3
T: Fell
ENGLAND 6
T: Williams, Taylor

21 Mar 1903
Athletic Ground, Richmond
ENGLAND 6
T: Dobson, Forrest
SCOTLAND 10
T: Dallas, Simson *DG:* Timms

19 Mar 1904
Inverleith, Edinburgh
SCOTLAND 6
T: Crabbie, Macdonald
ENGLAND 3
T: Vivyan

19 Mar 1905
Athletic Ground, Richmond
ENGLAND 0
SCOTLAND 8
T: Simson, Stronach *C:* Scott

17 Mar 1906
Inverleith, Edinburgh
SCOTLAND 3
T: Purves
ENGLAND 9
T: Mills, Raphael, Simpson

16 Mar 1907
Rectory Field, Blackheath
ENGLAND 3
T: Peters
SCOTLAND 8
T: Purves, Simson *C:* Geddes

21 Mar 1908
Inverleith, Edinburgh
SCOTLAND 16
T: Macleod (2) *C:* Geddes *DG:* Purves, Schulze
ENGLAND 10
T: Birkett, Slocock *C:* Lambert (2)

20 Mar 1909
Athletic Ground, Richmond
ENGLAND 8
T: Mobbs, Watson *C:* Palmer
SCOTLAND 18
T: Tennent (2), Gilray, Simson
C: Cunningham (3)

19 Mar 1910
Inverleith, Edinburgh
SCOTLAND 5
T: McPherson *C:* MacCallum
ENGLAND 14
T: Birkett (2), Berry, Ritson *C:* Chapman

18 Mar 1911
Twickenham
ENGLAND 13
T: Birkett, Lawrie, Wodehouse
C: Lagden (2)
SCOTLAND 8
T: Simson, Sutherland *C:* Cunningham

16 Mar 1912
Inverleith, Edinburgh
SCOTLAND 8
T: Sutherland, Usher *C:* MacCallum
ENGLAND 3
T: Holland

15 Mar 1913
Twickenham
ENGLAND 3
T: Brown
SCOTLAND 0

21 Mar 1914
Inverleith, Edinburgh
SCOTLAND 15
T: Will (2), Huggan *C:* Turner
DG: Bowie
ENGLAND 16
T: Lowe (3), Poulton *C:* Harrison (2)

20 Mar 1920
Twickenham
ENGLAND 13
T: Harris, Kershaw, Lowe
C: Greenwood (2)
SCOTLAND 4
DG: Bruce-Lockhart

19 Mar 1921
Inverleith, Edinburgh
SCOTLAND 0
ENGLAND 18
T: Brown, Edwards, King, Woods
C: Hammett (3)

18 Mar 1922
Twickenham
ENGLAND 11
T: Lowe (2), Davies *C:* Conway
SCOTLAND 5
T: Dykes *C:* Bertram

2 Apr 1923
Inverleith, Edinburgh
SCOTLAND 6
T: Gracie, McLaren
ENGLAND 8
T: Smallwood, Voyce *C:* Luddington

15 Mar 1924
Twickenham
ENGLAND 19
T: Catcheside, Myers, Wakefield
C: Conway (3)
SCOTLAND 0

21 Mar 1925
Murrayfield, Edinburgh
SCOTLAND 14
T: Nelson, Wallace *C:* Drysdale, Gillies
DG: Waddell
ENGLAND 11
T: Hamilton-Wickes, Wakefield
C: Luddington *PG:* Luddington

20 Mar 1926
Twickenham
ENGLAND 9
T: Tucker, Voyce, Webb
SCOTLAND 17
T: Smith (2), Waddell *C:* Waddell (2)
DG: Dykes

19 Mar 1927
Murrayfield
SCOTLAND 21
T: Smith (2), Dykes, Macpherson, Scott
ENGLAND 13
T: Gibbs, Laird *C:* Stanbury, Stark
PG: Stark

17 Mar 1928
Twickenham
ENGLAND 6
T: Hanley, Laird
SCOTLAND 0

16 Mar 1929
Murrayfield
SCOTLAND 12
T: Ian Smith (2), Brown, Nelson
ENGLAND 6
T: Meikle, Novis

15 Mar 1930
Twickenham
ENGLAND 0
SCOTLAND 0

21 Mar 1931
Murrayfield
SCOTLAND 28
T: Mackintosh (2), Smith (2), Ford, Logan *C:* Allan (5)
ENGLAND 19
T: Tallent (2), Reeve (2) *C:* Black (2)
PG: Black

19 Mar 1932
Twickenham
ENGLAND 16
T: Aavold (2), Black, Tanner *C:* Burland (2)
SCOTLAND 3
T: Smith

18 Mar 1933
Murrayfield
SCOTLAND 3
T: Fyfe
ENGLAND 0

17 Mar 1934
Twickenham
ENGLAND 6
T: Booth, Meikle
SCOTLAND 3
T: Shaw

16 Mar 1935
Murrayfield
SCOTLAND 10
T: Fyfe, Lambie *C:* Fyfe (2)
ENGLAND 7
T: Booth *DG:* Cranmer

21 Mar 1936
Twickenham
ENGLAND 9
T: Bolton, Candler, Cranmer
SCOTLAND 8
T: Shaw *C:* Fyfe *PG:* Fyfe

20 Mar 1937
Murrayfield
SCOTLAND 3
PG: Duncan Shaw
ENGLAND 6
T: Sever, Unwin

19 Mar 1938
Twickenham
ENGLAND 16
T: Unwin *DG:* Reynolds *PG:* Parker (3)
SCOTLAND 21
T: Renwick (2), Shaw (2), Dick
PG: Crawford (2)

18 Mar 1939
Murrayfield
SCOTLAND 6
T: Murdoch, Shaw
ENGLAND 9
PG: Heaton (3)

15 Mar 1947
Twickenham
ENGLAND 24
T: Bennett, Guest, Henderson, Holmes
C: Heaton (4)
SCOTLAND 5
T: Jackson *C:* Geddes

20 Mar 1948
Murrayfield
SCOTLAND 6
T: Drummond, Young
ENGLAND 3
PG: Uren

19 Mar 1949
Twickenham
ENGLAND 19
T: van Ryneveld (2), Guest, Hosking, Kennedy *C:* Travers (2)
SCOTLAND 3
PG: Wilson

18 Mar 1950
Murrayfield
SCOTLAND 13
T: Sloan (2), Abercrombie *C:* Gray (2)
ENGLAND 11
T: Smith (2) *C:* Hofmeyr *PG:* Hofmeyr

17 Mar 1951
Twickenham
ENGLAND 5
T: White *C:* Hook
SCOTLAND 3
T: Cameron

15 Mar 1952
Murrayfield
SCOTLAND 3
T: Johnston
ENGLAND 19
T: Evans, Kendall-Carpenter, Winn, Woodward *C:* Hall (2) *DG:* Agar

21 Mar 1953
Twickenham
ENGLAND 26
T: Bazley (2), Adkins, Butterfield, Stirling, Woodward *C:* Hall (4)
SCOTLAND 8
T: Henderson, Weatherstone
C: Thomson

20 Mar 1954
Murrayfield
SCOTLAND 3
T: Elgie
ENGLAND 13
T: Wilson (2), Young *C:* Gibbs (2)

19 Mar 1955
Twickenham
ENGLAND 9
T: Beer, Sykes *PG:* Hazell
SCOTLAND 6
T: Cameron *C:* Cameron

17 Mar 1956
Murrayfield
SCOTLAND 6
T: Stevenson *PG:* Smith
ENGLAND 11
T: Williams *C:* Currie *PG:* Currie (2)

16 Mar 1957
Twickenham
ENGLAND 16
T: Davies, Higgins, Thompson
C: Challis (2) *PG:* Challis
SCOTLAND 3
PG: Scotland

15 Mar 1958
Murrayfield
SCOTLAND 3
PG: Elliott
ENGLAND 3
PG: Hastings

21 Mar 1959
Twickenham
ENGLAND 3
PG: Risman
SCOTLAND 3
PG: Scotland

19 Mar 1960
Murrayfield
SCOTLAND 12
T: Arthur Smith *PG:* Scotland (3)
ENGLAND 21
T: Roberts, Syrett, Young *C:* Rutherford (3) *DG:* Sharp *PG:* Rutherford

18 Mar 1961
Twickenham
ENGLAND 6
T: Roberts *PG:* Horrocks-Taylor
SCOTLAND 0

17 Mar 1962
Murrayfield
SCOTLAND 3
PG: Scotland
ENGLAND 3
PG: Willcox

16 Mar 1963
Twickenham
ENGLAND 10
T: Drake-Lee, Sharp *C:* Willcox (2)
SCOTLAND 8
T: Glasgow *C:* Coughtrie *DG:* Scotland

21 Mar 1964
Murrayfield
SCOTLAND 15
T: Glasgow, Bruce, Telfer *C:* Wilson (3)
ENGLAND 6
T: Rogers *PG:* Hosen

20 Mar 1965
Twickenham
ENGLAND 3
T: Hancock
SCOTLAND 3
DG: Chisholm

19 Mar 1966
Murrayfield
SCOTLAND 6
T: Whyte *PG:* Blaikie
ENGLAND 3
DG: McFadyean

18 Mar 1967
Twickenham
ENGLAND 27
T: McFadyean (2), Taylor, Webb
C: Hosen (3) *DG:* Finlan *PG:* Hosen (2)
SCOTLAND 14
T: Hinshelwood, Turner *C:* Wilson
PG: Wilson (2)

16 Mar 1968
Murrayfield
SCOTLAND 6
DG: Connell *PG:* Wilson
ENGLAND 8
T: Coulman *C:* Hiller *PG:* Hiller

15 Mar 1969
Twickenham
ENGLAND 8
T: Duckham (2) *C:* Hiller
SCOTLAND 3
PG: Brown

21 Mar 1970
Murrayfield
SCOTLAND 14
T: Biggar, Turner *C:* Peter Brown
PG: Peter Brown (2)
ENGLAND 5
T: Spencer *C:* Hiller

20 Mar 1971
Twickenham
ENGLAND 15
T: Hiller, Neary *PG:* Hiller (3)
SCOTLAND 16
T: Peter Brown, Paterson, Rea *C:* Peter Brown (2) *DG:* Paterson

18 Mar 1972
Murrayfield
SCOTLAND 23
T: Peter Brown, MacEwan *DG:* Telfer
PG: Peter Brown (3), Arthur Brown
ENGLAND 9
PG: Old (3)

17 Mar 1973
Twickenham
ENGLAND 20
T: Dixon (2), Evans, Squires *C:* Jorden (2)
SCOTLAND 13
T: Steele (2) *C:* Irvine *PG:* Morgan

2 Feb 1974
Murrayfield
SCOTLAND 16
T: Irvine, Lauder *C:* Irvine *PG:* Irvine (2)
ENGLAND 14
T: Cotton, Neary *DG:* Rossborough
PG: Old

15 Mar 1975
Twickenham
ENGLAND 7
T: Morley *PG:* Bennett
SCOTLAND 6
PG: Morgan (2)

21 Feb 1976
Murrayfield
SCOTLAND 22
T: Lawson (2), Leslie *C:* Irvine
PG: Irvine (2)
ENGLAND 12
T: Maxwell *C:* Old *PG:* Old (2)

15 Jan 1977
Twickenham
ENGLAND 26
T: Kent, Slemen, Uttley, Young
C: Hignell (2) *PG:* Hignell (2)
SCOTLAND 6
PG: Irvine (2)

4 Mar 1978
Murrayfield
SCOTLAND 0
ENGLAND 15
T: Nelmes, Squires *C:* Young (2)
PG: Dodge

3 Feb 1979
Twickenham
ENGLAND 7
T: Slemen *PG:* Bennett
SCOTLAND 7
T: Rutherford *PG:* Irvine

15 Mar 1980
Murrayfield
SCOTLAND 18
T: Tomes, Rutherford *C:* Irvine (2)
PG: Irvine (2)
ENGLAND 30
T: Carleton (3), Slemen, Smith *C:* Hare (2) *PG:* Hare (2)

21 Feb 1981
Twickenham
ENGLAND 23
T: Davies, Slemen, Woodward *C:* Hare
PG: Hare (3)
SCOTLAND 17
T: Monro (2), Calder *C:* Irvine
PG: Irvine

16 Jan 1982
Murrayfield
SCOTLAND 9
DG: Rutherford *PG:* Irvine (2)
ENGLAND 9
PG: Dodge (2), Rose

5 Mar 1983
Twickenham
ENGLAND 12
DG: Horton *PG:* Hare (3)
SCOTLAND 22
T: Laidlaw, Smith *C:* Dods
DG: Robertson *PG:* Dods (3)

4 Feb 1984
Murrayfield
SCOTLAND 18
T: Johnston, Kennedy *C:* Dods (2)
PG: Dods (2)
ENGLAND 6
PG: Hare (2)

16 Mar 1985
Twickenham
ENGLAND 10
T: Smith *PG:* Andrew (2)
SCOTLAND 7
T: Robertson *PG:* Dods

15 Feb 1986
Murrayfield
SCOTLAND 33
T: Duncan, Rutherford, S Hastings *C:* G Hastings (3) *PG:* G Hastings (5)
ENGLAND 6
PG: Andrew (2)

4 Apr 1987
Twickenham
ENGLAND 21
T: Penalty try, Rose *C:* Rose (2)
PG: Rose (3)
SCOTLAND 12
T: Robertson *C:* G Hastings *PG:* G Hastings (2)

5 Mar 1988
Murrayfield
SCOTLAND 6
PG: G Hastings (2)
ENGLAND 9
PG: Webb (2) *DG:* Andrew

4 Feb 1989
Twickenham
ENGLAND 12
PG: Andrew (2), Webb (2)
SCOTLAND 12
T: Jeffrey *C:* Dods *PG:* Dods (2)

17 Mar 1990
Murrayfield
SCOTLAND 13
T: Stanger *PG:* Chalmers (3)
ENGLAND 7
T: Guscott *PG:* Hodgkinson

16 Feb 1991
Twickenham
ENGLAND 21
T: Heslop *C:* Hodkinson
PG: Hodgkinson (5)
SCOTLAND 12
PG: Chalmers (4)

18 Jan 1992
Murrayfield
SCOTLAND 7
T: White *PG:* G Hastings
ENGLAND 25
T: Underwood, Morris *C:* Webb
PG: Webb (4) *DG:* Guscott

ENGLAND v WALES

16 Dec 1882
St Helens, Swansea
WALES 0
ENGLAND 2g 4t
T: Wade (3), Bolton, Henderson, Thomson *C:* Evanson (2)

5 Jan 1884
Cardigan Fields, Leeds
ENGLAND 1g 2t
T: Rotherham, Twynam, Wade *C:* Bolton
WALES 1g
T: Allen *C:* Lewis

3 Jan 1885
St Helens, Swansea
WALES 1g 1t
T: Jordan (2) *C:* Taylor
ENGLAND 1g 4t
T: Hawcridge, Kindersley, Ryalls, Teggin, Wade *C:* Payne

2 Jan 1886
Rectory Field, Blackheath
ENGLAND 2t 1gm
T: Wade, Wilkinson *GM:* Stoddart
WALES 1g
T: Stadden *C:* Taylor

8 Jan 1887
Stradey Park, Llanelli
WALES 0
ENGLAND 0

15 Feb 1890
Crown Flatt, Dewsbury
ENGLAND 0
WALES 1t
T: Stadden

3 Jan 1891
Rodney Park, Newport
WALES 3
T: Pearson
ENGLAND 7
T: Christopherson (2), Budworth *C:* Alderson

2 Jan 1892
Rectory Field, Blackheath
ENGLAND 17
T: Alderson, Evershed, Hubbard, Nichol *C:* Lockwood (2), Alderson
WALES 0

7 Jan 1893
Cardiff Arms Park
WALES 12
T: Gould (2), Biggs *C:* Bancroft *PG:* Bancroft
ENGLAND 11
T: Marshall (3), Lohden *C:* Stoddart

6 Jan 1894
Birkenhead Park
ENGLAND 24
T: Bradshaw, Morfitt, Lockwood, Taylor *C:* Lockwood (3), Taylor *GM:* Taylor
WALES 3
T: Parfitt

5 Jan 1895
St Helens, Swansea
WALES 6
T: Elsey, Graham
ENGLAND 14
T: Carey, Leslie-Jones, Thomson, Woods *C:* Mitchell

4 Jan 1896
Rectory Field, Blackheath
ENGLAND 25
T: Cattell (2), Fookes (2), Morfitt (2), Mitchell *C:* Taylor, Valentine
WALES 0

9 Jan 1897
Rodney Parade, Newport
WALES 11
T: Pearson, Boucher, Jones *C:* Bancroft
ENGLAND 0

2 Apr 1898
Rectory Field, Blackheath
ENGLAND 14
T: Fookes (2), F Stout, P Stout *C:* Byrne
WALES 7
T: Huzzey *DG:* Huzzey

7 Jan 1899
St Helens, Swansea
WALES 29
T: Llewellyn (4), Huzzey (2) *C:* Bancroft (4)
ENGLAND 3
T: Robinson

6 Jan 1900
Kingsholm, Gloucester
ENGLAND 3
T: Nicholson
WALES 13
T: Hellings, Trew *C:* Bancroft (2) *PG:* Bancroft

5 Jan 1901
Cardiff Arms Park
WALES 13
T: Hodges, Nicholls, Williams *C:* Bancroft (2)
ENGLAND 0

11 Jan 1902
Rectory Field, Blackheath
ENGLAND 8
T: Dobson, Robinson *C:* Alexander
WALES 9
T: Gabe, Osborne *PG:* Strand-Jones

10 Jan 1903
St Helens, Swansea
WALES 21
T: Hodges (3), Owen, Pearson *C:* Strand-Jones (3)
ENGLAND 5
T: Dobson *C:* Taylor

9 Jan 1904
Welford Road, Leicester
ENGLAND 14
T: Elliot (2), Brettargh *C:* F Stout *PG:* Gamlin
WALES 14
T: Llewellyn, Morgan *C:* Winfield (2) *GM:* Winfield

14 Jan 1905
Cardiff Arms Park
WALES 25
T: Morgan (2), Gabe, Harding, Dick Jones, Llewellyn, Watkins *C:* Davies (2)
ENGLAND 0

13 Jan 1906
Athletic Ground, Richmond
ENGLAND 3
T: Hudson
WALES 16
T: Hodges, Maddocks, Morgan, C Pritchard *C:* Winfield (2)

12 Jan 1907
St Helens, Swansea
WALES 22
T: Maddocks (2), Williams (2), Brown, Gibbs *C:* Gibbs (2)
ENGLAND 0

18 Jan 1908
Ashton Gate, Bristol
ENGLAND 18
T: Birkett (2), Lapage, Williamson
C: Wood (2), Roberts
WALES 28
T: Gabe (2), Bush, Gibbs, Trew
C: Winfield (2), Bush *PG:* Winfield
DG: Bush

16 Jan 1909
Cardiff Arms Park
WALES 8
T: Hopkins, Williams *C:* Brancroft
ENGLAND 0

15 Jan 1910
Twickenham
ENGLAND 11
T: Chapman, Solomon *C:* Chapman
PG: Chapman
WALES 6
T: Gibbs, Webb

21 Jan 1911
St Helens, Swansea
WALES 15
T: Gibbs, Morgan, Spiller, Pugsley
PG: Birt
ENGLAND 11
T: Roberts, Kewney, Scholfield
C: Lambert

20 Jan 1912
Twickenham
ENGLAND 8
T: Brougham, Pym *C:* Chapman
WALES 0

18 Jan 1913
Cardiff Arms Park
WALES 0
ENGLAND 12
T: Coates, Pillman *C:* Greenwood
DG: Poulton

17 Jan 1914
Twickenham
ENGLAND 10
T: Brown, Pillman *C:* Chapman (2)
WALES 9
T: W Watts *C:* Bancroft *DG:* Hirst

17 Jan 1920
St Helens, Swansea
WALES 19
T: Powell, Shea *C:* Shea *DG:* Shea (2)
PG: Shea
ENGLAND 5
T: Day *C:* Day

15 Jan 1921
Twickenham
ENGLAND 18
T: Smallwood (2), Kershaw, Lowe
C: Hammett *DG:* Davies
WALES 3
T: Ring

21 Jan 1922
Cardiff Arms Park
WALES 28
T: Bowen, Delahay, Islwyn, Evans, Hiddlestone, Parker, Palmer, Richards, Whitfield *C:* Rees (2)
ENGLAND 6
T: Day, Lowe

20 Jan 1923
Twickenham
ENGLAND 7
T: Price *DG:* Smallwood
WALES 3
T: Michael

19 Jan 1924
St Helens, Swansea
WALES 9
T: Johnson, Tom Jones, Owen
ENGLAND 17
T: Catcheside (2), Jacob, Locke, Myers
C: Conway

17 Jan 1925
Twickenham
ENGLAND 12
T: Hamilton-Wickes, Kittermaster, Voyce
PG: Armstrong
WALES 6
T: Thomas, James

16 Jan 1926
Cardiff Arms Park
WALES 3
T: Andrews
ENGLAND 3
T: Wakefield

15 Jan 1927
Twickenham
ENGLAND 11
T: Corbett *C:* Stanbury *GM:* Corbett
PG: Stanbury
WALES 9
T: Andrews, Harding *PG:* Male

21 Jan 1928
St Helens, Swansea
WALES 8
T: Bartlett, Dai John *C:* Jones
ENGLAND 10
T: Taylor, Laird *C:* Richardson (2)

19 Jan 1929
Twickenham
ENGLAND 8
T: Wilkinson (2) *C:* Wilson
WALES 3
T: Morley

18 Jan 1930
Cardiff Arms Park
WALES 3
T: Jones-Davies
ENGLAND 11
T: Reeve (2) *C:* Black *PG:* Black

17 Jan 1931
Twickenham
ENGLAND 11
T: Burland *C:* Burland *PG:* Black (2)
WALES 11
T: Jones-Davies, Morley *C:* Bassett
GM: Powell

16 Jan 1932
St Helens, Swansea
WALES 12
T: Boon *C:* Bassett *DG:* Boon
PG: Bassett
ENGLAND 5
T: Coley *C:* Barr

21 Jan 1933
Twickenham
ENGLAND 3
T: Elliot
WALES 7
T: Boon *DG:* Boon

20 Jan 1934
Cardiff Arms Park
WALES 0
ENGLAND 9
T: Meikle (2), Warr

19 Jan 1935
Twickenham
ENGLAND 3
PG: Boughton
WALES 3
T: Wooller

18 Jan 1936
St Helens, Swansea
WALES 0
ENGLAND 0

16 Jan 1937
Twickenham
ENGLAND 4
DG: Sever
WALES 3
T: Wooller

15 Jan 1938
Cardiff Arms Park
WALES 14
T: McCarley, I Rees *C:* Jenkins
PG: Jenkins (2)
ENGLAND 8
T: Candler, Sever *C:* Freakes

21 Jan 1939
Twickenham
ENGLAND 3
T: Teden
WALES 0

18 Jan 1947
Cardiff Arms Park
WALES 6
T: Stephens, Evans
ENGLAND 9
T: White *C:* Gray *DG:* Hall

17 Jan 1948
Twickenham
ENGLAND 3
PG: Newman
WALES 3
T: Ken Jones

15 Jan 1949
Cardiff Arms Park
WALES 9
T: Les Williams, (2), Meredith
ENGLAND 3
DG: Hall

21 Jan 1950
Twickenham
ENGLAND 5
T: Smith *C:* Hofmeyr
WALES 11
T: Cale, Cliff Davies *C:* Lewis Jones
PG: Lewis Jones

20 Jan 1951
St Helens, Swansea
WALES 23
T: Matthews (2), Thomas (2), Ken Jones
C: Lewis Jones (4)
ENGLAND 5
T: Rittson-Thomas *C:* Hewitt

19 Jan 1952
Twickenham
ENGLAND 6
T: Agar, Woodward
WALES 8
T: Ken Jones (2) *C:* Malcolm Thomas

17 Jan 1953
Cardiff Arms Park
WALES 3
PG: Davies
ENGLAND 8
T: Cannell *C:* Hall *PG:* Woodward

16 Jan 1954
Twickenham
ENGLAND 9
T: Woodward (2), Winn
WALES 6
T: Rowlands *PG:* Rowlands

22 Jan 1955
Cardiff Arms Park
WALES 3
PG: Edwards
ENGLAND 0

21 Jan 1956
Twickenham
ENGLAND 3
PG: Allison
WALES 8
T: Davies, Robins *C:* Owen

19 Jan 1957
Cardiff Arms Park
WALES 0
ENGLAND 3
PG: Allison

18 Jan 1958
Twickenham
ENGLAND 3
T: Thompson
WALES 3
PG: TJ Davies

17 Jan 1959
Cardiff Arms Park
WALES 5
T: Bebb *C:* TJ Davies
ENGLAND 0

16 Jan 1960
Twickenham
ENGLAND 14
T: Roberts (2) *C:* Rutherford
PG: Rutherford (2)
WALES 6
PG: TJ Davies (2)

21 Jan 1961
Cardiff Arms Park
WALES 6
T: Bebb (2)
ENGLAND 3
T: Young

20 Jan 1962
Twickenham
ENGLAND 0
WALES 0

19 Jan 1963
Cardiff Arms Park
WALES 6
T: Hayward *PG:* Hodgson
ENGLAND 13
T: Owen, Phillips *C:* Sharp (2)
DG: Sharp

18 Jan 1964
Twickenham
ENGLAND 6
T: Perry, Ranson
WALES 6
T: Bebb (2)

16 Jan 1965
Cardiff Arms Park
WALES 14
T: S Watkins (2), H Morgan
ENGLAND 3
PG: Rutherford

15 Jan 1966
Twickenham
ENGLAND 6
T: Perry *PG:* Rutherford
WALES 11
T: Pask *C:* T Price *PG:* T Price (2)

15 Jan 1967
Cardiff Arms Park
WALES 34
T: TGR Davies (2), Jarrett, Morris, Bebb
C: Jarrett (5) *DG:* Raybould *PG:* Jarrett (2)
ENGLAND 21
T: Barton (2), Savage *PG:* Hosen (4)

20 Jan 1968
Twickenham
ENGLAND 11
T: McFadyean, Redwood *C:* Hiller
PG: Hiller
WALES 11
T: Edwards, Wanbon *C:* Jarrett
DG: John

12 Jan 1969
Cardiff Arms Park
WALES 30
T: MCR Richards (4), John *C:* Jarrett (3)
DG: John *PG:* Jarrett (2)
ENGLAND 9
PG: Hiller (3)

28 Feb 1970
Twickenham
ENGLAND 13
T: Duckham, Novak *C:* Hiller (2)
PG: Hiller
WALES 17
T: TM Davies, John, JPR Williams, Hopkins *C:* JPR Williams *DG:* John

16 Jan 1971
Cardiff Arms Park
WALES 22
T: TGR Davies (2), Bevan *C:* Taylor (2)
DG: John (2) *PG:* JPR Williams
ENGLAND 6
T: Hannaford *PG:* Rossborough

15 Jan 1972
Twickenham
ENGLAND 3
PG: Hiller
WALES 12
T: JPR Williams *C:* John *PG:* John (2)

20 Jan 1973
Cardiff Arms Park
WALES 25
T: JC Bevan (2), TGR Davies, Edwards, AJL Lewis *C:* Bennett *PG:* Taylor
ENGLAND 9
DG: Cowman *PG:* Doble

16 Mar 1974
Twickenham
ENGLAND 16
T: Duckham, Ripley *C:* Old *PG:* Old (2)
WALES 12
T: TM Davies *C:* Bennett *PG:* Bennett (2)

15 Feb 1975
Cardiff Arms Park
WALES 20
T: TGR Davies, Fenwick, JJ Williams
C: Martin *PG:* Martin (2)
ENGLAND 4
T: Horton

17 Jan 1976
Twickenham
ENGLAND 9
PG: Hignell (3)
WALES 21
T: JPR Williams (2), Edwards
C: Fenwick (3) *PG:* Martin

5 Mar 1977
Cardiff Arms Park
WALES 14
T: Edwards, JPR Williams *PG:* Fenwick (2)
ENGLAND 9
PG: Hignell (3)

4 Feb 1978
Twickenham
ENGLAND 6
PG: Hignell (2)
WALES 9
PG: Bennett (3)

17 Mar 1979
Cardiff Arms Park
WALES 27
T: E Rees, DS Richards, Ringer, MG Roberts, JJ Williams *C:* Martin, Fenwick
DG: WG Davies
ENGLAND 3
PG: Bennett

16 Feb 1980
Twickenham
ENGLAND 9
PG: Hare (3)
WALES 8
T: E Rees, Squire

17 Jan 1981
Cardiff Arms Park
WALES 21
T: WG Davies *C:* Fenwick *DG:* WG Davies *PG:* Fenwick (4)
ENGLAND 19
T: Hare *PG:* Hare (5)

6 Mar 1982
Twickenham
ENGLAND 17
T: Carleton, Slemen *PG:* Hare (3)
WALES 7
T: JR Lewis *DG:* WG Davies

5 Feb 1983
Cardiff Arms Park
WALES 13
T: Squire *DG:* Dacey *PG:* Wyatt (2)
ENGLAND 13
T: Carleton *DG:* Cusworth *PG:* Hare (2)

17 Mar 1984
Twickenham
ENGLAND 15
PG: Hare (5)
WALES 24
T: Hadley *C:* H Davies *PG:* H Davies (4) *DG:* Dacey

20 Apr 1985
Cardiff Arms Park
WALES 24
T: J Davies, Roberts *C:* Thorburn (2)
PG: Thorburn (3) *DG:* J Davies
ENGLAND 15
T: Smith *C:* Andrew *PG:* Andrew (2)
DG: Andrew

17 Jan 1986
Twickenham
ENGLAND 21
PG: Andrew (6) *DG:* Andrew
WALES 18
T: Bowen *C:* Thorburn *PG:* Thorburn (3) *DG:* J Davies

7 Mar 1987
Cardiff Arms Park
WALES 19
T: S Evans *PG:* Wyatt (4)
ENGLAND 12
PG: Rose (4)

6 Feb 1988
Twickenham
ENGLAND 3
PG: Webb
WALES 11
T: Hadley (2) *DG:* Davies

18 Mar 1989
Cardiff Arms Park
WALES 12
T: Hall *C:* Thorburn *PG:* Thorburn (2)
ENGLAND 9
PG: Andrew (2) *DG:* Andrew

17 Feb 1990
Twickenham
ENGLAND 34
T: Carling, Underwood (2), Hill
C: Hodgkinson (3) *PG:* Hodgkinson (4)
WALES 6
T: Davies *C:* Thorburn

19 Jan 1991
Cardiff Arms Park
WALES 6
PG: Thorburn, Jenkins
ENGLAND 25
T: Teague *PG:* Hodgkinson (7)

7 Mar 1992
Twickenham
ENGLAND 24
T: Carling, Skinner, Dooley *C:* Webb (3)
PG: Webb (2)
WALES 0

IRELAND v SCOTLAND

17 Feb 1883
Ormeau, Belfast
IRELAND 0
SCOTLAND 1g 1t
T: Reid, Somerville *C:* Maclagan

16 Feb 1884
Raeburn Place, Edinburgh
SCOTLAND 2g 2t
T: Peterkin, Tod, Don Wauchope, Asher
C: Berry (2)
IRELAND 1t
T: McIntosh

7 Mar 1885
Raeburn Place, Edinburgh
SCOTLAND 1g 2t
T: Reid, Peterkin, Don Wauchope
C: Veitch
IRELAND 0

20 Feb 1886
Raeburn Place, Edinburgh
SCOTLAND 3g 2t 1dg
T: Don Wauchope (2), Morrison (2), Macfarlan *C:* Macfarlan (3) *DG:* Asher
IRELAND 0

19 Feb 1887
Ormeau, Belfast
IRELAND 0
SCOTLAND 1g 2t 1gm
T: Maclagan, McEwan, Morton *C:* Berry
GM: Berry

10 Mar 1888
Raeburn Place, Edinburgh
SCOTLAND 1g
T: Macfarlan *C:* Berry
IRELAND 0

16 Feb 1889
Ormeau, Belfast
IRELAND 1dg
DG: Stevenson
SCOTLAND 0

22 Feb 1890
Raeburn Place, Edinburgh
SCOTLAND 1t 1dg
T: JE Orr *DG:* Boswell
IRELAND 0

21 Feb 1891
Ballynafeigh, Belfast
IRELAND 0
SCOTLAND 14
T: Wotherspoon (3), Clauss, MacGregor
C: Boswell (3) *DG:* McEwan

20 Feb 1892
Raeburn Place, Edinburgh
SCOTLAND 2
T: Millar
IRELAND 0

20 Feb 1893
Ballynafeigh, Belfast
IRELAND 0
SCOTLAND 0

24 Feb 1894
Lansdowne Road, Dublin
IRELAND 5
T: Wells *C:* CJ Lytle
SCOTLAND 0

2 Mar 1895
Raeburn Place, Edinburgh
SCOTLAND 6
T: Welsh, Campbell
IRELAND 0

15 Feb 1896
Lansdowne Road, Dublin
IRELAND 0
SCOTLAND 0

20 Feb 1897
Powderhall, Edinburgh
SCOTLAND 8
T: Turnbull *C:* TM Scott *PG:* TM Scott
IRELAND 3
T: Bulger

19 Feb 1898
Balmoral Showgrounds, Belfast
IRELAND 0
SCOTLAND 8
T: TM Scott (2) *C:* TM Scott

18 Feb 1899
Inverleith, Edinburgh
SCOTLAND 3
PG: Donaldson
IRELAND 9
T: Campbell, Reid, Sealy

24 Feb 1900
Lansdowne Road, Dublin
IRELAND 0
SCOTLAND 0

23 Feb 1901
Inverleith, Edinburgh
SCOTLAND 9
T: Gillespie, Welsh (2)
IRELAND 5
T: Doran *C:* Irvine

22 Feb 1902
Balmoral Showgrounds, Belfast
IRELAND 5
T: G Doran *C:* Corley
SCOTLAND 0

28 Feb 1903
Inverleith, Edinburgh
SCOTLAND 3
T: Crabbie
IRELAND 0

27 Feb 1904
Lansdowne Road, Dublin
IRELAND 3
T: Moffatt
SCOTLAND 19
T: Bedell-Sivright (2), Timms, Macdonald, Simson *C:* Macdonald (2)

25 Feb 1905
Inverleith, Edinburgh
SCOTLAND 5
T: Timms *C:* Forrest
IRELAND 11
T: Tedford, Wallace, Moffatt *C:* Maclear

24 Feb 1906
Lansdowne Road, Dublin
IRELAND 6
T: Parke, Robb
SCOTLAND 13
T: Beddell-Sivright, Munro
C: MacCallum (2) *GM:* MacLeod

23 Feb 1907
Inverleith, Edinburgh
SCOTLAND 15
T: Sanderson, Purves, Frew
C: MacLeod, Geddes (2)
IRELAND 3
PG: Parke

29 Feb 1908
Lansdowne Road, Dublin
IRELAND 16
T: Thrift (2), Thompson, Beckett
C: Parke, Hinton
SCOTLAND 11
T: MacLeod, Martin *C:* MacLeod
PG: MacLeod

27 Feb 1909
Inverleith, Edinburgh
SCOTLAND 9
T: Lindsay-Watson, McGregor, Kyle
IRELAND 3
PG: Parke

26 Feb 1910
Balmoral Showgrounds, Belfast
IRELAND 0
SCOTLAND 14
T: Dobson, Walter (2), Stuart
C: MacCallum

25 Feb 1911
Inverleith, Edinburgh
SCOTLAND 10
T: Simson, Angus *DG:* Munro
IRELAND 16
T: O'Callaghan, Foster, Adams, Quinn
C: Hinton, Lloyd

24 Feb 1912
Lansdowne Road, Dublin
IRELAND 10
T: Foster *DG:* Lloyd *PG:* Lloyd
SCOTLAND 8
T: Turner, Will *C:* MacCallum

22 Feb 1913
Inverleith, Edinburgh
SCOTLAND 29
T: Stewart (4), Usher, Bowie, Purves
C: Turner (4)
IRELAND 14
T: Schute, Stokes *C:* Lloyd (2)
DG: Lloyd

28 Feb 1914
Lansdowne Road, Dublin
IRELAND 6
T: Quinn, McNamara
SCOTLAND 0

28 Feb 1920
Inverleith, Edinburgh
SCOTLAND 19
T: Crole (2), Angus, Browning
C: Kennedy (2) *PG:* Kennedy
IRELAND 0

26 Feb 1921
Lansdowne Road, Dublin
IRELAND 9
T: Cussen, Stephenson, Cunningham
SCOTLAND 9
T: Hume, Sloan *C:* Maxwell

25 Feb 1922
Inverleith, Edinburgh
SCOTLAND 6
T: Bryce, Liddell
IRELAND 3
T: Clarke

24 Feb 1923
Lansdowne Road, Dublin
IRELAND 3
T: Cussen
SCOTLAND 13
T: Liddell, McQueen, Browning
C: Browning (2)

23 Feb 1924
Inverleith, Edinburgh
SCOTLAND 13
T: Waddell (2), Bertram *C:* Drysdale (2)
IRELAND 8
T: G Stephenson (2) *C:* G Stephenson

28 Feb 1925
Lansdowne Road, Dublin
IRELAND 8
T: H Stephenson *C:* Crawford
PG: Crawford
SCOTLAND 14
T: Wallace, McMyn *C:* Drysdale, Dykes
DG: Waddell

27 Feb 1926
Murrayfield, Edinburgh
SCOTLAND 0
IRELAND 3
T: Gage

26 Feb 1927
Lansdowne Road, Dublin
IRELAND 6
T: Pike, Ganly
SCOTLAND 0

25 Feb 1928
Murrayfield
SCOTLAND 5
T: Kerr *C:* Drysdale
IRELAND 13
T: Ganly, Davy, Stephenson
C: Stephenson (2)

23 Feb 1929
Lansdowne Road, Dublin
IRELAND 7
T: Arigho *DG:* Davy
SCOTLAND 16
T: Macpherson, Bannerman, I Smith, Simmers *C:* Dykes, Allan

22 Feb 1930
Murrayfield
SCOTLAND 11
T: Ford, Macpherson, Waters *C:* Waters
IRELAND 14
T: Davy (3), Crowe *C:* Murray

28 Feb 1931
Lansdowne Road, Dublin
IRELAND 8
T: Sugden, Pike *C:* Murray
SCOTLAND 5
T: Mackintosh *C:* Allan

27 Feb 1932
Murrayfield
SCOTLAND 8
T: Wood, Simmers *C:* Allan
IRELAND 20
T: Lightfoot (2), Hunt, Waide *C:* Murray (4)

1 Apr 1933
Lansdowne Road, Dublin
IRELAND 6
T: Crowe, Murray
SCOTLAND 8
DG: Jackson, Lind

24 Feb 1934
Murrayfield
SCOTLAND 16
T: Dick (2), Crawford *C:* Shaw (2)
PG: Allan
IRELAND 9
T: Russell (2), O'Connor

23 Feb 1935
Lansdowne Road, Dublin
IRELAND 12
T: O'Connor, Lawlor, Bailey, Ridgeway
SCOTLAND 5
T: Shaw *C:* Fyfe

22 Feb 1936
Murrayfield
SCOTLAND 4
DG: Murdoch
IRELAND 10
T: Walker, McMahon *DG:* Hewitt

27 Feb 1937
Lansdowne Road, Dublin
IRELAND 11
T: Alexander, McMahon, Moran
C: Bailey
SCOTLAND 4
DG: Wilson Shaw

26 Feb 1938
Murrayfield
SCOTLAND 23
T: Forrest (2), Macrae, Drummond
C: Crawford (2) *DG:* Dorward
PG: Drummond
IRELAND 14
T: Cromey, O'Loughlin, Moran, Morgan
C: Walker

25 Feb 1939
Lansdowne Road, Dublin
IRELAND 12
T: Moran, Torrens *PG:* McKibbin
GM: Sayers
SCOTLAND 3
T: Innes

22 Feb 1947
Murrayfield
SCOTLAND 0
IRELAND 3
T: Mullan

28 Feb 1948
Lansdowne Road, Dublin
IRELAND 6
T: Mullan, Kyle
SCOTLAND 0

26 Feb 1949
Murrayfield
SCOTLAND 3
PG: Allardice
IRELAND 13
T: McCarthy (2) *C:* Norton (2)
PG: Norton

25 Feb 1950
Lansdowne Road, Dublin
IRELAND 21
T: Blayney, Curtis, Crow *C:* Norton (3)
PG: Norton (2)
SCOTLAND 0

24 Feb 1951
Murrayfield
SCOTLAND 5
T: Sloan *C:* Thomson
IRELAND 6
T: O'Brien *DG:* Henderson

23 Feb 1952
Lansdowne Road, Dublin
IRELAND 12
T: Lane, Kyle, Henderson
PG: Henderson
SCOTLAND 8
T: Davison *C:* Thomson *PG:* Thomson

28 Feb 1953
Murrayfield
SCOTLAND 8
T: Henderson *C:* I Thomson *PG:* I Thomson
IRELAND 26
T: McCarthy, Byrne (3), Mortell, Kavanagh *C:* Gregg (4)

27 Feb 1954
Ravenhill, Belfast
IRELAND 6
T: Mortell (2)
SCOTLAND 0

26 Feb 1955
Murrayfield
SCOTLAND 12
T: Swann *DG:* Cameron *PG:* Elgie (2)
IRELAND 3
PG: Kelly

25 Feb 1956
Lansdowne Road, Dublin
IRELAND 14
T: Henderson, O'Reilly, Kyle, O'Meara
C: Pedlow
SCOTLAND 10
T: Michie, Smith *C:* McClung (2)

23 Feb 1957
Murrayfield
SCOTLAND 3
PG: Scotland
IRELAND 5
T: O'Sullivan *C:* Berkery

1 Mar 1958
Lansdowne Road, Dublin
IRELAND 12
T: Pedlow (2) *PG:* Henderson, Berkery
SCOTLAND 6
T: Smith, Weatherstone

28 Feb 1959
Murrayfield
SCOTLAND 3
PG: Scotland
IRELAND 8
T: Dooley *C:* Hewitt *PG:* Hewitt

27 Feb 1960
Lansdowne Road, Dublin
IRELAND 5
T: Wood *C:* Hewitt
SCOTLAND 6
T: Thomson *DG:* Scotland

25 Feb 1961
Murrayfield
SCOTLAND 16
T: Douglas, Ross (2) *C:* Scotland (2)
PG: Scotland
IRELAND 8
T: Kavanagh, Hewitt *C:* Moffett

24 Feb 1962
Lansdowne Road, Dublin
IRELAND 6
T: Hunter *PG:* Hunter
SCOTLAND 20
T: Smith (2), Cowan *C:* Scotland
PG: Coughtrie *PG:* Scotland (2)

23 Feb 1963
Murrayfield
SCOTLAND 3
PG: Coughtrie
IRELAND 0

22 Feb 1964
Lansdowne Road, Dublin
IRELAND 3
PG: Kiernan
SCOTLAND 6
PG: Wilson (2)

27 Feb 1965
Murrayfield
SCOTLAND 6
DG: Laughland *PG:* Wilson
IRELAND 16
T: McGrath, Young, Murphy *C:* Kiernan (2) *DG:* Gibson

26 Feb 1966
Lansdowne Road, Dublin
IRELAND 3
PG: Kiernan
SCOTLAND 11
T: Hinshelwood (2), Grant *C:* Wilson

25 Feb 1967
Murrayfield
SCOTLAND 3
PG: Wilson
IRELAND 5
T: Murphy *C:* Kiernan

24 Feb 1968
Lansdowne Road, Dublin
IRELAND 14
T: Duggan (2), Bresnihan *C:* Kiernan
PG: Kiernan
SCOTLAND 6
PG: Wilson (2)

Scotland's David McIvor is brought down by Nick Popplewell and Fergus Aherne during Scotland's 18–10 win at Lansdowne Road in 1992.

22 Feb 1969
Murrayfield
SCOTLAND 0
IRELAND 16
T: Duggan, McGann, Gibson, Bresnihan
C: Moroney (2)

28 Feb 1970
Lansdowne Road, Dublin
IRELAND 16
T: Molloy, Goodall, Gibson, Brown
C: Kiernan (2)
SCOTLAND 11
T: Lauder, MA Smith *C:* I Smith
DG: Robertson

27 Feb 1971
Murrayfield
SCOTLAND 5
T: Frame *C:* P Brown
IRELAND 17
T: Duggan (2), Grant *C:* Gibson
PG: Gibson (2)

24 Feb 1973
Murrayfield
SCOTLAND 19
T: Forsyth *DG:* Morgan (2), McGeechan
PG: Morgan (2)
IRELAND 14
T: McMaster, Kiernan *PG:* McGann (2)

2 Mar 1974
Lansdowne Road, Dublin
IRELAND 9
T: Milliken *C:* Gibson *PG:* McKinney
SCOTLAND 6
PG: Irvine (2)

1 Feb 1975
Murrayfield
SCOTLAND 20
T: Renwick, Steele *DG:* Morgan, McGeechan *PG:* Irvine (2)
IRELAND 13
T: Dennison, Grace *C:* McCombe
PG: McCombe

20 Mar 1976
Lansdowne Road, Dublin
IRELAND 6
PG: McGann (2)
SCOTLAND 15
DG: Wilson *PG:* Irvine (4)

19 Feb 1977
Murrayfield
SCOTLAND 21
T: Gammell (2), Madsen *DG:* Morgan
PG: Irvine (2)
IRELAND 18
T: Gibson *C:* Gibson *DG:* Quinn
PG: Gibson (2), Quinn

21 Jan 1978
Lansdowne Road, Dublin
IRELAND 12
T: McKinney *C:* Ward *PG:* Ward (2)
SCOTLAND 9
PG: Morgan (3)

3 Mar 1979
Murrayfield
SCOTLAND 11
T: Rutherford, Irvine *PG:* Irvine
IRELAND 11
T: Patterson (2) *PG:* Ward

2 Feb 1980
Lansdowne Road, Dublin
IRELAND 22
T: Keane, Kennedy *C:* Campbell
DG: Campbell *PG:* Campbell (3)
SCOTLAND 15
T: Johnston (2) *C:* Irvine (2) *PG:* Irvine

21 Mar 1981
Murrayfield
SCOTLAND 10
T: Hay *DG:* Rutherford *PG:* Irvine
IRELAND 9
T: Irwin *C:* Campbell *PG:* Campbell

20 Feb 1982
Lansdowne Road, Dublin
IRELAND 21
DG: Campbell *PG:* Campbell (6)
SCOTLAND 12
T: Rutherford *C:* Irvine *PG:* Renwick (2)

15 Jan 1983
Murrayfield
SCOTLAND 13
T: Laidlaw *DG:* Renwick *PG:* Dods (2)
IRELAND 15
T: Kiernan *C:* Campbell *PG:* Campbell (3)

3 Mar 1984
Lansdowne Road, Dublin
IRELAND 9
T: Kiernan *C:* Murphy *PG:* Murphy
SCOTLAND 32
T: Laidlaw (2), Penalty try, Roberston, Dods *C:* Dods *PG:* Dods (2)

2 Feb 1985
Murrayfield
SCOTLAND 15
PG: Dods (4) *DG:* Robertson
IRELAND 18
T: Ringland (2) *C:* Kiernan (2)
PG: Kiernan *DG:* Kiernan

15 Mar 1986
Lansdowne Road, Dublin
IRELAND 9
T: Ringland *C:* Kiernan *PG:* Kiernan
SCOTLAND 10
T: Laidlaw *PG:* G Hastings (2)

21 Feb 1987
Murrayfield
SCOTLAND 16
T: Laidlaw, Tukalo *C:* G Hastings
DG: Rutherford (2)
IRELAND 12
T: Lenehan *C:* Kiernan *PG:* Kiernan
DG: Kiernan

16 Jan 1988
Lansdowne Road, Dublin
IRELAND 22
T: Mullin, MacNeill, Bradley *C:* Kiernan (2) *PG:* Kiernan *DG:* Kiernan
SCOTLAND 18
T: Laidlaw, S Hastings *C:* G Hastings (2) *PG:* G Hastings (2)

4 Mar 1989
Murrayfield
SCOTLAND 37
T: Tukalo (3), Jeffrey, Cronin *C:* Dods (4) *PG:* Dods (3)
IRELAND 21
T: Mullin (2), Dunlea *C:* Kiernan (3)
PG: Kiernan

3 Feb 1990
Lansdowne Road, Dublin
IRELAND 10
T: JJ Fitzgerald *PG:* Kiernan (2)
SCOTLAND 13
T: White (2) *C:* Chalmers
PG: Chalmers

16 Mar 1991
Murrayfield
SCOTLAND 28
T: G Hastings, Stanger, S Hastings
C: Chalmers (2) *PG:* Chalmers (3), G Hastings
IRELAND 25
T: Crossan, Robinson, Geoghegan, Mullin *C:* BA Smith (3) *DG:* BA Smith

15 Feb 1992
Lansdowne Road, Dublin
IRELAND 10
T: Wallace *PG:* Keyes (2)
SCOTLAND 18
T: Stanger, Nicol *C:* G Hastings (2)
PG: G Hastings (2)

IRELAND v WALES

12 Apr 1884
Cardiff Arms Park
WALES 2t 1dg
T: Norton, Clapp *DG:* Stadden
IRELAND 0

12 Mar 1887
Birkenhead Park
WALES 1t 1dg
T: Morgan *DG:* Gould
IRELAND 3t
T: Montgomery (3)

3 Mar 1888
Lansdowne Road, Dublin
IRELAND 1g 1t 1dg
T: Warren, Shanahan *C:* Rambaut
DG: Carpendale
WALES 0

2 Mar 1889
St Helens, Swansea
WALES 0
IRELAND 2t
T: McDonnell, Cotton

1 Mar 1890
Lansdowne Road, Dublin
IRELAND 1g
T: Dunlop *C:* Roche
WALES 1g
T: C Thomas *C:* Bancroft

7 Mar 1891
Stradey Park, Llanelli
WALES 6
T: D Samuel *C:* Bancroft
IRELAND 4
T: Lee *DG:* Walkington

5 Mar 1892
Lansdowne Road, Dublin
IRELAND 9
T: Walsh (2), Davies *C:* Roche
WALES 0

11 Mar 1893
Stradey Park, Llanelli
WALES 2
T: Bert Gould
IRELAND 0

19 Mar 1894
Ballynafeigh, Belfast
IRELAND 3
PG: John Lytle
WALES 0

16 Mar 1895
Cardiff Arms Park
WALES 5
T: Pearson *C:* Bancroft
IRELAND 3
T: Crean

14 Mar 1896
Lansdowne Road, Dublin
IRELAND 8
T: Crean, Lytle *C:* Bulger
WALES 4 *DG:* Gould

18 Mar 1898
Limerick
IRELAND 3
PG: Bulger
WALES 11
T: Dobson, Huzzey *C:* Bancroft
PG: Bancroft

18 Mar 1899
Cardiff Arms Park
WALES 0
IRELAND 3
T: Doran

17 Mar 1900
Balmoral Showgrounds, Belfast
IRELAND 0
WALES 3
T: Davies

16 Mar 1901
St Helens, Swansea
WALES 10
T: Alexander (2) *C:* Bancroft (2)
IRELAND 9
T: J Ryan, Freear, Davidson

8 Mar 1902
Lansdowne Road, Dublin
IRELAND 0
WALES 15
T: Nicholls, Llewellyn, Llewellyn Lloyd
C: Brice *DG:* Nicholls

14 Mar 1903
Cardiff Arms Park
WALES 18
T: Llewellyn (2), Gabe, Morgan (2), Brice
IRELAND 0

2 Mar 1904
Balmoral Showgrounds, Belfast
IRELAND 14
T: Tedford (2), J Wallace, Thrift
C: Parke
WALES 12
T: Morgan (2), Gabe, Cliff Pritchard

11 Mar 1905
St Helens, Swansea
WALES 10
T: Wyndham Jones, Morgan *C:* Davies (2)
IRELAND 3
T: Robinson

10 Mar 1906
Balmoral Showgrounds, Belfast
IRELAND 11
T: Thrift, Wallace, Maclear *C:* Gardiner
WALES 6
T: Morgan, Gabe

9 Mar 1907
Cardiff Arms Park
WALES 29
T: Williams (3), Jones, Gabe, Bush
C: Winfield (2) *DG:* Bush *PG:* Winfield
IRELAND 0

14 Mar 1908
Balmoral Showgrounds, Belfast
IRELAND 5
T: Aston *C:* Parke
WALES 11
T: Williams (2), Gibbs *C:* Winfield

13 Mar 1909
St Helens, Swansea
WALES 18
T: J Jones, Hopkins, Watts, Trew
C: Bancroft (3)
IRELAND 5
T: Thompson *C:* Parke

12 Mar 1910
Lansdowne Road, Dublin
IRELAND 3
T: McIldowie
WALES 19
T: Williams (3), Gibbs, Dyke *DG: Bush*

11 Mar 1911
Cardiff Arms Park
WALES 16
T: T Evans, Webb, Gibbs *C:* Bancroft (2) *PG:* Bancroft
IRELAND 0

9 Mar 1912
Balmoral Showgrounds, Belfast
IRELAND 12
T: McIvor, Brown *C:* Lloyd *DG:* Lloyd
WALES 5
T: Davies *C:* Bancroft

8 Mar 1913
St Helens, Swansea
WALES 16
T: B Lewis (2), Jones *C:* Bancroft (2)
PG: Bancroft
IRELAND 13
T: T Quinn, Stewart *C:* Lloyd (2)
PG: Lloyd

14 Mar 1914
Balmoral Showgrounds, Belfast
IRELAND 3
T: Foster
WALES 11
T: Bedwelty Jones, Evans, Wetter
C: Lewis

13 Mar 1920
Cardiff Arms Park
WALES 28
T: B Williams, Jenkins, Whitfield, Parker
C: Jenkins (2), Wetter *DG:* Jenkins
IRELAND 4
DG: McFarland

12 Mar 1921
Balmoral Showgrounds, Belfast
IRELAND 0
WALES 6
T: M Thomas *PG:* Johnson

11 Mar 1922
St Helens, Swansea
WALES 11
T: Whitfield (2), I Evans *C:* Samuel
IRELAND 5
T: Stokes *C:* Wallis

10 Mar 1923
Lansdowne Road, Dublin
IRELAND 5
T: Cussen *C:* Crawford
WALES 4
DG: Powell

8 Mar 1924
Cardiff Arms Park
WALES 10
T: Richards, Pugh *DG:* Watkins
IRELAND 13
T: T Hewitt, F Hewitt, G Stephenson
C: Crawford (2)

14 Mar 1925
Ravenhill, Belfast
IRELAND 19
T: Millin, G Stephenson, Browne, H Stephenson *C:* G Stephenson (2)
PG: G Stephenson
WALES 3
T: Turnbull

13 Mar 1926
St Helens, Swansea
WALES 11
T: Harding, Hopkins, Herrera *C:* Rees
IRELAND 8
T: Hanrahan *C:* Stephenson
PG: Stephenson

12 Mar 1927
Lansdowne Road, Dublin
IRELAND 19
T: Stephenson (2), Ganly (2)
C: Stephenson (2) *PG:* Stephenson
WALES 9
T: Morgan *C:* Powell *DG:* Lewis

10 Mar 1928
Cardiff Arms Park
WALES 10
T: D John, A Jenkins *C:* I Jones (2)
IRELAND 13
T: Arigho (2), Ganly *C:* Stephenson (2)

9 Mar 1929
Ravenhill, Belfast
IRELAND 5
T: Davy *C:* Stephenson
WALES 5
T: Williams *C:* Parker

8 Mar 1930
St Helens, Swansea
WALES 12
T: Skym, Arthur Jones/Peacock (joint)
PG: Bassett
IRELAND 7
DG: Davy *PG:* Murray

14 Mar 1931
Ravenhill, Belfast
IRELAND 3
T: Siggins
WALES 15
T: Morley (2), Davey *C:* Bassett
DG: Ralph

12 Mar 1932
Cardiff Arms Park
WALES 10
T: Davey, Ralph *DG:* Ralph
IRELAND 12
T: Ross (2), Lightfoot, Waide

11 Mar 1933
Ravenhill, Belfast
IRELAND 10
T: Barnes *DG:* Davy *PG:* Siggins
WALES 5
T: Bowcott *C:* Jenkins

10 Mar 1934
St Helens, Swansea
WALES 13
T: Fear, Cowey, Jenkins *C:* Jenkins
IRELAND 0

9 Mar 1935
Ravenhill, Belfast
IRELAND 9
T: Doyle *PG:* Siggins, Bailey
WALES 3
PG: James

14 Mar 1936
Cardiff Arms Park
WALES 3
PG: Jenkins
IRELAND 0

3 Apr 1937
Ravenhill, Belfast
IRELAND 5
T: Bailey *C:* Walker
WALES 3
PG: Legge

12 Mar 1938
St Helens, Swansea
WALES 11
T: Taylor, Clement *C:* Legge
PG: Wooller
IRELAND 5
T: Moran *C:* McKibbin

11 Mar 1939
Ravenhill, Belfast
IRELAND 0
WALES 7
T: Willie Davies *DG:* Willie Davies

20 Mar 1947
St Helens, Swansea
WALES 6
T: B Evans *PG:* Tamplin
IRELAND 0

13 Mar 1948
Ravenhill, Belfast
IRELAND 6
T: Mullan, Daly
WALES 3
T: Bleddyn Williams

12 Mar 1949
St Helens, Swansea
WALES 0
IRELAND 5
T: McCarthy *C:* Norton

11 Mar 1950
Ravenhill, Belfast
IRELAND 3
PG: Norton
WALES 6
T: K Jones, Thomas

10 Mar 1951
Cardiff Arms Park
WALES 3
PG: Edwards
IRELAND 3
T: Kyle

8 Mar 1952
Lansdowne Road, Dublin
IRELAND 3
PG: Murphy
WALES 14
T: C Thomas, K Jones, Stephens
C: Lewis Jones *PG:* Lewis Jones

14 Mar 1953
St Helens, Swansea
WALES 5
T: Griffiths *C:* T Davies
IRELAND 3
T: Pedlow

13 Mar 1954
Lansdowne Road, Dublin
IRELAND 9
T: Gaston *PG:* Henderson, Kelly
WALES 12
DG: D Thomas *PG:* Evans (3)

12 Mar 1955
Cardiff Arms Park
WALES 21
T: Meredith, Griffiths, Morgan, Morris
C: Owen (3) *PG:* Owen
IRELAND 3
PG: Henderson

10 Mar 1956
Lansdowne Road, Dublin
IRELAND 11
T: Cunningham *C:* Pedlow *DG:* Kyle
PG: Pedlow
WALES 3
PG: Owen

9 Mar 1957
Cardiff Arms Park
WALES 6
PG: TJ Davies (2)
IRELAND 5
T: Kavanagh *C:* Pedlow

15 Mar 1958
Lansdowne Road, Dublin
IRELAND 6
T: O'Meara *PG:* Henderson
WALES 9
T: H Morgan, HV Meredith, Roberts

14 Mar 1959
Cardiff Arms Park
WALES 8
T: Ashton, M Price *C:* TJ Davies
IRELAND 6
T: O'Reilly *PG:* D Hewitt

12 Mar 1960
Lansdowne Road, Dublin
IRELAND 9
T: Murphy *PG:* Kelly (2)
WALES 10
T: Cresswell, Brace *C:* Morgan (2)

11 Mar 1961
Cardiff Arms Park
WALES 9
T: Richards *PG:* Richards (2)
IRELAND 0

17 Nov 1962
Lansdowne Road, Dublin
IRELAND 3
DG: English
WALES 3
PG: Hodgson

9 Mar 1963
Cardiff Arms Park
WALES 6
T: G Jones *DG:* Watkins
IRELAND 14
T: Casey *C:* Kiernan *DG:* English
PG: Kiernan (2)

7 Mar 1964
Lansdowne Road, Dublin
IRELAND 6
PG: Keogh (2)
WALES 15
T: S Watkins, Dawes, D Watkins
C: Bradshaw (3)

13 Mar 1965
Cardiff Arms Park
WALES 14
T: D Watkins, Bebb *C:* T Price *DG:* T Price *PG:* T Price
IRELAND 8
T: Flynn *C:* Kiernan *PG:* Kiernan

12 Mar 1966
Lansdowne Road, Dublin
IRELAND 9
T: Bresnihan *DG:* Gibson *PG:* Gibson
WALES 6
T: Prothero *PG:* Bradshaw

11 Mar 1967
Cardiff Arms Park
WALES 0
IRELAND 3
T: Duggan

9 Mar 1968
Lansdowne Road, Dublin
IRELAND 9
T: M Doyle *DG:* Gibson *PG:* Kiernan
WALES 6
DG: Edwards *PG:* D Rees

8 Mar 1969
Cardiff Arms Park
WALES 24
T: S Watkins, D Williams, Morris, Taylor
C: Jarrett (3) *DG:* John *PG:* Jarrett
IRELAND 11
T: Gibson *C:* Kiernan *PG:* Kiernan (2)

14 Mar 1970
Lansdowne Road, Dublin
IRELAND 14
T: Duggan, Goodall *C:* Kiernan
DG: McGann *PG:* Kiernan
WALES 0

13 Mar 1971
Cardiff Arms Park
WALES 23
T: TGR Davies (2), Edwards (2) *C:* John
DG: John *PG:* John (2)
IRELAND 9
PG: Gibson (3)

10 Mar 1973
Cardiff Arms Park
WALES 16
T: Shanklin, Edwards *C:* Bennett
PG: Bennett (2)
IRELAND 12
T: Gibson *C:* McGann *PG:* McGann (2)

2 Feb 1974
Lansdowne Road, Dublin
IRELAND 9
PG: Ensor (3)
WALES 9
T: JJ Williams *C:* Bennett *PG:* Bennett

15 Mar 1975
Cardiff Arms Park
WALES 32
T: Edwards, TGR Davies, Faulkner, JJ Williams, Bergiers *C:* Bennett (3)
IRELAND 4
T: Duggan

21 Feb 1976
Lansdowne Road, Dublin
IRELAND 9
PG: McGann (3)
WALES 34
T: TGR Davies (2), Edwards, Bennett
C: Bennett (3) *PG:* Bennett (3), Martin

15 Jan 1977
Cardiff Arms Park
WALES 25
T: Davies, JPR Williams, Burgess
C: Bennett (2) *DG:* Fenwick
PG: Bennett (2)
IRELAND 9
PG: Gibson (3)

4 Mar 1978
Lansdowne Road, Dublin
IRELAND 16
T: Moloney *DG:* Ward *PG:* Ward (3)
WALES 20
T: Fenwick, JJ Williams *PG:* Fenwick (4)

3 Feb 1979
Cardiff Arms Park
WALES 24
T: Martin, Ringer *C:* Fenwick (2)
PG: Fenwick (4)
IRELAND 21
T: McLennan, Patterson *C:* Ward (2)
PG: Ward (3)

15 Mar 1980
Lansdowne Road, Dublin
IRELAND 21
T: Irwin, O'Driscoll, Fitzgerald
C: Campbell (3) *PG:* Campbell
WALES 7
T: Blyth *PG:* Fenwick

21 Feb 1981
Cardiff Arms Park
WALES 9
DG: Pearce *PG:* Evans (2)
IRELAND 8
T: Slattery, MacNeill

23 Jan 1982
Lansdowne Road, Dublin
IRELAND 20
T: Ringland, Finn (2) *C:* Campbell
PG: Campbell (2)
WALES 12
T: Holmes *C:* G Evans *DG:* Pearce
PG: G Evans

5 Mar 1983
Cardiff Arms Park
WALES 23
T: T Wyatt, Holmes, E Rees *C:* Wyatt
PG: Wyatt (3)
IRELAND 9
PG: Campbell (2), MacNeill

4 Feb 1984
Lansdowne Road, Dublin
IRELAND 9
PG: Campbell (3)
WALES 18
T: Ackerman *C:* H Davies *PG:* H Davies (2), Bowen (2)

16 Mar 1985
Cardiff Arms Park
WALES 9
T: PI Lewis *C:* WG Davies *PG:* WG Davies
IRELAND 21
T: Crossan, Ringland *C:* Kiernan
PG: Kiernan (3)

15 Feb 1986
Lansdowne Road, Dublin
IRELAND 12
T: Ringland *C:* Kiernan *PG:* Kiernan (2)
WALES 19
T: PI Lewis, PT Davies *C:* Thorburn
PG: Thorburn (3)

4 Apr 1987
Cardiff Arms Park
WALES 11
T: I Evans, Norster *PG:* Wyatt
IRELAND 15
T: Dean, Mullin *C:* Kiernan (2)
PG: Kiernan

5 Mar 1988
Lansdowne Road, Dublin
IRELAND 9
T: Kingston *C:* Kiernan *PG:* Kiernan
WALES 12
T: Moriarty *C:* Thorburn *PG:* Thorburn
DG: Davies

4 Feb 1989
Cardiff Arms Park
WALES 13
T: M Jones *PG:* Thorburn (3)
IRELAND 19
T: Mannion, Dean *C:* Kiernan
PG: Kiernan (3)

24 Mar 1990
Lansdowne Road, Dublin
IRELAND 14
T: Smith, McBride, Kingston *C:* Kiernan
WALES 8
T: Ford, Llewellyn

18 Feb 1991
Cardiff Arms Park
WALES 21
T: Arnold, Jenkins *C:* Thorburn (2)
PG: Thorburn (2) *DG:* Jenkins
IRELAND 21
T: Clarke, Mullin, Geoghegan, Staples
C: BA Smith *DG:* BA Smith

18 Jan 1992
Lansdowne Road, Dublin
IRELAND 15
T: Wallace *C:* Keyes *PG:* Keyes (3)
WALES 16
T: S Davies *PG:* Jenkins (3)
DG: Stephens

SCOTLAND v WALES

8 Jan 1883
Raeburn Place, Edinburgh
SCOTLAND 3g
T: McFarlan (2), Don Wauchope
C: Maclagan (3)
WALES 1g
T: Judson *C:* Lewis

12 Jan 1884
Rodney Parade, Newport
WALES 0
SCOTLAND 1t 1dg
T: Ainslie *DG:* Asher

10 Jan 1885
Hamilton Crescent, Glasgow
SCOTLAND 0
WALES 0

9 Jan 1886
Cardiff Arms Park
WALES 0
SCOTLAND 2g 1t
T: Clay, Todd, AR Don Wauchope
C: Macleod (2)

26 Feb 1887
Raeburn Place, Edinburgh
SCOTLAND 4g 8t
T: Lindsay (5), Don Wauchope, Orr, Reid, Macmillan, McEwan, Maclagan, Morton *C:* Berry (2), Woodrow (2)
WALES 0

4 Feb 1888
Rodney Parade, Newport
WALES 1t
T: Pryce-Jenkins
SCOTLAND 0

2 Feb 1889
Raeburn Place, Edinburgh
SCOTLAND 2t
T: Orr, Ker
WALES 0

1 Feb 1890
Cardiff Arms Park
WALES 1t
T: Gould
SCOTLAND 1g 2t
T: Anderson, Boswell, Maclagan
C: McEwan

7 Feb 1891
Raeburn Place, Edinburgh
SCOTLAND 15
T: CE Orr, JE Orr, Goodhue, Clauss (2), Leggatt, Boswell *C:* McEwan *DG:* W Neilson, Stevenson
WALES 0

6 Feb 1892
St Helens, Swansea
WALES 2
T: Hannan
SCOTLAND 7
T: Boswell, Campbell *C:* Boswell

4 Feb 1893
Raeburn Place, Edinburgh
SCOTLAND 0
WALES 9
T: Bert Gould, Biggs, McCutcheon
C: Bancroft

3 Feb 1894
Rodney Parade, Newport
WALES 7
T: Fitzgerald *DG:* Fitzgerald
SCOTLAND 0

26 Jan 1895
Raeburn Place, Edinburgh
SCOTLAND 5
T: Gowans *C:* HO Smith
WALES 4
GM: Bancroft

25 Jan 1896
Cardiff Arms Park
WALES 6
T: Bowen, Gould
SCOTLAND 0

4 Mar 1899
Inverleith, Edinburgh
SCOTLAND 21
T: Gedge, Smith, Monypenny
DG: Lamond, Gedge *GM:* Thomson
WALES 10
T: Llewellyn Lloyd, Llewellyn
C: Bancroft (2)

27 Jan 1900
St Helens, Swansea
WALES 12
T: Llewellyn (2), Nicholls, Williams
SCOTLAND 3
T: Dykes

9 Feb 1901
Inverleith, Edinburgh
SCOTLAND 18
T: Gillespie (2), Turnbull, Flett
C: Gillespie (2), Flett
WALES 8
T: Llewellyn Lloyd, Boots *C:* Bancroft

1 Feb 1902
Cardiff Arms Park
WALES 14
T: Llewellyn (2), Gabe (2) *C:* Strand-Jones
SCOTLAND 5
T: Welsh *C:* Gillespie

7 Feb 1903
Inverleith, Edinburgh
SCOTLAND 6
T: Kyle *PG:* Timms
WALES 0

6 Feb 1904
St Helens, Swansea
WALES 21
T: Gabe, Jones, Morgan, Brice
C: Winfield (3) *PG:* Winfield
SCOTLAND 3
T: Orr

4 Feb 1905
Inverleith, Edinburgh
SCOTLAND 3
T: Little
WALES 6
T: Llewellyn (2)

3 Feb 1906
Cardiff Arms Park
WALES 9
T: Hodges, Cliff Pritchard, Maddocks
SCOTLAND 3
PG: MacLeod

2 Feb 1907
Inverleith, Edinburgh
SCOTLAND 6
T: Purves, Monteith
WALES 3
PG: Winfield

1 Feb 1908
St Helens, Swansea
WALES 6
T: Trew, Williams
SCOTLAND 5
T: Purves *C:* Geddes

6 Feb 1909
Inverleith, Edinburgh
SCOTLAND 3
PG: Cunningham
WALES 5
T: Trew *C:* Bancroft

5 Feb 1910
Cardiff Arms Park
WALES 14
T: Pugsley, Spiller, Baker, Ivor Morgan
C: Bancroft
SCOTLAND 0

4 Feb 1911
Inverleith, Edinburgh
SCOTLAND 10
T: Turner, Scott *DG:* Munro
WALES 32
T: Gibbs (3), Spiller (2), Williams (2), Rhys Thomas *C:* Dyke (2) *DG:* Spiller

3 Feb 1912
St Helens, Swansea
WALES 21
T: Hirst, Morgan, Plummer *C:* Bancroft (2) *DG:* Trew, Birt
SCOTLAND 6
T: Will, Milroy

1 Feb 1913
Inverleith, Edinburgh
SCOTLAND 0
WALES 8
T: C Lewis, T Jones *C:* C Lewis

7 Feb 1914
Cardiff Arms Park
WALES 24
T: Ivor Davies, Wetter, Hirst *C:* Bancroft (2) *DG:* Hirst, Lewis *PG:* Bancroft
SCOTLAND 5
T: Stewart *C:* Laing

7 Feb 1920
Inverleith, Edinburgh
SCOTLAND 9
T: Sloan *PG:* Kennedy (2)
WALES 5
T: Jenkins *C:* Jenkins

5 Feb 1921
St Helens, Swansea
WALES 8
DG Jenkins (2)
SCOTLAND 14
T: Thomson, Buchanan, Sloan
C: Maxwell *PG:* Maxwell

4 Feb 1922
Inverleith, Edinburgh
SCOTLAND 9
T: Browning (2) *PG:* Browning
WALES 9
T: Bowen *C:* Samuel *DG:* I Evans

3 Feb 1923
Cardiff Arms Park
WALES 8
T: Lewis *C:* A Jenkins *PG:* A Jenkins
SCOTLAND 11
T: Liddell, Stuart, Gracie *C:* Drysdale

2 Feb 1924
Inverleith, Edinburgh
SCOTLAND 35
T: Smith (3), Bryce, Bertram, Wallace, Waddell, Macpherson *C:* Drysdale (4)
PG: Drysdale
WALES 10
T: Griffiths, Ivor Jones *C:* Male (2)

7 Feb 1925
St Helens, Swansea
WALES 14
T: Hopkins, Jones, Cornish *C:* Parker
PG: Parker
SCOTLAND 24
T: Smith (4), Wallace (2) *C:* Drysdale
PG: Drysdale

6 Feb 1926
Murrayfield, Edinburgh
SCOTLAND 8
T: Waddell *C:* Drysdale *PG:* Gillies
WALES 5
T: Herrera *C:* Everson

5 Feb 1927
Cardiff Arms Park
WALES 0
SCOTLAND 5
T: Kerr *C:* Gillies

4 Feb 1928
Murrayfield
SCOTLAND 0
WALES 13
T: A Jenkins, Dai John, Roberts *C:* Male (2)

2 Feb 1929
St Helens, Swansea
WALES 14
T: Roberts (2), Morgan, Peacock *C:* Ivor Jones
SCOTLAND 7
DG: Dykes *PG:* Brown

1 Feb 1930
Murrayfield
SCOTLAND 12
T: Simmers (2) *C:* Waters *DG:* Waddell
WALES 9
T: G Jones *C:* Ivor Jones *DG:* G Jones

7 Feb 1931
Cardiff Arms Park
WALES 13
T: Morley, Thomas, Boon *C:* Bassett (2)
SCOTLAND 8
T: Crichton-Miller (2) *C:* Allan

6 Feb 1932
Murrayfield
SCOTLAND 0
WALES 6
T: Boon *PG:* Bassett

4 Feb 1933
St Helens, Swansea
WALES 3
T: Arthur
SCOTLAND 11
T: Smith, Jackson *C:* Fyfe *PG:* Fyfe

3 Feb 1934
Murrayfield
SCOTLAND 6
T: Logan *PG:* Ritchie
WALES 13
T: Cowey (2), Rees *C:* Jenkins (2)

2 Feb 1935
Cardiff Arms Park
WALES 10
T: Jones, Wooller *DG:* Jenkins
SCOTLAND 6
T: Thom, Shaw

1 Feb 1936
Murrayfield
SCOTLAND 3
T: Murray
WALES 13
T: Wooller, Davey, Jones *C:* Jenkins (2)

6 Feb 1937
St Helens, Swansea
WALES 6
T: Wooller
SCOTLAND 13
T: Wilson Shaw, Dick (2) *C:* Duncan Shaw (2)

5 Feb 1938
Murrayfield
SCOTLAND 8
T: Crawford *C:* Crawford *PG:* Crawford
WALES 6
T: McCarley (2)

4 Feb 1939
Cardiff Arms Park
WALES 11
T: M Davies, Travers *C:* Wooller *PG:* Wooller
SCOTLAND 3
PG: Crawford

1 Feb 1947
Murrayfield
SCOTLAND 8
T: Elliot *C:* Geddes *PG:* Geddes
WALES 22
T: K Jones (2), B Williams, Cleaver, L Williams *C:* Tamplin (2) *PG:* Tamplin

7 Feb 1948
Cardiff Arms Park
WALES 14
T: B Williams, Matthews, K Jones *C:* Tamplin *PG:* Tamplin
SCOTLAND 0

5 Feb 1949
Murrayfield
SCOTLAND 6
T: Gloag, Smith
WALES 5
T: Williams *C:* Trott

4 Feb 1950
St Helens, Swansea
WALES 12
T: Thomas, K Jones *DG:* Cleaver *PG:* Lewis Jones
SCOTLAND 0

3 Feb 1951
Murrayfield
SCOTLAND 19
T: Gordon (2), Dawson *C:* Inglis, Thomson *DG:* Kininmonth *PG:* Thomson
WALES 0

2 Feb 1952
Cardiff Arms Park
WALES 11
T: K Jones *C:* M Thomas *PG:* M Thomas (2)
SCOTLAND 0

7 Feb 1953
Murrayfield
SCOTLAND 0
WALES 12
T: B Williams (2), Jones *PG:* Davies

10 Apr 1954
St Helens, Swansea
WALES 15
T: Rhys Williams, Meredith, Ray Williams, Morgan *PG:* Evans
SCOTLAND 3
T: Henderson

5 Feb 1955
Murrayfield
SCOTLAND 14
T: Smith, Nicol *C:* Elgie *DG:* Docherty *PG:* Elgie
WALES 8
T: Brewer (2) *C:* Stephens

4 Feb 1956
Cardiff Arms Park
WALES 9
T: H Morgan, C Morgan, Davies
SCOTLAND 3
PG: Cameron

2 Feb 1957
Murrayfield
SCOTLAND 9
T: Smith *DG:* Dorward *PG:* Scotland
WALES 6
T: R Davies *PG:* T Davies

1 Feb 1958
Cardiff Arms Park
WALES 8
T: Wells, Collins *C:* T Davies
SCOTLAND 3
PG: A Smith

7 Feb 1959
Murrayfield
SCOTLAND 6
T: Bruce *PG:* Scotland
WALES 5
T: Price *C:* T Davies

6 Feb 1960
Cardiff Arms Park
WALES 8
T: Bebb *C:* Morgan *PG:* Morgan
SCOTLAND 0

11 Feb 1961
Murrayfield
SCOTLAND 3
T: A Smith
WALES 0

3 Feb 1962
Cardiff Arms Park
WALES 3
PG: Rees
SCOTLAND 8
T: Glasgow, ten Bos *C:* Scotland

2 Feb 1963
Murrayfield
SCOTLAND 0
WALES 6
DG: Rowlands *PG:* Hodgson

1 Feb 1964
Cardiff Arms Park
WALES 11
T: Bradshaw, Thomas *C:* Bradshaw
PG: Bradshaw
SCOTLAND 3
T: Laughland

6 Feb 1965
Murrayfield
SCOTLAND 12
DG: Simmers (2) *PG:* Wilson (2)
WALES 14
T: S Watkins, Gale *C:* T Price *PG:* T Price (2)

5 Feb 1966
Cardiff Arms Park
WALES 8
T: K Jones (2) *C:* Bradshaw
SCOTLAND 3
PG: Wilson

4 Feb 1967
Murrayfield
SCOTLAND 11
T: Hinshelwood, Telfer *C:* Wilson
DG: Chisholm
WALES 5
T: Watkins *C:* T Price

3 Feb 1968
Cardiff Arms Park
WALES 5
T: K Jones *C:* Jarrett
SCOTLAND 0

1 Feb 1969
Murrayfield
SCOTLAND 3
PG: Blaikie
WALES 17
T: John, Edwards, MCR Richards
C: Jarrett *PG:* Jarrett (2)

7 Feb 1970
Cardiff Arms Park
WALES 18
T: Daniel, Llewelyn, Dawes, Morris
C: Edwards (2), Daniel
SCOTLAND 9
T: Robertson *DG:* Robertson
PG: Lauder

6 Feb 1971
Murrayfield
SCOTLAND 18
T: Carmichael, Rea *PG:* Brown (4)
WALES 19
T: Taylor, Edwards, John, TGR Davies
C: John, Taylor *PG:* John

5 Feb 1972
Cardiff Arms Park
WALES 35
T: Edwards (2), Bergiers, TGR Davies, Taylor *C:* John (3) *PG:* John (3)
SCOTLAND 12
T: Clark *C:* P Brown *PG:* Renwick, P Brown

3 Feb 1973
Murrayfield
SCOTLAND 10
T: Telfer, Steele *C:* Morgan
WALES 9
PG: Bennett (2), Taylor

19 Jan 1974
Cardiff Arms Park
WALES 6
T: Cobner *C:* Bennett
SCOTLAND 0

1 Mar 1975
Murrayfield
SCOTLAND 12
DG: McGeechan *PG:* Morgan (3)
WALES 10
T: TP Evans *PG:* Fenwick (2)

7 Feb 1976
Cardiff Arms Park
WALES 28
T: JJ Williams, Edwards, TP Evans
C: Bennett (2) *DG:* Fenwick
PG: Bennett (3)
SCOTLAND 6
T: Irvine *C:* Morgan

19 Mar 1977
Murrayfield
SCOTLAND 9
T: Irvine *C:* Irvine *DG:* McGeechan
WALES 18
T: JJ Williams, Bennett *C:* Bennett (2)
PG: Bennett (2)

18 Feb 1978
Cardiff Arms Park
WALES 22
T: Edwards, Gravell, Fenwick, Quinnell
DG: Bennett *PG:* Bennett
SCOTLAND 14
T: Renwick, Tomes *PG:* Morgan (2)

20 Jan 1979
Murrayfield
SCOTLAND 13
T: Irvine *PG:* Irvine (3)
WALES 19
T: E Rees, Holmes *C:* Fenwick
PG: Fenwick (3)

1 Mar 1980
Cardiff Arms Park
WALES 17
T: Holmes, Keen, DS Richards *C:* Blyth
PG: Fenwick
SCOTLAND 6
T: Renwick *C:* Irvine

7 Feb 1981
Murrayfield
SCOTLAND 15
T: Tomes, Irvine (pen. try) *C:* Renwick (2) *PG:* Renwick
WALES 6
DG: Fenwick (2)

20 Mar 1982
Cardiff Arms Park
WALES 18
T: Butler *C:* G Evans *PG:* G Evans (4)
SCOTLAND 34
T: Calder, Renwick, Pollock, White, Johnston *C:* Irvine (4) *DG:* Renwick, Rutherford

19 Feb 1983
Murrayfield
SCOTLAND 15
T: Renwick *C:* Dods *PG:* Dods (3)
WALES 19
T: ST Jones, E Rees *C:* Wyatt
PG: Wyatt (3)

21 Jan 1984
Cardiff Arms Park
WALES 9
T: Titley *C:* H Davies *PG:* H Davies
SCOTLAND 15
T: Paxton, Aitken *C:* Dods (2)
PG: Dods

2 Mar 1985
Murrayfield
SCOTLAND 21
T: Paxton (2) *C:* Dods (2) *PG:* Dods
DG: Rutherford (2)
WALES 25
T: Pickering (2) *C:* Wyatt *PG:* Wyatt (4)
DG: WG Davies

1 Feb 1986
Cardiff Arms Park
WALES 22
T: Hadley *PG:* Thorburn (5) *DG:* J Davies
SCOTLAND 15
T: Duncan, Jeffrey, G Hastings *PG:* G Hastings

21 Mar 1987
Murrayfield
SCOTLAND 21
T: Beattie, Jeffrey *C:* G Hastings (2) *PG:* G Hastings (2) *DG:* Rutherford
WALES 14
T: M Jones *C:* Wyatt *PG:* Wyatt (2) *DG:* J Davies

20 Feb 1988
Cardiff Arms Park
WALES 25
T: Davies, Evans, Watkins *C:* Thorburn (2) *PG:* Thorburn *DG:* Davies (2)
SCOTLAND 20
T: Calder, Duncan *PG:* G Hastings (4)

21 Jan 1989
Murrayfield
SCOTLAND 23
T: Armstrong, White, Chalmers *C:* Dods *PG:* Dods (2) *DG:* Chalmers
WALES 7
T: Hall *PG:* Bowen

3 Mar 1990
Cardiff Arms Park
WALES 9
T: Emyr *C:* Thorburn *PG:* Thorburn
SCOTLAND 13
T: Cronin *PG:* Chalmers (3)

2 Feb 1991
Murrayfield
SCOTLAND 32
T: Chalmers, White (2), Armstrong *C:* Chalmers, G Hastings *PG:* Chalmers, G Hastings (2) *DG:* Chalmers
WALES 12
T: Ford *C:* Thorburn *PG:* Thorburn (2)

21 Mar 1992
Cardiff Arms Park
WALES 15
T: Webster *C:* Jenkins *PG:* Jenkins (3)
SCOTLAND 12
PG: G Hastings, Chalmers (2) *DG:* Chalmers

FRANCE v ENGLAND

3 Mar 1910
Parc des Princes, Paris
FRANCE 3
T: Communeau
ENGLAND 11
T: Hudson (2), Berry *C:* Chapman

28 Jan 1911
Twickenham
ENGLAND 37
T: Lambert (2), Pillman (2), Mann, A Stoop, Wodehouse *C:* Lambert (5) *PG:* Lambert (2)
FRANCE 0

8 Apr 1912
Parc des Princes, Paris
FRANCE 8
T: Dafau, Falliot *C:* Boyau
ENGLAND 18
T: Birkett, Brougham, Eddison, Roberts *C:* Pillman *DG:* Coverdale

25 Jan 1913
Twickenham
ENGLAND 20
T: Coates (3), Pillman (2), Poulton *C:* Greenwood
FRANCE 0

13 Apr 1914
Stade Colombes, Paris
FRANCE 13
T: Andre, Capmau, Lubin-Lebrere *C:* Besset (2)
ENGLAND 39
T: Poulton (4), Lowe (3), Davies, Watson *C:* Greenwood (6)

31 Jan 1920
Twickenham
ENGLAND 8
T: Davies *C:* Greenwood *PG:* Greenwood
FRANCE 3
T: Crabos

28 Mar 1921
Stade Colombes, Paris
FRANCE 6
PG: Crabos (2)
ENGLAND 10
T: Blakiston, Lowe *C:* Hammett (2)

25 Feb 1922
Twickenham
ENGLAND 11
T: Voyce *C:* Day *PG:* Day (2)
FRANCE 11
T: Cassayet, Got, Lasserre *C:* Crabos

2 Apr 1923
Stade Colombes, Paris
FRANCE 3
PG: Beguet
ENGLAND 12
T: Conway, Wakefield *C:* Luddington *DG:* Davies

23 Feb 1924
Twickenham
ENGLAND 19
T: Jacob (3), Catcheside, Young *C:* Conway (2)
FRANCE 7
T: Ballarin *DG:* Behoteguy

13 Apr 1925
Stade Colombes, Paris
FRANCE 11
T: Barthe, Besson, Cluchague *C:* Ducousso
ENGLAND 13
T: Hamilton-Wickes, Wakefield *C:* Luddington (2) *GM:* Luddington

27 Feb 1926
Twickenham
ENGLAND 11
T: Aslett (2), Kittermaster *C:* Francis
FRANCE 0

2 Apr 1927
Stade Colombes, Paris
FRANCE 3
T: Vellat
ENGLAND 0

25 Feb 1928
Twickenham
ENGLAND 18
T: Periton (2), Palmer (2) *C:* Richardson (3)
FRANCE 8
T: Galia, Jaureguy *C:* Verger

1 Apr 1929
Stade Colombes, Paris
FRANCE 6
T: Houdet, Ribere
ENGLAND 16
T: Aarvold (2), Gummer, Periton
C: Stanbury (2)

22 Feb 1930
Twickenham
ENGLAND 11
T: Periton, Reeve, Robson *C:* Black
FRANCE 5
T: Serin *C:* Ambert

6 Apr 1931
Stade Colombes, Paris
FRANCE 14
T: Clady, Galia *DG:* Baillette, Gerald
ENGLAND 13
T: Burland, Smeddle, Tallent *C:* Black (2)

19 Apr 1947
Twickenham
ENGLAND 6
T: Guest, Roberts
FRANCE 3
PG: Prat

29 Mar 1948
Stade Colombes, Paris
FRANCE 15
T: Pomathios, Prat, Soro *C:* Alvarez
DG: Bergougnan
ENGLAND 0

26 Feb 1949
Twickenham
ENGLAND 8
T: Cannell *C:* Holmes *DG:* Preece
FRANCE 3
DG: Alvarez

25 Feb 1950
Stade Colombes, Paris
FRANCE 6
T: Cazenave, Pilon
ENGLAND 3
T: Smith

24 Feb 1951
Twickenham
ENGLAND 3
T: Boobyer
FRANCE 11
T: Basquet, Prat *C:* Prat *DG:* Prat

5 Apr 1952
Stade Colombes, Paris
FRANCE 3
T: Pomathios
ENGLAND 6
PG: Hall (2)

28 Feb 1953
Twickenham
ENGLAND 11
T: Butterfield, Evans, Woodward *C:* Hall
FRANCE 0

10 Apr 1954
Stade Colombes, Paris
FRANCE 11
T: Boniface, M Prat *C:* J Prat *DG:* J Prat
ENGLAND 3
T: Wilson

26 Feb 1955
Twickenham
ENGLAND 9
T: Higgins *PG:* Hazell (2)
FRANCE 16
T: Baulon, Celaya *C:* Vannier (2) *DG:* J Prat (2)

14 Apr 1956
Stade Colombes, Paris
FRANCE 14
T: Dupuy, Pauthe *C:* Labazuy
PG: Labazuy (2)
ENGLAND 9
T: Thompson *PG:* Allison (2)

23 Feb 1957
Twickenham
ENGLAND 9
T: Jackson (2), Evans
FRANCE 5
T: Darrouy *C:* Vannier

1 Mar 1958
Stade Colombes, Paris
FRANCE 0
ENGLAND 14
T: Thompson (2), Jackson *C:* Hastings
PG: Hastings

28 Feb 1959
Twickenham
ENGLAND 3
PG: Hetherington
FRANCE 3
PG: Labazuy

27 Feb 1960
Stade Colombes, Paris
FRANCE 3
PG: Vannier
ENGLAND 3
T: Weston

25 Feb 1961
Twickenham
ENGLAND 5
T: Harding *C:* Willcox
FRANCE 5
T: Crauste *C:* Vannier

24 Feb 1962
Stade Colombes, Paris
FRANCE 13
T: Crauste (3) *C:* Albaladejo (2)
ENGLAND 0

23 Feb 1963
Twickenham
ENGLAND 6
PG: Willcox (2)
FRANCE 5
T: G Boniface *C:* Albaladejo

22 Feb 1964
Stade Colombes, Paris
FRANCE 3
T: Darrouy
ENGLAND 6
T: Phillips *PG:* Hosen

27 Feb 1965
Twickenham
ENGLAND 9
T: Payne *PG:* Rutherford (2)
FRANCE 6
T: Darrouy *PG:* Dedieu

26 Feb 1966
Stade Colombes, Paris
FRANCE 13
T: A Boniface, Gachassin, Graurin
ENGLAND 0

25 Feb 1967
Twickenham
ENGLAND 12
DG: Finlan *PG:* Hosen (3)
FRANCE 16
T: Dourthe, Duprat *C:* G Camberabero (2) *DG:* G Camberabero *PG:* G Camberabero

24 Feb 1968
Stade Colombes, Paris
FRANCE 14
T: Gachassin *C:* G Camberabero
DG: G Camberabero, Lacaze *PG:* G Camberabero
ENGLAND 9
DG: Weston *PG:* Hiller (2)

22 Feb 1969
Twickenham
ENGLAND 22
T: Fielding, Rollitt, Webb *C:* Hiller (2)
PG: Hiller (3)
FRANCE 8
T: Bonal *C:* Lacaze *DG:* Lacaze

18 Apr 1970
Stade Colombes, Paris
FRANCE 35
T: Berot, Bonal, Bourgarel, Dauga, Lux,

Trillo *C:* Villepreux (4) *DG:* Berot, Villepreux *PG:* Villepreux
ENGLAND 13
T: Spencer, Taylor *C:* Jorden (2)
PG: Jorden

27 Feb 1971
Twickenham
ENGLAND 14
T: Hiller *C:* Hiller *PG:* Hiller (3)
FRANCE 14
T: Bertranne, Cantoni *C:* Villepreux
DG: Berot *PG:* Villepreux

26 Feb 1972
Stade Colombes, Paris
FRANCE 37
T: Duprat (2), Biemouret, Lux, Sillieres, W Spanghero *C:* Villepreux (5)
PG: Villepreux
ENGLAND 12
T: Beese *C:* Old *PG:* Old (2)

24 Feb 1973
Twickenham
ENGLAND 14
T: Duckham (2) *PG:* Jorden (2)
FRANCE 6
T: Bertranne *C:* Romeu

2 Mar 1974
Parc des Princes, Paris
FRANCE 12
T: Romeu *C:* Romeu *DG:* Romeu
PG: Romeu
ENGLAND 12
T: Duckham *C:* Old *DG:* Evans
PG: Old

1 Feb 1975
Twickenham
ENGLAND 20
T: Duckham, Rossborough
DG: Rossborough *PG:* Rossborough (4)
FRANCE 27
T: Etchenique, Gourdon, Guilbert, Spanghero *C:* Paries (4) *PG:* Paries

20 Mar 1976
Parc des Princes, Paris
FRANCE 30
T: Paparemborde (2), Bastiat, Fouroux, Gourdon, Romeu *C:* Romeu (3)
ENGLAND 9
T: Dixon *C:* Butler *PG:* Butler

19 Feb 1977
Twickenham
ENGLAND 3
PG: Hignell
FRANCE 4
T: Sangali

21 Jan 1978
Parc des Princes, Paris
FRANCE 15
T: Averous, Gallion *C:* Aguirre (2)
PG: Aguirre
ENGLAND 6
DG: Old (2)

3 Mar 1979
Twickenham
ENGLAND 7
T: Bennett *PG:* Bennett
FRANCE 6
T: Costes *C:* Aguirre

2 Feb 1980
Parc des Princes, Paris
FRANCE 13
T: Averous, Rives *C:* Caussade
PG: Caussade
ENGLAND 17
T: Carleton, Preston *DG:* Horton (2)
PG: Hare

21 Mar 1981
Twickenham
ENGLAND 12
PG: Rose (4)
FRANCE 16
T: Lacans, Pardo *C:* Laporte
DG: Laporte (2)

20 Feb 1982
Parc des Princes, Paris
FRANCE 15
T: Pardo *C:* Sallefranque
DG: Lescarboura *PG:* Sallefranque (2)
ENGLAND 27
T: Woodward, Carleton *C:* Hare (2)
PG: Hare (5)

15 Jan 1983
Twickenham
ENGLAND 15
DG: Cusworth *PG:* Hare (4)
FRANCE 19
T: Esteve, Sella, Paparemborde
C: Blanco (2) *PG:* Camberabero

3 Mar 1984
Parc des Princes, Paris
FRANCE 32
T: Cordorniou, Sella, Esteve, Bergu, Gallion *C:* Lescarboura
PG: Lescarboura *DG:* Lescarboura
ENGLAND 18
T: Underwood, Hare *C:* Hare (2)
PG: Hare (2)

2 Feb 1985
Twickenham
ENGLAND 9
PG: Andrew (2) *DG:* Andrew
FRANCE 9
DG: Lescarboura (3)

15 Mar 1986
Parc des Princes, Paris
FRANCE 29
T: Sella, Blanco *Pen try:* Laporte
C: Laporte (2) *PG:* Laporte (3)
ENGLAND 10
T: Dooley *PG:* Barnes (2)

21 Feb 1987
Twickenham
ENGLAND 15
PG: Rose (4) *DG:* Andrew
FRANCE 19
T: Bonneval, Sella *C:* Berot *PG:* Berot (2) *DG:* Mesnel

16 Jan 1988
Parc des Princes, Paris
FRANCE 10
T: Rodriguez *PG:* Berot (2)
ENGLAND 9
PG: Webb (2) *DG:* Cusworth

4 Mar 1989
Twickenham
ENGLAND 11
T: Carling, Robinson *PG:* Andrew
FRANCE 0

3 Feb 1990
Parc des Princes, Paris
FRANCE 7
T: Lagisquet *PG:* Charvet
ENGLAND 26
T: Underwood, Guscott, Carling
C: Hodgkinson *PG:* Hodgkinson (4)

16 Mar 1991
Twickenham
ENGLAND 21
T: Underwood *C:* Hodgkinson
PG: Hodgkinson (4) *DG:* Andrew
FRANCE 19
T: Saint-Andre, Camberabero, Mesnel
C: Camberabero (2) *PG:* Camberabero

15 Feb 1992
Parc des Princes, Paris
FRANCE 13
T: Viars, Penaud *C:* Viars *PG:* Viars
ENGLAND 31
T: pen. try, Webb, Underwood, Morris
C: Webb (3) *PG:* Webb (3)

FRANCE v IRELAND

28 Mar 1910
Parc des Princes, Paris
FRANCE 3
T: Guillemin
IRELAND 8
T: Thompson, Smyth *C:* McClinton

25 Mar 1911
Mardyke, Cork
IRELAND 25
T: Quinn, O'Callaghan, Jackson (2), Heffernan *C:* Lloyd (3) *DG:* Lloyd
FRANCE 5
T: Failliot *C:* Dutour

1 Jan 1912
Parc des Princes, Paris
FRANCE 6
T: Paoli, Dufau
IRELAND 11
T: Taylor, Foster, Lloyd *C:* Taylor

24 Mar 1913
Mardyke, Cork
IRELAND 24
T: Quinn (3), Tyrrell (2), Patterson
C: Lloyd (3)
FRANCE 0

1 Jan 1914
Parc des Princes, Paris
FRANCE 6
T: Lacoste, Andre
IRELAND 8
T: Quinn, Wood *C:* Lloyd

3 Apr 1920
Lansdowne Road, Dublin
IRELAND 7
T: Price *DG:* Lloyd
FRANCE 15
T: Gayraud, Got (2), Jaureguy (2)

9 Apr 1921
Stade Colombes, Paris
FRANCE 20
T: Piteu (2), Cassayet, Boubee
C: Crabos (4)
IRELAND 10
T: Stokes (2) *C:* Wallis (2)

8 Apr 1922
Lansdowne Road, Dublin
IRELAND 8
T: G Stephenson *C:* Wallis *PG:* Wallis
FRANCE 3
T: Pascot

14 Apr 1923
Stade Colombes, Paris
FRANCE 14
T: Jaureguy (2), Beguet, Moreau
C: Beguet
IRELAND 8
T: Douglas, McClelland *C:* Crawford

26 Jan 1924
Lansdowne Road, Dublin
IRELAND 6
T: G Stephenson, Atkins
FRANCE 0

1 Jan 1925
Stade Colombes, Paris
FRANCE 3
T: Ribere
IRELAND 9
T: Sugden, G Stephenson
PG: Crawford

23 Jan 1926
Ravenhill, Belfast
IRELAND 11
T: Stephenson (2) *C:* Hewitt
PG: Stephenson
FRANCE 0

1 Jan 1927
Stade Colombes, Paris
FRANCE 3
T: Ribere
IRELAND 8
T: Davy *C:* Stephenson
PG: Stephenson

28 Jan 1928
Ravenhill, Belfast
IRELAND 12
T: Ganly (2), Arigho (2)
FRANCE 8
T: Ribere, H Behoteguy *C:* A Behoteguy

30 Dec 1928
Yves du Manor Stadium, Paris
FRANCE 0
IRELAND 6
T: Davy, Stephenson

25 Jan 1930
Ravenhill, Belfast
IRELAND 0
FRANCE 5
T: Samatan *C:* Ambert

1 Jan 1931
Stade Colombes, Paris
FRANCE 3
T: Ribere
IRELAND 0

25 Jan 1947
Lansdowne Road, Dublin
IRELAND 8
T: McKay *C:* Mullan *PG:* Mullan
FRANCE 12
T: Lassegue (2), Prat, Sorondo

1 Jan 1948
Stade Colombes, Paris
FRANCE 6
T: Basquet, Soro
IRELAND 13
T: Reid, McCarthy, Mullan *C:* Mullan (2)

29 Jan 1949
Lansdowne Road, Dublin
IRELAND 9
PG: Norton (3)
FRANCE 16
T: Basquet, Lassegue *C:* Prat (2)
DG: Prat (2)

28 Jan 1950
Stade Colombes, Paris
FRANCE 3
DG: Lauga
IRELAND 3
PG: Burges

27 Jan 1951
Lansdowne Road, Dublin
IRELAND 9
T: Nelson, Clifford *PG:* Henderson
FRANCE 8
T: Olive, Matheu *C:* Bertrand

26 Jan 1952
Stade Colombes, Paris
FRANCE 8
T: J Prat *C:* J Prat *PG:* J Prat
IRELAND 11
T: McCarthy (2) *C:* Notley
PG: Henderson

24 Jan 1953
Ravenhill, Belfast
IRELAND 16
T: Lawler, McCarthy, Kyle, Mortell
C: Gregg (2)
FRANCE 3
DG: Carabignac

23 Jan 1954
Stade Colombes, Paris
FRANCE 8
T: M Prat (2) *C:* J Prat
IRELAND 0

22 Jan 1955
Lansdowne Road, Dublin
IRELAND 3
PG: Henderson
FRANCE 5
T: Domenech *C:* Vannier

28 Jan 1956
Stade Colombes, Paris
FRANCE 14
T: Boniface, Baulon *C:* Vannier
DG: Vannier
IRELAND 8
T: O'Reilly *C:* Pedlow *PG:* Pedlow

26 Jan 1957
Lansdowne Road, Dublin
IRELAND 11
T: Brophy, Kyle *C:* Pedlow *PG:* Pedlow
FRANCE 6
PG: Vannier (2)

19 Apr 1958
Stade Colombes, Paris
FRANCE 11
T: Danos *C:* Labuzuy *DG:* Vannier
PG: Labuzuy
IRELAND 6
PG: Henderson (2)

18 Apr 1959
Lansdowne Road, Dublin
IRELAND 9
T: Brophy *DG:* English *PG:* Hewitt
FRANCE 5
T: Dupuy *C:* Lacaze

9 Apr 1960
Stade Colombes, Paris
FRANCE 23
T: Celaya, Domenech, Moncla, Rancoule *C:* Bouquet *DG:* Albaladejo (3)
IRELAND 6
T: Brophy (2)

15 Apr 1961
Lansdowne Road, Dublin
IRELAND 3
PG: Kiernan
FRANCE 15
T: Gachassin *DG:* Bouquet, Albaladejo
PG: Vannier, Albaladejo

14 Apr 1962
Stade Colombes, Paris
FRANCE 11
T: Mommejat, Lacaze, Crauste
C: Albaladejo
IRELAND 0

26 Jan 1963
Lansdowne Road, Dublin
IRELAND 5
T: O'Reilly *C:* Kiernan
FRANCE 24
T: G Boniface, Darrouy (3)
C: Albaladejo *DG:* Albaladejo, A Boniface

11 Apr 1964
Stade Colombes, Paris
FRANCE 27
T: Crauste, Lira, Darrouy (2), Arnaudet, Herrero *C:* Albaladejo (3) *DG:* Dedieu
IRELAND 6
T: Casey *DG:* Gibson

23 Jan 1965
Lansdowne Road, Dublin
IRELAND 3
T: Doyle
FRANCE 3
T: Darrouy

29 Jan 1966
Stade Colombes, Paris
FRANCE 11
T: Darrouy (2) *C:* Lacaze *PG:* Lacaze
IRELAND 6
DG: Kiernan *PG:* Gibson

15 Apr 1967
Lansdowne Road, Dublin
IRELAND 6
T: Molloy *PG:* Kiernan
FRANCE 11
T: Cabanier *C:* G Camberabero *DG:* G Camberabero (2)

27 Jan 1968
Stade Colombes, Paris
FRANCE 16
T: Campaes, Dauga *C:* Villepreux (2)
DG: Gachassin *PG:* Villepreux
IRELAND 6
PG: McCombe (2)

25 Jan 1969
Lansdowne Road, Dublin
IRELAND 17
T: Moroney *C:* Moroney *DG:* McGann
PG: Moroney (3)
FRANCE 9
T: Trillo *PG:* Villepreux (2)

24 Jan 1970
Stade Colombes, Paris
FRANCE 8
T: Sillieres *C:* Paries *DG:* Paries
IRELAND 0

30 Jan 1971
Lansdowne Road, Dublin
IRELAND 9
T: Grant *PG:* O'Driscoll (2)
FRANCE 9
DG: Berot *PG:* Villepreux (2)

29 Jan 1972
Stade Colombes, Paris
FRANCE 9
T: Lux *C:* Villepreux *PG:* Villepreux
IRELAND 14
T: Moloney, McLoughlin *PG:* Kiernan (2)

14 Apr 1973
Lansdowne Road, Dublin
IRELAND 6
PG: Gibson (2)
FRANCE 4
T: Phliponneau

19 Jan 1974
Parc des Princes, Paris
FRANCE 9
T: Boffelli *C:* Aguirre *PG:* Berot
IRELAND 6
PG: Ensor (2)

1 Mar 1975
Lansdowne Road, Dublin
IRELAND 25
T: Ensor, Grace, McBride *C:* McCombe (2) *DG:* McCombe (2) *PG:* McCombe
FRANCE 6
DG: Paries *PG:* Paries

7 Feb 1976
Parc des Princes, Paris
FRANCE 26
T: Pecune, Cholley, Fouroux, Rives
C: Rives, Bastiat *PG:* Romeu (2)
IRELAND 3
PG: Robbie

Frank Mesnel comes forward for France during the 44–12 victory over Ireland at Parc de Princes in 1992.

19 Mar 1977
Lansdowne Road, Dublin
IRELAND 6
PG: Gibson, Quinn
FRANCE 15
T: Bastiat *C:* Aguirre *PG:* Aguirre (2), Romeu

18 Feb 1978
Parc des Princes, Paris
FRANCE 10
T: Gallion *PG:* Aguirre (2)
IRELAND 9
PG: Ward (3)

20 Jan 1979
Lansdowne Road, Dublin
IRELAND 9
PG: Ward (3)
FRANCE 9
T: Caussade *C:* Aguirre *PG:* Aguirre

1 Mar 1980
Parc des Princes, Paris
FRANCE 19
T: Gourdon (2) *C:* Aguirre
DG: Pedeutour *PG:* Aguirre (2)
IRELAND 18
T: McLennan *C:* Campbell
DG: Campbell *PG:* Campbell

7 Feb 1981
Lansdowne Road, Dublin
IRELAND 13
T: MacNeill *PG:* Campbell (3)
FRANCE 19
T: Pardo *DG:* Laporte (2) *PG:* Laporte (2), Gabernet

20 Mar 1982
Parc des Princes, Paris
FRANCE 22
T: Blanco, Mesny *C:* Gabernet
PG: Blanco (2), Gabernet (2)
IRELAND 9
PG: Campbell (3)

19 Feb 1983
Lansdowne Road, Dublin
IRELAND 22
T: Finn (2) *C:* Campbell *PG:* Campbell (4)
FRANCE 16
T: Blanco, Esteve *C:* Blanco
PG: Blanco (2)

21 Jan 1984
Parc des Princes, Paris
FRANCE 25
T: Gallion, Sella *C:* Lescarboura
PG: Lescarboura (4) *DG:* Lescarboura
IRELAND 12
PG: Campbell (4)

2 Mar 1985
Lansdowne Road, Dublin
IRELAND 15
PG: Kiernan (5)
FRANCE 15
T: Esteve, Codorniou *C:* Lescarboura (2) *PG:* Lescarboura

1 Feb 1986
Parc des Princes, Paris
FRANCE 29
T: Berbizier, Marocco, Sella *C:* Laporte
PG: Laporte (3), Blanco *DG:* Lafond
IRELAND 9
PG: Kiernan (3)

21 Mar 1987
Lansdowne Road, Dublin
IRELAND 13
T: Ringland, Bradley *C:* Kiernan
PG: Kiernan
FRANCE 19
T: Champ (2) *C:* Berot *PG:* Berot (3)

20 Feb 1988
Parc des Princes, Paris
FRANCE 25
T: Blanco, Lagisquet, Camberabero, Caminati, Sella *C:* Camberabero
DG: Berot
IRELAND 6
PG: Kiernan (2)

21 Jan 1989
Lansdowne Road, Dublin
IRELAND 21
T: Mullin *C:* Kiernan *PG:* Kiernan (5)
FRANCE 26
T: Lagisquet (2), Blanco, Lafond
C: Lafond (2) *PG:* Lafond (2)

3 Mar 1990
Parc des Princes, Paris
FRANCE 31
T: Mesnel (2), Lagisquet
C: Camberabero (2) *PG:* Camberabero (5)
IRELAND 12
PG: Kiernan (4)

2 Feb 1991
Lansdowne Road, Dublin
IRELAND 13
T: SJ Smith *PG:* Kiernan (3)
FRANCE 21
T: Cabannes, Lagisquet
C: Camberabero (2) *PG:* Camberabero (3)

21 Mar 1992
Parc des Princes, Paris
FRANCE 44
T: Penaud (2), Viars (2), Cecillon, Cabannes, Sadourny *C:* Viars (5)
PG: Viars (2)
IRELAND 12
PG: McAleese (4)

FRANCE v SCOTLAND

22 Jan 1910
Inverleith, Edinburgh
SCOTLAND 27
T: Tennent (3), Robertson (2), Angus, Gowlland *C:* McCallum (3)
FRANCE 0

2 Jan 1911
Stade Colombes, Paris
FRANCE 16
T: Latterrade, Failliot (2), Peyretou *C:* Descamps (2)
SCOTLAND 15
T: MacCallum, Munro, Abercrombie *C:* Turner *DG:* Pearson

20 Jan 1912
Inverleith, Edinburgh
SCOTLAND 31
T: Gunn, Sutherland (2), Pearson, Will, Turner *C:* Turner (5) *PG:* Pearson
FRANCE 3
T: Communeau

1 Jan 1913
Parc des Princes, Paris
FRANCE 3
T: Sebedio
SCOTLAND 21
T: Stewart (3), Gordon (2) *C:* Turner (3)

1 Jan 1920
Parc des Princes, Paris
FRANCE 0
SCOTLAND 5
T: Crole *C:* Kennedy

22 Jan 1921
Inverleith, Edinburgh
SCOTLAND 0
FRANCE 3
T: Billac

2 Jan 1922
Stade Colombes, Paris
FRANCE 3
T: Jaureguy
SCOTLAND 3
T: Browning

20 Jan 1923
Inverleith, Edinburgh
SCOTLAND 16
T: McClaren (2), Bryce, Liddell *C:* Drysdale (2)
FRANCE 3
GM: Beguet

1 Jan 1924
Stade Pershing, Paris
FRANCE 12
T: Jaureguy, Piquirial, Galau, Moureu
SCOTLAND 10
T: Wallace *DG:* Waddell *PG:* Davies

24 Jan 1925
Inverleith, Edinburgh
SCOTLAND 25
T: Smith (4), Wallace (2), Gillies *C:* Gillies, Drysdale
FRANCE 4
DG: du Manoir

2 Jan 1926
Stade Colombes, Paris
FRANCE 6
T: Piquiral *C:* Gonnet
SCOTLAND 20
T: Wallace (3), MacMyn, Bannerman *C:* Drysdale *PG:* Gillies

22 Jan 1927
Murrayfield, Edinburgh
SCOTLAND 23
T: Waddell (2), Smith (2) *C:* Gillies (3), Drysdale *PG:* Gillies
FRANCE 6
T: Piquiral, Hutin

2 Jan 1928
Stade Colombes, Paris
FRANCE 6
T: Haget, Camel
SCOTLAND 15
T: Simmers, Paterson, Dykes, Douty, Scott

19 Jan 1929
Murrayfield
SCOTLAND 6
T: Paterson *PG:* Brown
FRANCE 3
T: Behoteguy

1 Jan 1930
Stade Colombes, Paris
FRANCE 7
T: Bioussa *DG:* Magnanou
SCOTLAND 3
T: Simmers

24 Jan 1931
Murrayfield
SCOTLAND 6
PG: Allan (2)
FRANCE 4
DG: Servole

1 Jan 1947
Stade Colombes, France
FRANCE 8
T: Lassegue, Terreau *C:* Prat
SCOTLAND 3
PG: Geddes

24 Jan 1948
Murrayfield
SCOTLAND 9
T: Jackson *PG:* Murdoch (2)
FRANCE 8
T: Lacaussade *C:* Alvarez *PG:* Prat

15 Jan 1949
Stade Colombes, Paris
FRANCE 0
SCOTLAND 8
T: Elliot, Kiminmonth *C:* Allardice

14 Jan 1950
Murrayfield
SCOTLAND 8
T: Macdonald, Budge *C:* Bruce-Lockhart
FRANCE 5
T: Merquey *C:* Prat

13 Jan 1951
Stade Colombes, Paris
FRANCE 14
T: Mias, Porthault *C:* Prat *PG:* Prat (2)
SCOTLAND 12
T: Rose (2) *PG:* Gray

12 Jan 1952
Murrayfield
SCOTLAND 11
T: Cordial *C:* Thomson *PG:* Thomson (2)
FRANCE 13
T: J Prat, Basquet *C:* J Prat (2) *PG:* J Prat

10 Jan 1953
Stade Colombes, Paris
FRANCE 11
T: Bordeau *C:* Bertrand *DG:* Carabignac *PG:* Bertrand
SCOTLAND 5
T: Rose *C:* Cameron

9 Jan 1954
Murrayfield
SCOTLAND 0
FRANCE 3
T: Brejassou

8 Jan 1955
Stade Colombes, Paris
FRANCE 15
T: Boniface, J Prat, Domenech, Dufau *PG:* Vannier
SCOTLAND 0

14 Jan 1956
Murrayfield
SCOTLAND 12
T: Kemp (2) *PG:* Smith, Cameron
FRANCE 0

12 Jan 1957
Stade Colombes, Paris
FRANCE 0
SCOTLAND 6
DG: Scotland *PG:* Scotland

11 Jan 1958
Murrayfield
SCOTLAND 11
T: Stevenson, Hastie *C:* Chisholm *PG:* Chisholm
FRANCE 9
T: Depuy *PG:* Vannier

10 Jan 1959
Stade Colombes, Paris
FRANCE 9
T: Moncia *DG:* Lacaze (2)
SCOTLAND 0

9 Jan 1960
Murrayfield
SCOTLAND 11
T: A Smith (2) *C:* Elliot *PG:* Elliot
FRANCE 13
T: Meyer, Mericq, Moncla *C:* Vannier (2)

7 Jan 1961
Stade Colombes, Paris
FRANCE 11
T: Boniface *C:* Albaladejo *DG:* Albaladejo *PG:* Albaladejo
SCOTLAND 0

13 Jan 1962
Murrayfield
SCOTLAND 3
PG: Smith
FRANCE 11
T: Rancoule *C:* Albaladejo *PG:* Albaladejo (2)

12 Jan 1963
Stade Colombes, Paris
FRANCE 6
DG: A Boniface *PG:* Albaladejo
SCOTLAND 11
T: Thomson *C:* Scotland *DG:* Scotland *PG:* Scotland

4 Jan 1964
Murrayfield
SCOTLAND 10
T: Laughland, Thomson *C:* Wilson (2)
FRANCE 0

9 Jan 1965
Stade Colombes, Paris
FRANCE 16
T: Gachassin, Pique, Darrouy (2) *C:* Dedieu (2)
SCOTLAND 8
T: Henderson (2) *C:* Scotland

15 Jan 1966
Murrayfield
SCOTLAND 3
T: Whyte
FRANCE 3
PG: Lacaze

14 Jan 1967
Stade Colombes, Paris
FRANCE 8
T: Duprat, Carrere *C:* Gachassin
SCOTLAND 9
DG: Simmers *PG:* Wilson (2)

13 Jan 1968
Murrayfield
SCOTLAND 6
T: Keith *PG:* Wilson
FRANCE 8
T: Duprat, Campaes *C:* G Camberabero

11 Jan 1969
Stade Colombes, Paris
FRANCE 3
PG: Villepreux
SCOTLAND 6
T: J Telfer *PG:* Blaikie

10 Jan 1970
Murrayfield
SCOTLAND 9
T: Smith *PG:* Lauder (2)
FRANCE 11
T: Dauga, Lux *C:* Paries *DG:* Paries

16 Jan 1971
Stade Colombes, Paris
FRANCE 13
T: Sillieres, Villepreux *C:* Villepreux (2) *PG:* Villepreux
SCOTLAND 8
T: Steele *C:* P Brown *PG:* Smith

15 Jan 1972
Murrayfield
SCOTLAND 20
T: Telfer, Renwick, Frame *C:* A Brown *DG:* Telfer *PG:* P Brown
FRANCE 9
T: Dauga *C:* Villepreux *PG:* Villepreux

13 Jan 1973
Parc des Princes, Paris
FRANCE 16
T: Dourthe *DG:* Romeu *PG:* Romeu (3)
SCOTLAND 13
T: Lawson *DG:* McGeechan *PG:* Brown (2)

16 Jan 1974
Murrayfield
SCOTLAND 19
T: McHarg, Dick *C:* Irvine *PG:* Morgan, Irvine (2)
FRANCE 6
DG: Romeu *PG:* Romeu

15 Jan 1975
Parc des Princes, Paris
FRANCE 10
T: Dourthe *DG:* Astre *PG:* Paries
SCOTLAND 9
PG: Irvine (3)

10 Jan 1976
Murrayfield
SCOTLAND 6
DG: Morgan *PG:* Renwick
FRANCE 13
T: Dubertrand *PG:* Romeu (3)

5 Mar 1977
Parc des Princes, Paris
FRANCE 23
T: Paco, Harize, Bertranne, Paparemborde *C:* Romeu (2) *PG:* Romeu
SCOTLAND 3
PG: Irvine

4 Feb 1978
Murrayfield
SCOTLAND 16
T: Shedden, Irvine *C:* Morgan
DG: Morgan *PG:* Morgan
FRANCE 19
T: Gallion, Haget *C:* Aguirre
PG: Aguirre (3)

17 Mar 1979
Parc des Princes, Paris
FRANCE 21
T: Belascain, Malquier (2) *DG:* Aguerre
PG: Aguerre, Aguirre
SCOTLAND 17
T: Robertson, Dickson, Irvine *C:* Irvine
PG: Irvine

16 Feb 1980
Murrayfield
SCOTLAND 22
T: Rutherford, Irvine (2) *C:* Irvine, Renwick *PG:* Irvine (2)
FRANCE 14
T: Gallion, Gabernet *DG:* Caussade
PG: Gabernet

17 Jan 1981
Parc des Princes, Paris
FRANCE 16
T: Blanco, Bertranne *C:* Caussade
PG: Vivies, Gabernet
SCOTLAND 9
T: Rutherford *C:* Renwick *PG:* Irvine

6 Mar 1982
Murrayfield
SCOTLAND 16
T: Rutherford *DG:* Renwick *PG:* Irvine (3)
FRANCE 7
T: Rives *PG:* Sallefranque

5 Feb 1983
Parc des Princes, Paris
FRANCE 19
T: Esteve (2) *C:* Blanco *PG:* Blanco (3)
SCOTLAND 15
T: Robertson *C:* Dods *DG:* Gossman (2) *PG:* Dods

17 Feb 1984
Murrayfield
SCOTLAND 21
T: Calder *C:* Dods *PG:* Dods (5)
FRANCE 12
T: Gallion *C:* Lescarboura
PG: Lescarboura *DG:* Lescarboura

16 Feb 1985
Parc des Princes, Paris
FRANCE 11
T: Blanco (2) *PG:* Lescarboura
SCOTLAND 3
PG: Dods

17 Jan 1986
Murrayfield
SCOTLAND 18
PG: G Hastings (6)
FRANCE 17
T: Berbizier, Sella *PG:* Laporte (2)
DG: Laporte

7 Mar 1987
Parc des Princes, Paris
FRANCE 28
T: Bonneval (3), Berot *PG:* Berot (3)
DG: Mesnel
SCOTLAND 22
T: Beattie, S Hastings *C:* G Hastings
PG: G Hastings (4)

6 Feb 1988
Murrayfield
SCOTLAND 23
T: G Hastings, Tukalo *PG:* G Hastings (4) *DG:* Cramb
FRANCE 12
T: Lagisquet *C:* Berot *PG:* Berot
DG: Lescarboura

19 Mar 1989
Parc des Princes, Paris
FRANCE 19
T: Berbizier, Blanco, Lagisquet *C:* Berot (2) *PG:* Berot
SCOTLAND 3
PG: Dods

17 Feb 1990
Murrayfield
SCOTLAND 21
T: Calder, Tukalo *C:* Chalmers (2)
PG: Chalmers (2), G Hastings
FRANCE 0

19 Jan 1991
Parc des Princes, Paris
FRANCE 15
PG: Camberabero (2)
DG: Camberabero (2), Blanco
SCOTLAND 9
PG: Chalmers (2) *DG:* Chalmers

7 Mar 1992
Murrayfield
SCOTLAND 10
T: Edwards *PG:* G Hastings (2)
FRANCE 6
PG: Lafond (2)

FRANCE v WALES

1 Jan 1910
St Helens, Swansea
WALES 49
T: Gibbs (3), Morgan (2), Maddocks (2), Trew, J Jones, Gronow *C:* Bancroft (8) *PG:* Bancroft
FRANCE 14
T: Lafite, Mauriat *C:* Menrath *PG:* Menrath (2)

28 Feb 1911
Parc des Princes, Paris
FRANCE 0
WALES 15
T: Morgan, Williams, Owen *C:* Bancroft (3)

25 Mar 1912
Rodney Parade, Newport
WALES 14
T: Davies (2), Plummer, Jones *C:* Thomas
FRANCE 8
T: Lessieur, Larribeau *C:* Boyau

27 Feb 1913
Parc des Princes, Paris
FRANCE 8
T: Failliot, Andre *C:* Struxiano
WALES 11
T: C Lewis, Davies, Williams *C:* C Lewis

2 Mar 1914
St Helens, Swansea
WALES 31
T: Wetter (2), Uzzell (2), Hirst, Rev. Davies, Evans *C:* Bancroft
FRANCE 0

17 Feb 1920
Stades Colombes, Paris
FRANCE 5
T: Jaureguy *C:* Struxiano
WALES 6
T: B Williams, Powell

26 Feb 1921
Cardiff Arms Park
WALES 12
T: J Williams, Hodder *PG:* Jenkins (2)
FRANCE 4
DG: Lasserre

23 Mar 1922
Stade Colombes, Paris
FRANCE 3
T: Jaureguy
WALES 11
T: Whitfield, Cummins, I Evans *C:* Jenkins

24 Feb 1923
St Helens, Swansea
WALES 16
T: Harding, M Thomas, Baker *C:* A Jenkins (2) *PG:* Rees
FRANCE 8
T: Lalande, Lasserre *C:* Larrieu

27 Mar 1924
Stade Colombes, Paris
FRANCE 6
T: Behoteguy, Lubin-Lebrere
WALES 10
T: Finch, Rickards *DG:* Griffiths

28 Feb 1925
Cardiff Arms Park
WALES 11
T: Finch (2), Delahay *C:* Parker
FRANCE 5
T: de Laborderie *C:* Ducousso

5 Apr 1926
Stade Colombes, Paris
FRANCE 5
T: Gerintes *C:* Gonnet
WALES 7
T: Watkins *DG:* Cornish

26 Feb 1927
St Helens, Swansea
WALES 25
T: Roberts (2), Harding (2), Thomas, Andrews, Morgan *C:* Male (2)
FRANCE 7
T: Prevost *DG:* Verger

9 Apr 1928
Stade Colombes, Paris
FRANCE 8
T: Houdet (2) *C:* A Behoteguy
WALES 3
T: Powell

25 Feb 1929
Cardiff Arms Park
WALES 8
T: Arthur, Barrell *C:* Parker
FRANCE 3
T: A Camel

21 Apr 1930
Stade Colombes, Paris
FRANCE 0
WALES 11
T: Skym *DG:* Morgan, Powell

28 Feb 1931
St Helens, Swansea
WALES 35
T: Ralph (2), Davey, Fender, Lang, Williams, Arthur *C:* Bassett (5) *DG:* Powell
FRANCE 3
T: Petit

22 Mar 1947
Stade Colombes, Paris
FRANCE 0
WALES 3
PG: Tamplin

21 Feb 1948
St Helens, Swansea
WALES 3
PG: O Williams
FRANCE 11
T: Basquet, Terreau, Pomathios *C:* Alvarez

26 Mar 1949
Stade Colombes, Paris
FRANCE 5
T: Lassegue *C:* Alvarez
WALES 3
T: K Jones

25 Mar 1950
Cardiff Arms Park
WALES 21
T: K Jones (2), John, Matthews *C:* Lewis Jones (3) *PG:* Lewis Jones
FRANCE 0

7 Apr 1951
Stade Colombes, Paris
FRANCE 8
T: Alvarez *C:* Prat *PG:* Alvarez
WALES 3
PG: K Jones

22 Mar 1952
St Helens, Swansea
WALES 9
DG: A Thomas *PG:* Lewis Jones (2)
FRANCE 5
T: Pomathios *C:* J Prat

28 Mar 1953
Stade Colombes, Paris
FRANCE 3
PG: Bertrand
WALES 6
T: Griffiths (2)

27 Mar 1954
Cardiff Arms Park
WALES 19
T: Griffiths, B Williams *C:* Evans (2)
PG: Evans (3)
FRANCE 13
T: Martine, Baulon *C:* J Prat (2) *PG:* J Prat

26 Mar 1955
Stade Colombes, Paris
FRANCE 11
T: Baulon *C:* Vannier *DG:* M Prat
PG: Vannier
WALES 16
T: Thomas, Morris *C:* Owen (2)
PG: Owen (2)

24 Mar 1956
Cardiff Arms Park
WALES 5
T: Williams *C:* Owen
FRANCE 3
T: Bouquet

23 Mar 1957
Stade Colombes, Paris
FRANCE 13
T: Dupuy, Prat, Sanac *C:* Bouquet (2)
WALES 19
T: Prosser, Howells, Faull, BV Meredith
C: TJ Davies (2) *PG:* TJ Davies

29 Mar 1958
Cardiff Arms Park
WALES 6
T: Collins *PG:* TJ Davies
FRANCE 16
T: Danos, Tarricq *C:* Labazuy (2)
DG: Vannier (2)

4 Apr 1959
Stade Colombes, Paris
FRANCE 11
T: Moncla (2) *C:* Labazuy *PG:* Labazuy
WALES 3
PG: TJ Davies

26 Mar 1960
Cardiff Arms Park
WALES 8
T: Cresswell *C:* N Morgan *PG:* N Morgan
FRANCE 16
T: Celaya, Lacroix, Meficq, Dupuy
C: Vannier, Albaladejo

25 Mar 1961
Stade Colombes, Paris
FRANCE 8
T: Boniface, Saux *C:* Vannier
WALES 6
T: Pask, Bebb

24 Mar 1962
Cardiff Arms Park
WALES 3
PG: Coslett
FRANCE 0

23 Mar 1963
Stade Colombes, Paris
FRANCE 5
T: G Boniface *C:* Albaladejo
WALES 3
PG: Hodgson

21 Mar 1964
Cardiff Arms Park
WALES 11
T: S Watkins *C:* Bradshaw
PG: Bradshaw (2)
FRANCE 11
T: Crauste *C:* Albaladejo
PG: Albaladejo (2)

27 Mar 1965
Stade Colombes, Paris
FRANCE 22
T: G Boniface (2), Herrero (2)
C: Dedieu (2) *DG:* Lasserre
PG: Dedieu
WALES 13
T: Dawes, S Watkins, Bebb *C:* T Price (2)

26 Mar 1966
Cardiff Arms Park
WALES 9
T: S Watkins *PG:* Bradshaw (2)
FRANCE 8
T: Duprat, Rupert *C:* Lacaze

1 Apr 1967
Stade Colombes, Paris
FRANCE 20
T: G Camberabero, Dauga, Dourthe
C: G Camberabero *DG:* G Camberabero (2) *PG:* G Camberabero
WALES 14
T: Bebb *C:* T Price *DG:* D Watkins
PG: T Price (2)

23 Mar 1968
Cardiff Arms Park
WALES 9
T: WK Jones *PG:* D Rees (2)
FRANCE 14
T: L Camberabero, Carrere *C:* G Camberabero *DG:* G Camberabero
PG: G Camberabero

22 Mar 1969
Stade Colombes, Paris
FRANCE 8
T: Campaes *C:* Villepreux
PG: Villepreux
WALES 8
T: Edwards, MCR Richards *C:* Jarrett

4 Apr 1970
Cardiff Arms Park
WALES 11
T: Morris *C:* JPR Williams *PG:* JPR Williams (2)
FRANCE 6
T: Cantoni, Bonal

27 Mar 1971
Stade Colombes, Paris
FRANCE 5
T: Dauga *C:* Villepreux
WALES 9
T: Edwards, John *PG:* John

25 Mar 1972
Cardiff Arms Park
WALES 20
T: TGR Davies, JC Bevan *PG:* John (4)
FRANCE 6
PG: Villepreux (2)

24 Mar 1973
Parc des Princes, Paris
FRANCE 12
DG: Romeu *PG:* Romeu (3)
WALES 3
DG: Bennett

16 Feb 1974
Cardiff Arms Park
WALES 16
T: JJ Williams *DG:* Edwards
PG: Bennett (3)
FRANCE 16
T: Lux *DG:* Romeu *PG:* Romeu (3)

18 Jan 1975
Parc des Princes, Paris
FRANCE 10
T: Gourdon *PG:* Taffary (2)
WALES 25
T: Fenwick, Cobner, TGR Davies, Edwards, G Price *C:* Fenwick
PG: Fenwick

6 Mar 1976
Cardiff Arms Park
WALES 19
T: JJ Williams *PG:* Bennett (2), Fenwick (2), Martin
FRANCE 13
T: Gourdon, Averous *C:* Romeu
PG: Romeu

Neil Jenkins (Wales) gets a hand to Sebastian Viars during the Five Nations Championship match against France at Cardiff Arms Park, won 12–9 by the French.

5 Feb 1977
Parc des Princes, Paris
FRANCE 16
T: Skrela, Harize *C:* Romeu *PG:* Romeu (2)
WALES 9
PG: Fenwick (3)

18 Mar 1978
Cardiff Arms Park
WALES 16
T: Bennett (2) *C:* Bennett
DG: Edwards, Fenwick
FRANCE 7
T: Skrela *DG:* Vivies

17 Feb 1979
Parc des Princes, Paris
FRANCE 14
T: Gourdon (2) *PG:* Aguirre (2)
WALES 13
T: Holmes *PG:* Fenwick (3)

19 Jan 1980
Cardiff Arms Park
WALES 18
T: E Rees, Holmes, DS Richards, G Price *C:* WG Davies
FRANCE 9
T: Marchal *C:* Caussade
DG: Caussade

7 Mar 1981
Parc des Princes, Paris
FRANCE 19
T: Gabernet *PG:* Laporte (3), Gabernet (2)
WALES 15
T: DS Richards *C:* G Evans *PG:* G Evans (3)

6 Feb 1982
Cardiff Arms Park
WALES 22
T: Holmes *PG:* G Evans (6)
FRANCE 12
T: Blanco *C:* Sallefranque
PG: Sallefranque, Martinez

19 Mar 1983
Parc des Princes, Paris
FRANCE 16
T: Esteve *DG:* Camberabero
PG: Blanco (3)
WALES 9
T: Squire *C:* Wyatt *PG:* G Evans

18 Feb 1984
Cardiff Arms Park
WALES 16
T: H Davies, Butler *C:* H Davies *PG:* H Davies (2)
FRANCE 21
T: Sella *C:* Lescarboura
PG: Lescarboura (4) *DG:* Lescarboura

30 Mar 1985
Parc des Princes, Paris
FRANCE 14
T: Esteve, Gallion *PG:* Lescarboura (2)
WALES 3
PG: Thorburn

1 Mar 1986
Cardiff Arms Park
WALES 15
PG: Thorburn (5)
FRANCE 23
T: Sella, Lafond (2), Blanco *C:* Laporte (2) *DG:* Laporte

7 Feb 1987
Parc des Princes, Paris
FRANCE 16
T: Mesnel, Bonneval *C:* Berot
PG: Berot (2)
WALES 9
PG: Thorburn (3)

19 Mar 1988
Cardiff Arms Park
WALES 9
T: Evans *C:* Thorburn *PG:* Thorburn
FRANCE 10
T: Lescarboura *PG:* Lafond (2)

18 Feb 1989
Parc des Princes, Paris
FRANCE 31
T: Blanco (2), Berbizier, Dintrans
C: Lafond (3) *PG:* Lafond (2)
DG: Mesnel
WALES 12
PG: Thorburn (4)

20 Jan 1990
Cardiff Arms Park
WALES 19
T: Titley *PG:* Thorburn (4) *DG:* Evans
FRANCE 29
T: Lafond, Sella, Camberabero, Lagisquet, Rodriguez *C:* Camberabero (3) *PG:* Camberabero

2 Mar 1991
Parc des Princes, Paris
FRANCE 36
T: Blanco, Saint-Andre, Mesnel, Roumat, Sella, Lafond *C:* Blanco, Camberabero (2) *PG:* Camberabero (2)
WALES 3
PG: Thorburn

1 Feb 1992
Cardiff Arms Park
WALES 9
PG: Jenkins (3)
FRANCE 12
T: Saint-Andre *C:* Lafond *PG:* Viars
DG: Penaud

OTHER MATCH

4 Sep 1991
Cardiff Arms Park
WALES 9
T: Collins *C:* Ring *PG:* Ring
FRANCE 22
T: Blanco, Camberabero, Saint-Andre
C: Camberabero (2) *PG:* Camberabero (2)

To inaugurate new floodlights

OTHER INTERNATIONALS

FRANCE v AUSTRALIA

1948
Paris
FRANCE 13
T: Basquet (2), Pomathios *C:* Alvarez (2)
AUSTRALIA 6
PG: Tonkin (2)

9 Mar 1958
Stades Colombes, Paris
FRANCE 19
T: Crauste, Quaglio, Rancoule *C:* A Labazuy (2)
AUSTRALIA 0

22 Aug 1961
Sydney
AUSTRALIA 8
T: Heinrich *C:* Elwood *PG:* Elwood
FRANCE 15
T: Lacroix, Pique, Bouguyon *DG:* P Albaladejo (2)

11 Feb 1967
Stade Colombes, Paris
FRANCE 20
T: L Camberabero *C:* G Camberabero *PG:* G Camberabero (4) *DG:* G Camberabero
AUSTRALIA 14
T: G Davis, Johnson *C:* Hawthorne *PG:* Hawthorne *DG:* Hawthorne

17 Aug 1968
Sydney
AUSTRALIA 11
T: Smith *C:* McGill *PG:* McGill *DG:* Ballesty
FRANCE 10
T: W Spanghero, Boujet *C:* Villepreux, Boujet

20 Nov 1971
Toulouse
FRANCE 11
T: Skrela, Bertranne *PG:* Villepreux
AUSTRALIA 13
T: L'Estrange (2) *C:* McGill *PG:* J McLean

17 Jun 1972
Sydney
AUSTRALIA 14
T: Taafe, Taylor *PG:* Fairfax (2)
FRANCE 14
T: Lux (2), Saisset *C:* Villepreux

23 Jun 1972
Brisbane
AUSTRALIA 15
PG: Fairfax (5)
FRANCE 16
T: Maso (2), W Spanghero *C:* Villepreux, Cabrol

24 Oct 1976
Bordeaux
FRANCE 18
T: Bertranne, Paparemborde, Cholley *C:* Droitecourt (3)
AUSTRALIA 15
PG: P McLean (4) *DG:* P McLean

31 Oct 1976
Parc des Princes, Paris
FRANCE 34
T: Harize, Averous, Bertranne, Aguirre, Rives, Cholley *C:* Aguirre (2) *PG:* Aguirre *DG:* Astre
AUSTRALIA 6
PG: P McLean (2)

5 Jul 1981
Ballymore, Brisbane
AUSTRALIA 17
T: Poidevin, O'Connor, Moon *C:* McLean *PG:* Richards
FRANCE 15
T: Mesney *C:* Gabernet *PG:* Blanco, Gabernet *DG:* Vivies

11 Jul 1981
Sydney Cricket Ground
AUSTRALIA 24
T: Hall, O'Connor *C:* PE McLean (2) *PG:* PE McLean (4)
FRANCE 14
T: Lacas, Elissalde *DG:* Elissalde, Sallefranque

13 Nov 1983
Clermont-Ferrand
FRANCE 15
PG: Lescarboura (3) *DG:* Lescarboura, Lafond
AUSTRALIA 15
T: Roche *C:* Campese *PG:* Campese *DG:* M Ella, Hawker

20 Nov 1983
Parc des Princes, Paris
FRANCE 15
T: Esteve *C:* Lescarboura *PG:* Gabernet, Lescarboura (2)
AUSTRALIA 6
PG: Campese *DG:* M Ella

21 Jun 1986
Sydney Cricket Ground
AUSTRALIA 27
T: Campese *C:* Lynagh *PG:* Lynagh (6) *DG:* Lynagh
FRANCE 14
T: Blanco (2), Sella *C:* Lescarboura

4 Nov 1989
Meinau Stadium, Strasbourg
FRANCE 15
PG: Camberabero (4) *DG:* Camberabero
AUSTRALIA 32
T: Horan (2), Williams, Campese *C:* Lynagh (2) *PG:* Lynagh (4)

11 Nov 1989
Stade Grimpooris, Lille
FRANCE 25
T: Lagisquet, Andrieu *C:* Lacroix
PG: Lacroix (5)
AUSTRALIA 19
T: Kearns, Farr-Jones *C:* Lynagh
PG: Lynagh (3)

9 Jun 1990
Sydney Football Stadium
AUSTRALIA 21
T: Martin *C:* Lynagh *PG:* Lynagh (5)
FRANCE 9
PG: Camberabero (3)

24 Jun 1990
Ballymore Oval, Brisbane
AUSTRALIA 48
T: Carozza, Cornish, Gavin, Little, Penalty try, Campese *C:* Lynagh (6)
PG: Lynagh (4)
FRANCE 31
T: Blanco (2), Armary, Lacombe
C: Camberabero (3) *PG:* Camberabero (3)

30 Jun 1990
Sydney Football Stadium
AUSTRALIA 19
T: Campese, Daly *C:* Lynagh
PG: Lynagh (2) *DG:* Lynagh
FRANCE 28
T: Camberabero, Mesnel
C: Camberabero *PG:* Camberabero (2), Blanco *DG:* Camberabero (3)

FRANCE v NEW ZEALAND

1 Jan 1906
Parc des Princes, Paris
FRANCE 8
T: Cessieux, Jerome *C:* Pujol
NEW ZEALAND 38
T: Wallace (3), Abbott (2), Hunter (2), Harper (2), Glasgow *C:* Wallace (2), Tyler, Abbott

18 Jan 1925
Stade des Ponts Jumeaux, Toulouse
FRANCE 6
T: Cassayet, Ribere
NEW ZEALAND 30
T: Cooke (2), White, Porter, Steele, Svenson, Irvine, Richardson *C:* Nicholls (3)

27 Feb 1954
Stade Colombes, Paris
FRANCE 3
T: J Prat
NEW ZEALAND 0

22 Jul 1961
Eden Park, Auckland
NEW ZEALAND 13
T: McKay, O'Sullivan *C:* DB Clarke (2)
DG: DB Clarke
FRANCE 6
DG: Albaladejo (2)

5 Aug 1961
Athletic Park, Wellington
NEW ZEALAND 15
T: Tremain *C:* DB Clarke (4)
FRANCE 3
T: Dupuy

19 Aug 1961
Lancaster Park, Christchurch
NEW ZEALAND 32
T: Graham, Little, Tremain, Meads, Yates *C:* DB Clarke *PG:* DB Clarke (3)
FRANCE 3
T: Crauste

8 Feb 1964
Stade Colombes, Paris
FRANCE 3
PG: Albaladejo
NEW ZEALAND 12
T: Caulton, Gray *PG:* Herewini
DG: Laidlaw

25 Nov 1967
Stade Colombes, Paris
FRANCE 15
T: Campaes *PG:* Villepreux (3)
DG: Gachassin
NEW ZEALAND 21
T: Going, Kirkpatrick, Dick, Steel
C: McCormick (3) *PG:* McCormick

13 Jul 1968
Lancaster Park, Christchurch
NEW ZEALAND 12
T: Kirton *PG:* McCormick (3)
FRANCE 9
PG: Villepreux (2) *DG:* Lacaze

27 Jul 1968
Athletic Park, Wellington
NEW ZEALAND 9
PG: McCormick (3)
FRANCE 3
PG: Villepreux

10 Aug 1968
Eden Park, Auckland
NEW ZEALAND 19
T: Going (2) *C:* McCormick (2)
PG: McCormick (2) *DG:* Cottrell
FRANCE 12
T: Trillo, Carrere, Lux *DG:* Dourthe

10 Feb 1973
Parc des Princes, Paris
FRANCE 13
T: Dourthe, Bertranne *C:* Romeu
PG: Romeu
NEW ZEALAND 6
PG: Karam (2)

11 Nov 1977
Stadium de Toulouse
FRANCE 18
T: Paparemborde *C:* Romeu
PG: Romeu (3) *DG:* Romeu
NEW ZEALAND 13
T: Williams *PG:* McKechnie, Williams
DG: Robertson

19 Nov 1977
Parc des Princes, Paris
FRANCE 3
PG: Romeu
NEW ZEALAND 15
T: Wilson *C:* McKechnie
PG: McKechnie, Seear *DG:* McKechnie

7 Jul 1979
Lancester Park, Christchurch
NEW ZEALAND 23
T: SS Wilson, Donaldson, Watts *C:* BW Wilson *PG:* BW Wilson (3)
FRANCE 9
T: Mesny *C:* Aguirre *DG:* Caussade

14 Jul 1979
Eden Park, Auckland
NEW ZEALAND 19
T: S Wilson, Mourie *C:* B Wilson *PG:* B Wilson (3)
FRANCE 24
T: Averous, Cordorniou, Caussade, Gallion *C:* Caussade *PG:* Aguirre *DG:* Caussade

14 Nov 1981
Stadium de Toulouse
FRANCE 9
PG: Laporte (2) *DG:* Gabernet
NEW ZEALAND 13
T: Wilson *PG:* Hewson (2) *DG:* Hewson

21 Nov 1981
Parc des Princes, Paris
FRANCE 6
PG: Laporte, Blanco
NEW ZEALAND 18
T: Shaw (pen. try), Wilson *C:* Hewson (2) *PG:* Hewson (2)

16 Jun 1984
Lancaster Park, Christchurch
NEW ZEALAND 10
T: Taylor *PG:* Hewson (2)
FRANCE 9
T: Blanco *C:* Lescarboura *PG:* Lescarboura

23 Jun 1984
Eden Park, Auckland
NEW ZEALAND 31
T: B Smith, Taylor, Dalton *C:* Hewson (2) *PG:* Hewson (5)
FRANCE 18
T: Lescarboura (2), Bonneval *PG:* Lescarboura (2)

28 Jun 1986
Lancaster Park, Christchurch
NEW ZEALAND 18
T: Brewer *C:* Cooper *PG:* Cooper (2) *DG:* Botica (2)
FRANCE 9
DG: Lescarboura (3)

8 Nov 1986
Stadium de Toulouse
FRANCE 7
T: Sella *PG:* Berot
NEW ZEALAND 19
T: W Shelford *PG:* Crowley (3) *DG:* Stone, Crowley

15 Nov 1986
Beaujoire Stadium, Nantes
FRANCE 16
T: Charvet, Lorieux *C:* Berot *PG:* Berot (2)
NEW ZEALAND 3
PG: Crowley

17 Jun 1989
Lancaster Park, Christchurch
NEW ZEALAND 25
T: Wright (2), A Whetton *C:* Fox (2) *PG:* Fox (3)
FRANCE 17
T: Blanco (2), Cecillon *C:* Berot *PG:* Berot

1 Jul 1989
Eden Park, Auckland
NEW ZEALAND 34
T: A Whetton, Stanley, Deans, Fitzpatrick *C:* Fox (3) *PG:* Fox (4)
FRANCE 20
T: Rouge-Thomas, Cecillon *PG:* Blanco (4)

3 Nov 1990
Stade Beaujoire, Nantes
FRANCE 3
PG: Camberabero
NEW ZEALAND 24
T: Innes, A Whetton *C:* Fox (2) *PG:* Fox (3) *DG:* Fox

10 Nov 1990
Parc des Princes, Paris
FRANCE 12
PG: Camberabero (3) *DG:* Camberabero
NEW ZEALAND 30
T: Crowley, M Jones *C:* Fox (2) *PG:* Fox (6)

FRANCE v SOUTH AFRICA

1913
Bordeaux
FRANCE 5
T: Bruneau *C:* Andre
SOUTH AFRICA 38
T: W Morkel, D Morkel (2), Francis, R Luyt, McHardy (2), Ledger, J Morkel *C:* D Morkel (2), G Morkel (2) *PG:* D Morkel

16 Feb 1952
Stade Colombes, Paris
FRANCE 3
DG: Carbignac
SOUTH AFRICA 25
T: Johnstone (2), Dinkelman, Muller, Delport, van Wik *C:* Muller, Johnstone *PG:* Johnstone

26 Jul 1958
Newlands, Cape Town
SOUTH AFRICA 3
T: Lochner
FRANCE 3
DG: Danos

16 Aug 1958
Ellis Park, Johhanesburg
SOUTH AFRICA 5
T: Fourie *C:* Gerber
FRANCE 9
PG: Lacaze *DG:* Lacaze, Martine

18 Feb 1961
Stade Colombes, Paris
FRANCE 0
SOUTH AFRICA 0

25 Jul 1964
Springs, South Africa
SOUTH AFRICA 6
T: Stewart *PG:* Stewart
FRANCE 8
T: Darrouy *C:* Albaladejo *PG:* Albaladejo

15 Jul 1967
Kingsmead, Durban
SOUTH AFRICA 26
T: Dirksen (2), Greyling (2), Ellis *C:* H de Villiers (4) *PG:* H de Villiers
FRANCE 3
T: Dourthe

22 Jul 1967
Free State Stadium, Bloemfontein
SOUTH AFRICA 16
T: Olivier, Dirksen, Engelbrecht *C:* H de Villiers (2) *PG:* Naude
FRANCE 3
PG: Villepreux

29 Jul 1967
Ellis Park, Johannesburg
SOUTH AFRICA 14
T: Olivier, Ellis *C:* Visagie *PG:* Naude (2)
FRANCE 19
T: Cabanier, Trillo *C:* G Camberabero (2) *DG:* G Camberabero (2) *PG:* Lacaze

12 Aug 1967
Newlands, Cape Town
SOUTH AFRICA 6
DG: Visagie *PG:* H de Villiers
FRANCE 6
T: Spanghero *PG:* G Camberabero

9 Nov 1968
Bordeaux
FRANCE 9
T: Douga (2), Bonal
SOUTH AFRICA 12
PG: Visagie (4)

16 Nov 1968
Stade Colombes, Paris
FRANCE 11
T: Cester *C:* Paries *DG:* Puget, Paries
SOUTH AFRICA 16
T: Engelbrecht, D de Villiers, Nomis *C:* Visagie (2) *PG:* Visagie

12 Jun 1971
Free State Stadium, Bloemfontein
SOUTH AFRICA 22
T: Muller, Viljoen *C:* McCallum (2) *PG:* McCallum (3) *DG:* Visagie
FRANCE 9
T: Trillo *PG:* Berot (2)

19 Jun 1971
Kings Park, Durban
SOUTH AFRICA 8
T: Cronje *C:* McCallum *DG:* Visagie
FRANCE 8
T: Bertranne *C:* Berot *DG:* Cantoni

23 Nov 1974
Stadium de Toulouse
FRANCE 4
T: Bertranne
SOUTH AFRICA 13
T: Stapelberg *PG:* Bosch (2), C Fourie

30 Nov 1974
Parc des Princes, Paris
FRANCE 8
T: Gourdon, Dourthe
SOUTH AFRICA 10
T: Stapelberg *PG:* Bosch (2)

21 Jun 1975
Free State Stadium, Bloemfontein
SOUTH AFRICA 38
T: Whipp, Grobler, Cockrell, Oosthuizen, Pope *C:* Bosch (2), Dawie Snyman *PG:* Bosch (3), Dawie Snyman
FRANCE 25
T: Skrela, Paparemborde, Averous, Harize *C:* Pesteil (3) *PG:* Pesteil

28 Jun 1975
Loftus Versveld, Pretoria
SOUTH AFRICA 33
T: C Fourie, Du Plessis *C:* Bosch (2) *PG:* Bosch (6), C Fourie
FRANCE 18
T: E Paparemborde *C:* Romeu *DG:* Romeu *PG:* Romeu (3)

8 Nov 1980
Loftus Versveld, Pretoria
SOUTH AFRICA 37
T: Pienaar, Germishuys, Serfontein, Stofberg, Kahts *C:* Botha (4) *PG:* Botha (3)
FRANCE 15
T: Dintrans *C:* Vivies *PG:* Vivies (3)

ENGLAND v NEW ZEALAND

2 Dec 1905
Crystal Palace, London
ENGLAND 0
NEW ZEALAND 15
T: McGregor (4), Newton

3 Jan 1925
Twickenham
ENGLAND 11
T: Cove-Smith, Kittermaster *C:* Conway *PG:* Corbett
NEW ZEALAND 17
T: Svenson, Steel, Parker, MJ Brownlie *C:* Nicholls *PG:* Nicholls

4 Jan 1936
Twickenham
ENGLAND 13
T: Obolensky (2), Sever *DG:* Cranmer
NEW ZEALAND 0

30 Jan 1954
Twickenham
ENGLAND 0
NEW ZEALAND 5
T: Dalzell *C:* Scott

25 May 1963
Eden Park, Auckland
NEW ZEALAND 21
T: Caulton (2), DB Clarke *C:* DB Clarke (3) *PG:* DB Clarke *DG:* DB Clarke
ENGLAND 11
T: Ranson *C:* Hosen *PG:* Hosen (2)

1 Jun 1963
Lancaster Park, Christchurch
NEW ZEALAND 9
T: McKay, Walsh *GM:* DB Clarke
ENGLAND 6
T: Phillips *PG:* Hosen

4 Jan 1964
Twickenham
ENGLAND 0
NEW ZEALAND 14
T: Caulton, Meads *C:* DB Clarke *PG:* DB Clarke (2)

4 Nov 1967
Twickenham
ENGLAND 11
T: Lloyd (2) *C:* Rutherford *PG:* Larter
NEW ZEALAND 23
T: Kirton (2), Birtwistle, Laidlaw, Dick *C:* McCormick (4)

6 Jan 1973
Twickenham
ENGLAND 0
NEW ZEALAND 9
T: Kirkpatrick *C:* Karam *DG:* Williams

15 Sep 1973
Eden Park, Auckland
NEW ZEALAND 10
T: Barry, Hurst *C:* Lendrum
ENGLAND 16
T: Squires, Stevens, Neary *C:* Rossborough (2)

25 Nov 1978
Twickenham
ENGLAND 6
PG: Hare *DG:* Hare
NEW ZEALAND 16
T: Oliver, Johnstone *C:* McKechnie
PG: McKechnie (2)

24 Nov 1979
Twickenham
ENGLAND 9
PG: Hare (3)
NEW ZEALAND 10
T: Fleming *PG:* RG Wilson (2)

19 Nov 1983
Twickenham
ENGLAND 15
T: Colclough *C:* Hare *PG:* Hare (3)
NEW ZEALAND 9
T: Davie *C:* Deans *PG:* Deans

1 Jun 1985
Lancaster Park, Christchurch
NEW ZEALAND 18
PG: Crowley (6)
ENGLAND 13
T: Harrison, Teague *C:* Barnes
PG: Barnes

8 Jun 1985
Athletic Park, Wellington
NEW ZEALAND 42
T: Green (2), Kirwan, Mexted, Shaw, Hobbs *C:* Crowley (3) *PG:* Crowley (3)
DG: Smith
ENGLAND 15
T: Hall, Harrison *C:* Barnes (2)
DG: Barnes

SCOTLAND v NEW ZEALAND

18 Nov 1905
Inverleith, Edinburgh
SCOTLAND 7
T: MacCallum *DG:* ED Simson
NEW ZEALAND 12
T: Smith (2), Glasgow, Cunningham

23 Nov 1935
Murrayfield
SCOTLAND 8
T: Fyfe, Dick *C:* Murdoch
NEW ZEALAND 18
T: Caughey (3), Hadley *C:* Gilbert (3)

13 Feb 1954
Murrayfield
SCOTLAND 0
NEW ZEALAND 3
PG: Scott

18 Jan 1964
Murrayfield
SCOTLAND 0
NEW ZEALAND 0

2 Dec 1967
Murrayfield
SCOTLAND 3
DG: Chisholm
NEW ZEALAND 14
T: MacRae, Davis *C:* McCormick
PG: McCormick (2)

16 Dec 1972
Murrayfield
SCOTLAND 9
PG: Irvine (2) *DG:* McGeechan
NEW ZEALAND 14
T: Wyllie, Batty, Going *C:* Karam

14 Jun 1975
Eden Park, Auckland
NEW ZEALAND 24
T: Williams (2), Macdonald, Robertson
C: Karam (4)
SCOTLAND 0

9 Dec 1978
Murrayfield
SCOTLAND 9
T: Hay *C:* Irvine *DG:* McGeechan
NEW ZEALAND 18
T: Seear, Robertson *C:* McKechnie (2)
PG: McKechnie (2)

10 Nov 1979
Murrayfield
SCOTLAND 6
PG: Irvine (2)
NEW ZEALAND 20
T: SS Wilson, Dunn, Loveridge, Mexted
C: RG Wilson

13 Jun 1981
Carisbrook, Dunedin
NEW ZEALAND 11
T: Wilson, Loveridge *PG:* Hewson
SCOTLAND 4
T: Deans

20 Jun 1981
Eden Park, Auckland
NEW ZEALAND 40
T: Wilson (3), Hewson (2), Robertson, Mourie *C:* Hewson (6)
SCOTLAND 15
T: Hay *C:* Irvine *PG:* Irvine (2)
DG: Renwick

12 Nov 1983
Murrayfield
SCOTLAND 25
T: Pollock *PG:* Dods (5) *DG:* Rutherford (2)
NEW ZEALAND 25
T: Hobbs, Fraser (2) *C:* Deans (2)
PG: Deans (3)

16 Jun 1990
Carisbrook, Dunedin
NEW ZEALAND 31
T: Kirwan (2), Crowley, Fox, Jones
C: Fox (4) *PG:* Fox
SCOTLAND 16
T: Lineen, Gray, Sole *C:* G Hastings (2)

23 Jun 1990
Eden Park, Auckland
NEW ZEALAND 21
T: Loe *C:* Fox *PG:* Fox (5)
SCOTLAND 18
T: Stanger, Moore *C:* G Hastings (2)
PG: G Hastings (2)

IRELAND v NEW ZEALAND

25 Nov 1905
Lansdowne Road, Dublin
IRELAND 0
NEW ZEALAND 15
T: Deans (2), McDonald *C:* Wallace (3)

1 Nov 1924
Lansdowne Road, Dublin
IRELAND 0
NEW ZEALAND 6
T: Svenson *PG:* Nicholls

7 Dec 1935
Lansdowne Road, Dublin
IRELAND 9
T: Beamish *PG:* Bailey, Siggins
NEW ZEALAND 17
T: Mitchell, Oliver, Hart *C:* Gilbert
PG: Gilbert (2)

9 Jan 1954
Lansdowne Road, Dublin
IRELAND 3
PG: Henderson
NEW ZEALAND 14
T: Clark, Stuart *C:* Scott *PG:* Scott
DG: Scott

7 Dec 1963
Lansdowne Road, Dublin
IRELAND 5
T: Fortune *C:* Kiernan
NEW ZEALAND 6
T: Tremain *PG:* Clarke

20 Jan 1973
Lansdowne Road, Dublin
IRELAND 10
T: Grace *PG:* McGann (2)
NEW ZEALAND 10
T: Going, Wyllie *C:* Karam

23 Nov 1974
Lansdowne Road, Dublin
IRELAND 6
PG: Ensor (2)
NEW ZEALAND 15
T: Karam *C:* Karam *PG:* Karam (3)

5 Jun 1976
Athletic Park, Wellington
NEW ZEALAND 11
T: BJ Robertson, Kirkpatrick *PG:* Mains
IRELAND 3
T: Dalton *DG:* Bruce (2)

4 Nov 1978
Lansdowne Road, Dublin
IRELAND 6
PG: Ward (2)
NEW ZEALAND 10
T: Dalton *DG:* Bruce (2)

18 Nov 1989
Lansdowne Road, Dublin
IRELAND 6
PG: Smith (2)
NEW ZEALAND 23
T: Gallagher, Wright, Shelford *C:* Fox
PG: Fox (3)

30 May 1992
Carisbrook, Dunedin
NEW ZEALAND 24
T: Bunce (2), Henderson, Clarke
C: G Cooper (4)
IRELAND 21
T: Cunningham (2), Staples
C: Russell (3) *PG:* Russell

6 Jun 1992
Athletic Park, Wellington
NEW ZEALAND 59
T: Bunce (2), Pene (2), I Jones, Clarke, Timu, M Cooper (2), Kirwan, Strachan
C: M Cooper (6) *PG:* M Cooper
IRELAND 6
T: Furlong *C:* Russell

WALES v NEW ZEALAND

16 Dec 1905
Cardiff Arms Park
WALES 3
T: Morgan
NEW ZEALAND 0

29 Nov 1925
St Helens, Swansea
WALES 0
NEW ZEALAND 19
T: Irvine (2), MJ Brownlie, Svenson
C: Nicholls (2) *PG:* Nicholls

21 Dec 1935
Cardiff Arms Park
WALES 13
T: Rees-Jones (2), Davey *C:* Jenkins (2)
NEW ZEALAND 12
T: Ball (2) *C:* Gilbert *DG:* Gilbert

19 Dec 1953
Cardiff Arms Park
WALES 13
T: Judd, K Jones *C:* Rowlands (2)
PG: Rowlands
NEW ZEALAND 8
T: Clark *C:* Jarden *PG:* Jarden

21 Dec 1963
Cardiff Arms Park
WALES 0
NEW ZEALAND 6
PG: Clarke *DG:* Watt

11 Nov 1967
Cardiff Arms Park
WALES 6
PG: Gale *DG:* John
NEW ZEALAND 13
T: Birtwistle, Davis *C:* McCormick (2)
PG: McCormick

31 May 1969
Lancaster Park, Christchurch
NEW ZEALAND 19
T: Dick, McLeod, Lochore, Gray
C: McCormick (2) *PG:* McCormick
WALES 0

14 Jun 1969
Eden Park, Auckland
NEW ZEALAND 33
T: Skudder, MacRae, Kirkpatrick
C: McCormick (3) *PG:* McCormick (5)
DG: McCormick
WALES 12
T: MCR Richards, Jarrett *PG:* Jarrett (2)

2 Dec 1972
Cardiff Arms Park
WALES 16
T: JC Bevan *PG:* Bennett (4)
NEW ZEALAND 19
T: Murdoch *PG:* Karam (5)

11 Nov 1978
Cardiff Arms Park
WALES 12
PG: WG Davies (3), Fenwick
NEW ZEALAND 13
T: SS Wilson *PG:* McKechnie (3)

1 Nov 1980
Cardiff Arms Park
WALES 3
PG: Fenwick
NEW ZEALAND 23
T: Mourie, Fraser, Allen, Reid
C: Rollerson (2) *PG:* Rollerson

28 May 1988
Lancaster Park, Christchurch
NEW ZEALAND 52
T: Kirwan (4), Wright (2), G Whetton, Deans, Shelford, Gallagher *C:* Fox (6)
WALES 3
PG: Ring

11 Jun 1988
Eden Park, Auckland
NEW ZEALAND 54
T: Wright (2), Jones, Deans, McDowell, Kirwan (2), Taylor *C:* Fox (8) *PG:* Fox (2)
WALES 9
T: J Davies *C:* Ring *PG:* Ring

4 Nov 1989
Cardiff Arms Park
WALES 9
PG: Thorburn (3)
NEW ZEALAND 34
T: Innes (2), Wright, Bachop *C:* Fox (3)
PG: Fox (4)

BRITISH ISLES v NEW ZEALAND

13 Aug 1904
Athletic Park, Wellington
NEW ZEALAND 9
T: D McGregor (2) *PG:* Wallace
GREAT BRITAIN 3
PG: Harding

21 Jun 1930
Carisbrook, Dunedin
NEW ZEALAND 3
T: Hart
GREAT BRITAIN 6
T: Reeve, Morley

5 Jul 1930
Lancaster Park, Christchurch
NEW ZEALAND 13
T: Hart, Oliver *C:* Nicholls (2)
GM: Nicholls
GREAT BRITAIN 10
T: Aarvold (2) *C:* Prentice (2)

26 Jul 1930
Eden Park, Auckland
NEW ZEALAND 15
T: McLean (2), Lucas *C:* Strang
DG: Nicholls
GREAT BRITAIN 10
T: Bowcott, Aarvold *C:* Jones, Black

9 Aug 1930
Athletic Park, Wellington
NEW ZEALAND 22
T: Porter (2), Cooke (2), Strang, Batty
C: Strang (2)
GREAT BRITAIN 8
T: Novis *C:* Black *PG:* Parker

27 May 1950
Carisbrook, Dunedin
NEW ZEALAND 9
T: Roper, Elvidge *PG:* Scott
BRITISH ISLES 9
T: Kyle, Jones *PG:* Robins

10 Jun 1950
Lancaster Park, Christchurch
NEW ZEALAND 8
T: Crowley, Roper *C:* Haig
BRITISH ISLES 0

1 Jul 1950
Athletic Park, Wellington
NEW ZEALAND 6
T: Elvidge *PG:* Scott
BRITISH ISLES 3
PG: Robins

29 Jul 1950
Eden Park, Auckland
NEW ZEALAND 11
T: Wilson, Henderson *C:* Scott
DG: Scott
BRITISH ISLES 8
T: KL Jones *C:* BL Jones *PG:* BL Jones

18 Jul 1959
Carisbrook, Dunedin
NEW ZEALAND 18
PG: DB Clarke (6)
BRITISH ISLES 17
T: Price (2), O'Reilly, Jackson
C: Risman *PG:* Hewitt

15 Aug 1959
Athletic Park, Wellington
NEW ZEALAND 11
T: Caulton (2), DB Clarke *C:* DB Clarke
BRITISH ISLES 8
T: Young *C:* Davies *PG:* Davies

29 Aug 1959
Lancaster Park, Christchurch
NEW ZEALAND 22
T: Caulton (2), Meads, Urbahn *C:* DB Clarke (2) *PG:* DB Clarke *DG:* DB Clarke
BRITISH ISLES 8
T: Hewitt *C:* Faull *PG:* Faull

19 Sep 1959
Eden Park, Auckland
NEW ZEALAND 6
PG: DB Clarke (2)
BRITISH ISLES 9
T: O'Reilly, Jackson, Risman

16 Jul 1966
Carisbrook, Dunedin
NEW ZEALAND 20
T: McLeod, Williment, Lochore
C: Williment *PG:* Williment (2)
DG: Herewini
BRITISH ISLES 3
PG: Wilson

6 Aug 1966
Athletic Park, Wellington
NEW ZEALAND 16
T: Tramian, CE Meads, Steel
C: Williment (2) *PG:* Williment
BRITISH ISLES 12
PG: Wilson (3) *DG:* Watkins

27 Aug 1966
Lancaster Park, Christchurch
NEW ZEALAND 19
T: Nathan (2), Steel *C:* Williment (2)
PG: Williment (2)
BRITISH ISLES 6
T: Lamont, D Watkins

10 Sep 1966
Eden Park, Auckland
NEW ZEALAND 24
T: Nathan, Dick, MacRae, Steel
C: Williment (3) *PG:* Williment
DG: Herewini
BRITISH ISLES 11
T: Hinshelwood, McFadyean *C:* Wilson
PG: Wilson

27 Jun 1971
Carisbrook, Dunedin
NEW ZEALAND 3
PG: McCormick
BRITISH ISLES 9
T: McLaughlan *PG:* John (2)

10 Jul 1971
Lancaster Park, Christchurch
NEW ZEALAND 22
T: Burgess (2), Going, Kirkpatrick, Williams (pen. try) *C:* Mains (2)
PG: Mains
BRITISH ISLES 12
T: TGR Davies (2) *PG:* John *DG:* John

31 Jul 1971
Athletic Park, Wellington
NEW ZEALAND 3
T: Mains
BRITISH ISLES 13
T: TGR Davies, John *C:* John (2)
DG: John

14 Aug 1971
Eden Park, Auckland
NEW ZEALAND 14
T: Cottrell, Lister *C:* Mains *PG:* Mains (2)
BRITISH ISLES 14
T: Dixon *C:* John *PG:* John (2)
DG: JPR Williams

18 Jun 1977
Athletic Park, Wellington
NEW ZEALAND 16
T: Going, Johnstone, Batty *C:* Williams (2)
BRITISH ISLES 12
PG: Bennett (3), Irvine

9 Jul 1977
Lancaster Park, Christchurch
NEW ZEALAND 9
PG: Williams (3)
BRITISH ISLES 13
T: JJ Williams *PG:* Bennett (3)

30 Jul 1977
Carisbrook Park, Dunedin
NEW ZEALAND 19
T: Kirkpatrick, Haden *C:* Wilson
PG: Wilson (2) *DG:* Robertson
BRITISH ISLES 7
T: Duggan *PG:* Irvine

13 Aug 1977
Eden Park, Auckland
NEW ZEALAND 10
T: Knight *PG:* Wilson (2)
BRITISH ISLES 9
T: Morgan *C:* Morgan *PG:* Morgan

4 Jun 1983
Lancaster Park, Christchurch
NEW ZEALAND 16
T: M Shaw *PG:* Hewson (3)
DG: Hewson
BRITISH ISLES 12
PG: Campbell (3) *DG:* Campbell

18 Jun 1983
Athletic Park, Wellington
NEW ZEALAND 9
T: Loveridge *C:* Hewson *PG:* Hewson
BRITISH ISLES 0

2 Jul 1983
Carisbrook Park, Dunedin
NEW ZEALAND 15
T: S Wilson *C:* Hewson *PG:* Hewson (3)
BRITISH ISLES 8
T: Baird, Rutherford

16 Jul 1983
Eden Park, Auckland
NEW ZEALAND 38
T: S Wilson (3), Hewson, Hobbs, Haden
C: Hewson (4)
BRITISH ISLES 6
PG: G Evans (2)

ENGLAND v AUSTRALIA

1909
Blackheath
ENGLAND 3
T: Mobbs
AUSTRALIA 9
T: Russell (2), N Rowe

3 Jan 1948
Twickenham
ENGLAND 0
AUSTRALIA 11
T: Windon (2), Walker *C:* Tonkin

1 Feb 1958
Twickenham
ENGLAND 9
T: Phillips, Jackson *PG:* Hetherington
AUSTRALIA 6
PG: Lenehan *DG:* Curley

4 Jun 1963
Sydney Sports Ground
AUSTRALIA 18
T: Jones, Walsham, Heinrich, Davis
C: Ryan (3)
ENGLAND 9
T: Phillips, Clarke, Godwin

8 Jan 1967
Twickenham
ENGLAND 11
T: Ashby *C:* Hosen *PG:* Hosen (2)
AUSTRALIA 23
T: Brass, Catchpole *C:* Lenehan
PG: Lenehan, Hawthorne
DG: Hawthorne (3)

18 Nov 1973
Twickenham
ENGLAND 20
T: Old, Neary, Ripley *C:* Rossborough
PG: Rossborough (2)
AUSTRALIA 3
PG: Fairfax

24 May 1975
Sydney Cricket Ground
AUSTRALIA 16
T: Loane *PG:* Brown (2) *DG:* Brown, Wright
ENGLAND 9
T: Squires *PG:* Butler *DG:* Butler

31 May 1975
Ballymore, Brisbane
AUSTRALIA 30
T: Price, Smith, Weatherstone, Fay, Monaghan *C:* Brown, Wright
PG: Brown, Wright
ENGLAND 21
T: Squires, Uttley *C:* Old (2) *PG:* Old (3)

3 Jan 1976
Twickenham
ENGLAND 23
T: Corless, Duckham, Lampowski
C: Hignell *PG:* Hignell (3)
AUSTRALIA 6
PG: PE McLean (2)

2 Jan 1982
Twickenham
ENGLAND 15
T: Jeavons *C:* Dodge *PG:* Rose (3)
AUSTRALIA 11
T: Moon (2) *PG:* McLean

3 Nov 1984
Twickenham
ENGLAND 3
PG: Barnes
AUSTRALIA 19
T: M Ella, Poidevin, Lynagh *C:* Lynagh (2) *PG:* Lynagh

29 May 1988
Ballymore, Brisbane
AUSTRALIA 22
T: Williams *PG:* Lynagh (6)
ENGLAND 16
T: Underwood, Bailey *C:* Webb
PG: Webb (2)

12 Jun 1988
Concord Oval, Sydney
AUSTRALIA 28
T: Campese, G Ella, Lynagh, Carter
C: Lynagh (3) *PG:* Lynagh (2)
ENGLAND 8
T: Richards, Underwood

5 Nov 1988
Twickenham
ENGLAND 28
T: Underwood (2), Morris, Halliday
C: Webb (3) *PG:* Webb (2)
AUSTRALIA 19
T: Leeds, Campese, Grant *C:* Lynagh (2) *PG:* Lynagh

27 Jul 1991
Sydney Football Stadium
AUSTRALIA 40
T: Campese (2), Ofahengaue (2), Roebuck *C:* Lynagh (4) *PG:* Lynagh (4)
ENGLAND 15
T: Guscott *C:* Webb *PG:* Webb (3)

IRELAND v AUSTRALIA

6 Dec 1947
Lansdowne Road, Dublin
IRELAND 3
PG: Quinn
AUSTRALIA 16
T: Allan, Windon, Burke, Tonkin
C: McMaster, Allan

18 Jan 1958
Lansdowne Road, Dublin
IRELAND 9
T: Henderson, Dawson *PG:* Pedlow
AUSTRALIA 6
T: Phelps, Summons

21 Jan 1967
Lansdowne Road, Dublin
IRELAND 15
T: Duggan, Gibson *PG:* Kiernan
DG: Gibson (2)
AUSTRALIA 8
T: Boyce *C:* Lenehan *DG:* Hawthorne

13 May 1967
Sydney Cricket Ground
AUSTRALIA 5
T: Catchpole *C:* Lenehan
IRELAND 11
T: McGrath, Walsh *C:* Kiernan
DG: Kiernan

26 Oct 1968
Lansdowne Road, Dublin
IRELAND 10
T: Bresnihan, Goodall *C:* Kiernan, Moroney
AUSTRALIA 3
T: Ballesty

17 Jan 1976
Lansdowne Road, Dublin
IRELAND 10
T: McMaster *PG:* Robbie (2)
AUSTRALIA 20
T: Ryan, T Shaw, Weatherstone *C:* PE McLean *PG:* PE McLean

3 Jun 1979
Ballymore, Brisbane
AUSTRALIA 12
T: Moon *C:* PE McLean *PG:* PE McLean (2)
IRELAND 27
T: Patterson (2) *C:* Campbell (2)
PG: Campbell (3) *DG:* Campbell (2)

16 Jun 1979
Sydney Cricket Ground
AUSTRALIA 3
PG: P McLean
IRELAND 9
PG: Campbell (3)

21 Nov 1981
Lansdowne Road, Dublin
IRELAND 12
PG: Ward (4)
AUSTRALIA 16
T: O'Connor *PG:* P McLean (3)
DG: Gould

10 Nov 1984
Lansdowne Road, Dublin
IRELAND 9
PG: Kiernan (3)
AUSTRALIA 16
T: M Ella *PG:* Lynagh *DG:* M Ella (2), Lynagh

SCOTLAND v AUSTRALIA

24 Nov 1947 *Murrayfield*
SCOTLAND 7
PG: McDonald *DG:* Hepburn
AUSTRALIA 16
T: Kearney, Tonkin, Howell, Cooke *C:* Piper (2)

15 Feb 1958 *Murrayfield*
SCOTLAND 12
T: Weatherstone, Stevenson *PG:* AR Smith (2)
AUSTRALIA 8
T: Thornett, Donald *C:* Lenehan

17 Dec 1966 *Murrayfield*
SCOTLAND 11
T: Chisholm, Boyle *C:* Wilson *PG:* Wilson
AUSTRALIA 5
T: Brass *C:* Lenehan

2 Nov 1968 *Murrayfield*
SCOTLAND 9
T: Hinshelwood *PG:* Blaikie (2)
AUSTRALIA 3
PG: Brass

6 Jun 1970 *Sydney Cricket Ground*
AUSTRALIA 23
T: Batterham (2), Cole (2), Hipwell, Rosenblum *C:* McGill *PG:* McGill
SCOTLAND 3
PG: Lauder

6 Dec 1975 *Murrayfield*
SCOTLAND 10
T: Renwick, Dick *C:* Morgan
AUSTRALIA 3
PG: McLean

19 Dec 1981 *Murrayfield*
SCOTLAND 24
T: Renwick *C:* Irvine *PG:* Irvine (5) *DG:* Rutherford
AUSTRALIA 15
T: Poidevin, Moon, Slack *PG:* PE McLean

3 Jul 1982 *Ballymore, Brisbane*
AUSTRALIA 7
T: Hawker *PG:* Hawker
SCOTLAND 12
T: Robertson *C:* Irvine *PG:* Irvine *DG:* Rutherford

10 Jul 1982 *Sydney Cricket Ground*
AUSTRALIA 33
T: Gould (2), O'Connor *C:* PE McLean (3) *PG:* PE McLean (5)
SCOTLAND 9
PG: Irvine (3)

8 Dec 1984 *Murrayfield*
SCOTLAND 12
PG: Dods (4)
AUSTRALIA 37
T: Campese (2), Farr-Jones, M Ella *C:* Lynagh (3) *PG:* Lynagh (5)

19 Nov 1988 *Murrayfield*
SCOTLAND 13
T: G Hastings, Robertson *C:* G Hastings *PG:* G Hastings
AUSTRALIA 32
T: Lawton (2), Campese (2), Gourley *C:* Lynagh (3) *PG:* Lynagh (2)

13 Jun 1992 *Sydney Football Stadium*
AUSTRALIA 27
T: Campese (2), Carozza, Lynagh *C:* Lynagh *PG:* Lynagh (3)
SCOTLAND 12
T: Wainwright *C:* G Hastings *PG:* G Hastings (2)

21 Jun 1992 *Ballymore, Brisbane*
AUSTRALIA 37
T: Carozza (2), Horan (2), Eales *C:* Lynagh *PG:* Lynagh (5)
SCOTLAND 13
T: Lineen, Sole *C:* Chalmers *PG:* Chalmers

WALES v AUSTRALIA

12 Dec 1908
Cardiff Arms Park
WALES 9
T: Travers, Hopkins *PG:* Winfield
AUSTRALIA 6
T: Richards, Russell

20 Dec 1947
Cardiff Arms Park
WALES 6
PG: Tamplin (2)
AUSTRALIA 0

4 Jan 1958
Cardiff Arms Park
WALES 9
T: Collins *PG:* TJ Davies *DG:* CR James
AUSTRALIA 3
T: Miller

3 Dec 1966 *Cardiff Arms Park*
WALES 11
T: Dawes, Morgan *C:* Price *PG:* Price
AUSTRALIA 14
T: Lenehan,Cardy *C:* Hawthorne *PG:* Lenehan *DG:* Hawthorne

21 Jun 1969 *Sydney Cricket Ground*
AUSTRALIA 16
T: McGill, Smith *C:* McGill (2) *PG:* McGill (2)
WALES 19
T: Davies, Taylor, Morris *C:* Jarrett (2) *PG:* Jarrett (2)

10 Nov 1973 *Cardiff Arms Park*
WALES 24
T: TGR Davies, Morris, Windsor *PG:* Bennett (4)
AUSTRALIA 0

21 Dec 1975
Cardiff Arms Park
WALES 24
T: JJ Williams (3), Edwards *C:* Fenwick (2), Martin *PG:* Fenwick
AUSTRALIA 3
PG: P McLean

11 Jun 1978
Ballymore, Brisbane
AUSTRALIA 18
T: Crowe *C:* P McLean *PG:* P McLean (4)
WALES 8
T: TGR Davies, B Williams

17 Jun 1978
Sydney Cricket Ground
AUSTRALIA 19
T: Loane *PG:* P McLean (3) *DG:* P McLean, Monaghan
WALES 17
T: Holmes, TGR Davies *PG:* WG Davies *DG:* WG Davies

5 Dec 1981
Cardiff Arms Park
WALES 18
T: RD Moriarty *C:* G Evans *PG:* G Evans *DG:* WG Davies
AUSTRALIA 13
T: Slack, M Cox *C:* P McLean *PG:* P McLean

24 Nov 1984
Cardiff Arms Park
WALES 9
T: Bishop *C:* Wyatt *PG:* Wyatt
AUSTRALIA 28
T: Lawton, Tuynman, M Ella, Lynagh *C:* Gould (3) *PG:* Gould (2)

21 Jul 1991 *Ballymore, Brisbane*
AUSTRALIA 63
T: Lynagh (2), Kearns (2), Gavin (2), Ofahengaue, Horan, Roebuck, Campese, Egerton, Little *C:* Lynagh (6) *PG:* Lynagh
WALES 6
PG: Thorburn, A Davies

AUSTRALIA v BRITISH ISLES

30 Aug 1930
Sydney Cricket Ground
AUSTRALIA 6
T: Malcolm, McGhie
BRITISH ISLES 5
T: Novis *C:* Prentice

19 Aug 1950
Brisbane Cricket Ground
AUSTRALIA 6
T: Cross *PG:* Gardner
BRITISH ISLES 19
T: Jones, Williams *C:* Jones (2) *PG:* Jones (2) *DG:* Jones

26 Aug 1950
Sydney Cricket Ground
AUSTRALIA 3
T: Burke
BRITISH ISLES 24
T: Nelson (2), Kyle, Macdonald, John *C:* Robins (2), Jones *PG:* Jones

6 Jun 1959
Brisbane Exhibition Ground
AUSTRALIA 6
PG: Donald (2)
BRITISH ISLES 17
T: O'Reilly, Smith *C:* Risman *PG:* Hewitt (2) *DG:* Scotland

13 Jun 1959
Sydney Sports Ground
AUSTRALIA 3
PG: Donald
BRITISH ISLES 24
T: Price (2), Risman, O'Reilly, Dawson *C:* Hewitt (2) *PG:* Scotland

28 May 1966
Sydney Cricket Ground
AUSTRALIA 8
T: Miller *C:* Ruebner *PG:* Ruebner
BRITISH ISLES 11
T: Kennedy, McLoughlin *C:* Rutherford *PG:* Rutherford

4 Jun 1966
Lang Park, Brisbane
AUSTRALIA 0
BRITISH ISLES 31
T: Jones (2), Bebb, Watkins, Murphy *C:* Wilson (5) *PG:* Wilson *DG:* Watkins

1 Jul 1989
Sydney Football Stadium
AUSTRALIA 30
T: Walker, Gourley, Maguire, Martin *C:* Lynagh (4) *DG:* Lynagh
BRITISH ISLES 12
PG: G Hastings (2), Chalmers *DG:* Chalmers

8 Jul 1989
Ballymore, Brisbane
AUSTRALIA 12
T: Martin *C:* Lynagh *PG:* Lynagh (2)
BRITISH ISLES 19
T: G Hastings, Guscott *C:* Andrew *PG:* G Hastings, Andrew *DG:* Andrew

15 Jul 1989
Sydney Football Stadium
AUSTRALIA 18
T: Williams *C:* Lynagh *PG:* Lynagh (4)
BRITISH ISLES 19
T: Evans *PG:* G Hastings (5)

ENGLAND v SOUTH AFRICA

8 Dec 1906
Crystal Palace
ENGLAND 3
T: Brooks
SOUTH AFRICA 3
T: Millar

4 Jan 1913
Twickenham
ENGLAND 3
T: Poulton
SOUTH AFRICA 9
T: JWH Morkel *PG:* DFT Morkel (2)

2 Jan 1932
Twickenham
ENGLAND 0
SOUTH AFRICA 7
T: Bergh *DG:* Brand

5 Jan 1952
Twickenham
ENGLAND 3
T: Winn
SOUTH AFRICA 8
T: Du Toit *C:* Muller *PG:* Muller

7 Jan 1961
Twickenham
ENGLAND 0
SOUTH AFRICA 5
T: Hopwood *C:* Du Preez

20 Dec 1969
Twickenham
ENGLAND 11
T: Larter, Pullin *C:* Hiller *PG:* Hiller
SOUTH AFRICA 8
T: Greyling *C:* Visagie *PG:* Visagie

3 Jun 1972
Ellis Park, Johannesburg
SOUTH AFRICA 9
PG: Snyman (3)
ENGLAND 18
T: Morley *C:* Doble *PG:* Doble (4)

2 Jun 1984
Boet Erasmus Stadium, Port Elizabeth
SOUTH AFRICA 33
T: Gerber, C Du Plessis, Louw
C: Heunis (3) *PG:* Heunis (5)
ENGLAND 15
PG: Hare (4) *DG:* Horton

9 Jun 1984
Ellis Park, Johannesburg
SOUTH AFRICA 35
T: Gerber (3), Stofberg, Sonnekus, Tobias *C:* Heunis (3), Tobias
PG: Heunis
ENGLAND 9
PG: Hare (3)

IRELAND v SOUTH AFRICA

24 Nov 1906
Belfast
IRELAND 12
T: Mclear, Sugar (2) *PG:* Parke
SOUTH AFRICA 15
T: Loubser (2), Krige, AC Stegmann
PG: Joubert

30 Nov 1912
Lansdowne Road, Dublin
IRELAND 0
SOUTH AFRICA 38
T: JA Stegmann (3), McHardy (3), J Morkel (2), Francis, Millar *C:* G Morkel (3), Luyt

19 Dec 1931
Lansdowne Road, Dublin
IRELAND 3
PG: McMahon
SOUTH AFRICA 8
T: Zimmerman, Waring *C:* Osler

8 Dec 1951
Lansdowne Road, Dublin
IRELAND 5
T: Browne *C:* Murphy
SOUTH AFRICA 17
T: Van Wyk (2), Ochse, Van Schoor
C: Geffin *DG:* Brewis

17 Dec 1960
Lansdowne Road, Dublin
IRELAND 3
PG: Kiernan
SOUTH AFRICA 8
T: Gainsford, H Van Zyl *C:* Lockyear

13 May 1961
Newlands, Cape Town
SOUTH AFRICA 24
T: Greenwood (2), Hopwood, BP Van Zyl (2) *C:* Nimb (3) *PG:* Nimb
IRELAND 8
T: Kiernan *C:* Kiernan *PG:* Kiernan

6 Apr 1965
Lansdowne Road, Dublin
IRELAND 9
T: McGrath *PG:* Kiernan (2)
SOUTH AFRICA 6
T: Mans *PG:* Stewart

10 Jan 1970
Lansdowne Road, Dublin
IRELAND 8
T: Duggan *C:* Kiernan *PG:* Kiernan
SOUTH AFRICA 8
T: Greyling *C:* HO de Villiers *PG:* HO de Villiers

30 May 1981
Newlands, Cape Town
SOUTH AFRICA 23
T: Gerber (2), Louw *C:* Botha
PG: Botha (2)
IRELAND 15
T: McGrath, McLennan *C:* Campbell (2)
PG: Campbell

6 Jun 1981
King's Park, Durban
IRELAND 10
T: O'Brien *PG:* Quinn (2)
SOUTH AFRICA 12
PG: Botha *DG:* Botha (3)

WALES v SOUTH AFRICA

1 Dec 1906
St Helens, Swansea
WALES 0
SOUTH AFRICA 11
T: Joubert, Loubser, Raaf *C:* Joubert

14 Dec 1912
Cardiff Arms Park
WALES 0
SOUTH AFRICA 3
PG: DFT Morkel

5 Dec 1931
St Helens, Swansea
WALES 3
T: Will Davies
SOUTH AFRICA 8
T: Daneel, Bergh *C:* Osler

22 Dec 1951
Cardiff Arms Park
WALES 3
T: BL Williams
SOUTH AFRICA 6
T: Ochse *PG:* Brewis

3 Dec 1960
Cardiff Arms Park
WALES 0
SOUTH AFRICA 3
PG: Oxlee

23 May 1964
Kings Park, Durban
SOUTH AFRICA 24
T: Marais, Hopwood, Smith *C:* Oxlee (3)
PG: Oxlee (2) *DG:* Wilson
WALES 3
PG: Bradshaw

24 Jan 1970
Cardiff Arms Park
WALES 6
T: Edwards *PG:* Edwards
SOUTH AFRICA 6
T: Nomis *PG:* HO de Villiers

SCOTLAND v SOUTH AFRICA

17 Nov 1906
Hampden Park, Glasgow
SCOTLAND 6
T: MacLeod, Purves
SOUTH AFRICA 0

23 Nov 1912
Inverleith, Edinburgh
SCOTLAND 0
SOUTH AFRICA 16
T: McHardy, JA Stegmann (2), WH Morkel *C:* PG Morkel, DTF Morkel

16 Jan 1932
Murrayfield, Edinburgh
SCOTLAND 3
T: Lind
SOUTH AFRICA 6
T: Osler, Craven

24 Nov 1951
Murrayfield
SCOTLAND 0
SOUTH AFRICA 44
T: Durand, Van Schoor, C Koch (2), Delport, Van Wyk, Muller, Dinkelmann, Lategan *C:* Geffin (7) *DG:* Brewis

30 Apr 1960
Boet Erasmus, Port Elizabeth
SOUTH AFRICA 18
T: Van Zyl (2), Gerike, Van Jaarscveldt *C:* Gerber (3)
SCOTLAND 10
T: Bruce, Smith *C:* Smith (2)

21 Jan 1961
Murrayfield
SCOTLAND 5
T: Smith *C:* Scotland
SOUTH AFRICA 12
T: Hopwood, Claassen *PG:* Du Preez (2)

17 Apr 1965
Murrayfield
SCOTLAND 8
T: Shackleton *C:* Wilson *DG:* Chisholm
SOUTH AFRICA 5
T: Engelbrecht *C:* Mans

6 Dec 1969
Murrayfield
SCOTLAND 6
T: ISG Smith *PG:* ISG Smith
SOUTH AFRICA 3
PG: Visagie

BRITISH ISLES v SOUTH AFRICA

30 Jul 1891
Crusader Ground, Port Elizabeth
SOUTH AFRICA 0
BRITISH ISLES 4
T: Aston, Whittaker *C:* Rotherham

28 Aug 1891
Kimberley
SOUTH AFRICA 0
BRITISH ISLES 3
DG: Mitchell

5 Sep 1891
Newlands, Cape Town
SOUTH AFRICA 0
BRITISH ISLES 4
T: Aston, Maclagan *C:* Rotherham

30 Jul 1896
Crusader Ground, Port Elizabeth
SOUTH AFRICA 0
BRITISH ISLES 8
T: Carey, Bulger *C:* Byrne

22 Aug 1896
Johannesburg
SOUTH AFRICA 8
T: Samuels (2) *C:* Cope
BRITISH ISLES 17
T: Todd, Crean, Hancock *C:* Byrne (2) *DG:* Mackie

29 Aug 1896
Kimberley
SOUTH AFRICA 3
T: Jones
BRITISH ISLES 9
T: Mackie *C:* Byrne *DG:* Byrne

5 Sep 1896
Newlands, Cape Town
SOUTH AFRICA 5
T: Larard *C:* Hepburn
BRITISH ISLES 0

26 Aug 1903
Johannesburg
SOUTH AFRICA 10
T: Dobbin, Sinclair *C:* Heatlie (2)
BRITISH ISLES 10
T: Skrimshire, Cave *C:* Gillespie (2)

5 Sep 1903
Kimberley
SOUTH AFRICA 0
BRITISH ISLES 0

12 Sep 1903
Newlands, Cape Town
SOUTH AFRICA 8
T: Barry, Reid *C:* Heatlie
BRITISH ISLES 0

6 Aug 1910
Johannesburg
SOUTH AFRICA 14
T: De Villiers, DFT Morkel, F Luyt, Hahn *C:* DFT Morkel
BRITISH ISLES 10
T: Foster, Spoors *DG:* Jones

27 Aug 1910
Crusader Ground, Port Elizabeth
SOUTH AFRICA 3
T: Mills
BRITISH ISLES 8
T: Spoors, Neale *C:* Pillman

3 Sep 1910
Newlands, Cape Town
SOUTH AFRICA 21
T: Roos, F Luyt, Allport, Reyneke *C:* DFT Morkel (3) *PG:* DFT Morkel
BRITISH ISLES 5
T: Spoors *C:* Pillman

16 Aug 1924
Kingsmead, Durban
SOUTH AFRICA 7
T: Aucamp *DG:* Osler
BRITISH ISLES 3
T: Whitley

23 Aug 1924
Johannesburg
SOUTH AFRICA 17
T: Starke, Mostert, Van Druten, Albertyn
C: Osler *PG:* Osler
BRITISH ISLES 0

17 Sep 1924
Crusader Ground, Port Elizabeth
SOUTH AFRICA 3
T: Van Druten
BRITISH ISLES 3
T: Cunningham

20 Sep 1924
Newlands, Cape Town
SOUTH AFRICA 16
T: Starke (2), Bester, Slater *DG:* Starke
BRITISH ISLES 9
T: Boyce, Harris *PG:* Boyce

6 Aug 1938
Johannesburg
SOUTH AFRICA 26
T: Williams (2), SC Louw, Harris
C: Brand (4) *PG:* Brand (2)
BRITISH ISLES 12
PG: Jenkins (3), Taylor

3 Sep 1938
Crusader Ground, Port Elizabeth
SOUTH AFRICA 19
T: Du Toit, Lochner, Bester *C:* Turner (2) *PG:* Turner (2)
BRITISH ISLES 3
T: Duff

10 Sep 1938
Newlands, Cape Town
SOUTH AFRICA 16
T: Turner, Bester, Lotz *C:* Turner (2)
PG: Turner
BRITISH ISLES 21
T: Jones, Dancer, Alexander, Duff
C: McKibbin *PG:* McKibbin *DG:* Grieve

6 Aug 1955
Ellis Park, Johannesburg
SOUTH AFRICA 22
T: Briers (2), Swart, Koch *C:* Van der Schyff (2) *PG:* Van der Schyff (2)
BRITISH ISLES 23
T: Pedlow, Butterfield, Morgan, Greenwood, O'Reilly *C:* Cameron (4)

20 Aug 1955
Newlands, Cape Town
SOUTH AFRICA 25
T: Van Vollenhoven (3), Rosenburg, Dryburgh, Briers, Ackermann
C: Dryburgh (2)
BRITISH ISLES 9
T: Butterfield, B Meredith *PG:* Cameron

3 Sep 1955
Loftus Versveld, Pretoria
SOUTH AFRICA 6
PG: Dryburgh (2)
BRITISH ISLES 9
T: Butterfield *PG:* Baker *DG:* Butterfield

24 Sep 1955
Crusader Ground, Port Elizabeth
SOUTH AFRICA 22
T: Briers (2), Ulyate, Van Vollenhoven, Reteif *C:* Dryburgh (2) *DG:* Ulyate
BRITISH ISLES 8
T: Greenwood, O'Reilly *C:* Pedlow

23 Jun 1962
Ellis Park, Johannesburg
SOUTH AFRICA 3
T: Gainsford
BRITISH ISLES 3
T: DK Jones

21 Jul 1962
Durban
SOUTH AFRICA 3
PG: Oxlee
BRITISH ISLES 0

4 Aug 1962
Newlands, Cape Town
SOUTH AFRICA 8
T: Oxlee *C:* Oxlee *PG:* Oxlee
BRITISH ISLES 3
DG: Sharp

25 Aug 1962
Free State Stadium, Bloemfontein
SOUTH AFRICA 34
T: Roux (2), Wyness, Gainsford, H Van Zyl, Claassen *C:* Oxlee (5) *PG:* Oxlee (2)
BRITISH ISLES 14
T: Cowan, Rowlands, Campbell-Lamerton *C:* Willcox *PG:* Willcox

8 Jun 1968
Loftus Versveld, Pretoria
SOUTH AFRICA 25
T: Naude, De Villiers, Du Preez
C: Visagie (2) *PG:* Visagie (2), Naude (2)
BRITISH ISLES 20
T: McBride *C:* Kiernan *PG:* Kiernan (5)

22 Jun 1968
Boet Erasmus, Port Elizabeth
SOUTH AFRICA 6
PG: Naude, Visagie
BRITISH ISLES 6
PG: Kiernan (2)

13 Jul 1968
Newlands, Cape Town
SOUTH AFRICA 11
T: Lourens *C:* Visagie *PG:* Visagie, Naude
BRITISH ISLES 6
PG: Kiernan (2)

27 Jul 1968
Ellis Park, Johannesburg
SOUTH AFRICA 19
T: Roux, Ellis, Olivier, Nomis *C:* Visagie (2) *DG:* Gould
BRITISH ISLES 6
PG: Kiernan (2)

8 Jun 1974
Newlands, Cape Town
SOUTH AFRICA 3
DG: D Snyman
BRITISH ISLES 12
PG: Bennett (3) *DG:* Edwards

22 Jun 1974
Loftus Versveld, Pretoria
SOUTH AFRICA 9
PG: Bosch (2) *DG:* Bosch
BRITISH ISLES 28
T: JJ Williams (2), Bennett, Brown, Miliken *C:* Bennett *PG:* Bennett
DG: McGeechan

13 Jul 1974
Boet Erasmus, Port Elizabeth
SOUTH AFRICA 9
PG: J Snyman (3)
BRITISH ISLES 26
T: Brown, JJ Williams (2) *C:* Irvine
PG: Irvine (2) *DG:* Bennett (2)

27 Jul 1974
Ellis Park, Johannesburg
SOUTH AFRICA 13
T: Cronje *PG:* J Snyman (3)
BRITISH ISLES 13
T: Uttley, Irvine *C:* Bennett *PG:* Irvine

31 May 1980
Newlands, Cape Town
SOUTH AFRICA 26
T: Louw, W Du Plessis, Van Heerden, Germishuys, Serfontein *C:* Botha (3)
BRITISH ISLES 22
T: Price *PG:* Ward (5) *DG:* Ward

14 Jun 1980
Free State Stadium, Bloemfontein
SOUTH AFRICA 26
T: Louw, Stofberg, Germishuys, Pienaar
C: Botha (2) *PG:* Botha (2)
BRITISH ISLES 19
T: O'Driscoll, Gravell *C:* G Davies
PG: G Davies (2), Irvine

28 Jun 1980
Boet Erasmus, Port Elizabeth
SOUTH AFRICA 12
T: Germishuys *C:* Botha *PG:* Botha
DG: Botha
BRITISH ISLES 10
T: Hay *PG:* Campbell (2)

12 Jul 1980
Loftus Versveld, Pretoria
SOUTH AFRICA 13
T: W du Plessis *PG:* Pienaar (2), Botha
BRITISH ISLES 17
T: C Williams, Irvine, O'Driscoll
C: Campbell *PG:* Campbell

AUSTRALIA v SOUTH AFRICA

8 Jul 1933
Newlands, Cape Town
SOUTH AFRICA 17
T: Bergh (2), Craven, Osler *C:* Brand
PG: Brand
AUSTRALIA 3
PG: Billman

22 Jul 1933
Durban
SOUTH AFRICA 6
T: Waring *PG:* Brand
AUSTRALIA 21
T: Loudon, Cerutti, Bennett, Sturtridge
C: Billman (3) *PG:* Billman

12 Jul 1933
Johannesburg
SOUTH AFRICA 12
T: M Louw, Turner *C:* Brand *DG:* Osler
AUSTRALIA 3
T: Cowper

26 Aug 1933
Boet Erasmus, Port Elizabeth
SOUTH AFRICA 11
T: White, S Louw *C:* Osler *PG:* Brand
AUSTRALIA 0

2 Sep 1933
Free State Stadium, Bloemfontein
SOUTH AFRICA 4
DG: Brand
AUSTRALIA 15
T: Kelleher, Steggle, Bridle *C:* Ross
DG: Cowper

26 Jun 1937
Sydney Cricket Ground
AUSTRALIA 5
T: Towers *C:* Towers
SOUTH AFRICA 9
T: Bastard, Bergh *PG:* Brand

17 Jul 1937
Sydney Cricket Ground
AUSTRALIA 17
T: Hodgson, Kelaher, O'Brien *C:* Rankin
PG: Rankin (2)
SOUTH AFRICA 26
T: Van Reenen (2), Bergh, Babrow, Williams, White *C:* Brand (4)

22 Aug 1953
Ellis Park, Johannesburg
SOUTH AFRICA 25
T: Lategan, Marais, Oelofse, Durand, Muller *C:* Marais, Buchler *PG:* Marais, Buchler
AUSTRALIA 3
PG: Sweeney

5 Sep 1953
Newlands, Cape Town
SOUTH AFRICA 14
T: Ochse, Van Wyk, Durand, Koch
C: Marais
AUSTRALIA 18
T: Jones, Phipps, Cross, Johnson
C: Colbert (2), Stapleton

19 Sep 1953
Durban
SOUTH AFRICA 18
T: R Bekker, Roussow, Van Wyk, H Bekker *C:* Rens (3)
AUSTRALIA 8
T: Cross *C:* Colbert *PG:* Solomon

26 Sep 1953
Crusader Ground, Port Elizabeth
SOUTH AFRICA 22
T: Koch, Oelofse *C:* Rens *PG:* Rens (2)
DG: Marais, Buchler
AUSTRALIA 9
T: Stapleton *PG:* Barker (2)

26 May 1956
Sydney Cricket Ground
AUSTRALIA 0
SOUTH AFRICA 9
T: Nel, Reteif *PG:* Viviers

2 Jun 1956
Brisbane
AUSTRALIA 0
SOUTH AFRICA 9
T: Dryburgh, Reteif *DG:* Von Vollenhoven

5 Aug 1961
Ellis Park, Johannesburg
SOUTH AFRICA 28
T: Van Zyl (3), Gainsford, Engelbrecht, Oxlee, Pelser, Hopwood *C:* Claassen (2)
AUSTRALIA 3
PG: Dowse

12 Aug 1961
Boet Erasmus, Port Elizabeth
SOUTH AFRICA 23
T: Van Zyl, Roux, Oxlee *C:* Oxlee
PG: Oxlee (3) *DG:* Wilson
AUSTRALIA 11
T: Cleary *C:* Dowse *PG:* Dowse (2)
DG: Dowse

13 Jul 1963
Loftus Versveld, Pretoria
SOUTH AFRICA 14
T: Bedford, Cilliers *C:* Oxlee *PG:* Oxlee (2)
AUSTRALIA 3
T: McMullen

10 Aug 1963
Newlands, Cape Town
SOUTH AFRICA 5
T: Penalty try *C:* Oxlee
AUSTRALIA 9
T: Boyce *PG:* Casey *DG:* Hawthorne

24 Aug 1963
Ellis Park, Johannesburg
SOUTH AFRICA 9
PG: Smith (3)
AUSTRALIA 11
T: Williams *C:* Casey *PG:* Casey
DG: Casey

7 Sep 1963
Boet Erasmus, Port Elizabeth
SOUTH AFRICA 22
T: Gainsford, Naude, Malan *C:* Oxlee (2) *PG:* Oxlee (2), Naude
AUSTRALIA 6
PG: Casey *DG:* Hawthorne

19 Jun 1965
Sydney Cricket Ground
AUSTRALIA 18
T: Lenehan, S Boyce *PG:* Ellwood (4)
SOUTH AFRICA 11
T: Engelbrecht (2) *PG:* Naude

26 Jun 1965
Lang Park, Brisbane
AUSTRALIA 12
PG: Ellwood (2), Lenehan (2)
SOUTH AFRICA 8
T: Gainsford, Truter *C:* Naude

2 Aug 1969
Ellis Park, Johannesburg
SOUTH AFRICA 30
T: Nomis, Roux(2), Ellis, Greyling
C: Visagie (3) *PG:* Visagie (3)
AUSTRALIA 11
T: Forman *C:* Rosenblum
PG: Rosenblum (2)

16 Aug 1969
Kings Park, Durban
SOUTH AFRICA 16
T: Engelbrecht (2), Visagie *C:* Visagie (2) *PG:* Visagie (2)
AUSTRALIA 9
PG: Ballesty (3)

6 Sep 1969
Newlands, Cape Town
SOUTH AFRICA 11
T: Ellis, Visagie *C:* Visagie *PG:* Visagie
AUSTRALIA 3
PG: Ballesty

21 Sep 1969
Free State Stadium, Bloemfontein
SOUTH AFRICA 19
T: Olivier (2), Roux *C:* Visagie (2)
PG: Visagie (2)
AUSTRALIA 8
T: Knight *C:* Ballesty *PG:* Ballesty

17 Jul 1971
Sydney Cricket Ground
AUSTRALIA 11
T: R McLean *C:* McGill *PG:* McGill (2)
SOUTH AFRICA 19
T: H Viljeon, J Viljeon, Ellis *C:* McCullum (2) *PG:* McCullum *DG:* Visagie

31 Jul 1971
Brisbane Exhibition Ground
AUSTRALIA 6
PG: McGill (2)
SOUTH AFRICA 14
T: Visagie (2), H Viljeon *C:* McCullum
PG: McCullum

7 Aug 1971
Sydney Cricket Ground
AUSTRALIA 6
T: Cole *PG:* J McLean
SOUTH AFRICA 18
T: Cronje, Visagie, Ellis *C:* Visagie (3)
PG: Visagie

AUSTRALIA v NEW ZEALAND

15 Aug 1903
Sydney Cricket Ground
AUSTRALIA 3
PG: Wickham
NEW ZEALAND 22
T: Asher, Tyler, RW McGregor
C: Wallace *PG:* Wallace *GM:* Wallace (2)

2 Sep 1905
Tahuna Park, Dunedin
NEW ZEALAND 14
T: McMinn (2), Wrigley, Cross
C: Francis
AUSTRALIA 3
T: McLean

20 Jul 1907
Sydney Cricket Ground
AUSTRALIA 6
PG: Carmichael *GM:* Carmichael
NEW ZEALAND 26
T: Mitchinson (3), Seeling, Hughes, Francis *C:* Wallace (4)

3 Aug 1907
Woolloongabba Ground, Brisbane
AUSTRALIA 5
T: Messenger *C:* Messenger
NEW ZEALAND 14
T: Wallace (2), Seeling, Francis
C: Wallace

10 Aug 1907
Sydney Cricket Ground
AUSTRALIA 5
T: Wood *C:* Messenger
NEW ZEALAND 5
T: Mitchinson *C:* Wallace

25 Jun 1910
Sydney Cricket Ground
AUSTRALIA 0
NEW ZEALAND 6
T: Wilson, Fuller

27 Jun 1910
Sydney Cricket Ground
AUSTRALIA 11
T: Gilbert (2), Hodgens *C:* Row
NEW ZEALAND 0

2 Jul 1910
Sydney Cricket Ground
AUSTRALIA 13
T: Gilbert, Row *C:* Row (2) *PG:* Row
NEW ZEALAND 28
T: Burns (2), Stohr (2), Paterson, Mitchinson, Mitchell, Paton *C:* O'Leary (2)

6 Sep 1913
Athletic Park, Wellington
NEW ZEALAND 30
T: Lynch (3), McKenzie (2), Murray, Gray, Roberts *C:* Roberts (3)
AUSTRALIA 5
T: Carr *C:* McMahon

13 Sep 1913
Carisbrook, Dunedin
NEW ZEALAND 25
T: Brown, Cummings, Hasell, Taylor, Wilson *C:* O'Leary (3) *DG:* O'Leary
AUSTRALIA 13
T: Jones (2), Suttor *C:* Simpson (2)

20 Sep 1913
Lancaster Park, Christchurch
NEW ZEALAND 5
T: Fanning *C:* O'Leary
AUSTRALIA 16
T: Suttor (2), Jones, Thompson
C: Hughes (2)

18 Jul 1914
Sydney Sports Ground
AUSTRALIA 0
NEW ZEALAND 5
T: McNeece *C:* Graham

1 Aug 1914
Brisbane Cricket Ground
AUSTRALIA 0
NEW ZEALAND 17
T: Taylor (3), RW Roberts, Lynch *C:* EJ Roberts

15 Aug 1914
Sydney Sports Ground
AUSTRALIA 7
T: Wogan *DG:* Dwyer
NEW ZEALAND 22
T: RW Roberts (2), Francis (2), McKenzie, Taylor *C:* RW Roberts, EJ Roberts

6 Jul 1929
Sydney Cricket Ground
AUSTRALIA 9
T: Gordon *PG:* Lawton (2)
NEW ZEALAND 8
T: Oliver *C:* Nepia *PG:* Nepia

20 Jul 1929
Exhibition Ground, Brisbane
AUSTRALIA 17
T: McGhie, Crossman, Ford *C:* Lawton *PG:* Lawton (2)
NEW ZEALAND 9
T: Grenside, Porter *PG:* Cundy

27 Jul 1929
Sydney Cricket Ground
AUSTRALIA 15
T: JA Ford, King *PG:* Lawton (2), Towers
NEW ZEALAND 13
T: McWilliams, Stringfellow, Grenside *C:* Lilburne (2)

12 Sep 1931
Eden Park, Auckland
NEW ZEALAND 20
T: Hart, Ball *C:* Bush *PG:* Bush (4)
AUSTRALIA 13
T: Towers (2), Cowper *C:* Ross (2)

2 Jul 1932
Sydney Cricket Ground
AUSTRALIA 22
T: Cerutti (2), Bridle, Cowper *C:* Lawton (2) *PG:* Lawton (2)
NEW ZEALAND 17
T: Bullock-Douglas, Hore, Purdue *C:* Pollock (2) *DG:* Pollock

16 Jul 1932
Exhibition Ground, Brisbane
AUSTRALIA 3
T: Steggall
NEW ZEALAND 21
T: Bullock-Douglas (2), Ball, Page *C:* Pollock *DG:* Collins *DG:* Pollock

23 Jul 1932
Sydney Cricket Ground
AUSTRALIA 13
T: Hemmingway, Bridle, Cowper *C:* Ross, Cowper
NEW ZEALAND 21
T: Kilby, McLean, Solomon, Manchester, Palmer *C:* Collins (2), Pollock

11 Aug 1934
Sydney Cricket Ground
AUSTRALIA 25
T: Towers (2), Bridle, McLean *C:* Ross (2) *PG:* Ross (3)
NEW ZEALAND 11
T: Hore, Knight, Max *C:* Collins

25 Aug 1934
Sydney Cricket Ground
AUSTRALIA 3
T: Loudon
NEW ZEALAND 3
T: Hore

5 Sep 1936
Athletic Park, Wellington
NEW ZEALAND 11
T: Hart, Hadley, Watt *C:* Pollock
AUSTRALIA 6
T: McLaughlin *PG:* Rankin

12 Sep 1936
Carisbrook, Dunedin
NEW ZEALAND 36
T: Mitchell (2), Hart (2), Reid (2), Rankin (2), Watt *C:* Pollock (4) *PG:* Pollock
AUSTRALIA 13
T: McLaughlin, Bridle *C:* Rankin *PG:* Rankin

23 Jul 1938
Sydney Cricket Ground
AUSTRALIA 9
PG: Carpenter (3)
NEW ZEALAND 24
T: Saxton (2), Sullivan, Parkhill *C:* Taylor (3) *PG:* Taylor

6 Aug 1938
Exhibition Ground, Brisbane
AUSTRALIA 14
T: Carpenter (2), Collins *C:* Carpenter *PG:* Carpenter
NEW ZEALAND 20
T: Phillips, Milliken, Bowman, Mitchell *C:* Taylor (2) *DG:* Morrison

13 Aug 1938
Sydney Cricket Ground
AUSTRALIA 6
T: Ramsay *PG:* Hayes
NEW ZEALAND 14
T: Saxton, Bowman *C:* Taylor *PG:* Taylor (2)

14 Sep 1946
Carisbrook, Dunedin
NEW ZEALAND 31
T: Argus (2), Haig, Elliott, Finlay, Smith, White *C:* Scott (5)
AUSTRALIA 8
T: Eastes, Allan *C:* Livermore

28 Sep 1946
Eden Park, Auckland
NEW ZEALAND 14
T: Elvidge *C:* Scott *PG:* Scott (3)
AUSTRALIA 10
T: Eastes, MacBride *C:* Piper (2)

14 Jun 1947
Exhibition Ground, Brisbane
AUSTRALIA 5
T: Cornforth *C:* Piper
NEW ZEALAND 13
T: Frazer (pen. try), Argus, Arnold *C:* Scott (2)

28 Jun 1947
Sydney Cricket Ground
AUSTRALIA 14
T: McLean *C:* Allan *PG:* Allan (3)
NEW ZEALAND 27
T: Argus, Kearney, Mason *C:* Scott (3) *PG:* Thornton (3)

3 Sep 1949
Athletic Park, Wellington
NEW ZEALAND 6
T: Moore *PG:* Kelly
AUSTRALIA 11
T: Garner (2), Windon *C:* Cawsey

24 Sep 1949
Eden Park, Auckland
NEW ZEALAND 9
T: Roper *DG:* Smith *PG:* O'Callaghan
AUSTRALIA 16
T: Solomon, Windon, Emery *C:* Allan, Cawsey *PG:* Allan

23 Jun 1951
Sydney Cricket Ground
AUSTRALIA 0
NEW ZEALAND 8
T: Skinner *C:* Cockerill *PG:* Cockerill

7 Jul 1951
Sydney Cricket Ground
AUSTRALIA 11
T: Tooth, Shehadie *C:* Rothwell *PG:* Rothwell
NEW ZEALAND 17
T: Jarden (2), NL Wilson, Lynch *C:* Cockerill *DG:* Lynch

21 Jul 1951
Brisbane Cricket Ground
AUSTRALIA 6
PG: Rothwell, Cottrell
NEW ZEALAND 16
T: Tanner, Lynch, Bell, Haig
C: Cockerill (2)

6 Sep 1952
Lancaster Park, Christchurch
NEW ZEALAND 9
T: Fitzgerald, White *PG:* Bell
AUSTRALIA 14
T: Stapleton, Barker, Windon *C:* Cottrell
DG: Solomon

13 Sep 1952
Athletic Park, Wellington
NEW ZEALAND 15
T: Hotop, Robinson *PG:* Jarden, Bowden *DG:* Hotop
AUSTRALIA 8
T: Windon *C:* Cottrell *PG:* Cottrell

29 Aug 1955
Athletic Park, Wellington
NEW ZEALAND 16
T: Clark, Vodanovich, Jarden *C:* Jarden (2) *PG:* Jarden
AUSTRALIA 8
T: Jones *C:* Tooth *PG:* Stapleton

3 Sep 1955
Carisbrook, Dunedin
NEW ZEALAND 8
T: Jarden *C:* Jarden *DG:* Elsom
AUSTRALIA 0

17 Sep 1955
Eden Park, Auckland
NEW ZEALAND 3
T: Jarden
AUSTRALIA 8
T: Stapleton, Hughes *C:* Stapleton

25 May 1957
Sydney Cricket Ground
AUSTRALIA 11
T: Cross *C:* Tooth *PG:* Tooth (2)
NEW ZEALAND 25
T: McEwan, Hemi, McMullen, Walsh
C: DB Clarke (2) *PG:* DB Clarke (3)

1 Jun 1957
Exhibition Ground, Brisbane
AUSTRALIA 9
T: Morton *PG:* Tooth (2)
NEW ZEALAND 22
T: Dixon, McMullen, Brown, Meads
C: DB Clarke (2) *DG:* Brown *GM:* DB Clarke

23 Aug 1958
Athletic Ground, Wellington
NEW ZEALAND 25
T: Whineray (2), Walsh (2), Graham, McMullen, Jones *C:* DB Clarke (2)
AUSTRALIA 3
T: Ellwood

6 Sep 1958
Lancaster Park, Christchurch
NEW ZEALAND 3
T: Brown
AUSTRALIA 6
T: Morton *PG:* Curley

20 Sep 1958
Epsom Showgrounds, Auckland
NEW ZEALAND 17
T: Meads *C:* DB Clarke *PG:* DB Clarke (4)
AUSTRALIA 8
T: Carroll *C:* Curley *PG:* Curley

26 May 1962
Exhibition Ground, Brisbane
AUSTRALIA 6
PG: Scott (2)
NEW ZEALAND 20
T: BA Watt (2), MacEwan, Tremain
C: DB Clarke *PG:* DB Clarke *DG:* DB Clarke

4 Jun 1962
Sydney Cricket Ground
AUSTRALIA 5
T: RN Thornett *C:* Scott
NEW ZEALAND 14
T: Nathan, Watt *C:* DB Clarke *PG:* DB Clarke (2)

25 Aug 1962
Athletic Park, Wellington
NEW ZEALAND 9
T: Morrisey *PG:* DB Clarke (2)
AUSTRALIA 9
PG: Chapman (3)

8 Sep 1962
Carisbrook, Dunedin
NEW ZEALAND 3
PG: Clarke
AUSTRALIA 0

22 Sep 1962
Eden Park, Auckland
NEW ZEALAND 16
T: Morrissey, Heeps, Herewini
C: Clarke (2) *DG:* Herewini
AUSTRALIA 8
T: Lenehan *C:* Chapman
PG: Chapman

15 Aug 1964
Carisbrook, Dunedin
NEW ZEALAND 14
T: McLeod *C:* Williment *PG:* Williment (2) *DG:* Moreton
AUSTRALIA 9
T: Marks *PG:* Casey (2)

22 Aug 1964
Lancaster Park, Christchurch
NEW ZEALAND 18
T: Murdoch, Moreton, Rangi, Gray
C: Clarke (3)
AUSTRALIA 3
T: Marks

29 Aug 1964
Athletic Park, Wellington
NEW ZEALAND 5
T: Murdoch *C:* Clarke
AUSTRALIA 20
T: ES Boyce (2) *C:* Casey *PG:* Casey (3) *DG:* Hawthorne

19 Aug 1967
Athletic Park, Wellington
NEW ZEALAND 29
T: Steel (2), Davis, Tremain *C:* Williment (4) *PG:* Williment (2) *DG:* Herewini
AUSTRALIA 9
T: Batterham (2) *PG:* Batterham

15 Jun 1968
Sydney Cricket Ground
AUSTRALIA 11
T: Cardy *C:* McGill *PG:* McGill (2)
NEW ZEALAND 27
T: Kirkpatrick (3), Kirton, Steel, Laidlaw
C: McCormick (3) *PG:* McCormick

22 Jun 1968
Ballymore Oval, Brisbane
AUSTRALIA 18
T: Hipwell *PG:* McGill (5)
NEW ZEALAND 19
T: Lister, Thorne, Davis (pen. try)
C: McCormick (2) *PG:* McCormick (2)

19 Aug 1972
Athletic Park, Wellington
NEW ZEALAND 29
T: Dougan, Going, Sutherland, Williams, PJ Whiting *C:* Morris (3) *DG:* Morris
AUSTRALIA 6
PG: JJ McLean (2)

2 Sep 1972
Lancaster Park, Christchurch
NEW ZEALAND 30
T: Kirkpatrick (2), Sutherland, PJ Whiting, Williams *C:* Morris (2) *PG:* Morris (2)
AUSTRALIA 17
T: JJ McLean (2), Cole *C:* JJ McLean *DG:* Richardson

16 Sep 1972
Eden Park, Auckland
NEW ZEALAND 38
T: Kirkpatrick, Sutherland, Scown, Going, Whiting, Williams *C:* Morris (4) *PG:* Morris (2)
AUSTRALIA 3
PG: JJ McLean

25 May 1974
Sydney Cricket Ground
AUSTRALIA 6
T: Price *C:* PE McLean
NEW ZEALAND 11
T: DJ Robertson, Kirkpatrick *PG:* Karam

1 Jun 1974
Ballymore Oval, Brisbane
AUSTRALIA 16
T: Hipwell, Monaghan *C:* PE McLean *PG:* PE McLean (2)
NEW ZEALAND 16
T: Hurst, Leslie *C:* Karam *PG:* Karam (2)

8 Jun 1974
Sydney Cricket Ground
AUSTRALIA 6
PG: PE McLean (2)
NEW ZEALAND 16
T: Kirkpatrick, Batty, Stevens *C:* Karam (2)

19 Aug 1978
Athletic Park, Wellington
NEW ZEALAND 13
T: Williams *PG:* BW Wilson (3)
AUSTRALIA 12
T: Batch *PG:* Wright (2)

26 Aug 1978
Lancaster Park, Christchurch
NEW ZEALAND 22
T: Taylor, Seear, SS Wilson *C:* BW Wilson (2) *PG:* BW Wilson *DG:* Bruce
AUSTRALIA 6
PG: Wright *DG:* Wright

9 Sep 1978
Eden Park, Auckland
NEW ZEALAND 16
T: Ashworth, SS Wilson *C:* McKechnie *PG:* McKechnie (2)
AUSTRALIA 30
T: Cornelsen (4), Pearse *C:* Wright, Melrose *PG:* Wright *DG:* Melrose

28 Jul 1979
Sydney Cricket Ground
AUSTRALIA 12
PG: PE McLean (3) *DG:* Melrose
NEW ZEALAND 6
PG: Wilson *DG:* Taylor

21 Jun 1980
Sydney Cricket Ground
AUSTRALIA 13
T: Hawker, Martin *C:* Gould *DG:* Ella
NEW ZEALAND 9
PG: Codlin (3)

28 Jun 1980
Ballymore Oval, Brisbane
AUSTRALIA 9
T: Moon *C:* Gould *PG:* Gould
NEW ZEALAND 12
T: Reid *C:* Codlin *PG:* Codlin (2)

12 Jul 1980
Sydney Cricket Ground
AUSTRALIA 26
T: Grigg (2), O'Connor, Carson *C:* Gould (2) *PG:* Gould *DG:* Ella
NEW ZEALAND 10
T: Fraser *PG:* Codlin (2)

14 Aug 1982
Lancaster Park, Christchurch
NEW ZEALAND 23
T: Mexted, Mourie, Pokere, Fraser *C:* Hewson (2) *PG:* Hewson
AUSTRALIA 16
T: Hawker, Campese *C:* Gould *PG:* Gould (2)

28 Aug 1982
Athletic Park, Wellington
NEW ZEALAND 16
T: Shaw, Fraser *C:* Hewson *PG:* Hewson (2)
AUSTRALIA 19
T: GA Ella, Campese *C:* Gould *PG:* Gould (3)

11 Sep 1982
Eden Park, Auckland
NEW ZEALAND 33
T: Hewson, Shaw *C:* Hewson (2) *PG:* Hewson (5) *DG:* Hewson, Smith
AUSTRALIA 18
T: Gould *C:* Gould *PG:* Gould (3) *DG:* Hawker

20 Aug 1983
Sydney Cricket Ground
AUSTRALIA 8
T: Slack, Poidevin
NEW ZEALAND 18
T: Taylor *C:* Hewson *PG:* Hewson (4)

21 Jun 1984
Sydney Cricket Ground
AUSTRALIA 16
T: Reynolds, Moon *C:* M Ella *PG:* M Ella *DG:* Gould
NEW ZEALAND 9
PG: Hewson (2) *DG:* Hewson

4 Aug 1984
Ballymore Oval, Brisbane
AUSTRALIA 15
T: M Ella *C:* M Ella *PG:* M Ella (2), Campese
NEW ZEALAND 19
T: Pokere *PG:* Deans (5)

18 Aug 1984
Sydney Cricket Ground
AUSTRALIA 24
T: Campese *C:* M Ella *PG:* M Ella (5), Campese
NEW ZEALAND 25
T: Stone, Clamp *C:* Deans *PG:* Deans (5)

29 Jun 1985
Eden Park, Auckland
NEW ZEALAND 10
T: Green *PG:* Crowley (2)
AUSTRALIA 9
T: Black *C:* Lynagh *PG:* Lynagh

9 Aug 1986
Athletic Park, Wellington
NEW ZEALAND 12
T: Brooke-Cowden *C:* Cooper *PG:* Cooper (2)
AUSTRALIA 13
T: Campese, Burke *C:* Lynagh *PG:* Lynagh

23 Aug 1986
Carisbrook, Dunedin
NEW ZEALAND 13
T: Kirk *PG:* Cooper (2) *DG:* Cooper
AUSTRALIA 12
PG: Lynagh (3) *DG:* Lynagh

6 Sep 1986
Eden Park, Auckland
NEW ZEALAND 9
PG: Crowley (3)
AUSTRALIA 22
T: Leeds, Campese *C:* Lynagh *PG:* Lynagh (4)

3 Jul 1988
Concord Oval, Sydney
AUSTRALIA 7
T: Williams *PG:* Lynagh
NEW ZEALAND 32
T: Kirwan (2), Schuster, A Whetton, McDowell *C:* Fox (3) *PG:* Fox (2)

16 Jul 1988
Ballymore, Brisbane
AUSTRALIA 19
T: Grant, Williams *C:* Leeds *PG:* Leeds (3)
NEW ZEALAND 19
T: Jones, Kirwan, Wright *C:* Fox (2) *PG:* Fox

30 Jul 1988
Concord Oval, Sydney
AUSTRALIA 9
T: Walker *C:* Lynagh *PG:* Leeds
NEW ZEALAND 30
T: Gallagher, Kirwan, Deans *C:* Fox (3) *PG:* Fox (4)

21 Jul 1990
Lancaster Park, Christchurch
NEW ZEALAND 21
T: Fitzpatrick, Innes, Crowley, Kirwan *C:* Fox *PG:* Fox
AUSTRALIA 6
PG: Lynagh (2)

4 Aug 1990
Eden Park, Auckland
NEW ZEALAND 27
T: Fitzpatrick, Brooke, Bachop *C:* Fox (3) *PG:* Fox (2) *DG:* Fox
AUSTRALIA 17
T: Horan, Ofahengaue *PG:* Lynagh (2) *DG:* Lynagh

18 Aug 1990
Athletic Park, Wellington
NEW ZEALAND 9
PG: Fox (2) *DG:* Fox
AUSTRALIA 21
T: Kearns *C:* Lynagh *PG:* Lynagh (5)

10 Aug 1991
Sydney Football Stadium
AUSTRALIA 21
T: Gavin, Egerton *C:* Lynagh (2) *PG:* Lynagh (3)
NEW ZEALAND 12
T: I Jones *C:* Fox *PG:* Fox (2)

24 Aug 1991
Eden Park, Auckland
NEW ZEALAND 6
PG: Fox (2)
AUSTRALIA 3
PG: Lynagh

SOUTH AFRICA v NEW ZEALAND

13 Aug 1921
Carisbrook, Dunedin
NEW ZEALAND 13
T: Belliss, Steel, Storey *C:* MF Nicholls
SOUTH AFRICA 5
T: van Heerden *C:* PG Morkel

27 Aug 1921
Eden Park, Auckland
NEW ZEALAND 5
T: McLean *C:* Nicholls
SOUTH AFRICA 9
T: Sendin *C:* PG Morkel

17 Sep 1921
Athletic Park, Wellington
NEW ZEALAND 0
SOUTH AFRICA 0

30 Jun 1928
Kingsmead, Durban
SOUTH AFRICA 17
T: Slater *PG:* BL Osler (2) *DG:* BL Osler (2)
NEW ZEALAND 0

21 Jul 1928
Ellis Park, Johannesburg
SOUTH AFRICA 6
PG: Osler *GM:* Mostert
NEW ZEALAND 7
PG: Lindsay *DG:* Strang

18 Aug 1928
Crusader Ground, Port Elizabeth
SOUTH AFRICA 11
T: Nel, de Jongh, Daneel *C:* Osler
NEW ZEALAND 6
T: Stewart, Grenside

1 Sep 1928
Newlands, Cape Town
SOUTH AFRICA 5
T: van der Westhuizen *C:* Osler
NEW ZEALAND 13
T: Swain *PG:* Nicholls (2) *DG:* Nicholls

14 Aug 1937
Athletic Park, Wellington
NEW ZEALAND 13
T: Dick *PG:* Trevathan (2) *DG:* Trevathan
SOUTH AFRICA 7
T: Williams *DG:* White

4 Sep 1937
Lancaster Park, Christchurch
NEW ZEALAND 6
T: Sullivan (2)
SOUTH AFRICA 13
T: Turner, Bastard *C:* Brand (2) *PG:* Brand

25 Sep 1937
Eden Park, Auckland
NEW ZEALAND 6
PG: Trevathan (2)
SOUTH AFRICA 17
T: Babrow (2), Bergh, Williams, Turner *C:* Brand

16 Jul 1949
Newlands, Cape Town
SOUTH AFRICA 15
PG: Geffin (5)
NEW ZEALAND 11
T: Henderson *C:* Scott *DG:* Kearney *PG:* Scott

13 Aug 1949
Ellis Park, Johannesburg
SOUTH AFRICA 12
T: Brewis, Lategan *DG:* Brewis *PG:* Geffin
NEW ZEALAND 6
DG: Kearney *PG:* Scott

3 Sep 1949
Kingsmead Ground, Durban
SOUTH AFRICA 9
PG: Geffin (3)
NEW ZEALAND 3
T: Goddard

17 Sep 1949
Crusader Ground, Port Elizabeth
SOUTH AFRICA 11
T: du Toit *C:* Geffin *PG:* Geffin *DG:* Brewis
NEW ZEALAND 8
T: Johnstone, Elvidge *C:* Scott

14 Jul 1956
Carisbrook, Dunedin
NEW ZEALAND 10
T: White, Jarden *C:* Jarden (2)
SOUTH AFRICA 6
T: Howe *PG:* Dryburgh

4 Aug 1956
Athletic Park, Wellington
NEW ZEALAND 3
T: Brown
SOUTH AFRICA 8
T: Reteif, du Rand *C:* Viviers

18 Aug 1956
Lancaster Park, Christchurch
NEW ZEALAND 17
T: Dixon, Jarden, White *C:* DB Clarke *PG:* DB Clarke (2)
SOUTH AFRICA 10
T: Lochner, Rosenberg *C:* Viviers (2)

1 Sep 1956
Eden Park, Auckland
NEW ZEALAND 11
T: Jones *C:* DB Clarke *PG:* DB Clarke (2)
SOUTH AFRICA 5
T: Dryburgh *C:* Viviers

25 Jun 1960
Ellis Park, Johannesburg
SOUTH AFRICA 13
T: H van Zyl (2) *C:* Dryburgh, Lockyear *PG:* Lockyear
NEW ZEALAND 0

23 Jul 1960
Newlands, Cape Town
SOUTH AFRICA 3
T: Oxlee
NEW ZEALAND 11
T: Meads *C:* DB Clarke *PG:* DB Clarke *DG:* DB Clarke

13 Aug 1960
Free State Stadium, Bloemfontein
SOUTH AFRICA 11
T: Oxlee *C:* Lockyear *PG:* Lockyear (2)
NEW ZEALAND 11
T: McMullen *C:* Clarke *PG:* Clarke (2)

27 Aug 1960
Boet Erasmus Stadium, Port Elizabeth
SOUTH AFRICA 8
T: Pelser *C:* Lockyear *PG:* Lockyear
NEW ZEALAND 3
PG: DB Clarke

31 Jul 1965
Athletic Park, Wellington
NEW ZEALAND 6
T: Birtwistle, Tremain
SOUTH AFRICA 3
DG: Oxlee

21 Aug 1965
Carisbrook, Dunedin
NEW ZEALAND 13
T: Tremain, McLeod, Rangi *C:* Williment (2)
SOUTH AFRICA 0

4 Sep 1965
Lancaster Park, Christchurch
NEW ZEALAND 16
T: Tremain, Rangi, Moreton *C:* Williment (2) *PG:* Williment
SOUTH AFRICA 19
T: Gainsford (2), Brynard (2) *C:* Naude (2) *PG:* Naude

18 Sep 1965
Eden Park, Auckland
NEW ZEALAND 20
T: Smith (2), Conway, Birtwistle, Gray *C:* McCormick *DG:* Herewini
SOUTH AFRICA 3
PG: Naude

25 Jul 1970
Loftus Versveld Stadium, Pretoria
SOUTH AFRICA 17
T: de Villiers, Nomis *C:* McCallum *PG:* McCallum *DG:* Visagie
NEW ZEALAND 6
T: Williams *PG:* McCormick

8 Aug 1970
Newlands, Cape Town
SOUTH AFRICA 8
T: Jansen *C:* McCallum *PG:* McCallum
NEW ZEALAND 9
T: Laidlaw, Kirkpatrick *PG:* McCormick

29 Aug 1970
Boet Erasmus Stadium, Port Elizabeth
SOUTH AFRICA 14
T: Muller (2) *C:* McCallum *PG:* McCallum (2)
NEW ZEALAND 3
PG: Williams

12 Sep 1970
Ellis Park, Johannesburg
SOUTH AFRICA 20
T: Visagie, Muller *C:* McCallum *PG:* McCallum (4)
NEW ZEALAND 17
T: Williams *C:* Kember *PG:* Kember (4)

24 Jul 1976
Kings Park, Durban
SOUTH AFRICA 16
T: Germishuys, Krantz *C:* Bosch *PG:* Bosch *DG:* Robertson
NEW ZEALAND 7
T: Jaffray *PG:* Williams

14 Aug 1976
Free State Stadium, Bloemfontein
SOUTH AFRICA 9
PG: Bosch (3)
NEW ZEALAND 15
T: Morgan *C:* Going *PG:* Going (2) *DG:* Bruce

4 Sep 1976
Newlands, Cape Town
SOUTH AFRICA 15
T: Oosthuizen *C:* Bosch *PG:* Bosch (2) *DG:* Snyman
NEW ZEALAND 10
T: BJ Robertson *PG:* Williams (2)

18 Sep 1976
Ellis Park, Johannesburg
SOUTH AFRICA 15
T: Kritzinger *C:* Bosch *PG:* Bosch (2) *DG:* Bosch
NEW ZEALAND 14
T: Kirkpatrick, Going *PG:* Williams *DG:* Bruce

15 Aug 1981
Lancaster Park, Christchurch
NEW ZEALAND 14
T: Rollerson, Wilson, Shaw *C:* Rollerson
SOUTH AFRICA 9
T: Bekker *C:* HE Botha *DG:* HE Botha

29 Aug 1981
Athletic Park, Wellington
NEW ZEALAND 12
PG: Hewson (4)
SOUTH AFRICA 24
T: Germishuys *C:* Botha *PG:* Botha (5) *DG:* Botha

12 Sep 1981
Eden Park, Auckland
NEW ZEALAND 25
T: Wilson, Knight *C:* Rollerson *PG:* Hewson (3), Rollerson *DG:* Rollerson
SOUTH AFRICA 22
T: Mordt (3) *C:* Botha (2) *PG:* Botha (2)

THE WORLD CUP

Now firmly established as rugby's major event, the World Cup has become the focal point of the international calendar. So much so that some 'friendly' internationals are now often used as mere warm-up matches for the World Cup. The first World Cup was held in New Zealand and Australia from 22 May to 20 June 1987 with the final at Eden Park, Auckland won by New Zealand, who beat France 29–9 in the final. The second World Cup was held in the United Kingdom, Ireland and France from 3 October to 2 November 1991, with Australia beating England 12–6 in the final at Twickenham.

1987

POOL 1

23 May 1987 *Concord Oval, Sydney*
AUSTRALIA 19
T: Campese (50 min), Poidevin (60 min) *C:* Lynagh (60 min) *PG:* Lynagh (21, 30, 64 min)
ENGLAND 6
T: Harrison (47 min) *C:* Webb (47 min)
AUSTRALIA: Gould; Grigg, Slack (capt), Papworth, Campese; Lynagh, Farr-Jones; Rodriguez, Lawton, McIntyre, Cutler, Campbell, Poidevin, Coker, Tuynman
Replacement: James for Gould (78 min)
ENGLAND: Rose; Harrison (Capt), Simms, Salmon, Underwood; Williams, Harding; Rendall, Moore, Pearce; Dooley, Redman; Winterbottom, Rees, Richards
Replacement: Webb for Rose (2 min)
Referee: KH Lawrence (New Zealand)
Attendance: 17 896

24 May 1987 *Ballymore, Brisbane*
UNITED STATES 21
T: Purcell (26 min), Nelson (38 min), Lambert (70 min) *C:* Nelson (26, 38, 70 min) *PG:* Nelson (20 min)
JAPAN 18
T: Taumoefolau (16, 30 min), Yoshinaga (72 min) *PG:* Yoshinaga (36 min), Kutsuki (54 min)
UNITED STATES: Nelson; Purcell, Higgins, Helu, Lambert; Clarkson, Saunders; Bailey, Everett, Paoli; Lambert, Swords; Burlingham (capt), Warhurst, Vizard
JAPAN: Mukai; Taumoefolau, Yoshinaga, Onuki, Kutsuki; Hirao, Ikuta; Yasumi, Fujita, Horaguchi; Miyamoto, Hayashi (capt), Oyagi, Latu, Chida
Referee: G Maurette (France)
Attendance: 4500

30 **May 1987** *Concord Oval, Sydney*
ENGLAND 60
T: Underwood (31, 56 min), Rees (39 min) Salmon (47 min), Richards (49 min), Simms (64 min), Harrison (68, 70, 80 min), Redman (79 min) *C:* Webb (39, 47, 49, 64, 70, 79,80 min) *PG:* Webb (8, 16 min)
JAPAN 7
T: Miyamoto (7 min) *PG:* Matsuo (25 min)
ENGLAND: Webb; Harrison (capt), Simms, Salmon, Underwood; Williams, Harding; Rendall, Moore, Chilcott; Bainbridge, Redman; Rees, Winterbottom, Richards
Replacements: Clough for Simms (68 min), Andrew for Williams (77 min)
JAPAN: Murai; Taumoefolau,Kutsuki, Matsuo, Onuki; Hirao, Hagimoto; Kimura, Fujita, Horaguchi; Oyagi, Kurihara; Miyamoto, Chida, Hayashi (capt)
Referee: R Horquet (France)
Attendance: 5500

31 May 1987 *Ballymore, Brisbane*
AUSTRALIA 47
T: Penalty try (7 min), Smith (24 min), Slack (40 min), Leeds (43, 80 min), Papworth (56 min), Campese (65 min), Codey (70 min) *C:* Lynagh (7,24, 40, 65, 70, 80 min) *PG:* Lynagh (2 min)
UNITED STATES 12
T: Nelson (53 min) *C:* Nelson (53 min) *PG:* Nelson (32 min) *DG:* Horton (75 min)
AUSTRALIA: Leeds; Campese, Slack (capt), Papworth, Burke; Lynagh, Smith; Lillicrap, Lawton, McIntyre, Coker, Campbell, Miller, Tuynman, Codey
UNITED STATES: Nelson; Higgins, Helu, Vinick, Hein; Horton, Dickson; Horvath, Johnson, Paoli; Swords, Shiflet; Finkel, Vizard, Ridnell
Replacements: Saunders for Dickson (35 min), Lambert for Shiflet (24 min)
Referee: JB Anderson (Scotland)
Attendance: 8300

3 Jun 1987 *Concord Oval, Sydney*
ENGLAND 34
T: Winterbottom (23, 45 min), Harrison (61 min), Dooley (79 min) *C:* Webb (23, 45, 79 min) *PG:* Webb (10, 31, 47, 54 min)
UNITED STATES 6
T: Purcell (65 min) *C:* Nelson (65 min)
ENGLAND: Webb; Harrison (capt), Clough, Salmon, Bailey; Andrew, Hill; Chilcott, Dawe, Pearce; Bainbridge, Dooley; Rees, Winterbottom, Richards
UNITED STATES: Nelson; Purcell, Higgins, Vinick, Hein;

Clarkson, Saunders; Brendel, Everett, Bailey; Causey, Burlingham (capt); Finkel, Vizard, Lambert
Referee: KVJ Fitzgerald (Australia)
Attendance: 15 000

3 Jun 1987 *Concord Oval, Sydney*
AUSTRALIA 42
T: Slack (8, 77 min), Tuynman (21 min), Burke (33, 80 min), Grigg (46 min), Hartill (55 min), Campese (60 min) *C:* Lynagh (21, 33, 46, 77, 80 min)
JAPAN 23
T: Kutsuki (12 min), Okidoi (23 min), Fujita (73 min) *C:* Okidoi (12 min) *PG:* Okidoi (2, 66 min) *DG:* Okidoi (57 min)
AUSTRALIA: Campese; Grigg, Slack, Cook, Burke; Lynagh, Smith; Rodriguez, McBail, Hartill; Cutler, Reynolds; Poidevin (capt), Tuynman, Codey
Replacements: Papworth for Cook (17 min), Campbell for Tuynman (69 min)
JAPAN: Mukai; Taumoefolau, Yoshinaga, Kutsuki, Okidoi; Hirao, Ikuta; Kimura, Fujita, Aizawa; Sakuraba, Hayashi (capt), Miyamoto, Latu, Kawese
Referee: JM Fleming (Scotland)
Attendance: 15 000

POOL 1 FINAL TABLE

	P	W	D	L	F	A	Pts
Australia	3	3	0	0	108	41	6
England	3	2	0	1	100	32	4
United States	3	1	0	2	39	99	2
Japan	3	0	0	3	48	123	0

POOL 2

24 May 1987 *McLean Park, Napier*
CANADA 37
T: Stuart (3 min), Frame (15, 26 min), Vaesen (43, 76 min), Palmer (68, 72 min) *C:* Wyatt (3, 26 min), Rees (72 min) *PG:* Rees (70 min)
TONGA 4
T: Valu (45 min)
CANADA: Wyatt, Palmer, Vaesen, McTavish, Woods; Rees, Stuart; Evans, Cardinal, Handson; van den Brink, de Goede (capt); Frame, Radu, Robertson
TONGA: Etaiki; A'Si, Kuteki'Aho, Mohi, Fiela; Liava'A, Fifita; Moto'Apauaka, Afu, Tupou; Fine, Tu'Ihalamaka; Tuuta, Fotu, Valu (capt)
Replacements: Vaipulu for A'Si (22 min), Tahaafe for Tu'Ihalamaka (28 min)
Referee: CT Norling (Wales)
Attendance: 8000

25 May 1987 *Athletic Park, Wellington*
WALES 13
T: Ring (55 min) *PG:* Thorburn (43 min) *DG:* Davies (61, 65 min)
IRELAND 6
PG: Kiernan (39, 40 min)
WALES: Thorburn; I Evans, Devereux, Ring, Hadley; J Davies, Jones; Whitefoot, K Phillips, S Evans; Norster, R Moriarty (capt); Collins, P Moriarty, Roberts
IRELAND: McNeill; Ringland, Mullin, Kiernan, Crossan; Dean, Bradley; Orr, Kingston, Fitzgerald; Anderson, Lenihan (capt); McGrath, Matthews, Spillane
Replacement: Glennon for Matthews (35 min)
Referee: KVJ Fitzgerald (Australia)
Attendance: 17 500

29 May 1987 *Showgrounds Oval, Palmerston North*
WALES 29
T: Webbe (4, 12, 71 min), Hadley (40 min) *C:* Thorburn (4, 71 min) *DG:* J Davies (64 min)
TONGA 16
T: Fiela (40 min), Etaiki (76 min) *C:* Liava'a (76 min) *PG:* Amone (34 min), Liava'a (80 min)
WALES: Thorburn; Webbe, Ring, Hopkins, Hadley; Dacey, Jones; Buchanan, K Phillips, S Evans; Richards, R Moriarty (capt); P Moriarty, P Davies, Roberts
Replacements: Blackmore for S Evans (40 min), J Davies for Dacey (58 min)
TONGA: Etaiki; Vunipola, Mohi, Kuteki'Aho, Fiela; Amone, Fifita; Tupou, Afu, Lutua; Fine, Tu'ungafasi; Tu'uta, Filise, Valu (capt)
Replacements: Va'eno for Tupou (44 min), Liava'a for Amone (67 min)
Referee: DJ Bishop (New Zealand)
Attendance: 10 000

30 May 1987 *Carisbrook, Dunedin*
IRELAND 46
T: Bradley (10 min), Crossan (28, 65 min), Spillane (70 min), Ringland (78 min), McNeill (79 min) *C:* Kiernan (10, 65, 70, 78, 79 min) *PG:* Kiernan (39, 57 min) *DG:* Kiernan (5 min), Ward (75 min)
CANADA 19
T: Cardinal (56 min) *PG:* Rees (2, 18, 48 min) *DG:* Rees (25 min)
IRELAND: McNeill; Ringland, Mullin, Kiernan, Crossnan; Ward, Bradley; Orr, McDonald, Fitzgerald; Lenihan (capt), Anderson; McGrath, Collins, Spillane
Replacement: Kingston for McDonald (65 min)
CANADA: Wyatt; Palmer, Lecky, McTavish, Woods; Rees, Stuart; Evans, Cardinal, Handson; de Goede (capt), Hindson; Frame, Radu, Ennis
Referee: FA Howard (England)
Attendance: 10 000

3 Jun 1987 *Ballymore Oval, Brisbane*
WALES 40
T: I Evans (3, 43, 65, 80 min), Bowen (49 min), Devereux (57 min), Hadley (67 min), A Phillips (81 min)
C: Thorburn (3, 43, 49, 65 min)
CANADA 9
PG: Rees (1, 26, 34 min)
WALES: Thorburn; I Evans, Devereux, Bowen, Hadley; J Davies (capt), Giles; Whitefoot, A Phillips, Blackmore; Norster, Sutton; P Moriarty, P Davies, Roberts
Replacements: Hopkins for Bowen (72 min), R Moriarty for P Moriarty (77 min)
CANADA: Wyatt, Palmer, Lecky, Woods, Gray; Rees, Stuart;McKellar,Svoboda, Handson; de Goede (capt), Hindson; Frame, Breen, Ennis
Replacement: Tucker for Stuart (52 min)
Referee: DJ Bishop (New Zealand)
Attendance: 12 000

3 Jun 1987 *Ballymore Oval, Brisbane*
IRELAND 32
T: McNeill (15, 76 min), Mullin (35, 56, 76 min) *C:* Ward (35, 56, 72 min) *PG:* Ward (3, 41 min)
TONGA 9
PG: Amone (24, 48, 75 min)
IRELAND: McNeill; Ringland, Mullin, Irwin, Crossan; Ward, Bradley; Langbroek, Kingston, McCoy; Lenihan (capt), Anderson; Matthews, Francis, McGrath
TONGA: Etaiki; Fiela, Mohi, Kuteki'Aho, Liava'a; Amone, Fifita; Tupou, Fungeraka, Lutua; Fine, Tu'ungafasi; Valu (capt), Felise, Kakato
Referee: G Maurette (France)
Attendance: 3000

POOL 2 FINAL TABLE

	P	W	D	L	F	A	Pts
Wales	3	3	0	0	82	31	6
Ireland	3	2	0	1	84	41	4
Canada	3	1	0	2	65	90	2
Tonga	3	0	0	3	29	98	0

POOL 3

22 May 1987 *Eden Park, Auckland*
NEW ZEALAND 70
T: Penalty try (12 min), Jones (30 min), Kirk (38, 73 min), Taylor (45 min), Green (48, 54 min), McDowell (65 min), Kirwan (68, 72 min), Stanley (76 min), A Whetton (80 min) *C:* Fox (12, 45, 54, 65, 68, 72, 73, 80 min) *PG:* Fox (20, 60 min)
ITALY 6
PG: Collodo (40 min) *DG:* Collodo (38 min)
NEW ZEALAND: Gallagher; Kirwan, Stanley, Taylor, Green; Fox, Kirk (capt); McDowell, Fitzpatrick, Loe; Pierce, G Whetton; A Whetton, Jones, Shelford
ITALY: Ghizzoni; Mascioletti, Collodo, Gaetenillo, Cuttita; Ambrosio, Lorigiola; Rossi, Morelli, Lupini; Berni, Gardin; Farina, Innocenti (capt), Artuso
Referee: RJ Fordham (Australia)
Attendance: 20 000

24 May 1987 *Rugby Park, Hamilton*
FIJI 28
T: Gale (17 min), Naiviliwasa (38 min), Nalaga (46 min), Savai (80 min) *C:* Koroduadua (17, 46 min), Rokowailoa (80 min) *PG:* Koroduadua (21, 62 min)
ARGENTINA 9
T: Travaglini (82 min) *C:* Porta (82 min) *PG:* Porta (50 min)
FIJI: Koroduadua; Nalaga, T Cama, Tuvula, E Naituku; Rokowailoa, Tabulutu; Namoro, Naiviliwasa, S Naituku; Rakoroi (capt), Savai; Gale, Qoro, Sanday
Replacements: Nawalus for Tabulatu (25 min), Vunivalu for Gale (58 min)
ARGENTINA: Salvat; Campo, Cuesta Silva, Turnes, J Lanza; Porta (capt), Gomez; Morel, Cash, Molina; Branca, Milano; Mostany, Allen, Travaglini
Replacement: Schiavio for Milano (53 min)
Referee: JM Fleming (Scotland)
Attendance: 12 000

27 May 1987 *Lancaster Park, Christchurch*
NEW ZEALAND 74
T: Green (2, 12, 25, 39 min), Gallagher (5, 57, 60, 76 min), Kirk (32 min), Kirwan (45 min), Penalty try (50 min), A Whetton (70 min)*C:* Fox (2, 5, 12, 32, 39, 45, 50, 57, 70, 76 min) *PG:* Fox (20, 23 min)
FIJI 13
T: Savai (79 min) *PG:* Koroduadua (16, 49, 61 min)
NEW ZEALAND: Gallagher; Kirwan, Stanley, Taylor, Green; Fox, Kirk (capt); McDowell, Fitzpatrick, Drake; Anderson, G Whetton; A Whetton, Jones, Shelford
FIJI: Koroduadua; Tuvulu, Lovokulu, Kubu, T Cama; Rokowailoa, Nawalu; Taga, Rakai, Volavola; J Cama, Savai; Kididromo, Vunivalu, Rakoroi (capt)
Referee: WD Bevan (Wales)
Attendance: 24 000

28 May 1987 *Lancaster Park, Christchurch*
ARGENTINA 25
T: J Lanza (38 min), Gomez (79 min)*C:* Porta (80 min) *PG:* Porta (16, 20, 53, 56, 74 min)
ITALY 16
T: Innocenti (50 min), Cuttita (60 min) *C:* Collodo (50 min) *PG:* Collodo (25, 55 min)
ARGENTINA: Salvat; J Lanza, Cuesta Silva, Madero, P Lanza; Porta (capt), Yanguela; Dengra, Cash, Molina; Branca, Carrosio; Schiavio, Allen, Travaglini
Replacement: Gomez for Yanguela (65 min)
ITALY: Tebaldi; Mascioletti, Gaetaniello, Barba, Cuttita; Collodo, Lorigiola; Rossi, Galeazzo, Lupini; Gardin, Gollela; Pavin, Innocenti (capt), Zanon
Referee: RC Quittenton (England)
Attendance: 5000

31 May 1987 *Carisbrook, Dunedin*
ITALY 18
T: Cuttita (11 min), Cucchiella (44 min), Mascioletti (58 min) *PG:*Collodo (36 min) *DG:* Collodo (4 min)
FIJI 15
T: Naiviliwasa (67 min) *C:* Koroduadua (67 min) *PG:* Koroduadua (49, 62 min) *DG:* Qoro (31 min)
ITALY: Tebaldi; Mascioletti, Gaeteniello, Barba, Cuttita; Collodo, Ghini; Cucchiella, Romagnoli, Lupini; Gardin, Collela; Dolfato, Innocenti (capt), Farina
FIJI: Koroduadua; T Cama, Salusalu, Mitchell, Tuvula; Rakowailoa, Nawalu; Volavola, Naiviliwasa, Naituku; Nadolo, Sanday, Savai, Qoro, Rakoroi (capt)
Replacements: Natluku for Tuvulu (20 min), Kubu for Natluku (62 min)
Referee: KH Lawrence (New Zealand)
Attendance: 6000

31 May 1987 *Carisbrook, Dunedin*
NEW ZEALAND 46
T: Kirk (13 min), Brooke (39 min), Stanley (49 min), Earl (67 min), Crowley (71 min), A Whetton (75 min) *C:* Fox (39, 75) *PG:* Fox (6)
ARGENTINA 15
T: J Lanza (57 min) *C:* Porta (57 min) *PG:* Porta (16, 30, 36 min)
NEW ZEALAND: Crowley; Kirwan, Stanley, McCahill, Wright; Fox, Kirk (capt); Loe,Fitzpatrick, Drake; Pierce, G Whetton; A Whetton, Brooke, Earl
ARGENTINA: Angaut; Campo, Madero, Turnes, J Lanza; Porta (capt), Gomez; Dengra, Cash, Molina; Branca, Carrosio; Allen, Schiavio, Travaglini

Replacements: Mostany for Travaglini (44 min), P Lanza for Turnes (65 min)
Referee: RC Quittenton (England)
Attendance: 30 000

POOL 3 FINAL TABLE

	P	W	D	L	F	A	Pts
New Zealand	3	3	0	0	190	34	6
Fiji	3	1	0	2	56	101	2
Italy	3	1	0	2	40	110	2
Argentina	3	1	0	2	49	90	2

POOL 4

23 May 1987 *Eden Park, Auckland*
ROMANIA 21
T: Paraschiv (72 min), Toader (76 min), Hodorca (80 min) *PG:* Alexandru (23, 44, 48 min)
ZIMBABWE 20
T: Tsimba (7, 63 min), Neill (17 min) *C:* Ferreira (63 min) *PG:* Ferreira (27, 54 min)
ROMANIA: Toader; Marin, David, Tofan, Lungu; Alexandru, Paraschiv (capt); Bucan, Grigore, Leonte; Dumitras, L Constantin; S Constantin, Raducanu, Mariaru
Replacements: Hodorca for Marin (5 min), Ion for Alexandru (60 min)
ZIMBABWE: Ferreira; Kaulbach, K. Graham, Tsimba, Barrett; Brown, Jellicoe (capt); Elcombe, Bray, Tucker; D. Buitendag, Martin; Sawyer, Gray, Neill
Replacement: A Buitendag for Tsimba (67 min)
Referee: SR Hilditch (Ireland)
Attendance: 4000

23 May 1987 *Lancaster Park, Christchurch*
SCOTLAND 20
T: White (2 min), Duncan (80 min) *PG:* G Hastings (12,22, 36, 45 min)
FRANCE 20
T: Sella (50 min), Berbizier (58 min), Blanco (65 min) *C:* Blanco (65 min) *PG:* Blanco (24, 33 min)
SCOTLAND: G Hastings; Duncan, Robertson, Wyllie, Tukalo; Rutherford, Laidlaw; Milne, Deans (capt), Sole; White, Tomes, F Calder, Jeffrey, Paxton
Replacement: Tait for Rutherford (17 min)
FRANCE: Blanco; Lagisquet, Sella, Charvet, Esteve; Mesnel, Berbizier; Garuet, Dubroca (capt), Ondarts; Condom, Lorieux, Erbani, Champ, Rodriguez
Referee: FA Howard (England)
Attendance: 17 000

28 May 1987 *Athletic Park, Wellington*
FRANCE 55
T: Charvet (18, 78 min), Sella (26 min), Andrieu(42 min), Camberabero (45 min), Erbani (53 min), Laporte (57 min), Lagisquet (68, 75 min) *C:* Laporte (18, 26, 42, 53, 57, 68, 75, 78 min) *PG:* Laporte (50 min)
ROMANIA 12
PG: Bezuscu (15, 23, 31, 34 min)
FRANCE: Blanco; Lagisquet, Sella, Charvet, Andrieu; Laporte, Berbizier, Garuet, Dubroca (capt), Armary; Haget, Condom, Champ, Erbani, Carminati
Replacement: Camberabero for Blanco (14 min)
ROMANIA: Ion; Toader, Tofan, David, Lungu; Bezuscu, Paraschiv (capt); Opris, Ilca, Pascu; L Constantin, Veres; Necula, Raducanu, Dimitru
Replacement: Grigore for Ilca (12 min)
Referee: DJ Fordham (Australia)
Attendance: 5500

30 May 1987 *Athletic Ground, Wellington*
SCOTLAND 60
T: Tait (4, 38 min), Duncan (10, 61 min), Oliver (17 min), G Hastings (25 min), Paxton (31, 45 min), Jeffrey (74 min) *C:* G Hastings (4, 10, 21, 25, 31, 38, 45, 74 min)
ZIMBABWE 21
T: D Buitendag (48 min) *C:* Grobler (48 min) *PG:* Grobler 13, 35, 56, 63, 66 min)
SCOTLAND: G Hastings; Duncan, Tait, Robertson, Tukalo; Wyllie, Oliver; Sole, Deans (capt), Milne; Tomes, Campbell-Lamerton; Jeffrey, F Calder, Paxton
ZIMBABWE: Ferreira; S Graham, A Buitendag, K Graham, Barrett; Grobler, Jellicoe (capt); Elcombe, Bray, Tucker; Martin, Sawyer; Gray, D Buitendag, Neill
Referee: DIH Burnett (Ireland)
Attendance: 5000

2 Jun 1987 *Eden Park, Auckland*
FRANCE 70
T: Modin (4, 13, 57 min), Dubroca (17 min), Rodriguez (38, 73 min), Charvet (52, 56 min), Camberabero (61, 67, 75 min), Laporte (77 min), Esteve (62 min)*C:* Camberabero (4, 13, 17, 52, 56, 57, 61, 67, 77 min)
ZIMBABWE 12
T: Kaulbach (66 min) *C:* Grobler (66 min) *PG:* Grobler (4, 69 min)
FRANCE: Camberabero; Andrieu, Bonneval, Charvet, Esteve; Mesnel, Modin; Tolot, Dubroca (capt), Ondarts; Lorieux, Condom; Carminati, Joinel, Rodriguez
Replacements: Sella for Bonneval (20 min), Laporte for Sella (43 min)
ZIMBABWE: Ferreira; Kaulbach, Tsimba, K Graham, Barrett; Grobler, Jellicoe (capt); Elcombe, Gray, Tucker; Martin, Sawyer; Gray, D Buitendag, Neill
Replacements: Nicholls for Elcombe (27 min), Kloppers for Martin (37 min)
Referee: WD Bevan (Wales)
Attendance: 4000

2 Jun 1987 *Carisbrook, Dunedin*
SCOTLAND 55
T: Tait (5, 23 min), Jeffrey (18, 40, 42 min), Duncan (22 min), G Hastings (68, 80 min), Tukalo (78 min) *C:* G Hastings (4, 17, 20, 22, 37, 42, 65, 78 min) *PG:* Hastings (15 min)
ROMANIA 28
T: Murariu (40, 80 min), Toader (48 min) *C:* Alexandru (48 min), Ion (80 min) *PG:* Alexandru (33, 56, 62, 68 min)
SCOTLAND: G Hastings; Duncan, Tait, S Hastings, Tukalo, Wyllie, Laidlaw; Sole, Deans (capt), Rowan; White, Tomes; Jeffrey, F Calder, Paxton
Replacements: Cramb for S Hastings (1 min), Campbell-Lamerton for Tomes (42 min)
ROMANIA: Ion; Pilotschi, Lungu, Tofan; Alexandru, Paraschiv (capt); Bucan, Grigore, Leonte; S Constantin, L Constantin; Murariui, Dumitras, Raducanu
Replacement: Dumitri for Raducanu (20 min)
Referee: S Hilditch (Ireland)
Attendance: 10 000

POOL 4 FINAL TABLE

	P	W	D	L	F	A	Pts
France	3	2	1	0	145	44	5
Scotland	3	2	1	0	135	69	5
Romania	3	1	0	2	61	130	2
Zimbabwe	3	0	0	3	53	151	0

QUARTER FINALS

6 Jun 1987 *Lancaster Park, Christchurch*
NEW ZEALAND 30
T: A Whetton (51 min), Gallagher (70 min) *C:* Fox (51, 70 min) *PG:* Fox (18, 25, 38, 58, 60, 67 min)
SCOTLAND 3
PG: G Hastings (18 min)
NEW ZEALAND: Gallagher; Kirwan, Stanley, Taylor, Green; Fox, Kirk (capt); McDowell, Fitzpatrick, Drake; Pierce, G Whetton; A Whetton, Jones, Shelford
Replacement: McCahill for Taylor (17 min)
SCOTLAND: G Hastings; Duncan, Tait, Robertson, Tukalo; Wyllie, Laidlaw; Sole, Deans (capt), Milne; White, Tomes; Turnbull, F Calder, Paxton
Referee: DIH Burnett (Ireland)
Attendance: 30 000

7 Jun 1987 *Concord Oval, Sydney*
AUSTRALIA 33
T: McIntyre (14 min), Smith (17 min), Burke (22, 63 min) *C:* Lynagh (14, 17, 22, 63 min) *PG:* Lynagh (2, 8, 50 min)
IRELAND 15
T: McNeill (69 min), Kiernan (80 min) *C:* Kiernan (69, 80 min) *PG:*Kiernan (57 min)
AUSTRALIA: Campese; Grigg,Slack (capt), Papworth, Burke; Lynagh, Farr-Jones; Lillicrap, Lawton, McIntyre; Cutler, Campbell; Poidevin, Miller, Tuynman
Replacement: Smith for Farr-Jones (5 min)
IRELAND: McNeill; Ringland, Mullin, Kiernan, Crossan; Dean, Bradley; Orr, Kingston, Fitzpatrick; Lenihan (capt), Anderson; Matthews, McGrath, Spillane
Replacement: Francis for Spillane (57 min), Irwin for Mullin (67 min)
Referee: JB Anderson (Scotland)
Attendance: 17 800

7 Jun 1987 *Concord Oval, Sydney*
FRANCE 31
T: Lorieux (20 min), Rodriguez (30, 40 min), Lagisquet (76 min) *C:* Laporte (20, 30, 76 min) *PG:* Laporte (9. 17 min) *DG:* Laporte (80 min)
FIJI 16
T: Qoro (15 min), Damu (78 min) *C:* Koroduadua (78 min) *PG:* Koroduadua (38, 64 min)
FRANCE: Blanco; Charvet, Sella, Mesnel, Lagisquet; Laporte, Berbizier; Ondarts, Dubroca (capt), Garuet; Haget, Lorieux; Champ, Erbani, Rodriguez
Replacement: Camberabero for Blanco (79 min)
FIJI: Kubu; Damu, Salusalu, T Cama, Mitchell; Koroduadua, Nawalu; Namoro, Rakai, Naituku; Rakaroi (capt), Savai; Sanday, Qoro, Naiviliwasa
Replacements: Rokiowailoa for Savai (45 min), Lovoruku for Qoro (53 min)
Referee: CT Norling (Wales)
Attendance: 12 000

8 Jun 1987 *Ballymore Oval, Brisbane*
WALES 16
T: Roberts (23 min), Jones (45 min), Devereux (80 min) *C:* Thorburn (23, 80 min)
ENGLAND 3
PG: Webb (73 min)
WALES: Thorburn; I Evans, Devereux, Bowen, Hadley; J Davies, Jones; Buchanan, A Phillips, Young; R Moriarty (capt), Norster; Collins, Roberts, P. Moriarty
Replacements: Richards for Norster (73 min)
ENGLAND: Webb; Harrison (capt), Simms, Salmon, Underwood; Williams, Harding; Rendall, Moore, Pearce; Dooley, Redman; Winterbottom, Rees, Richards
Replacement: Chilcott for Rendall (24 min)
Referee: R Horquet (France)
Attendance: 15 000

SEMI FINALS

13 Jun 1987 *Concord Oval, Sydney*
FRANCE 30
T: Lorieux (40 min), Sella (44 min), Lagisquet (54 min), Blanco (80 min) *C:* Camberabero (40, 44, 54, 80 min) *PG:* Camberabero (59, 79 min)
AUSTRALIA 24
T: Campese (46 min), Codey (64 min) *C:* Lynagh (46, 64 min) *PG:* Lynagh (7, 29, 76 min) *DG:* Lynagh (4 min)
FRANCE: Blanco; Camberabero, Sella, Charvet, Lagisquet; Mesnel, Berbizier; Ondarts, Dubroca (capt), Garuet; Lorieux, Condom; Champ, Erbani, Rodriguez
AUSTRALIA: Campese; Grigg, Slack (capt), Papworth, Burke; Lynagh, Farr-Jones; Lillicrap, Lawton, McIntyre; Campbell, Cutler; Miller, Poidevin, Coker
Replacements: Herbert for Papworth (8 min), Codey for Campbell (20 min)
Referee: JB Anderson (Scotland)
Attendance: 17 800

14 Jun 1987 *Ballymore Oval, Brisbane*
NEW ZEALAND 49
T: Shelford (2, 73 min), Drake (8 min), Kirwan (22, 25 min), A Whetton (59 min), Stanley (62 min), Brooke-Cowden (68 min) *C:* Fox (2, 8, 22, 25, 59, 62, 73 min) *PG:* Fox (35 min)
WALES 6
T: Devereux (55 min) *C:* Thorburn (55 min)
NEW ZEALAND: Gallagher; Kirwan, Stanley, Taylor, Green; Fox, Kirk (capt);Drake, Fitzpatrick, McDowell; Pierce, G Whetton; A. Whetton, Brooke-Cowden, Shelford
Replacement: McCahill for Stanley (73 min)
WALES: Thorburn; I Evans, Devereux, Bowen, Hadley; J Davies, Jones; Buchanan, K Phillips, Young; Richards, R Moriarty (capt); Collins, P Davies, P Moriarty
Replacement: Sutton for Collins (40 min)
Sending-off: Richards (71 min)
Referee: KVJ Fitzgerald (Australia)
Attendance: 25 000

THIRD PLACE MATCH

18 Jun 1987 *Rotorua International Stadium*
WALES 22
T: Roberts (29 min), P Moriarty (40 min), Hadley (80 min) *C:* Thorburn (40, 80 min) *PG:* Thorburn (5, 43 min)

AUSTRALIA 21
T: Burke (31 min), Grigg (39 min) *C:* Lynagh (31, 39 min) *PG:* Lynagh (12, 46 min) *DG:* Lynagh (54 min)
WALES: Thorburn; I Evans, Devereux, Ring, Hadley; J Davies, Jones, Buchanan, A Phillips, Blackmore; R Moriarty (capt), Sutton; Roberts, Webster, P Moriarty
AUSTRALIA: Leeds; Grigg, Burke, Slack (capt), Campese; Lynagh, Smith; Lillicrap, Lawton, McIntyre; Cutler, Coker; Poidevin, Codey, Tuynman
Replacements: Farr-Jones for Grigg (46 min), Rodriguez for Lillicrap (76 min)
Sending-off: Codey (5 min)
Referee: FA Howard (England)
Attendance: 20 000

FINAL

20 Jun 1987 *Eden Park, Auckland*
NEW ZEALAND 29
T: Jones (17 min), Kirk (63 min), Kirwan (66 min) *C:* Fox (17 min) *PG:* Fox (46, 56, 69, 77 min) *DG:* Fox (14 min)
FRANCE 9
T: Berbizier (80 min) *C:* Camberabero (80 min) *PG:* Camberabero (44 min)
NEW ZEALAND: Gallagher; Kirwan, Stanley, Taylor, Green; Fox, Kirk (capt); McDowell, Fitzpatrick, Drake; Pierce, G Whetton; A Whetton, Jones, Shelford
FRANCE: Blanco; Camberabero, Sella. Charvet, Lagisquet; Mesnel, Berbizier; Ondarts, Dubroca (capt), Garuet; Lorieux, Condom; Champ, Erbani, Rodriguez
Referee: KVJ Fitzgerald (Australia)
Attendance: 48 0350

David Kirk with the Webb Ellis Trophy – New Zealand's World Cup triumph, 1987

1991

POOL 1

3 Oct 1991 *Twickenham*
ENGLAND 12
PG: Webb (1, 14, 29 min) *DG:* Andrew (40 min)
NEW ZEALAND 18
T: M Jones (50 min) *C:* Fox (50 min) *PG:* Fox (3 min, 8 min, 24 min, 53 min)
ENGLAND: Webb; Underwood, Carling (capt), Guscott, Oti; Andrew, Hill; Leonard, Moore, Probyn; Ackford, Dooley; Teague, Winterbottom, Richards
NEW ZEALAND: Wright; Kirwan, Innes, McCahill, Timu; Fox, Bachop; McDowell, Fitzpatrick, Loe; I Jones, G Whetton (capt); A Whetton, M Jones, Brooke
Replacement: Earl for Brooke (69 min)
Referee: JM Fleming (Scotland)
Attendance: 57 000

5 Oct 1991 *Cross Green, Otley*
ITALY 30
T: Barba (3 min), Francescato (43 min), Vaccari (64 min), Gaetaniello (75 min)*C:* Dominguez (3, 43, 64, 75 min) *PG:* Dominguez (38, 80 min)
USA 9
T: Swords (68 min) *C:* Williams (68 min) *PG:* Williams (30 min)
ITALY: Troiani; Vaccari, Gaetaniello, Barba, Marcello Cuttitta; Dominguez, Francescato; Massimo Cuttitta, Pivetta, Properzi Curti; Favaro, Croci; Saetti, Checchinato, Zanon (capt)
USA: Nelson; Hein, Williams, Higgins, Whitaker; DeJong, Daily; Lippert, Flay, Paoli; Swords, Leversee; Vizard (capt), Farley, Ridnell
Replacement: Lipman for Vizard (58 min)
Referee: OE Doyle (Ireland)
Attendance: 7500

8 Oct 1991 *Kingsholm, Gloucester*
NEW ZEALAND 46
T: Earl (22 min), Wright (25, 29, 80 min), Purvis (45 min), Timu (53 min), Tuigamala (73 min), Innes (78 min)*C:* Preston (29, 45, 78, 80 min) *PG:* Preston (15, 39 min)
USA 6
PG: Williams (35, 56 min)
NEW ZEALAND: Wright; Timu, Innes, McCahill, Tuigamala; Preston, Bachop; McDowell, Fitzpatrick, Purvis; I Jones, G Whetton (capt); A Whetton, M Jones, Earl
USA: Sheehy; Hein, Williams, Burke, Whitaker; O'Brien, Pidcock; Lippert, Johnson, Mottram; Swords (capt), Tunnacliffe; Sawicki, Lipman, Ridnell
Replacement: Manga for Lippert (50 min)
Referee: E Sklar (Argentina)
Attendance: 12 000

8 Oct 1991 *Twickenham*
ENGLAND 36
T: Underwood (11 min), Guscott (40, 49 min) Webb (61 min)*C:* Webb (11, 40, 49, 61 min) *PG:* Webb (2, 8, 15, 24 min)
ITALY 6
T: Marcello Cuttitta (58 min) *C:* Dominguez (58 min)

ENGLAND: Webb; Oti, Carling (capt), Guscott, Underwood, Andrew, Hill; Leonard, Moore, Probyn; Ackford, Redman; Teague
Replacement: Rendall for Probyn (58 min)
ITALY: Troiani; Vaccari, Barba, Gaetaniello, Marcello Cuttitta; Dominguez, Francescato; Massimo Cuttita, Pivetta, Properzi Curti; Favaro, Croci; Saetti, Giovanelli, Zanon (capt)
Replacement: Bonomi for Troiani (46 min)
Referee: JB Anderson (Scotland)
Attendance: 30 000

11 Oct 1991 *Twickenham*
ENGLAND 37
T: Underwood (8, 80 min), Carling (32 min), Skinner (62 min), Heslop (68 min) *C:* Hodgkinson (8, 32, 62, 68 min) *PG:* Hodgkinson (5, 12, 25 min)
USA 9
T: Nelson (47 min) *C:* Williams (47 min) *PG:* Williams (20 min)
ENGLAND: Hodgkinson; Heslop, Carling (capt), Halliday, Underwood; Andrew, Hill; Leonard, Olver, Pearce; Redman, Dooley; Skinner, Rees, Richards
USA: Nelson; Hein, Williams, Higgins, Sheehy; O'Brien, Pidcock; Manga, Flay, Mottram; Swords (capt), Tunnacliffe; Lipman, Farley, Ridnell
Replacements: DeJong for Higgins (40 min), Wilkinson for Farley (75 min)
Referee: LJ Peard (Wales)
Attendance: 45 000

13 Oct 1991 *Welford Road, Leicester*
NEW ZEALAND 31
T: Brooke (1 min), Innes (26 min), Tuigamala (43 min), Hewett (65 min) *C:* Fox (1, 43, 65 min)) *PG:* Fox (6, 15, 53 min)
ITALY 21
T: Marcello Cuttitta (57 min), Bonomi (76 min) *C:* Dominguez (57, 76 min) *PG:* Dominguez (23, 52, 70 min)
NEW ZEALAND: Wright; Kirwan, Innes, Little, Tuigamala; Fox, Hewett; McDowell, Fitzpatrick, Loe; I Jones, G Whetton (capt); A Whetton, Carter, Brooke
Replacement: Philpott for Wright (73 min)
ITALY: Vaccari; Venturi, Gaetaniello, Dominguez, Marcello Cuttitta; Bonomi, Francescato; Massimo Cuttitta, Pivetta (capt), Properzi Curti; Favaro, Croci; Bottacchiari, Giovanelli, Checchinato
Replacement: Grespan for Properzi Curti (44 min)
Referee: KVJ Fitzgerald (Austria)
Attendance: 16 200

POOL 1 FINAL TABLE

	P	W	D	L	F	A	Pts
New Zealand	3	3	0	0	95	39	9
England	3	2	0	1	85	33	7
Italy	3	1	0	2	57	76	5
USA	3	0	0	3	24	113	3

POOL 2

5 Oct 1991 *Murrayfield*
SCOTLAND 47
T: S Hastings (12 min), Stanger (30 min), Chalmers (35 min), Penalty try (43 min), White (64 min), Tukalo (67 min), G Hastings (69 min) *C:* G Hastings (35, 43, 64, 67, 69 min) *PG:* Chalmers (18 min), G Hastings (48, 55 min)
JAPAN 9
T: Hosokawa (39 min) *C:* Hosokawa (39 min) *PG:* Hosokawa (20 min)
SCOTLAND: G Hastings; Stanger, S Hastings, Lineen, Tukalo; Chalmers, Armstrong; Sole (capt), Allan, Burnell; Gray, Weir; Jeffrey, Calder, White
Replacements: Wyllie for Chalmers (68 min)
JAPAN: Hosokawa; Masuho, Kutsuki, Hirao (capt), Yoshida; Matsuo, Murata; Ohta, Kunda, Takura; Hayashi, Tifaga; Kajihara, Nakashima, Latu
Referee: E Morrison (England)
Attendance: 60 000

6 Oct 1991 *Lansdowne Road, Dublin*
IRELAND 55
T: Robinson (8, 37, 62, 70 min), Geoghegan (39 min), Popplewell (57, 79 min), Curtis (74 min) *C:* Keyes (8, 37, 39, 57 min) *PG:* Keyes (3, 12, 16, 20, 33 min)
ZIMBABWE 11
T: Dawson (64 min), Schultz (80 min) *PG:* Ferreira (52 min)
IRELAND: Staples; Geoghegan, Cunningham, Curtis, Crossan; Keyes, Saunders; Popplewell, Smith, D Fitzgerald; Lenihan, Francis; Matthews (capt), Hamilton, Robinson
ZIMBABWE: Currin (capt); Brown, Tsimba, Letcher, Walters; Kuhn, Ferreira; Hunter, Beattie, Garvey; Demblon, Martin; Botha, Dawson, Catterall
Replacement: Schultz for Kuhn (30 min)
Referee: KH Lawrence (New Zealand)
Attendance: 40 000

9 Oct 1991 *Lansdowne Road, Dublin*
IRELAND 32
T: O'Hara (13 min), Mannion (28, 66 min), Staples (40 min) *C:* Keyes (28, 40 min) *PG:* Keyes (9, 46, 48, 53 min)
JAPAN 16
T: Hayashi (35 min), Kajihara (61 min), Yoshida (79 min) *C:* Hosokawa (35, 79 min)
IRELAND: Staples; Clarke, Mullin, Curtis, Crossan; Keyes, Saunders; J Fitzgerald, Kingston (capt), Halpin; Galwey, Francis; O'Hara, Hamilton, Mannion
Replacement: Cunningham for Crossan (63 min)
JAPAN: Hosokawa; Masuho, Kutsuki, Hirao (capt), Yoshida; Matsuo, Horikoshi; Ohta, Fujita, Takura' Hayashi, Oyagi; Tifaga, Kajihara, Latu
Replacements: Kunda for Fujita (52 min), Miyamoto for Tifaga (75 min)
Referee: L Colati (Fiji)
Attendance: 30 000

9 Oct 1991 *Murrayfield*
SCOTLAND 51
T: Tukalo (3, 62, 70 min), Turnbull (30 min), Stanger (41 min), Weir (79 min), White (80 min) *C:* Dods (3, 30, 37, 62, 70 min) *PG:* Dods (24, 52 min) *DG:* Wyllie (46 min)
ZIMBABWE 12
T: Garvey (2, 33 min) *C:* Currin (2, 33 min)
SCOTLAND: Dods (capt); Stanger, S Hastings, Lineen, Tukalo; Wyllie, Oliver; Watt, K Milne, Burnell; Cronin, Weir; Turnbull, Marshall, White
Replacement: Chalmers for Stanger (78 min)
ZIMBABWE: Currin (capt); Schultz, Tsimba, Letcher, Walters; Brown, MacMillan; Nicholls, Beattie, Garvey; Martin,

Nguruve; Muirhead, Dawson, Catterall
Replacements: Hunter for Garvey (45 min), Chimbima for Walters (56 min), Roberts for Hunter (78 min)
Referee: D Reordan (USA)
Attendance: 35 000

12 Oct 1991 *Murrayfield*
SCOTLAND 24
T: Shiel (55 min), Armstrong (75 min)*C:* G Hastings (55, 75 min) *PG:* G Hastings (14, 28, 63 min) *DG:* Chalmers (24 min)
IRELAND 15
PG: Keyes (4, 19, 32, 45 min) *DG:* Keyes(37 min)
SCOTLAND: G Hastings; Stanger, S Hastings, Lineen, Tukalo; Chalmers, Armstrong; Sole (capt), Allan, Burnell; Gray, Weir; Jeffrey, Calder, White
Replacement: Shiel for Chalmers (47 min)
IRELAND: Staples; Geoghegan, Mullin, Curtis, Crossan; Keyes, Saunders; Popplewell, Smith, D Fitzgerald; Lenihan, Francis; Matthews (capt), Hamilton, Robinson
Referee: FA Howard (England)
Attendance: 60 000

14 Oct 1991 *Ravenhill, Belfast*
JAPAN 52
T: Horikoshi (22 min), Yoshida (30, 58 min), Masuho (52, 64 min), Kutsuki (70, 78 min), Tifaga (72 min), Matsuo (80 min)*C:* Hosokawa (30, 52, 58, 70, 80 min) *PG:* Hosokawa (4, 37 min)
ZIMBABWE 8
JAPAN: Hosokawa; Masuho, Kutsuki, Hirao (capt), Yoshida; Matsuo, Horikoshi; Ohta, Kunda, Takura; Hayashi, Oyagi; Tifaga, Kajihara, Latu
ZIMBABWE: Currin (capt); Schultz, Tsimba, Letcher, Walters; Brown, MacMillan; Nicholls, Beattie, Garvey; Martin, Botha; Nguruve, Dawson, Catterall
Replacement: Roberts for Garvey (68 min)
Referee: R Hourquet (France)
Attendance: 9000

POOL 2 FINAL TABLE

	P	W	D	L	F	A	Pts
Scotland	3	3	0	0	122	36	9
Ireland	3	2	0	1	102	51	7
Japan	3	1	0	2	77	87	5
Zimbabwe	3	0	0	3	31	158	3

POOL 3

4 Oct 1991 *Stradley Park, Llanelli*
AUSTRALIA 32
T: Campese (7, 69 min), Horan (30, 76 min), Kearns (41 min) *C:* Lynagh (30, 69, 76 min) *PG:* Lynagh (15, 17 min)
ARGENTINA 19
T: Teran (32, 65 min) *C:* del Castillo (65 min) *PG:* del Castillo (59 min) *DG:* Arbizu (19, 74 min)
AUSTRALIA: Roebuck; Campese, Little, Horan, Egerton; Lynagh, Farr-Jones (capt); Daly, Kearns, McKenzie; McCall, Coker; Poidevin, Ofahengaue, Eales
Replacement: Nuciflora for Kearns (49 min)
ARGENTINA: del Castillo; Teran, Laborde, Garcia Simon, Cuesta Silva; Arbizu, Camardon; Mendez, Le Fort, Cash; Sporleder, Llanes; Garreton (capt), Santamarina, Carreras
Replacement: Bosch for Le Fort (41 min)
Referee: DJ Bishop (New Zealand)
Attendance: 11 000

6 Oct 1991 *Cardiff Arms Park*
WALES 13
T: Emyr (62 min), I Evans (80 min)*C:* Ring (62 min) *PG:* Ring (23 min)
WESTERN SAMOA 16
T: Vaega (42 min), Vaifale (51 min) *C:* Vaea (42 min) *PG:* Vaea (19, 77 min)
WALES: Clement; I Evans (capt), Gibbs, Hall, Emyr; Ring, R Jones; Griffiths, Waters, Delaney; May, Moseley; Lewis, Collins, P Davies
Replacements: Morris for May (30 min), Rayer for Clement (47 min), Jenkins for Collins (51 min)
WESTERN SAMOA: Aiolupo; Lima, Vaega, Dunce, Tagaloa; Bachop, Vaea; Fatialofa (capt), Toomalatai, Alaalatoa; Birtwhistle, Keenan; Vaifale, Perelini, Lam
Referee: P Robin (France)
Attendance: 45 000

9 Oct 1991 *Pontypool Park, Pontypool*
AUSTRALIA 9
PG: Lynagh (3, 38, 73 min)
WESTERN SAMOA 3
PG: Vaea (65 min)
AUSTRALIA: Roebuck; Campese, Herbert, Horan, Flett; Lynagh, Farr-Jones (capt); Lillicrap, Kearns, Crowley; Coker, Cutler; Miller, Nasser, Eales
Replacement: Slattery for Farr-Jones (11 min)
WESTERN SAMOA: Aiolupo; Lima, Vaega, Bunce, Fa'amasino; Bachop, Vaea; Fatialofa (capt), Toomalatai, Alaalatoa; Birtwhistle, Keenan; Paramore, Kaleopa, Perelini
Replacement: Tagaloa for Lima (50 min)
Referee: E Morrison (England)
Attendance: 15 000

9 Oct 1991 *Cardiff Arms Park*
WALES 16
T: Arnold (73 min) *PG:* Ring (8, 21, 37 min), Rayer (73 min)
ARGENTINA 7
T: Garcia Simon (75 min) *PG:* del Castillo (65 min)
Wales: Rayer; I Evans (capt), Gibbs, Hall, Emyr; Ring, Jones; Griffiths, Jenkins, Delaney; Arnold, Moseley; Lewis, Webster, P Davies
ARGENTINA: del Castillo; Teran, Laborde, Garcia Simon, Cuesta Silva; Arbizu, Camardon; Mendex, Le Fort, Molina: Sporleder, Llanes; Garreton (capt), Santamarina, Carreras
Referee: R Hourquet (France)
Attendance: 35 000

12 Oct 1991 *Cardiff Arms Park*
WALES 3
AUSTRALIA 38
T: Roebuck (35, 79 min), Slattery (46 min), Campese (49 min), Horan (76 min), Lynagh (78 min) *C:* Lynagh (46, 49, 76, 79 min) *PG:* Lynagh (9, 29 min)
WALES: Clement; I Evans (capt), Gibbs, Hall, Emyr; Ring, Jones; Griffiths, Jenkins, Delaney; Arnold, Moseley; Lewis, Webster, P Davies
Replacements: D Evans for Emyr (77 min), Rayer for Gibbs (79 min)
AUSTRALIA: Roebuck; Campese, Little, Horan, Egerton;

Brian Beattie of Zimbabwe gets the ball out despite the attentions of Scotland's Kenny Milne in their Pool 2 match at Murrayfield.

Lynagh (capt), Slattery; Daly, Kearns, McKenzie; McCall, Eales; Poidevin, Miller, Ofahengaue
Referee: KH Lawrence (New Zealand)
Attendance: 54 000

13 Oct 1991 *Sardis Road, Pontypridd*
WESTERN SAMOA 35
T: Tagaloa (20, 73 min), Lima (40, 79 min), Bunce (57 min), Bachop (76 min) *C:* Vaea (20, 40, 73, 76 min) *PG:* Vaea (29 min)
ARGENTINA 12
T: Teran (35 min) *C:* Arbizu (35 min) *PG:* Laborde (14 min), Arbizu (34 min)
WESTERN SAMOA: Aiolupo; Lima, Vaega, Bunce, Tagaloa; Bachop, Vaea; Fatialofa (capt), Toomalatai, Alaalatoa; Birtwhistle, Keenan; Vaifale, Perelini, Lam
ARGENTINA: Angaut; Teran, Laborde, Garcia Simon, Cuesta Silva; Arbizu, Camardon; Aguirre, Bosch, Cash; Sporleder, Buabse; Irarrazaval, Garreton (capt), Santamarina
Replacements: Meson for Angaut (52 min), Carreras for Irarrazaval (58 min)
Referees: JB Anderson and JM Fleming – Anderson injured hamstring and replaced at half time
Attendance: 8500

POOL 3 FINAL TABLE

	P	W	D	L	F	A	Pts
Australia	3	3	0	0	79	25	9
Western Samoa	3	2	0	1	54	34	7
Wales	3	1	0	2	32	61	5
Argentina	3	0	0	0	38	83	3

POOL 4

4 Oct 1991 *Stade de la Mediterranee, Beziers*
FRANCE 30
T: Penalty try (60 min), Saint Andre (63 min), Roumat (69 min), Lafond (76 min)*C:* Camberabero (60 min) *PG:* Camberabero (25, 34, 45, 52 min)
ROMANIA 3
PG: Nichitean (54 min)
FRANCE: Blanco (capt); Saint Andre, Lacroix, Mesnel, Lagisquet; Camberabero, Galthie; Lascube, Marocco, Ondarts; Cadieu, Roumat; Champ, Cabannes, Benazzi
Replacement: Lafond for Lagisquet (48 min)
ROMANIA: Dumitru; Sasu, Lungu, Sava, Racean; Nichitean, Neaga; Leonte, Ion, Stan; Ciorascu, Cojocariu; Dinu, Guranescu, Dumitras (capt)
Referee: LJ Peard (Wales)
Attendance: 22 000

5 Oct 1991 *Parc Municipal Saint-Leon, Bayonne*
CANADA 13
T: S Stewart (20 min)*PG:* Rees (35, 67, 72 min)
FIJI 3
DG: Serevi (13 min)
CANADA: S Stewart; Palmer, C Stewart, Lecky, Gray; Rees, Tynan; Evans, Spiers, Jackart; Robertsen, Hadley; Charron, MacKinnon, Ennis (capt)
FIJI: Koroduadua; Seru, Aria, Nadruki, Lovo; Serevi, Tabulutu; Taga (capt), Naivilawasa, Naituivau; Savai, Domoni; Kato, Dere, Tawake
Replacement: Baleiwai for Naivilawasa (75 min)
Referee: KVJ Fitzgerald (Australia)
Attendance: 5000

8 Oct 1991 *Stade Lesdiguieres, Grenoble*
FRANCE 33
T: Sella (12, 71 min), Lafond (33, 40, 68 min), Camberabero (59 min) *C:* Camberabero (12, 40, 71 min) *PG:* Camberabero (18 min)
FIJI 9
T: Naruma (74 min) *C:* Koroduadua (74 min) *PG:* Koraduadua (1 min)
FRANCE: Blanco (capt); Lafond, Sella, Mesnel, Saint Andre; Camberabero, Galthie; Lascube, Marocco, Ondarts; Cadieu, Roumat; Champ, Cabannes, Benazzi
FIJI: Koroduadua; Seru, Aria, Naisoro, Lovo; Serevi, Vosanibole; Taga (capt), Balewai, Vuli; Savai, Domoni; Naruma, Dere, Tawake
Replacements: Volavola for Taga (10 min), Tabulutu for Vosanibole (40 min)
Referee: WD Bevan (Wales)
Attendance: 17 500

9 Oct 1991 *Stade Municipal, Toulouse*
CANADA 19
T: MacKinnon (43 min), Ennis (48 min)*C:* Wyatt (48 min) *PG:* Wyatt (38, 55 min) *DG:* Rees (71 min)
ROMANIA 11
T: Lungu (68 min), Sasu (80 min) *PG:* Nichitean (40 min)
CANADA: Palmer, S Stewart, Lecky,C Stewart; Rees, Tynan; Evans, Svoboda, Jackart; Vanden Brink, Hadley; Breen MacKinnon, Ennis
ROMANIA: Dumitru; Sasu, Lungu, Fulina, Racean; Nichitean, Neaga; Leonte, Ion, Stan; Ciorascu, Cojocariu; Dinu, Doja, Dumitras (capt)
Replacements: Brinza for Doja (20 min), Sava for Dumitru (37 min), Vlad for Leonte (70 min)
Referee: AR McNeill (Australia)
Attendance: 10 000

12 Oct 1991 *Stade Municipal, Brive*
ROMANIA 17
T: Ion (35 min), Dumitras (51 min), Sasu (55 min) *C:* Racean (51 min) *PG:* Racean (39 min)
FIJI 15
PG: Turuva (8, 70 min) *DG:* Rabaka (27, 42 min), Turuva (48 min)
ROMANIA: Racean; Sasu, Lungu, Fulina, Colceriu; Nichitean, Neaga; Stan, Ion, Vlad; Cojocariu, Ciorascu; Dinu, Marin, Dumitras (capt)
Replacement: Ivanciuc for Nichitean (51 min)
FIJI: Turuva; Seru, Nadruku, Naisoro, Vonolagi; Rabaka, Tabulutu; Vuli, Balewai, Volavola; Savai, Nadolo; Tawake, Dere (capt), Olsson
Replacements: Naituivau for Volavola (31 min), Narumu for Olsson (41 min)
Referee: OE Doyle (Ireland)
Attendance: 8500

13 Oct 1991 *Stade Armandie, Agen*
FRANCE 19
T: Lafond (10 min), Saint Andre (47 min) *C:* Camberabero (10 min) *PG:* Camberabero (4 min), Lacroix (68, 74 min)

CANADA 13
T: Wyatt (40 min) *PG:* Wyatt (26 min), Rees (78 min) *DG:* Rees (60 min)
FRANCE: Blanco (capt); Lafond, Sella, Mesnel, Saint Andre; Camberabero, Galthie; Lascube, Marocco, Ondarts; Cadieu, Roumat; Champ, Cabannes, Benazzi
Replacements: Lacroix for Camberabero (40 min), Sadourny for Sella (47 min)
CANADA: Wyatt (capt); Palmer, C Stewart, Woods, Gray; Rees, Tynan; Evans, Svoboda, Jackart; Robertsen, Hadley; Charron, MacKinnon, Ennis
Replacements: Vanden Brink for Robertsen (23 min), S Stewart for Wyatt (46 min)
Referee: SR Hilditch (Ireland)
Attendance: 15 000

POOL 4 FINAL TABLE

	P	W	D	L	F	A	Pts
France	3	3	0	0	82	25	9
Canada	3	2	0	1	45	33	7
Romania	3	1	0	2	31	64	5
Fiji	3	0	0	3	27	63	3

QUARTER FINALS

19 Oct 1991 *Murrayfield*
SCOTLAND 28
T: Stanger (30 min), Jeffrey (39, 70 min)*C:* G Hastings (39, 70 min) *PG:* G Hastings (17, 56, 63, 70 min)
WESTERN SAMOA 6
PG: Vaea (6 min) *DG:* Bachop (58 min)
SCOTLAND: G Hastings; Stanger, S Hastings, Shiel, Tukalo; Chalmers, Armstrong; Sole (capt), Allan, Burnell; Gray, Weir; Jeffrey, Calder, White
WESTERN SAMOA: Aiolupo; Lima, Vaega, Bunce, Tafaloa; Bachop, Vaea; Fatialofa (capt), Toomalatai, Alaalatoa; Birtwhistle, Ioane; Vaifale, Perelini, Lam
Referee: WD Bevan (Wales)
Attendance: 60 000

19 Oct 1991 *Parc des Princes, Paris*
FRANCE 10
T: Lafond (51 min) *PG:* Lacroix (16, 22 min)

ENGLAND 19
T: Underwood (19 min), Carling (80 min) *C:* Webb (80 min) *PG:* Webb (6, 9, 75 min)
FRANCE: Blanco (capt); Lafond, Sella, Mesnel, Saint Andre; Lacroix, Galthie; Ondarts, Marocco, Lascube; Roumat, Cadieu; Champ, Cabannes, Cecillon
ENGLAND: Webb; Heslop, Carling (capt), Guscott, Underwood; Andrew, Hill; Leonard, Moore, Probyn; Ackford, Dooley; Skinner, Winterbottom, Teague
Referee: DJ Bishop (New Zealand)
Attendance: 48 000

20 Oct 1991 *Lansdowne Road, Dublin*
IRELAND 18
T: Hamilton (75 min)*C:* Keyes (75 min) *PG:* Keyes (26, 34, 63 min) *DG:* Keyes (51 min)
AUSTRALIA 19
T: Campese (17, 53 min), Lynagh (79 min) *C:* Lynagh (17, 53 min) *PG:* Lynagh (45 min)
IRELAND: Staples; Geoghegan, Mullin, Curtis, Clarke; Keyes, Saunders; Popplewell, Smith, D Fitzgerald; Lenihan, Francis; Matthews (capt), Hamilton, Robinson
AUSTRALIA: Roebuck; Campese, Little, Horan, Egerton; Lynagh, Farr-Jones (capt); Daly, Kearns, McKenzie; McCall, Eales; Poidevin, Miller, Ofahengaue
Replacement: Slattery for Farr-Jones (18 min)
Referee: JM Fleming (Scotland)
Attendance: 54 500

20 Oct 1991 *Stade du Nord, Lille*
NEW ZEALAND 29
T: Timu (9, 75 min), McCahill (19 min), Brooke (39 min), Kirwan (55 min) *C:* Fox (9, 19, 39 min) *PG:* Fox (27 min)
CANADA 13
T: Tynan (60 min), Charron (80 min) *C:* Wyatt (80 min) *PG:* Wyatt (33 min)
NEW ZEALAND: Timu; Kirwan, Innes, McCahill, Tuigamala; Fox, Bachop; McDowell, Fitzpatrick, Loe; I Jones, G Whetton (capt); A Whetton, Henderson, Brooke
CANADA: Wyatt (capt); S Stewart, C Stewart, Woods, Gray; Rees, Tynan; Evans, Speirs, Szabo; Vanden Brink, Hadley; Charron, MacKinnon, Ennis
Referee: FA Howard (England)
Attendance: 30 360

Michael Jones, New Zealand's explosive flanker, watches from the stands as his team-mates play their quarter-final against Canada. Jones refused to compromise his beliefs by playing on a Sunday and missed the semi-final for the same reason.

SEMI FINALS

26 Oct 1991 *Murrayfield*
SCOTLAND 6
PG: G Hastings (9, 32 min)
ENGLAND 9
PG: Webb (34, 57 min) *DG:* Andrew (75 min)
SCOTLAND: G Hastings; Stanger, S Hastings, Lineen, Tukalo; Chalmers, Armstrong; Sole (capt), Allan, Burnell; Gray, Weir; Jeffrey, Calder, White
ENGLAND: Webb; Halliday, Carling (capt), Guscott, Underwood; Andrew, Hill; Leonard, Moore, Probyn; Ackford, Dooley; Skinner, Winterbottom, Teague
Referee: KVJ Fitzgerald (Australia)
Attendance: 60 000

27 Oct 1991 *Lansdowne Road, Dublin*
AUSTRALIA 16
T: Campese (6 min), Horan (35 min)*C:* Lynagh (35 min) *PG:* Lynagh (13, 61 min)
NEW ZEALAND 6
PG: Fox (42, 71 min)
AUSTRALIA: Roebuck; Campese, Little, Horan, Egerton; Lynagh, Farr-Jones (capt); Daly, Kerns, McKenzie; McCall, Eales; Poidevin, Ofahengaue, Coker
NEW ZEALAND: Crowley; Kirwan, Innes, McCahill, Timu; Fox, Bachop; McDowell, Fitzpatrick, Loe; I Jones, G Whetton (capt); A Whetton, Carter, Brooke
Referee: JM Fleming (Scotland)
Attendance: 54 500

Two vital moments from the semi-final at Murrayfield. Gavin Hastings (top) misses a vital penalty opportunity to put Scotland into the lead, while Rob Andrew (above) drops the goal that puts England into the final.

Above *Tony Daly scores the only try of the 1991 final for Australia.*

THIRD PLACE MATCH

30 Oct 1991 *Cardiff Arms Park*
NEW ZEALAND 13
T: Little (77 min) *PG:* Preston (15, 34, 54 min)
SCOTLAND 6
PG: G Hastings (4, 74 min)
NEW ZEALAND: Wright; Kirwan, Innes, Little, Tuigamala; Preston, Bachop; McDowell, Fitzpatrick, Loe; I Jones, G Whetton (capt); Earl, M Jones, Brooke
Replacement: Philpott for Tuigamala (40 min)
SCOTLAND: G Hastings; Stanger, S Hastings,Lineen, Tukalo; Chalmers, Armstrong; Sole (capt), Allan, Burnell; Gray, Weir; Jeffrey,Calder, White
Replacement: Dods for Stanger (50 min)
Referee: G Hastings (Ireland)
Attendance: 37 000

FINAL

2 Nov 1991 *Twickenham*
ENGLAND 6
PG: Webb (60, 71 min)
AUSTRALIA 12
T: Daly (30 min) *C:* Lynagh (30 min) *PG:* Lynagh (27, 65 min)
ENGLAND: Webb; Halliday, Carling (capt), Guscott, Underwood; Andrew, Hill; Leonard, Moore, Probyn; Ackford, Dooley; Skinner, Winterbottom, Teague
AUSTRALIA: Roebuck; Campese, Little, Horan, Egerton; Lynagh, Farr-Jones (capt); Daly, Kearns, McKenzie; McCall, Eales; Poidevin, Ofahengaue, Coker
Referee: WD Bevan (Wales)
Attendance: 56 208

Below *Captain Nick Farr-Jones (left) and David Campese with the Webb Ellis Trophy.*

WORLD CUP 1991

	TRIES	CONVERSIONS
Scotland	20	14
New Zealand	19	11
Australia	17	11
France	13	5
Ireland	13	7
Japan	13	8
England	11	9
Western Samoa	8	5
Italy	7	7
Zimbabwe	6	2
Canada	6	2
Romania	5	1
Argentina	4	2
Wales	3	1
USA	2	2
Fiji	1	1

PENALTY GOALS

(Number of penalties attempted are in brackets)

17 (29) England
16 (22) Ireland (29) Scotland
15 (23) New Zealand
12 (25) Australia
10 (16) France
8 (14) Canada
6 (12) Wales
5 (6) Italy (19) Western Samoa
4 (13) Argentina (10) USA
3 (11) Fiji (9) Romania
2 (5) Japan
1 (7) Zimbabwe

DROP GOALS

(Number of drop goals attempted are in brackets)

4 (4) Fiji
2 (6) Argentina (4) Canada (4) England (2) Ireland (5) Scotland
1 (1) Japan (5) Western Samoa
0 (0) Australia (2) France (1) Italy (0) New Zealand (2) USA (2) Romania (3) Wales (1) Zimbabwe

The final was watched by 15.3 million people in the UK.

Attendances: The total figure for the 1991 World Cup was 1 007 760 compared with 604 500 at the 1987 World Cup. The lowest attendance at the 1991 World Cup was 5000 for Fiji v Canada at Bayonne, while 60 000 were reported to have watched the final.

Average gates for the Pool matches: 26 025

Average gates for the knock out stages: 48 895

Leading points scorer: 68 Ralph Keyes (Ireland)

Leading try scorers: **6** David Campese (Australia) and Jean-Baptiste Lafond (France)

WORLD CUP RECORDS

Highest Score
74 New Zealand 74 Fiji 13, Christchurch, 1987
Biggest Winning Margin
64 New Zealand 70 Italy 6, Auckland, 1987

Most tries in a match
4 Ieuan Evans (Wales) v Canada 1987
4 Craig Green (NZ) v Fiji, 1987
4 John Gallagher (NZ) v Fiji, 1987
4 Brian Robinson (Ireland) v Zimbabwe, 1991

Most points
170 Grant Fox (NZ) (1987, 1991)
148 Michael Lynagh (Aus) (1987, 1991)
123 Gavin Hastings (Sco) (1987, 1991)
99 Jon Webb (Eng) (1987, 1991)
85 Didier Camberabero (Fra) (1987, 1991)
68 Ralph Keyes (Ire) (1991)

Most tries
10 David Campese (Aus) (1987, 1991)
7 John Kirwan (NZ) (1987, 1991)
6 Rory Underwood (Eng) (1987, 1991)
6 J-B Lafond (Fra) (1991)
6 Craig Green (NZ) (1987)

Most dropped goals
3 Jonathan Davies (Wales) (1987)

Most penalties
27 Grant Fox (NZ) (1987, 1991)
22 Michael Lynagh (Aus) (1987, 1991)
21 Jon Webb (Eng) (1987, 1991)
19 Gavin Hastings (Sco) (1987, 1991)
16 Ralph Keyes (Ire) (1991)

Most penalties in a game
6 Grant Fox (NZ) v Argentina (1987)
6 Grant Fox (NZ) v Scotland (1987)
5 Ralph Keyes (Ire) v Zimbabwe (1991)

Most points in a match
30 Didier Camberabero (Fra) v Zimbabwe (1987)
27 Gavin Hastings (Sco) v Romania (1987)
26 Grant Fox (NZ) v Fiji (1987)
23 Ralph Keyes (Ire) v Zimbabwe (1991)

THE BARBARIAN CLUB

In 1948, the Barbarians arranged, at short notice, a match against the touring Australians at Twickenham. The match, to boost Australian funds for the return journey home, was such a success that it quickly became the ideal final showpiece match at the end of each tour – a non-international match where the tourists and Barbarians can – more often than not – indulge in the traditional open play that is the feature of Barbarian matches. Results against major touring teams are listed.

Right *Hugo Porta of Argentina in action for the Barbarians against South Africa.*

BARBARIANS RESULTS

31 January 1948 *Cardiff*
BARBARIANS 9 AUSTRALIA 6
BARBARIANS: RF Trott; MF Turner, BL Williams, WB Cleaver, CB Holmes; TA Kemp, H Tanner (capt); H Walker, KD Mullen, IC Henderson, J Mycock, WE Tamplin, WID Elliot, SV Perry, MR Steele-Bodger.
Scorers – T: Steele-Bodger, Holmes, Tanner
AUSTRALIA: BJ Piper; AEJ Tonkin, T Allan (capt), MJ Howell, JWT MacBride; EG Broad, CT Burke; E Tweedale, WL Dawson, N Shehadie, PA Hardcastle, GM Cooke DH Kellar, AJ Buchan, CJ Windon.
Scorers: T: Tonkin *PG:* Tonkin
Referee: AS Bean

26 January 1952 *Cardiff*
BARBARIANS 3 SOUTH AFRICA 17
BARBARIANS: G Williams; JE Woodward, BL Williams, LB Cannell, KJ Jones; CI Morgan, WR Willis; RV Stirling, DM Davies, JMcGK Kendall-Carpenter, ER John, JE Nelson (capt), VG Roberts, JRG Stephens, WID Elliot.
Scorer – T: Elliot
SOUTH AFRICA: AC Keevy; FP Marais, RAM Van Schoor, MT Lategan, JK Ochse; PG Johnstone, PA du Toit; FE van der Ryst, W Delport, HJ Bekker, E Dinklemann, JM du Rand, SP Fry, HSV Muller (capt), CJ van Wyk.
Scorers – T: Ochse, van Wyk *C:* Keevy *PG:* Keevy (2), Johnstone
Referee: MJ Dowling

20 February 1954 *Cardiff*
BARBARIANS 5 NEW ZEALAND 19
BARBARIANS: I King; KJ Jones, J Butterfield, WPC Davies, GM Griffiths; CI Morgan, WR Willis (capt); CR Jacobs, E Evans, JH Smith, RC Hawkes, JRG Stephens, RCC Thomas, S Judd, DF White
Scorers – T: Griffiths *C:* King.
NEW ZEALAND: RWH Scott; MJ Dixon, JT Fitzgerald, RA Jarden, BBJ Fitzpatrick; RG Bowers, K Davis; KL Skinner, RC Hemi, HL White, DO Oliver, RA White, GN Dalzell, RC Stuart (capt), WA McCaw.
Scorers – T: Davis, Dixon, White, Jarden *C:* Jarden (2) *DG:* Scott
Referee: I David

22 February 1958 *Cardiff*
BARBARIANS 11 AUSTRALIA 6
BARBARIANS: RWT Chisholm; AR Smith, GT Wells, MS Phillips, AJF O'Reilly; CI Morgan (capt), AA Mulligan; N Shehadie, AR Dawson, CR Jacobs, RWD Marques, WR Evans, PGD Robbins, J Faull, A Robson
Scorers – T: Evans, Phillips, Dawson *C:* Faull.
AUSTRALIA: TG Curley; AR Morton, R Phelps, JK Lenehan, KJ Donald; RM Harvey, DM Connor; RAL Davidson (capt), R Meadows, GN Vaughan, DM Emanuel, AR Miller, JE Thornett, NM Hughes, WJ Gunter
Scorers – T: Emanuel, Donald.
Referee: GA Walker
N.B. Australian prop forward Nick Shehadie who played for Australia v Barbarians in 1948 becomes the first player to appear both for and against the Barbarians in this fixture.

4 February 1961 *Cardiff*
BARBARIANS 6 SOUTH AFRICA 0
BARBARIANS: HJ Mainwaring; AJF O'Reilly, HM Roberts, BJ Jones, JRC Young; RAW Sharp, WR Watkins; BGM Wood, AR Dawson (capt), S Millar, WRE Evans, B Price, MG Culliton, WGD Morgan, HJ Morgan.
Scorers – T: WGD Morgan, HJ Morgan
SOUTH AFRICA: LG Wilson; BP van Zyl, JP Engelbrecht, JL Gainsford, MJG Antelme; DA Stewart, P de W Uys; SP Kuhn, GF Malan; JL Myburgh, GH van Zyl, AS Malan (capt), PJ van Zyl, HJM Pelser, DJ Hopwood.
Referee: MF Turner

15 February 1964 *Cardiff*
BARBARIANS 3 NEW ZEALAND 36
BARBARIANS: S Wilson; SJ Watkins, MS Phillips, MK Flynn, CP Simpsom; RAW Sharpe, SJS Clarke; LJ Cunningham, AR Dawson (capt), IJ Clarke,E Jones, B Price, MG Culliton, AEI Pask, DP Rogers.
Scorer – DG: IJ Clarke
NEW ZEALAND: DB Clarke; MJ Dick, PF Little, DA Arnold, RW Caulton; BA Watt, CR Laidlaw; WJ Whineray (capt), D Young, KF Gray, AJ Stewart, CE Meads, DJ Graham, KR Tremain, WJ Nathan.
Scorers – T: Nathan (2), Tremain, Meads, Graham, Dick, Caulton, Whineray *C:* Clarke (6)
Referee: DG Walters)
N.B. Ian Clarke follows Nick Shehadie 1958 as a touring player to play for the Barbarians against his own side. Ian and Don, the All-Blacks full-back are brothers.

28 January 1967 *Cardiff*
BARBARIANS 11 AUSTRALIA 17
BARBARIANS: S Wilson; SJ Watkins, TGR Davies, FPK Bresnihan, PB Glover; D Watkins, RM Young; N Suddon, KW Kennedy, AB Carmichael, B Price, WJ. McBride, NA Murphy (capt), JW Telfer, JP Fisher.
Scorers – T: Kennedy, Penalty try *C:* Wilson *PG:* Wilson
AUSTRALIA: JK Lenehan; ES Boyce, RJ Marks, JE Brass, R Webb; PF Hawthorne, KW Catchpole; JE Thornett (capt), PG Johnson, AR Miller, RG Teitzel, M Purcell, GV Davis, JF O'Gorman, J Guerassimoff.
Scorers – T: Boyce (2), Hawthorne, O'Gorman, Webb *C:* Lenehan
Referee: RW Gilliland

16 December 1967 *Twickenham*
BARBARIANS 6 NEW ZEALAND 11
BARBARIANS: S. Wilson (capt); WK Jones, RH Lloyd, TGR Davies, RE Webb; B John, GO Edwards; CH Norris, FA Laidlaw, AL Horton, M Wiltshire, PJ Larter, D Grant, GA Sherriff, RB Taylor.
Scorers – T: Lloyd *DG:* Wilson
NEW ZEALAND: WF McCormick; MJ Dick, WL Davis, IR Macrae, AG Steel; EW Kirton, CR Laidlaw; BL Muller, BE McLeod, KF Gray, SC Strahan, EC Meads, KR Tremain, BJ Lochore (capt), WJ Nathan.
Scorers T: Steel, Macrae *C:* McCormick *DG:* Kirton
Referee: M Joseph

31 January 1970 *Twickenham*
BARBARIANS 12 SOUTH AFRICA 21
BARBARIANS: JPR Williams; ATA Duggan, JS Spencer, CMH Gibson, DJ Duckham; B John, GO Edwards (capt); KE Fairbrother, FAL Laidlaw, DB Llewellyn, AM Davis, IS Gallacher, JJ Jeffrey, RJ Arneil, TM Davies.
Scorers – T: Arneil, Duckham, Duggan, Fairbrother
SOUTH AFRICA: HO de Villiers; SH Nomis, OA Roux, JP van der Merwe, AE van der Watt; MJ Lawless, DJ de Villiers (capt); JFK Marais, CH Cockrell, JL Myburgh, FCH du Preez, IJ de Klerk, PJF Greyling, JH Ellis, MW Jennings.
Scorers – T: Ellis (2), van der Watt *C:* DJ de Villiers (3) *PG:* DJ de Villiers *DG:* Lawless
Referee: GC Lamb

27 January 1973 *Cardiff*
BARBARIANS 23 NEW ZEALAND 11
BARBARIANS: JPR Williams, DJ Duckham, SJ Dawes (capt), CMH Gibson, JC Bevan; P Bennett, GO Edwards; RJ McLoughlin, JV Pullin, AB Carmichael, WJ McBride, RM Wilkinson, TP David, JF Slattery, DL Quinnell.
Scorers – T: Edwards, Slattery, Bevan, Williams *C:* Bennett (2) *PG:* Bennett
NEW ZEALAND: JF Karam; BG Williams, BJ Robertson, IA Hurst, GB Batty; RE Burgess, SM Going; GJ Whiting, RA Urlich, KK Lambert, HH MacDonald, PJ Whiting, AI Scown, AJ Wyllie, IA Kirkpatrick (capt).
Replacement: GL Colling (for Going after 60 mins)
T: Batty (2) *PG:* Karam
Referee: G Domercq

30 November 1974 *Twickenham*
BARBARIANS 13 NEW ZEALAND 13
BARBARIANS: AR Irvine; TGR Davies, PJ Warfield, PS Preece, DJ Duckham; JD Bevan, GO Edwards; J McLaughlan, RW Windsor, FE Cotton, WJ McBride (capt), GL Brown, RM Uttley, JF Slattery, TM Davies.
Scorers – T: TM Davies *PG:* Irvine (3)
NEW ZEALAND: JF Karam; BG Williams, BJ Robertson, IA Hurst, GB Batty; DJ Robertson, SM Going; KK Lambert, RW Norton, KJ Tanner, PJ Whiting, HH MacDonald, IA Kirkpatrick, KW Stewart, AR Leslie (capt).
Scorers – T: Leslie, Williams *C:* Karam *PG:* Karam
Referee: G Domercq

24 January 1976 *Cardiff*
BARBARIANS 19 AUSTRALIA 7
BARBARIANS: AR Irvine; TGR Davies, RWR Gravell, CMH Gibson, JJ Williams; P Bennett, GO Edwards; FMD Knill, PJ Wheeler, AB Carmichael, GL Brown, AJ Martin, JF Slattery, TP Evans, TM Davies (capt).
Scorers – T: Bennett, Wheeler, JJ Williams *C:* Bennett (2) *PG:* Bennett
AUSTRALIA: JC Hindmarsh; JR Ryan, RD L'Estrange, GA Shaw (capt), LE Monaghan; LJ Weatherstone, RG Hauser; JEC Meadows, CM Carberry, R Graham, G Fay, RA Smith, GK Pearse, AA Shaw, ME Loane.
Replacements: WA McKid (for Monaghan), DW Hillhouse (for Loane)
Scorers – T: Ryan *PG:* Hindmarsh
Referee: G Domercq

Andre Joubert (South Africa) in Barbarian colours at Murrayfield in 1991.

16 December 1978 *Cardiff*
BARBARIANS 16 NEW ZEALAND 18
BARBARIANS: AR Irvine; HE Rees, RN Hutchings, JM Renwick, MAC Slemen; P Bennett, DB Williams; W Dickinson, PJ Wheeler, PA Orr, WB Beaumont, AJ Martin, J-P Rives, J-C Skrela, DL Quinnell (capt).
Replacement: BG Nelmes (for Orr)
Scorers – T: Slemen (2) *C:* Bennett *PG:* Bennett (2)
NEW ZEALAND: BJ McKechnie; BG Williams, BJ Robertson, WM Osborne, SS Wilson; EJ Dunn, DS Loveridge; GA Knight, AM Dalton, BR Johnstone, AM Haden, FJ Oliver, LM Rutledge GNK Mourie (capt), J.K. Fleming.
Replacement: JC Ashworth (for Johnstone)
Scorers – T: Johnstone, Rutledge, Williams *PG:* Rutledge *DG:* Dunn
Referee: NR Sanson

9 January 1982 *Cardiff*
BARBARIANS v AUSTRALIA
Match abandoned owing to heavy snow.

15 December 1984 *Cardiff*
BARBARIANS 30 AUSTRALIA 37
BARBARIANS: S Blanco; ST Smith, B Mullin, RA Ackerman, R Underwood; WG Davies (capt), J Gallion; PA Orr, MJ Watkins, IG Milne, RL Norster, DG Lenihan, S McGaughey, G Rees, W Anderson.
Scorers – T: Milne, Smith, Underwood, Gallion, Blanco *C:* Davies (2) *PG:* Davies (2)
AUSTRALIA: RG Gould; MJ Hawker, AG Slack (capt), MP Lynagh, DI Campese; MG Ella, PA Cox; S Pilecki, TA Lawton, AJ McIntyre, SAG Cutler, SA Williams, SP Poidevin, RJ Reynolds, C Roche.
Scorers – T: Poidevin (2), Williams, Hawker, Gould, Slack *C:* Lynagh (5) *PG:* Lynagh
Referee: R Hourquet

26 Nov 1988 *Cardiff*
BARBARIANS 22 AUSTRALIA 40
BARBARIANS: AG Hastings; MDF Duncan, C Laity, MG Ring, R Underwood; J Davies, RN Jones; DMB Sole, SJ Smith, D Young, WA Dooley, RL Norster, PM Matthews (capt), IAM Paxton, RA Robinson.
T: Duncan, Hastings, Robinson, Laity *C:* Hastings (3)
AUSTRALIA: AJS Leeds; AS Niuqila, MT Cook, LF Walker, DI Campese; MP Lynagh, NC Farr-Jones (capt); R Lawton, TA Lawton, AJ McIntyre, SAG Cutler, D Frawley, JS Miller, SP Tuynman, SR Gourley.
Scorers – T: Campese (2), Miller, Lynagh, Walker, Tuynman *C:* Lynagh (5) *PG:* Lynagh (2)
Referee: G Maurette

25 Nov 1989 *Twickenham*
BARBARIANS 10 NEW ZEALAND 21
BARBARIANS: AG Hastings; T Underwood, S Hastings, JC Guscott, R Underwood; A Clement, NC Farr-Jones; DMB Sole (capt), BC Moore, D Young, WA Dooley, PJ Ackford, PM Matthews, PT Davies, GW Rees.
Replacement: BJ Mullin for Guscott
T: Matthews *PG:* AG Hastings (2)
NEW ZEALAND: JA Gallagher; CR Innes, WJ Schuster, WK Little, TJ Wright; GJ Fox, GTM Bachop; SC McDowell, SBT Fitzpatrick, RW Loe, MJ Pierce, G Whetton, AT Earl, WT Shelford (capt), MP Brewer.
Replacement: ZV Brooke for Shelford
T: Innes, Brooke, Loe *C:* Fox (3) *PG:* Fox
Referee: CT Norling

INTERNATIONAL BOARD COUNTRIES

There have been many changes in the basic structure of virtually every major rugby playing nation in the world over the last few years. In the home nations, England, Ireland and Wales have joined Scotland in organising of their club programme into a league set up. In South Africa, the Lion Cup and the Toyota Cup have added a knock out cup competition and a club championship to the schedule.

New Zealand, once reliant on the Ranfurly Shield, has had the National Championship as the backbone of its provincial rugby since 1976, while Australia has benefited from the growth of rugby in the Australian Capital Territory, and with the experiment of an all-Australian club final.

Everywhere changes are being made to improve the domestic programme. This chapter traces not only the growth of the game in the major countries but includes results from the major competitions in the leading rugby nations, the International Board members (Australia, England, France, Ireland, New Zealand, Scotland, South Africa and Wales).

AUSTRALIA

FOUNDATION: 1949
Honours: 1991 World Cup winners, 1987 World Cup fourth
Most points: 721 MP Lynagh, 260 PE McLean, 235 DI Campese
Most Tries: 48 DI Campese
Largest victories: Points 67–9 v USA 1990
Margin 63–6 v Wales 1991
Heaviest defeat: 3–38 v New Zealand 1972
Clubs: 350
Players: 11 500
Population: 16 125 00
Main stadia: Sydney Football ground (cap 50 000), Ballymore, Brisbane (25 500)
Colours: Gold jerseys, green shorts
Headquarters: Australian Rugby Football Union
PO Box 333
Kingsford
New South Wales 2032

MILESTONES

1829 First football matches reported at the Sydney barracks, where soldiers 'amused themselves with a game called football' according to the Sydney Monitor of July 25.
1856 Thomas Wills returned to Australia from playing cricket for Kent, MCC and Cambridge University, and was appalled by the lack of fitness amongst cricketers. Wills organised 'rugby' but derivations of his keep fit exercises became the basis of Australian Rules football.
1864 Foundation of Sydney University rugby club as one of the oldest in the world. First match was against the British warships. The University adhere to Webb Ellis rules.
1865 Sydney Football Club had a match reported in the Sydney Morning Herald on June 19, with 30 players joining in a match at Hyde Park.
1869 Wallaroo Club founded and refounded in 1870 after only five players turned up to the first meeting. Monty Arnold was the first character at the club and it was he who instigated the first Australian ball, by persuading a local saddler to make a plausible copy of the original English Gilbert ball. The Gilbert ball was unobtainable in Australia.
1874 The Southern Rugby Union was founded to organise rules and clubs. The first clubs in the Southern RU were Balmain, Camden College, Kings School, Newington College, Goulburn, Sydney University, Wallaroo, Waratah and North Shore.
1880 Southern RU controlled as many as 100 clubs. Sydney University included Sir Edmund Barton, first Prime Minister of Australia, in their teams.

Australia's future, the Sydney Football Stadium.

1882 First tour by a selection of the clubs in the Southern RU to New Zealand – boat trip took five days.
Queensland Rugby Union founded – sent team to Sydney for first fixture with NSW which was won 28–4 by NSW before a crowd of 4000.
1883 Queensland RU formally constituted a year later.
1887 Ipswich won the first Queensland Championship.
1888 First visit by British Isles team (not Lions as this was an invited team, not selected on merit). Tour captain RL Seddon lost his life in a boating accident on the Hunter River, NSW, with AE Stoddart, the England cricketer, taking over as captain.
First rugby played in Victoria between Melbourne and North Melbourne.
1892 New South Wales Rugby Union formed – but only really changed its name from the Southern RU, which had previously controlled the game in NSW. The Queensland RU dropped the occasional reference to Northern Rugby Union.
1899 First representative Australian team – beat Great Britain 13–3 at the Sydney Cricket Ground. Britain won other three matches 11–0, 11–10 and 13–0.
1900 Glebe won the first Sydney Championship.
1903 On August 15, the first official international played by both Australia and New Zealand resulted in a 22–3 win for New Zealand at the Sydney Cricket Ground. Australia wore the NSW colours of light blue.
1908 First tour to Britain by Australian team, who chose the name Wallabies themselves. Their first mascot was a live snake, who died just before their first defeat at Llanelli. While on tour Australia won the Olympic rugby gold medal beating the English champion county, Cornwall, in the final by 32–3. Rugby league had become very popular in 1908 with meetings setting up a professional tour; consequently the Wallabies team was understrength. The Australian rugby league and rugby union teams had plans for a match, but the Union constitution forbade it.
1910 Rugby league in ascendancy in New South Wales and Queensland – payment for travelling vast distances appealed.
1919–28 No club football in Queensland – Queensland RU disbanded and reformed in 1928.
1927–8 Waratah's tour of Britain revived interest in rugby union, especially in the armed forces. Waratah were NSW based and revival continued in Queensland and Victoria.
1929 Australian revival continued with 3–0 win over New Zealand.
1933 Australia won two Test series in South Africa with a side containing players from NSW, and also Queensland (10) and Victoria (3).
1934 Australia won Bledisloe Cup for first time against New Zealand. The Cup had been donated for competition in 1931 between Australia and New Zealand by Lord Bledisloe, Governor-General of New Zealand from 1930–4.
1939 Wallabies toured Britain but tour was cancelled before a match could be played owing to commencement of World War II.
1948 Australia became the first tourists to play the Barbarians in the traditional end of tour fixture – the Australians needed this extra fixture to fund their return journey.
1949 Australian Rugby Union founded to harmonise the two major states, NSW and Queensland, and to develop the game in other states.
1980 Australian Schools side perform Grand Slam in Britain.
1984 First Australian team to complete the Grand Slam with wins over the four home nations on tour in Britain.
1991 Australia beat Wales by 63–6 – a record between major rugby playing nations. NSW earlier beat Wales 71–8.
Australia complete 1991 by winning the second Rugby World Cup with 12–6 win over England in the final.

INTERNATIONAL RECORDS

Most capped player

DI Campese	66	1982–92

In individual positions

Full-back		
RG Gould	25	1980–87
Wing		
DI Campese	50 (66)[1]	1982–92
Centre		
AG Slack	39	1978–87
Fly-half		
MP Lynagh	47 (55)[2]	1984–92
Scrum-half		
NC Farr-Jones	54 (55)[3]	1984–92
Prop		
AJ McIntyre	38	1982–89
Hooker		
PG Johnson	42	1959–71
Lock		
SAG Cutler	40	1982–92
Flanker		
SP Poidevin	59	1980–92
No 8		
SN Tuynman	28 (34)[4]	1983–92

[1] Campese has played 16 times as full-back
[2] Lynagh has played 7 times as a centre and once as a replacement full-back
[3] Farr-Jones was capped once as a replacement wing
[4] Tuynman played 6 times as a flanker

Australia's 1991 World Cup victory was based around the suburban strengths of Sydney and Brisbane, with New South Wales and Queensland providing the entire World Cup squad. The Premiership in both these cities are the two leagues from which the national XVs are drawn. But there is increasing activity away from the major centres.

David Campese: Milan, Randwick and Australia.

New South Wales

FOUNDATION: 1874 (as Southern Rugby Union)
No of clubs: 127
No of players: 4050
Record win against overseas opposition: 71–8 v Wales 1991
Number of Internationals: 159
Ground: Waratah Park, Sydney

MILESTONES

1829 Reports of a game between soldiers at the Sydney barracks on 25 July
1863 Sydney University founded
1865 Sydney RFC and Australian RFC founded
1867 Military and Civil Service RFC founded
1870 Wallaroo RFC founded
1874 The Southern Rugby Union founded to organise up to 100 clubs in the area. This was a forerunner of the NSW Rugby Union. The Union also had to contend with the standardisation of rules, which were chaotic
1882 First match against Queensland – NSW believed to have won by 26–3
1888 Northern section of the Southern RU opened at Newcastle

SYDNEY PREMIERSHIP WINNERS

1900 Glebe
1901 Glebe and Sydney University (University)
1902 Western Suburbs (Wests)
1903 Eastern Suburbs (Easts)
1904 University
1905 South Sydney
1906, 1907 Glebe
1908 Newtown
1909 Glebe
1910, 1911 Newtown
1912 Glebe
1913 Easts
1914 Glebe
1915–1918 No competition
1919, 1920 University
1921 Easts
1922 Manly
1923, 1924 University
1925 Glebe–Balmain
1926, 1927, 1928 University
1929 Wests
1930 Randwick
1931 Easts
1932 Manly
1933 Northern Suburbs (Norths)
1934 Randwick
1935 Norths
1936 Drummoyne
1937 University
1938 Randwick
1939 University
1940 Randwick
1941 Easts
1942, 1943 Manly
1944 Easts
1945 University
1946, 1947 Easts
1948 Randwick
1949 Gordon
1950 Manly
1951 University
1952 Gordon
1953, 1954, 1955 University
1956 Gordon
1957 St George
1958 Gordon
1959 Randwick
1960 Norths
1961, 1962 University
1963, 1964 Norths
1965, 1966, 1967 Randwick
1968 University
1969 Easts
1970 University
1971 Randwick
1972 University
1973, 1974 Randwick
1975 Norths
1976 Gordon
1977 Parramatta
1978, 1979, 1980, 1981, 1982 Randwick
1983 Manly
1984 Randwick
1985, 1986 Parramatta
1987, 1988, 1989, 1990,1991 Randwick

Randwick

That no one has yet devised a system by which the world club champions can be decided fairly, is perhaps the only reason why Randwick are not unquestionably the world's top club. Currently the outstanding team in the Southern Hemisphere, the fact that the seasons are different from their Northern Hemisphere foes, means that no particular club side is match fit at exactly the same time.

Randwick is a southern suburb of Sydney. Close to the Randwick racecourse, their original base was the Randwick Oval – a ground with no proper facilities. The club's shirt colours were taken from the myrtle green of the local tram.

The club reached the first grade (or first division) in 1923, and won their first Premiership in 1930. Under the founders, Wally Meagher and Owen Crossman, who toured New Zealand in 1923 with New South Wales, the club defined its playing policy as an open, Barbarian style which has carried forward to this day. Seven Randwick players were in the 1947–8 Wallabies that met the Barbarians in the first of the closing tour matches.

After World War II, the club continued to thrive with the famous Catchpole–Hawthorne half back partnership, the Windons, the Ellas and the base of the 1991 World Cup squad amongst those continuing the tradition. That Randwick has continued to dominate Australian rugby, despite the massive defection of players to Rugby League, speaks volumes for the coaching set up, and the fact that players from all over the continent are attracted by their reputation.

New South Wales Country

FOUNDATION: 1955
No of clubs: 33
No of players: 930
Record win against overseas opposition:
Major 14–13 v England 1975
Other 97–20 v Japan 1975
Number of Internationals: 16

MILESTONES

1910 Larry Dwyer, from Orange, won the first of his seven caps for Australia – the first from the outback to play for Australia. He later captained his country.
1946 NSW Country advisory committee formed to investigate possibility of forming a Union
1953 First tours to Melbourne and Adelaide
1955 NSW Country Union formed
1959 Newcastle break away to form their own Union

David Cody

The most capped of those who represented NSW Country, he was similar to many others before him who learnt the game in Country before progressing to the city. Amongst those before Cody was former captain John Hipwell.

But Cody returned to Bathurst and Orange to pursue business interests. He was born 7 July 1957, and won 13 caps from 1983–1987. He played in the 1987 World Cup, but gained unwanted notoriety by being sent off in the third place match with Wales after just five minutes.

Queensland

FOUNDATION: 1883 (as Northern Rugby Union)
No of clubs: 86
No of players: 2250
Record win against overseas opposition:
68-11 v Italy 1981
Number of internationals: 102
Ground: Ballymore Oval, Brisbane

MILESTONES

1867 Brisbane RFC is the first club to be formed in Queensland
1878 Excelsior is second Queensland club
1882 First inter state match with New South Wales
1883 Queensland Rugby Union formed to administer three clubs in Brisbane, with further centres at Rockhampton, Toowoomba, Gympie and Maryborough
1910 Rugby league the dominant sport in Queensland
1919 Queensland RU folded after World War I
1929 Queensland RU resumed inter state matches with NSW

BRISBANE PREMIERSHIP WINNERS

1887 Ipswich Rangers
1888 Union Harriers
1889, 1890 Wallaroos
1891 Acoma
1892 Past and Present Grammar
1893, 1894 Boomerangs
1895, 1896, 1897 City
1898, 1899 Past Grammar
1900 City
1901, 1902, 1903, 1904 North Brisbane Electorate
1904 Vally (shared)
1905–14 Official competition suspended
1915 Brothers
1916–28 No competition
1929 YMCA
1930, 1931, 1932 Brisbane University (University)
1933 YMCA
1934 University
1935, 1936, 1937 Eagle Junction
1938 University
1939 YMCA
1940–1945 Competition suspended
1946 Christian Brothers School Old Boys (Brothers)
1947, 1948 University
1949, 1950, 1951 Brothers
1952 University
1953 Brothers
1954, 1955, 1956, 1957 University
1958 Southern Districts (Souths)
1959 Brothers
1960 University
1961 GPS Old Boys
1962 University
1963 Teachers
1964, 1965 University
1966 Brothers
1967 University
1968 Brothers
1969, 1970 University
1971 Brothers
1972 GPS
1973, 1974, 1975 Brothers
1976 Teachers
1977 Western Districts (Wests)
1978 Brothers
1979 University
1980, 1981, 1982, 1983, 1984 Brothers
1985, 1986 Wests
1987, 1988, 1989, 1990 University
1991 Souths

The Ballymore Oval Ground at Brisbane, Queensland.

Brisbane University

The most successful club in Queensland, the University XV is open to both past and present students of the University. The club was started in 1912, a year after the University was founded. Initially the club was not successful, and preferred to play Rugby League.

University won the 1928 and 1929 Premierships when Rugby Union began again in Queensland, and have since won more Premiership titles than any other club in Queensland. There was a solid representation of University players in the 1991 World Cup winning squad.

Queensland Country

FOUNDATION: 1965
No of clubs: 29
No of players: 900
Record win against overseas opposition: 35-3 v Soviet Union 1990
Number of internationals: –

MILESTONES

1888 British tourists played four matches in Queensland
1965 Wide Bay, Gold Coast and Darling Downs, who had separate unions, formed the Queensland Country Union
1966 Townsville joined QCRU
1968 Rockhampton and Cairns joined QCRU
1971 Mount Isa joined QCRU
1976 Mackay and District joined QCRU
1978 Central Highlands joined QCRU

Australian Capital Territory

FOUNDATION: 1974
No of clubs: 10
No of players: 650
Record win against overseas opposition:
Major 21-20 v Wales 1978
Other 35-3 v Argentina 1983
Number of internationals: 8
Ground: Canberra Raiders Stadium

MILESTONES

1870 Clubs already formed in Bungendore, Gundaroo, Captain's Flat, Sutton and Ginnindera
1873 Goulborn RFC formed
1878 Queanbeyan RFC formed
1938 First interclubs competition
1974 ACT separated from the NSW Country Union to form their own Union
1975 LJ Weatherstone (Wests) becomes ACT's first international
1982 David Campese (Queanbeyan Whites) gains first cap against New Zealand to herald the start of a record breaking career
1989–92 Seven ACT members either capped or members of the full Wallabies touring parties – making ACT easily the third ranked rugby state in Australia

South Australia

FOUNDATION: 1932
No of clubs: 16
No of players 725
Record win against overseas opposition: –
Number of internationals: –
Ground: Bailey ground, Adelaide

MILESTONES

1930 First games between staff of the Adelaide Advertizer
1932 South Australian RU founded with just two clubs, but only one, Adelaide RFC, was properly constituted
1958 Malcolm van Gelder became the first to win Wallaby selection from South Australia, when selected to tour New Zealand
1974 New Zealand beat South Australia 117–6

Tasmania

FOUNDATION: 1966
No of clubs: 11
No of players: 525
Record win against overseas opposition: –
Number of internationals: –
Ground: Queenborough Oval, Hobart

MILESTONES

1926 Two New Zealand ship crews demonstrated the game at Hobart
1932 Clubs in Launceston, Glen Dhu, Alhambra and Wellington in the north of the Island
1933 University of Tasmania at Hobart is the first club in the south, Harlequins are formed in the same year
1951 Island club competition – final between winners of the North (Launceston and District) and South (Hobart) leagues
1954–1959 League system prevailed but folded because of excessive travel costs. Reverted to 1951 format

Victoria

FOUNDATION: 1888 (as Melbourne RU)
No of clubs: 22
No of players: 1130
Record win against overseas opposition: –
Number of internationals: 13
Ground: Olympic Park, Melbourne

MILESTONES

1888 First British team spent much time in Melbourne but played more Australian Rules than Rugby Union
First match in Melbourne between North Melbourne and Melbourne
New Zealand Maoris stopped on way to, and way from, Britain where they played 74 games
1889 Victoria sent first team to play New South Wales at Sydney
1894 Victoria beat NSW 3–0 with a side of New Zealanders, South Africans and Britons; employers sacked Victorians who played rugby instead of Australian Rules
1909 First Melbourne club competition – St Kilda, Melbourne, South Melbourne, North Melbourne and University entered
1926 Victoria RU reorganise club competition after World War I to ward off threat of clubs joining Rugby League
1933 Four Victorians in Australian party to South Africa
1939 Three Victorians from one club, Power House, in party to tour England. The tour was called off after the arrival in Britain because of War.
1962 Olympic Park, No. 2 Ground, secured as home for Victoria RU

Western Australia

FOUNDATION: 1893
No of clubs: 16
No of players: 940
Record win against overseas opposition:
33-23 v USA 1990
Number of internationals: 1
Ground: Perry Lakes, Perth

Robert Thompson

Western Australia's only international, he was capped three times – against South Africa, France and Fiji in 1971–2. Thompson scored 18 points for Western Australia against South Africa earlier on the tour. He was unusual in that he was a goal-kicking hooker.

Thompson was a Maori, who played for Bay of Plenty, before marrying a radiographer who was posted to Perth. He broke his leg badly in 1969, and only took up goal kicking to strengthen the leg. In 1972, he moved to Sydney to play for Northern Suburbs and NSW, but although he toured New Zealand in 1972 with the Wallabies, he did not play any further international rugby.

MILESTONES

1868 First games in Swan River Colony among servicemen and ships crews in Fremantle
1893 Formation of first Western Australian Rugby Union – mining communities had brought the game from the major cities in Australia
1914 WARU ceased due to World War I
1928 WARU revived to cater for growth of the game at Perth, Fremantle and the mining communities
1962 Commonwealth Games at Perth, with its improved airport facilities, opened the region to stop-over games for various British, French, South African, New Zealand and Australian touring teams.
1971 Perry Lakes Stadium gives WARU a base to accommodate touring sides, and to house offices of WARU

Inter-State Rugby

QUEENSLAND V NEW SOUTH WALES

Played 261, New South Wales have won 175, Queensland 73, 13 draws.

Highest score:

New South Wales	47	(47–16) Sydney, 1929
Queensland	48	(48–10) Sydney, 1979

Biggest Winning Margin

New South Wales	45	(45–0) Sydney, 1955
		(45–0) Sydney, 1961
Queensland	38	(42–4) Sydney, 1976
		(48–10) Sydney, 1979

Most points in a game

58 (Queensland 48, NSW 10) Sydney 1979

AUSTRALIAN PREMIERSHIP

Held on four occasions before 1991 when the event was suspended due to participation in the World Cup by many of the players who would have contested the Premiership. The winners of the Sydney and Brisbane club competitions meet in an all-Australian final.

Winners

1987	Randwick
1988	Randwick
1989	Queensland University
1990	Randwick
1991	Not contested

ENGLAND

FOUNDATION: 1871
Honours: 1991 World Cup runners-up
Grand Slam: 1913, 1914, 1921, 1923, 1924, 1928, 1957, 1980, 1991, 1992
International Championship: 19 (outright)
Triple Crown: 17
Most Points: 246 JM Webb, 240 WH Hare, 203 SD Hodgkinson
Most Tries: 35 R Underwood, 18 CN Lowe, 13 JC Guscott
Largest victory: 60–7 v Japan 1987
Heaviest defeat: 15–42 v New Zealand 1985
Clubs: 1705 (1111 in Courage Leagues)
Players: 375 000
Population: 46 450 000
Main stadia: Twickenham (cap: 54 500), Welford Road, Leicester (16 100)
Colours: All white
Headquarters: Rugby Football Union
Twickenham
Middlesex
TW1 1DZ

MILESTONES

1823 William Webb Ellis, 'with a fine disregard of the rules of football as played in his time', first took the ball and ran with it thus originating the distinctive feature of the rugby game at Rugby School.

1843 A rugby club was formed at Guys Hospital.

1845 The first set of rules drawn up at Rugby School.

1851 William Gilbert made a 'Rugby School football' which was on view at the International Exhibition at London.

1863 Richmond v Blackheath in the game's oldest regular fixture.

1871 January 26, the Rugby Football Union was formed at the Pall Mall Restaurant on the corner of Pall Mall East and Cockspur Street (now no more) in London – to formulate acceptable rules and to accept a challenge from Scotland for an international match. Present at the first meeting were Blackheath, Richmond, Civil Service, Wellington College, Harlequins, Guy's Hospital, Kings College and St Paul's School plus the following now defunct clubs – West Kent, Ravenscourt Park, Marlborough Nomads, Wimbledon Hornets, Gipsies, Law, Flamingoes, Clapham Rovers, Queen's House, Lausanne, Addison, Mohicans and Belsize Park.

March 7, first rugby international between Scotland and England at Raeburn Place, Edinburgh. Scotland won by a goal and a try to a try

1872 William Webb Ellis died – he is buried at Menton, near

England's record points scorer, Jonathan Webb, in World Cup action against Scotland at Murrayfield.

Monaco, in Southern France.
First University match won by Oxford against Cambridge at the Parks, Oxford, by a goal and a try to nil on February 10.
England's first home international – at Kennington Oval – against Scotland
1875 Hospitals Cup competition started
1877 Calcutta Cup struck and awarded for competition between England and Scotland
1889 County Championship started
1893 'Broken time' dispute which led to breakaway by Northern clubs of Cheshire, Lancashire and Yorkshire – the Northern Union (later the Rugby League) formed
1907 Twickenham site purchased by the Rugby Union.
1909 First rugby match at Twickenham on October 2: Harlequins 14 Richmond 10.
1910 First international at Twickenham – England beat Wales.
1914 England win their first back to back Grand Slam after winning in 1913.
1924 England win second back to back Grand Slam following win in 1923.
1926 Harlequins won first Middlesex sevens competition.
1938 First televised international – England v Scotland at Twickenham.
1947 Number of rugby clubs affiliated to Rugby Football Union passes 1000 for the first time.
1954 St Luke's College, Exeter become the first to top 1000 points in a club season with 1082 points
1964 Clubs affiliated to the Rugby Football Union pass 2000 for the first time with 2034 registered
1972 First Rugby Football Union Knockout Cup – won by Gloucester
1985 First club leagues set up in England
1991 England reach World Cup final losing 12–6 in the final to Australia at Twickenham
1992 England win third back to back Grand Slam following similar achievements in 1914 and 1924

INTERNATIONAL CAPS

Most capped player		
R Underwood	55	1984–92
In individual positions		
Full Back		
JM Webb	27	1987–92
Wing		
R Underwood	55	1984–92
Centre		
WDC Carling	36	1988–92
Fly-half		
CR Andrew	47 (48)[1]	1985–92
Scrum-half		
RJ Hill	29	1984–91
Prop		
GS Pearce	36	1979–91
Hooker		
JV Pullin	42	1966–76
Lock		
WA Dooley	50	1985–92
Flanker		
P Winterbottom	52	1982–92
No 8		
D Richards	33	1986–92

[1] Andrew played one game as full-back

LEADING POINTS SCORERS

	Caps	Points
JM Webb	27	246
WH Hare	25	240
SD Hodgkinson	14	203
CR Andrew	48	148
R Underwood	55	140
RB Hiller	19	138

Top right *England's record try scorer, Rory Underwood, in the day job as an RAF pilot.*

Above *Dusty Hare of Leicester and England in his daytime job as a farmer.*

COURAGE LEAGUES

The mammoth task of integrating over 1000 clubs into National leagues began in the mid-1980s. The competition, sponsored by the brewers John Courage, began in 1987, but there had been unofficial leagues in the previous two seasons to determine which clubs were placed in the respective divisions for the start of the competition. Below the National league, the competition is run in regions with a system of promotion and relegation to the three national divisions.

Division One

1987–88

	P	W	D	L	F	A	Pts
Leicester	10	9	0	1	225	133	37
Wasps	11	8	1	2	218	136	36
Harlequins	11	6	1	4	261	128	30
Bath	11	6	1	4	197	156	30
Gloucester	10	6	1	3	206	121	29
Orrell	11	5	1	5	192	153	27
Moseley	11	5	0	6	167	170	26
Nottingham	11	4	1	6	146	170	24
Bristol	10	4	1	5	171	145	23
Waterloo	10	4	0	6	123	208	22
Coventry	11	3	1	7	139	246	21
Sale	11	0	0	11	95	374	11

1988–89

	P	W	D	L	F	A	Pts
Bath	11	10	0	1	263	98	20
Gloucester	11	7	1	3	215	112	15
Wasps	11	7	1	3	206	138	15
Nottingham	11	6	1	4	142	122	13
Orrell	11	6	1	4	148	157	13
Leicester	11	6	1	4	189	199	13
Bristol	11	6	0	5	188	117	12
Harlequins	11	5	0	6	194	184	10
Rosslyn Park	11	5	0	6	172	208	10
Moseley	11	3	0	8	113	242	6
Waterloo	11	1	1	9	120	235	3
Liverpool St Helens	11	1	0	10	116	254	2

1989–90

	P	W	D	L	F	A	Pts
Wasps	11	9	0	2	250	106	18
Gloucester	11	8	1	2	214	139	17
Bath	11	8	0	3	258	104	16
Saracens	11	7	1	3	168	167	15
Leicester	11	6	0	5	248	184	12
Nottingham	11	6	0	5	187	148	12
Harlequins	11	6	0	5	218	180	12
Orrell	11	5	0	6	221	132	10
Bristol	11	4	0	7	136	144	8
Rosslyn Park	11	4	0	7	164	243	8
Moseley	11	2	0	9	138	258	4
Bedford	11	0	0	11	70	467	0

1990–91

	P	W	D	L	F	A	Pts
Bath	12	11	0	1	280	104	22
Wasps	12	9	1	2	252	151	19
Harlequins	12	8	0	4	267	162	16
Leicester	12	8	0	4	244	140	16
Orrell	12	7	0	5	247	105	14
Gloucester	12	6	0	6	207	163	12
Rosslyn Park	12	6	0	6	216	174	12
Nottingham	12	6	0	6	138	194	12
Northampton	12	5	1	6	149	254	11
Saracens	12	5	0	7	151	228	10
Bristol	12	4	1	7	135	219	9
Moseley	12	1	1	10	113	244	3
Liverpool St Helens	12	0	0	12	88	349	0

1991–92

	P	W	D	L	F	A	Pts
Bath*	12	10	1	1	277	126	20
Orrell	12	10	0	2	204	95	20
Northampton	12	9	1	2	209	136	19
Gloucester	12	7	1	4	193	168	15
Saracens	12	7	1	4	176	165	15
Leicester	12	6	1	5	262	216	13
Wasps	12	6	0	6	177	180	12
Harlequins	12	5	1	6	213	207	11

The Recreation Ground at Bath, home of England's most successful club side.

London Irish	12	3	3	6	147	237	9
Bristol	12	4	0	8	192	174	8
Rugby	12	2	3	7	124	252	7
Nottingham	12	2	1	9	133	204	5
Rosslyn Park	12	0	1	11	111	258	1

* Bath 1 pt deducted

FIRST DIVISION RECORDS

The **biggest win and winning margin** in the First Division is 76–0 by Bath against Bedford in 1989–90. Bath scored a record 14 tries.

The **biggest away win** is 71–8 by Harlequins, also against Bedford in 1989–90. Harlequins scored 11 tries.

Jeremy Guscott and Tony Swift both scored 4 tries for Bath against Bedford and Stuart Barnes converted 10 tries – both are First Division records.

NATIONAL KNOCKOUT CUP

England's national knockout cup began life as the Rugby Football Union club competition in the 1971–2 season. Sponsorship from John Player Special began in the 1975–6 season, with Pilkington Glass taking over in 1988.

1971–2
Semi-finals: Coventry 6, Gloucester 6*
Moseley 18, Wilmslow 10
*Gloucester win on 'away team' rule
Final: GLOUCESTER 17 MOSELEY 6
GLOUCESTER: EJF Stephens; RJ Clewes, JA Bayliss, R Morris, J Dix; T Palmer, MH Booth; MA Burton, MJ Nicholls (capt), RJ Cowling, A Brinn, JS Jarrett, JA Watkins, MJ Potter, R Smith
Scorers – T: Dix, Morris *PG:* Stephens *DG:* Palmer, Booth
MOSELEY: SA Doble; K Hatter, MK Swain, CW McFadyan, R Kerr; JF Finlan, JG Webster (capt); CC Morrell, DE Lane, J Griffiths, R Morris, NE Horton, TJ Smith, JC White, IN Pringle.
Scorers – T: Swain *C:* Doble
Referee: R Lewis

1972–3
Semi-finals: London Welsh 15, Bristol 18
Sale 6 Coventry 35
Final: COVENTRY 27 BRISTOL 15
COVENTRY: PA Rossborough; DJ Duckham (capt), CS Wardlow, GW Evans, PS Preece; AR Cowman, WJ Gittings; KE Fairbrother, JD Gray, JM Broderick, RN Creed, BF Ninnes, IR Darnell, J Barton, BC Holt
Scorers – T: Barton, Duckham, Evans, Gray *C:* Rossborough *PG:* Rossborough (2) *DG:* Cowman
BRISTOL: PM Knight; MJW Dandy, CJ Williams, RJ Swaffield, AJ Morley; AH Nicholls (capt), AFA Pearn; AJ Rodgers, JV Pullin, MJ Fry, AC Munden, DEJ Watt, RJ Orledge, RC Hannaford, DM Rollitt
Scorers – PG: Pearn (5)
Referee: RF Johnson

1973–4
Semi-finals: Coventry 23, Rosslyn Park 4
Orrell 3, London Scottish 12
Final: COVENTRY 26 LONDON SCOTTISH 6
COVENTRY: PA Rossborough; RC Barnwell, D Foulks, BJ Corless, DJ Duckham (capt); AR Cowman, WJ Gittings; KE Fairbrother, J Gallagher, JM Broderick, R Walker, BF Ninnes, IR Darnell, LJ Rolinson, R Cardwell
Scorers – T: Duckham (2), Barnwell, Gittings *C:* Rossborough (2) *PG:* Rossborough (2)
LONDON SCOTTISH: GB Stevenson; DG Fowlie, AAS Friell, AG Biggar, RR Keddie; DE Bell, RD Crerar; AE Corstorphine, DA Pickering, MS Lovett, RA McKenzie, AF McHarg, G Fraser, MA Biggar (capt), CW Thorburn.
Scorer – DG: Bell (2)
Referee: MH Titcomb

1974–5
Semi-finals: Bedford 13, Coventry 6
Morpeth 6, Rosslyn Park 28
Final: BEDFORD 28 ROSSLYN PARK 12
BEDFORD: AM Jorden; R Demming, JM Howard, R Chadwick, D Wyatt; WN Bennett, A Lewis; CJ Bailward, N Barker, B Keen, EF Edwards, RM Wilkinson, C Hooker, AJ Hollins, DP Rogers (capt)
Scorers – T: Demming (2), Wyatt, Bailward, Keen *C:* Bennett (4)
ROSSLYN PARK: RA Codd; RG Fisher, CD Saville, MB Bazalgette, DJ McKay; PA Treseder, LE Weston; RL Barlow, P d'A Keith-Roach (capt), NP Hinton, PG Anderson, ND Mantell, AK Rodgers, AG Ripley, G Link
Scorers – T: McKay (2), Fisher
Referee: RF Johnson

1975–6
Semi-finals: Sale 3, Gosforth 12
Rosslyn Park 12, Wakefield 6
Final: GOSFORTH 23 ROSSLYN PARK 14
GOSFORTH: B Patrick; SM Griffin, JK Britten, HE Patrick, JS Gustard; RW Breakey, M Young (capt); AJ Cutter, DF Madsen, C White, AJ Preston, TC Roberts, JJO Short, PJ Dixon, D Robinson
Scorers – T: B Patrick, Roberts, Gustard, Robinson *C:* Young (2) *PG:* Young
ROSSLYN PARK: PA Treseder; MP Bulpitt, CP Kent, S Fluskey, JL Moyes; CS Ralston, LE Weston; NP Hinton, P d'A Keith-Roach (capt), G Lloyd-Roberts, R Mordell, AK Rodgers, ND Mantell, AG Ripley, D Starling
Replacement: L Byrne (for Treseder after 33 mins)
Scorers – T: Ripley, Bulpitt *PG:* Weston *DG:* Ralston
Referee: NR Sanson

1976–7
Semi-finals: London Welsh 12, Gosforth 18
Waterloo 11, Saracens 6
Final: GOSFORTH 27 WATERLOO 11
GOSFORTH: B Patrick; JS Archer, HE Patrick, JK Britten, JS Gustard; RW Breakey, M Young; AJ Cutter, DF Madsen, C White, D Robinson, J Hedley, TC Roberts, RM Uttley (capt), PJ Dixon
Scorers – T: Robinson (2), Dixon, Archer, Hedley *C:* B Patrick (2) *PG:* B Patrick
WATERLOO: SG Tickle; JN Spaven, GT Jackson, SF Christopherson, MA Flett; I Ball, DJ Carfoot; D Reed, CD Fisher (capt), F Blackhurst, K Hancock, KF Short, MF Billingham, L Connor, K Lunt

Scorers – T: Christopherson, Tickle *PG:* Ball
Referee: PE Hughes

1977–8
Semi-finals: Leicester 25, Coventry 16
Harlequins 6, Gloucester 12
Final: GLOUCESTER 6 LEICESTER 3
GLOUCESTER: PE Butler; RJ Clewes, BJ Vine, R Jardine, RR Mogg; CG Williams, PR Howell; MA Burton, SGF Mills, GAF Sargent, JA Watkins (capt), SB Boyle, JH Fidler, JF Simonett, VJ Wooley
Scorers – T: Mogg *C:* Butler
LEICESTER: WH Hare; MJ Duggan, PW Dodge, BP Hall (capt), RG Barker; B Jones, S Kenney; SP Redfern, PJ Wheeler, RE Needham, SR Johnson, NJ Joyce, AG Hazlerigg, GJ Adey, DJ Forfar.
Scorer – PG: Hare
Referee: RC Quittenton

1978–9
Semi-finals: Gosforth 3, Moseley 6
Wasps 7, Leicester 43
Final: LEICESTER 15 MOSELEY 12
LEICESTER: WH Hare; M Newton, T Burwell, PW Dodge, RC Barnwell; L Cusworth, S Kenney; SP Redfern, PJ Wheeler (capt), RJ Cowling, SR Johnson, NJ Joyce, AG Hazlerigg, GJ Adey, IR Smith
Scorers – T: Kenney *C:* Hare *PG:* Hare (2) *DG:* Hare
MOSELEY: R Akenhead; A Thomas, MK Swain, BJ Corless, R Laird; MJ Cooper (capt), CJ Gifford; KJ Astley, GNK Cox, WH Greaves, NC Jeavons, R Field, B Ayre, DR Nutt, JD Beale
Replacements: A Watson-Jones (for Corless after 30 mins), S King (for Nutt after 50 mins).
Scorers – T: Laird *C:* Akenhead *PG:* Akenhead *DG:* Cooper
Referee: A Welsby

1979–80
Semi-finals: Harlequins 9, Leicester 16
Rosslyn Park 6, London Irish 6
London Irish won on 'away team' rule
Final: LEICESTER 21, LONDON IRISH 9
LEICESTER: WH Hare, RC Barnwell, CR Woodward, PW Dodge, TR Burwell; L Cusworth, S Kenney; SP Redfern, PJ Wheeler (capt), RJ Cowling, SR Johnson, NJ Joyce, NK Gillingham, GJ Adey, IR Smith.
Scorers – *PG:* Hare (4) *DG:* Cusworth (2), Hare
LONDON IRISH: DA Leopold; R McKibbin, AR McKibbin, P O'Donnell, CA Meanwell; HC Condon, BW Murphy; L White, GG Beringer, JA Newberry, JB O'Driscoll (capt), JM Sheehan, MJ Smythe, KS Short, W Jones.
Scorers – T: Smythe *C:* Meanwell *PG:* Meanwell
Referee: CJ High

1980–81
Semi-finals: London Scottish 12, Leicester 18 (a.e.t.)
Gosforth 24, Moseley 3
Final: LEICESTER 22, GOSFORTH 15
LEICESTER: WH Hare, K Williams, PW Dodge, CR Woodward, RC Barnwell; L Cusworth, S Kenney; SP Redfern, PJ Wheeler (capt), RJ Cowling, SR Johnson, NJ Joyce, N Jackson, GJ Adey, IR Smith.
Scorers – T: Kenney, Barnwell, Hare *C:* Hare (2) *PG:* Hare (2)
GOSFORTH: B Patrick; JS Archer, RW Breakey, AJ MacMillan, NH McDowell; D Johnson, M Young; JAH Bell, R Cunningham, C. White (capt), SM Smith, TC Roberts, S Bainbridge, JL Butler, TR Anderson.
Scorers – T: Cunningham *C:* Johnson *PG:* Johnson (2), Patrick
Referee: RC Quittenton

1981–2
Semi-finals: Moseley 12, Leicester 4
Coventry 9, Gloucester 18
Final: GLOUCESTER 12, MOSELEY 12 (After extra time: title shared)
GLOUCESTER: P Ford; P Pritchard, PA Taylor, SG Parsloe, RR Mogg; L Jones, SJW Baker; PJ Blakeway, SGF Mills (capt), M Preedy, J Gadd, SB Boyle, J Orwin, M Teague, M Longstaff
Replacements: GAF Sargent (for Preedy after 40 mins), P Wood (for Longstaff after 65 mins).
Scorers – PG: Ford (4)
MOSELEY: MJ Cooper; JM Goodwin, JE Desborough, DW Shorrock, RD Lawson; MH Perry, IS Sutherland; SD Adcaster, GNJ Cox, TF Corless, DG Warren, JS Davidson, A Recardo, DR Nutt (capt), NC Jeavons.
Scorers – PG: Perry (3) *DG:* Perry
Referee: RC Quittenton

1982–3
Semi-finals: Coventry 3, Bristol 23
London Scottish 9, Leicester 30
Final: BRISTOL 28, LEICESTER 22
BRISTOL: IH Duggan; AJG Morley, RA Knibbs, ST Hogg, JF Carr; S Barnes, RM Harding; RJ Doubleday, MK Bogira, A Shepard, P Polledri, NJC Pomphrey, AH Troughton, R Hesford, M Rafter (capt).
Replacement: DJ Palmer (for Bogira after 29 mins)
Scorers – T: Carr (2), Hogg, Hesford *C:* Barnes (3) *PG:* Barnes
LEICESTER: I Dobson; B Evans, PW Dodge, CR Woodward, RC Barnwell; L Cusworth, NC Youngs; SB Redfern, PJ Wheeler, SP Redfern, SR Johnson (capt), MV Foulkes-Arnold, NK Gillingham, IR Smith, D Richards.
Replacement: I Bates (for Barnwell after 37 mins)
Scorers – T: Evans, Smith *C:* Cusworth *PG:* Cusworth (4)
Referee: RC Quittenton

1983–4
Semi-finals: Bristol 21, Harlequins 18
Nottingham 3, Bath 12
Final: BATH 10, BRISTOL 9
BATH: CR Martin; DM Trick, JA Palmer, A Rees, B Trevaskis; JP Horton, RJ Hill; GJ Chilcott, R Cunningham, MR Lee, N Gaymond, NC Redman, RA Spurrell (capt), JP Hall, PD Simpson.
Scorers – T: Simpson *PG:* Palmer *DG:* Horton
BRISTOL: PC Cue; AJG Morley, RA Knibbs, ST Hogg, JF Carr; S Barnes, RM Harding; RJ Doubleday, DJ Palmer, A Sheppard, P Polledri, NJC Pomphrey, PJ Stiff, M Rafter (capt), DL Chidgey.
Scorers – T: Harding *C:* Barnes *PG:* Barnes
Referee: RC Quittenton

1984–5
Semi-finals: Coventry 10, London Welsh 10*
Gloucester 11, Bath 12
*London Welsh won on 'more tries' rule
Final: BATH 24, LONDON WELSH 15
BATH: CR Martin; DM Trick, JA Palmer, SJ Halliday, B Trevaskis; JP Horton, RJ Hill; GJ Chilcott, G Bess, MR Lee, N Gaymond, NC Redman, RA Spurrell (capt), JP Hall, PD Simpson
Replacement: JC Guscott (for Trevaskis after 40 mins).
Scorers – T: Trick, Chilcott *C:* Palmer (2) *PG:* Palmer (4)
LONDON WELSH: M Ebsworth; J Hughes, RA Ackerman, D Fouhy, CFW Rees (capt); C Price, MHJ Douglas; TW Jones, B Light, B Bradley, E Lewis, J Collins, S Russell, M Watkins, K Bowring.
Scorers – PG: Price (5)
Referee: RC Quittenton

1985–6
Semi-finals: Leicester 6, Bath 10
Wasps 11, London Scottish 3
Final: BATH 25, WASPS 17
BATH: CR Martin; DM Trick, JA Palmer (capt), SJ Halliday, AH Swift; S Barnes, RJ Hill; GJ Chilcott, G Dawe, MR Lee, JSC Morrison, NC Redman, RA Spurrell, JP Hall, PD Simpson.
Scorers – T: Swift, Spurrell, Hill, Simpson *C:* Trick (3) *PG:* Trick
WASPS: NC Stringer; ST Smith, RM Cardus (capt), R Pellow, MD Bailey; GL Rees, SM Bates; G Holmes, A Simmons, JA Probyn, J Bonner, MCF Pinnegar, M Rigby, D Pegler, MA Rose.
Replacement: P Balcombe (for Bates after 36 mins).
Scorers – T: Stringer, Pellow, Balcombe *C:* Stringer *PG:* Stringer
Referee: FA Howard

1986–7
Semi-finals: Orrell 7, Bath 31
Wasps 13, Leicester 6
Final: BATH 19, WASPS 12
BATH: CR Martin; AH Swift, JA Palmer, SJ Halliday, B Trevaskis; S Barnes, RJ Hill (capt); DMB Sole, RGR Dawe, GJ Chilcott, JSC Morrison, NC Redman, A Robinson, JP Hall, DW Egerton.
Replacements: JC Guscott (for Swift after 45 mins), G Bess (for Dawe after 25 mins).
Scorers – T: Redman (2), Halliday *C:* Barnes (2) *PG:* Barnes
WASPS: GH Davies; ST Smith, KG Simms, RAP Lozowski, MD Bailey; CR Andrew, SM Bates; PAG Rendall, A Simmons, JA Probyn, MCF Pinnegar, J Bonner, MA Rigby, DJ Pegler (capt), MA Rose.
Scorers – T: Davies *C:* Andrew *PG:* Andrew *DG:* Andrew
Referee: FA Howard

1987–8
Semi-finals: Harlequins 20, Wasps 16 after extra time
Bristol 34, Moseley 6
Final: HARLEQUINS 28, BRISTOL 22
HARLEQUINS: SE Thresher; AT Harriman, JLB Salmon, WDC Carling, EG Davis; AL Thompson, RHQB Moon; PS Curtis, CJ Olver (capt), AR Mullins, NGB Edwards, PJ Ackford, MG Skinner, TP Bell, RS Langhorn.
Scorers – T: Carling (2), Harriman *C:* Thresher, Salmon *PG:* Salmon (3), Thresher
BRISTOL: JM Webb; JF Carr, RA Knibbs, DG Thomas, IH Duggan; ST Hogg, RM Harding; CA Phillips, DJ Palmer, RJ Doubleday, NJC Pomphrey (capt), AG Blackmore, AF Dun, W Hone, P Collings.
Scorers – T: Duggan, penalty try *C:* Webb *PG:* Webb (3) *DG:* Knibbs
Referee: FA Howard

1988–9
Semi-finals: Bath 6, Gloucester 3
Leicester 16, Harlequins 7
Final: BATH 10, LEICESTER 6
BATH: JA Palmer; AH Swift, SJ Halliday, JC Guscott, FK Sagoe; S Barnes (capt), RJ Hill; GJ Chilcott, RGR Dawe, MR Lee, JSC Morrison, DF Cronin, RA Robinson, JP Hall, DW Egerton.
Replacement: PD Simpson for Egerton (52 mins)
Scorers – T: Barnes *PG:* Barnes (2)
LEICESTER: WH Hare; BJ Evans, PW Dodge (capt). I Bates, R Underwood; L Cusworth, A Kardooni; S Redfern, T Thacher, WP Richardson, MV Foulkes-Arnold, T Smith, JM Wells, IR Smith, D Richards.
Scorers – PG: Hare (2)
Referee: FA Howard

1989–90
Semi-finals: Bath 21, Moseley 7
Gloucester 17, Northampton 12
Final: BATH 48, GLOUCESTER 6
BATH: J Callard; AH Swift, SJ Halliday, JC Guscott, A Adebayo; S Barnes (capt), RJ Hill; VE Ubogu, RGR Dawe, GJ Chilcott, NC Redman, DF Cronin, RA Robinson, DW Egerton, K Withey.
Replacement: S Knight for Hill (70 mins)
Scorers – T: Swift (2), Withey, Guscott, Callard, Dawe, Redman, Ubogu *C:* Barnes (4), Halliday *PG:* Barnes (2)
GLOUCESTER: T Smith; D Morgan, D Caskie, R Mogg, J Breeze; M Hamlin (capt), M Hannaford; M Preedy, K Dunn, R Pascall, N Scrivens, J Brain, J Gadd, MC Teague, I Smith
Scorers – T: Dunn *C:* T Smith
Referee: FA Howard

1990–91
Semi-finals: Harlequins 22, Nottingham 18*
*after extra time
Northampton 18, Orrell 10
Final: HARLEQUINS 25, NORTHAMPTON 13
HARLEQUINS: S Thresher; AT Harriman, WDC Carling, SJ Halliday, E Davis; D Pears, R Glenister; J Leonard, BC Moore, A Mullins, T Coker, PJ Ackford, MG Skinner, R Langhorn, PJ Winterbottom (capt).
Scorers – T: Langhorn, Harriman, Halliday, Glenister *C:* Pears (3) *PG:* Pears
NORTHAMPTON: I Hunter; F Packman, J Thame, P Moss, H Thorneycroft; J Steele, R Nancekivell; G Baldwin, CJ Olver, GS Pearce (capt), C Hall, J Etheridge, P Alston, T Rodber, P Pask.
*Replacements:*B Ward for Packman, D Elkington for Nancekivell

Damien Cronin wins a line-out for Bath during their Pilkington Cup Final record win, 48–6 against Gloucester in 1990.

Scorers – T: Moss *PG:* Steele (3)
Referee: E Morrison

1991–2
Semi-finals: Harlequins 15, Leicester 9
Gloucester 18, Bath 27 after extra time
Final: BATH 15, HARLEQUINS 12 *after extra time*
BATH: JM Webb; AH Swift, PR de Glanville, JC Guscott, JA Fallon; S Barnes, RJ Hill; GJ Chilcott, RGR Dawe, VE Obogu; M Haag, NC Redman; RA Robinson (capt), S Ojomoh, BB Clarke
Scorers – T: de Glanville *C:* Webb *PG:* Webb (2) *DG:* Barnes
HARLEQUINS: D Pears; MA Wedderburn, SJ Halliday, WDC Carling, EG Davis; AP Challinor, TC Luxton; MJ Hobley, BC Moore, AR Mullins; NGB Edwards, PJ Ackford; MP Russell, PJ Winterbottom (capt), CMA Sheasby
Scorers – T: Winterbottom *C:* Pears *PG:* Pears (2)
Referee: FA Howard

CUP RECORDS

Bath have appeared in **most finals** (7) winning all seven in 1984, 1985, 1986, 1987, 1989, 1990 and 1992.
Leicester were the first club to **win three finals in succession**, from 1979–81, while Bath were the first club to win on **four** consecutive occasions, from 1984–7.
Leicester have appeared in six finals, in 1978, 1979, 1980, 1981, 1983 and 1989 and were the first club to **appear** in four successive finals – they lost their first final in 1978, before winning the next three.

Two players have been in **seven** English Knock-out Cup winning teams – Richard Hill and Gareth Chilcott of Bath have appeared in the winning teams in 1984, 1985, 1986, 1987, 1989, 1990 and 1992. Stuart Barnes (Bristol and Bath) and Simon Halliday (Bath and Harlequins) have also appeared in seven finals – winning on six occasions.

In the final, the most points by a team, the most tries by a team, and the biggest points margin by a team were all set in **1990** when Bath beat Gloucester 48–6, scoring eight tries.

The **most points by a player** in the final is **16** by John Palmer of Bath in the 1985 final – Colyn Price (London Welsh) scored 15 points in the same match. Alan Pearn (Bristol) also scored 15 points in the 1973 final. Both Price and Pearn kicked five penalties, the record for a final.

No individual has scored more than two tries in a final. Three **forwards** have scored tries in the final: David Robinson (flanker) for Gosforth in 1977, Nigel Redman (lock) for Bath in 1990, and Peter Winterbottom (flanker) for Harlequins in 1992.

The **most conversions** in a final is four by Neil Bennett (Bedford) in 1975 and by Stuart Barnes (Bath) in 1990.

The **most dropped goals** in a final is two by Les Cusworth (Leicester) in 1980. Stuart Barnes' dropped goal in 1992 was the last action of the final, which included extra time.

The only **drawn** final was in 1982 when Gloucester and Moseley shared the Cup for six months each.

Three players have been **sent off** in Cup finals – Nigel Horton (lock) by Ron Lewis in 1972 for Moseley; Bob Mordell (flanker) by Norman Sanson in 1977 for Rosslyn Park, and John Gadd (flanker) by Fred Howard in 1990 for Gloucester.

Two finals, thus far, have required **extra time** of 10 minutes each way, in 1991 and 1992.

There have been conflicting opinions (as in Wales) as to the **record attendance** in the Cup final. The 1988–9 figure for the Bath v Leicester final was given as 59300. The current (1992) capacity for Twickenham – to comply with the Taylor Report safety regulations – is 56202.

Two **referees** have taken charge of six finals – Roger Quittenton (Worthing) and Fred Howard (Liverpool).

The **highest score** at any stage of the Cup is Gloucester's 87–6 win over Exeter University in the 1985–6 competition.

COUNTY CHAMPIONSHIP FINALS

1st SYSTEM

1889 Yorkshire, undefeated, declared champions by the Rugby Union
1890 Yorkshire, undefeated, declared champions

2nd SYSTEM

	Champions	**Group Winners**
1891	Lancashire	Gloucestershire, Surrey, Yorkshire
1892	Yorkshire	Kent, Lancashire, Midlands
1893	Yorkshire	Cumberland, Devon, Middlesex
1894	Yorkshire	Gloucestershire, Lancashire, Midlands
1895	Yorkshire	Cumberland, Devon, Midlands

3rd SYSTEM

	Champions	**Runners-Up**	**Venue**
1896	Yorkshire	Surrey	Richmond
1897	Kent	Cumberland	Carlisle
1898	Northumberland	Midlands	Coventry

1899	Devon	Northumberland	Newcastle
1900	Durham	Devon	Exeter
1901	Devon	Durham	West Hartlepool
1902	Durham	Gloucestershire	Gloucester
1903	Durham	Kent	West Hartlepool
1904	Kent	Durham	Blackheath
1905	Durham	Middlesex	West Hartlepool
1906	Devon	Durham	Exeter
1907	Devon/Durham		West Hartlepool and Exeter
1908	Cornwall	Durham	Redruth
1909	Durham	Cornwall	West Hartlepool
1910	Gloucestershire	Yorkshire	Gloucester
1911	Devon	Yorkshire	Headingley
1912	Devon	Northumberland	Devonport
1913	Gloucestershire	Cumberland	Carlisle
1914	Midlands	Durham	Leicester
1915–19	*Suspended owing to First World War*		
1920	Gloucestershire	Yorkshire	Bradford

4th SYSTEM

	Winners		**Runners-Up**	**Venue**
1921	Gloucestershire	31–4	Leicestershire	Gloucester
1922	Gloucestershire	19–0	North Midlands	Birmingham
1923	Somerset	8–6	Leicestershire	Bridgwater
1924	Cumberland	14–3	Kent	Carlisle
1925	Leicestershire	14–6	Gloucestershire	Bristol
1926	Yorkshire	15–14	Hampshire	Bradford
1927	Kent	22–12	Leicestershire	Blackheath
1928	Yorkshire	12–8	Cornwall	Bradford
1929	Middlesex	9–8 *–*	Lancashire	Twickenham, Blundellsands
1930	Gloucestershire	13–7	Lancashire	Blundellsands
1931	Gloucestershire	10–9	Warwickshire	Gloucester
1932	Gloucestershire	9–3	Durham	Blaydon
1933	Hampshire	18–7	Lancashire	Boscombe
1934	East Midlands	10–0	Gloucestershire	Northampton
1935	Lancashire	14–0	Somerset	Bath
1936	Hampshire	13–6	Northumberland	Gosforth
1937	Gloucestershire	5–0	East Midlands	Bristol
1938	Lancashire	24–12	Surrey	Blundellsands
1939	Warwickshire	8–3	Somerset	Weston-super-Mare
1940–6	*Suspended owing to Second World War*			
1947	Lancashire	14–3	Gloucestershire	Gloucester
1948	Lancashire	5–0	Eastern Counties	Cambridge
1949	Lancashire	9–3	Gloucestershire	Blundellsands
1950	Cheshire	5–0	East Midlands	Birkenhead Park
1951	East Midlands	10–0	Middlesex	Northampton
1952	Middlesex	9–6	Lancashire	Twickenham
1953	Yorkshire	11–3	East Midlands	Bradford
1954	Middlesex	24–6	Lancashire	Blundellsands
1955	Lancashire	14–8	Middlesex	Twickenham
1956	Middlesex	13–9	Devon	Twickenham
1957	Devon	12–3	Yorkshire	Plymouth
1958	Warwickshire	16–8	Cornwall	Coventry
1959	Warwickshire	14–9	Gloucestershire	Bristol
1960	Warwickshire	9–6	Surrey	Coventry
1961	Cheshire	0–0	Devon	Plymouth
	Cheshire	5–3	Devon	Birkenhead Park
1962	Warwickshire	11–6	Hampshire	Twickenham
1963	Warwickshire	13–10	Yorkshire	Coventry
1964	Warwickshire	8–6	Lancashire	Coventry
1965	Warwickshire	15–9	Durham	Hartlepool
1966	Middlesex	6–0	Lancashire	Blundellsands
1967	Durham	14–14, 0–0 *Championship shared*	Surrey	Twickenham/Durham

1968	Middlesex	9–6	Warwickshire	Twickenham
1969	Lancashire	11–9	Cornwall	Redruth
1970	Staffordshire	11–9	Gloucestershire	Burton-on-Trent
1971	Surrey	14–3	Gloucestershire	Gloucester
1972	Gloucestershire	11–6	Warwickshire	Coventry
1973	Lancashire	17–12	Gloucestershire	Blundellsands
1974	Gloucestershire	22–12	Lancashire	Blundellsands
1975	Gloucestershire	13–9	Eastern Counties	Gloucester
1976	Gloucestershire	24–9	Middlesex	Richmond
1977	Lancashire	17–6	Middlesex	Blundellsands
1978	North Midlands	10–7	Gloucestershire	Moseley
1979	Middlesex	19–6	Northumberland	Twickenham
1980	Lancashire	21–15	Gloucestershire	Vale of Lune
1981	Northumberland	15–6	Gloucestershire	Gloucester
1982	North Midlands	13–7	Lancashire	Moseley
1983	Gloucestershire	19–7	Yorkshire	Bristol
1984	Gloucestershire	36–18	Somerset	Twickenham
1983	Middlesex	12–9	Notts, Lincs and Derby	Twickenham
1986	Warwickshire	16–6	Kent	Twickenham
1987	Yorkshire	22–11	Middlesex	Twickenham
1988	Lancashire	23–18	Warwickshire	Twickenham
1989	Durham	13–9	Cornwall	Twickenham
1990	Lancashire	32–9	Middlesex	Twickenham
1991	Cornwall	29–20	Yorkshire	Twickenham
1992	Lancashire	9–6	Cornwall	Twickenham

COUNTY CHAMPIONSHIP RECORDS

Most points in a season
253 Lancashire 1979–80
Most tries in a season
42 Lancashire 1979–80
Most county career points
462 Peter Butler (Gloucestershire)

Most wins
15 Gloucestershire, Lancashire
Highest score in final
36–18 Glos v Somerset, 1984
Most points in final
24 PE Butler, Gloucestershire, 1976

In 1912 Devon set three final records – the biggest winning points margin (29), the most tries (7) and the most tries by a player (4 by PJ Baker).

FRANCE

FOUNDATION: 1920
Honours: 1987 World Cup runners-up
Grand Slam: 1968, 1977, 1981, 1987
International Championship: 9 (outright)
Most points: 334 D Camberabero, 265 J-P Romeu, 225 S Blanco
Most tries: 38 S Blanco, 25 P Sella, 20 P Lagisquet
Largest victory: 70–12 v Zimbabwe 1987
Heaviest defeat: Points 14–49 v Wales 1910
Margin 5–47 v Wales 1909
Clubs: 1782
Players: 218 500 *Population:* 55 324 000
Main stadia: Parc des Princes, Paris (cap: 49 500), Stade Municipal, Toulouse (35 000). Football stadia at Nantes (52 500), Strasbourg (48 500) and Lille (36 500) have been used for recent internationals.
Colours: Blue shirts, white shorts
Headquarters: Federation Francaise de Rugby
7 Cite d'Antin
75009 Paris

EARLY MILESTONES

1870 First recorded game in France played by English students at Le Havre.
1877 First recorded game in Paris, again played by English students.
1885 French team tour Britain and play the Civil Service at Dulwich, London.
1892 First French Championship final – Racing Club de France beat Stade Francais 4–3 in a match refereed by the founder of the modern Olympic movement, Baron Pierre de Coubertin.
1899 First French champions from the provinces – Stade Bordelais UC from Bordeaux.
1904 France introduce Rugby at the Olympic Games.
1906 First official international on January 1 – France lose 38–6 to New Zealand at Parc des Princes, Paris.
1910 France join the four Home Nations in the International Championship.
1911 France beat Scotland 16–15 at Stade Colombes, Paris to record their first international victory.
1920 FFR (Federation de France Rugby) founded.

Serge Blanco homing in on the Welsh defence – his 38 tries in internationals are a record for France.

INTERNATIONAL RECORDS

Most capped player

S Blanco	93	1980–91

In individual positions

Full back		
S Blanco	81 (93)[1]	1980–91
Wing		
P Lagisquet	46	1983–92
Centre		
P Sella	75 (82)[2]	1982–92
Fly-half		
J-P Romeu	33 (34)[3]	1972–77
Scrum-half		
P Berbizier	56	1981–91
Prop		
R Paparemborde	55	1975–83
Hooker		
P Dintrans	50	1979–90
Lock		
J Condom	61	1982–90
Flanker		
J-P Rives	59	1975–84
No. 8		
G Basquet	33	1945–52

[1] Blanco played 12 games as a wing
[2] Sella has won 6 caps as a wing, and one as a full-back
[3] Romeu was capped once as a replacement full-back

FRENCH CHAMPIONSHIP FINALS

The French Championship has one consistent theme – that it has a final each season at the Parc des Princes. Quite how clubs qualify is another matter, the system changes virtually every season. The rough format is for teams to play in leagues at the start of the season, the qualifiers then moving into knockout stages. The number of leagues, number of qualifiers, and format of the knockout stages, change with bewildering regularity.

The championship began in 1892, making it perhaps the oldest senior club competition in the world.

1892 Racing Club de France 4, Stade Francais 3
1893 Stade Francais 7, Racing Club de France 3
1894 Stade Francais 18, Inter-Nos 0
1895 Stade Francais 16, Paris Olympique 0
1896 Paris Olympique 12, Stade Francais 0
1897 Stade Francais won group
1898 Stade Francais won group
1899 Stade Bordelais UC 5, Stade Francais 3
1900 Racing Club de France 37, Stade Bordelais UC 3
1901 Stade Francais beat Stade Bordelais UC on disqualification
1902 Racing Club de France 6, Stade Bordelais UC 0
1903 Stade Francais 16, Stade Toulousain 8
1904 Stade Bordelais UC 3, Stade Francais 0
1905 Stade Bordelais UC 12, Stade Francais 3
1906 Stade Bordelais UC 9, Stade Francais 0
1907 Stade Bordelais UC 14, Stade Francais 3
1908 Stade Francais 16, Stade Bordelais UC 3
1909 Stade Bordelais UC 17, Stade Toulousain 0
1910 FC Lyon 13, Stade Bordelais UC 8
1911 Stade Bordelais UC 14, SCUF 0
1912 Stade Toulousain 8, Racing Club de France 6
1913 Bayonne 31, SCUF 8
1914 Perpignan 8, Tarbes 7
1920 Tarbes 8, Racing Club de France 3

1921 Perpignan 5, Stade Toulousain 0
1922 Stade Toulousain 6, Bayonne 0
1923 Stade Toulousain 3, Bayonne 0
1924 Stade Toulousain 3, Perpignan 0
1925 Perpignan 5, Carcassonne 0
1926 Stade Toulousain 11, Perpignan 0
1927 Stade Toulousain 19, Stade Francais 9
1928 Pau 6, Quillan 4
1929 Quillan 11, Lezignan 8
1930 Agen 4, Quillan 0
1931 Toulon 6, Lyon OU 3
1932 Lyon OU 9, Narbonne 3
1933 Lyon OU 10, Narbonne 3
1934 Bayonne 13, Bairritz 8
1935 Biarritz 3, Perpignan 0
1936 Narbonne 6, Montferrand 3
1937 Vienne 13, Montferrand 7
1938 Perpignan 11, Biarritz 6
1939 Biarritz 6, Perpignan 0
1943 Bayonne 3, Agen 0
1944 Perpignan 20, Bayonne 5
1945 Agen 7, Lourdes 3
1946 Pau 11, Lourdes 0
1947 Stade Toulousain 10, Agen 3
1948 Lourdes 11, Toulon 3
1949 Castres 14, Mont de Marsan 3
1950 Castres 11, Racing Club de France 8
1951 Carmaux 14, Tarbes 12
1952 Lourdes 20, Perpignan 11
1953 Lourdes 21, Mont de Marsan 16
1954 Grenoble 5, Cognac 3
1955 Perpignan 11, Lourdes 6
1956 Lourdes 20, Dax 0
1957 Lourdes 16, Racing Club de France 13
1958 Lourdes 25, Mazamet 8
1959 Racing Club de France 8, Mont de Marsan 3
1960 Lourdes 14, Beziers 11
1961 Beziers 6, Dax 3
1962 Agen 14, Beziers 11
1963 Mont de Marsan 9, Dax 6
1964 Pau 14, Beziers 0
1965 Agen 15, Brive 8
1966 Agen 9, Dax 8
1967 Montauban 11, Begles 3
1968 Lourdes 9, Toulon 9 (Lourdes won on tries)
1969 Begles 11, Stade Toulousain 9
1970 La Voulte 3, Montferrand 0
1971 Beziers 15, Toulon 9
1972 Beziers 9, Brive 0
1973 Tarbes 18, Dax 12
1974 Beziers 16, Narbonne 14
1975 Beziers 13, Brive 12
1976 Agen 13, Beziers 10
1977 Beziers 12, Perpignan 4
1978 Beziers 31, Montferrand 9
1979 Narbonne 10, Bagneres 0
1980 Beziers 10, Stade Toulousain 6
1981 Beziers 22, Bagneres 13
1982 Agen 18, Bayonne 9
1983 Beziers 14, Nice 6
1984 Beziers 21, Agen 21*
1985 Stade Toulousain 36, Toulon 22 (after extra time)
1986 Stade Toulousain 16, Agen 6
1987 Toulon 15, Racing Club de France 12
1988 Agen 9, Tarbes 3
1989 Toulouse 18, Toulon 12
1990 Racing Club de France 22, Agen 12
1991 Belges-Bordeaux 19, Toulouse 10
1992 Toulon 19, Biarritz 14

IRELAND

FOUNDATION: 1874 and 1879
Honours: Grand Slam 1948
International Championship: 10 (outright)
Triple Crown: 6
Most points: 308 MJ Kiernan, 243 SO Campbell
Most tries: 15 BJ Mullin, 14 GV Stephenson
Largest victory: 60–0 v Romania 1986
Heaviest defeat: 6–59 v New Zealand 1992
Players: 12 500
Population: 3 515 000
Main stadia: Lansdowne Road, Dublin (cap: 54 500), Ravenhill, Belfast (11 500)
Colours: Green jerseys, white shorts
Headquarters: Irish Rugby Football Union
62 Lansdowne Road
Dublin 4
Republic of Ireland

MILESTONES

1807 William Webb Ellis born in Manchester, his father was a member of the First Dragoon Guards stationed in Ireland at the time.
1854 Trinity College, Dublin founded – first Irish club. The first secretary was RH Scott who was educated at Rugby School. Trinity was the second oldest rugby club in the world.
1868 Trinity College set up their own rules – one of the compilers was Charles Barrington, a relative of Jonah Barrington, former world number one squash player.
1874 Irish Rugby Union formed in Dublin, but Ulster were not informed as to the whereabouts of the meeting, and so did not join. Somewhat miffed, Ulster attempted to play to their own rules, but with little seriousness.
1875 Ireland's first international was played against England at the Oval with the 'moral assistance' of Ulster on February 19.
1878 Lansdowne Road used for internationals, two years after it was first used as an international athletics venue.
1879 Ireland's 'second' foundation, this time including Ulster. This led to two centenaries being celebrated – in 1974 and again in 1979.
1882 Leinster Senior Cup began.
1885 Ulster Senior Cup began.
1886 Munster provincial Cup began.
1896 Connacht Cup began.
1948 Ireland win Grand Slam for first time (and only time to date).
1949 Ireland complete a two year record of winning seven out of eight Five Nations matches, bringing two Triple Crowns and a Grand Slam.
1974 Willie John McBride captains British Lions on unbeaten tour of South Africa. Retired with world record number of caps, later overtaken by team mate Mike Gibson.
1990 First All Ireland league competition. Prior to that, all league competitions were organised by the four provinces, Ulster, Leinster, Munster and Connacht.

ALL IRELAND CHAMPIONSHIP

1990–91

	P	W	D	L	F	A	Pts
Cork Constitution	8	7	0	1	119	78	14
Garryowen	8	6	0	2	120	76	12
Lansdowne	8	6	0	2	133	99	12
Shannon	8	5	0	3	108	99	10
Ballymena	8	3	1	4	113	115	7
Instonians	8	3	1	4	99	116	7
St Mary's College	8	2	0	6	91	106	4
Wanderers	8	2	0	6	83	112	4
Malone	8	1	0	7	80	145	2

1991–92

	P	W	D	L	F	A	Pts
Garryowen	8	7	0	1	162	91	14
Shannon	8	5	1	2	101	88	11
Ballymena	8	5	1	2	101	96	11
Old Wesley	8	4	0	4	83	91	8
Young Munster	8	3	1	4	71	72	7
St Mary's College	8	3	0	5	78	78	6
Cork Constitution	8	3	0	5	100	112	6
Lansdowne	8	2	1	5	93	92	5
Instonians	8	2	0	6	68	137	4

Michael Kiernan, Ireland's record points scorer.

INTERNATIONAL RECORDS

Most capped player

CMH Gibson	69	1964–79

In individual positions

Full-back

TJ Kiernan	54	1960–73

Wing

KD Crossan	41	1982–92

Centre

BJ Mullin	45	1984–92

Fly-half

JW Kyle	46	1947–58

Scrum-half

M Sugden	28	1925–31

Prop

PA Orr	58	1976–87

Hooker

KW Kennedy	45	1965–75

Lock

WJ McBride	63	1962–75

Flanker

JF Slattery	61	1970–84

No. 8

WP Duggan	39 (41)[1]	1975–84

[1] Duggan won 2 caps as a flanker

SENIOR CUP

Before the advent of the All Ireland League, the Senior Cups were the most prestigious club competitions. The Cups will remain an integral part of the Irish club season.

Team	Wins	Years
Leinster		
Trinity	21	1882, 1883, 1884, 1886, 1887, 1890, 1893, 1895, 1896, 1897, 1898, 1900, 1905, 1907, 1908, 1912, 1913, 1920, 1921, 1926, 1960
Wanderers	12	1885, 1888, 1894, 1906, 1922, 1947, 1954, 1973, 1978, 1982, 1984, 1990
Bective Rangers	12	1889, 1892, 1910, 1914, 1923, 1925, 1932, 1934, 1935, 1955, 1956, 1962
Lansdowne	21	1891, 1901, 1903, 1904, 1922, 1927, 1928, 1929, 1930, 1931, 1933, 1949, 1950, 1953, 1972, 1979, 1980, 1981, 1986, 1989, 1991
Monkstown	2	1899, 1902
Old Wesley	2	1909, 1985
University College	7	1924, 1938, 1948, 1963, 1964, 1970, 1977
Clontarf	1	1936
Blackrock College	8	1937, 1939, 1957, 1961, 1975, 1983, 1988, 1992
Old Belvedere	10	1940, 1941, 1942, 1943, 1944, 1945, 1946, 1951, 1952, 1968
St Mary's College	5	1958, 1969, 1971, 1974, 1987
Terenure College	2	1966, 1967
Ulster		
NIFC	18	1885, 1893, 1894, 1895, 1896, 1897, 1898, 1899, 1901, 1902, 1908, 1920, 1930, 1935, 1939, 1955, 1969, 1973
Queen's University	21	1886, 1887, 1890, 1891, 1892, 1900, 1903, 1909, 1912, 1921, 1924, 1925, 1932, 1933, 1936, 1937, 1947, 1951, 1959, 1960, 1981
Lisburn	1	1888
Albion	1	1889
Malone	7	1904, 1905, 1907, 1971, 1984, 1988, 1992
Collegians	7	1910, 1913, 1926, 1952, 1961, 1962, 1983
Knock	1	1911
Instonians	18	1922, 1923, 1927, 1928, 1929, 1931, 1934, 1938, 1946, 1948, 1949, 1950, 1954, 1956, 1957, 1958, 1965, 1979
CIYMS	6	1953, 1966, 1967, 1972, 1974, 1978
Ballymena	7	1963, 1970, 1975, 1977, 1989, 1990, 1991
Dungannon	2	1964, 1968
Bangor	3	1980, 1982, 1986
Ards	2	1985, 1987
Munster		
Bandon	1	1886
Queen's College	5	1887, 1888, 1897, 1900, 1901
Garryowen	31	1889, 1890, 1891, 1892, 1893, 1894, 1895, 1896, 1898, 1899, 1902, 1903, 1904, 1909, 1911, 1914, 1920, 1924, 1925, 1926, 1932, 1934, 1940, 1947, 1952, 1954, 1969, 1971, 1974, 1975, 1979
Cork Constitution	22	1905, 1906, 1907, 1910, 1922, 1923, 1929, 1933, 1942, 1943, 1946, 1957, 1961, 1963, 1964, 1967, 1970, 1972, 1973, 1983, 1985, 1989
University College, Cork	12	1912, 1913, 1935, 1936, 1937, 1939, 1941, 1950, 1951, 1955, 1965, 1981
Dolphin	6	1921, 1931, 1944, 1945, 1948, 1956
Bohemians	4	1927, 1958, 1959, 1962
Young Munster	5	1930, 1938, 1980, 1984, 1990
Sunday's Well	2	1949, 1953
Shannon	9	1960, 1977, 1978, 1982, 1986, 1987, 1988, 1991, 1992
Highfield	2	1966, 1968
Connacht		
Galway Town	5	1896, 1906, 1911, 1913, 1922
Queen's College, Galway	7	1897, 1899, 1903, 1904, 1905, 1907, 1908
Galway Grammar, School	1	1898
University College, Galway	27	1909, 1910, 1912, 1923, 1924, 1925, 1930, 1932, 1935, 1936, 1937, 1939, 1940, 1942, 1944, 1945, 1946, 1953, 1961, 1962, 1964, 1966, 1967, 1970, 1974, 1987, 1989
Sligo Town	1	1914
Galwegians	23	1926, 1927, 1928, 1929, 1938, 1943, 1952, 1956, 1957, 1958, 1959, 1960, 1963, 1965, 1968, 1969, 1971, 1973, 1975, 1980, 1981, 1983, 1986
Loughrea	1	1931
Corinthians	12	1933, 1934, 1941, 1947, 1949, 1954, 1972, 1978, 1982, 1984, 1985, 1988
Ballinsloe	3	1948, 1950, 1992
Ballina	2	1951, 1979
Athlone	4	1966, 1977, 1990, 1991

NEW ZEALAND

FOUNDATION: 1892
Honours: 1987 World Cup winners, 1991 World Cup third
Most points: 533 GJ Fox, 207 DB Clarke, 201 AR Hewson
Most tries: 32 JJ Kirwan, 20 TJ Wright, 19 SS Wilson
Largest victories: Points 74–13 v Fiji 1987
Margin 70–6 v Italy 1987
Heaviest defeats: Points 16–30 v Australia 1978
Margin 0–17 v South Africa 1928
Clubs: 1000
Players: 182 500
Population: 3 107 000
Main stadia: Eden Park, Auckland (cap: 58 000), Lancaster Park, Christchurch (52 500), Athletic Park, Wellington (45 000), Dunedin (35 000)
Colours: All black
Headquarters: New Zealand Rugby Union
PO Box 2172
Wellington

MILESTONES

1870 Match between Nelson College and Nelson Football Club played on May 14, first played under Rugby rules. Formation of first club at Nelson, South Island, by Charles John Munroe (son of the Speaker of the House of Representatives) and others. Munroe had returned from public school at Sherborne (England). On September 12 Nelson beat Wellington at Petone by two goals to one.
1871 Wellington followed by Wanganui (1872) Auckland (1873) Hamilton (1874) – became new rugby playing centres.
1875 First tour – Combined Auckland clubs visited Wellington, Dunedin, Christchurch, Nelson and Taranaki for two week tour.
1879 First Unions formed in Canterbury and Wellington to organise the interests of the clubs in their areas.
1882 First overseas tourists arrived – New South Wales.
1884 First New Zealand team selected for tour of New South Wales. Played 9 Won 9.
1888 First visit to New Zealand by a British team.
1888–9 First tour to Great Britain by New Zealand, who also visited Australia after beginning tour in New Zealand. Still the longest ever tour in rugby history, encompassing 74 matches.
1892 New Zealand Rugby Football Union founded.
1893 First tour by New Zealand under auspices of NZRFU (to Australia).
1897 First North Island v South Island match at Wellington – North winning 16–3.
1902 Ranfurly Shield was presented to the NZRFU by the Governor of New Zealand, the Earl of Ranfurly, for inter provincial competition. Auckland, with an unbeaten record, were declared the first winners of the Shield on September 14. The NZRFU were allowed to make the rules, stipulating that challenges would be accepted by the holder.
1903 First full international played by New Zealand – August 15 at Sydney Cricket Ground after several 'inter colonial matches'. New Zealand won 22–3.
1904 First New Zealand home international on August 13 at Athletic Park, Wellington – beat Great Britain 9–3.
1905–6 First visit to British Isles, France and North America by fully representative New Zealand team – won 34 of 35 matches, losing only to Wales 3–0 at Cardiff in controversial circumstances.
1905 The term 'The All Blacks' coined for the first time by British Press.
1921 First visit by South African team.
1924–5 'The Invincibles' win every match on their tour to Great Britain, France and British Columbia – played and won 32 matches with 868 points to 115.
1926 First radio commentary of a rugby match – George Allardyce commentated live on game between Christchurch and High School Old Boys.
1928 First New Zealand tour of South Africa.
1929 First time that New Zealand lost all matches in an international series – lost to Australia 9–8, 17–9, 15–13.
1931 Lord Bledisloe, the Governor General of New Zealand, donated the Bledisloe Cup for competition between Australia and New Zealand. Lord Bledisloe was Governor General from 1930 to 1934.
1949 New Zealand played six tests – four against South Africa and two against Australia – and lost the lot, including 11–3 to Australia and 9–3 to South Africa both on September 3.
1971 British Lions visit New Zealand and return with a 2–1 win in the four match series with one drawn.
1972 First televised match from overseas – Wales v New Zealand at Cardiff.
1975 National Championship set up with 11 teams in Division 1, and with two second divisions – one on each island.
1987 New Zealand win inaugural World Cup with 29–9 win over France in the final.

FIRST DIVISION RECORDS

The most points scored in a season is 434 points by Auckland in 1984. Auckland also scored a record 70 tries that season . . . The highest points score by a team, and the highest winning margin, is Auckland's 84–3 win against Counties in 1984 . . . The most points scored by an individual in a match is 32 by GJ Cooper (Otago) v Hawke's Bay in 1991. Cooper scored four tries and kicked five conversions and two penalty goals . . . The most tries scored by an individual in a match is 5 by TJ Wright (Auckland) v Manawatu in 1984 and by R Gordon (Waikato) v Southland in 1990 . . . The most penalties kicked by an individual in a match is 8 by KJ Crowley (Taranaki) v North Auckland in 1990 . . . The most points scored in a season by an individual is 176 points by GJ Fox (Auckland) in 1990 . . . The most tries in a season by an individual is 15 tries by TJ Wright (Auckland) in 1984.

Previous page *Richard Loe in the hick of the action for New Zealand luring the opening match of the 1991 World Cup, an 18–12 win for the All Blacks against England.*

Right *Canada v Fiji under floodlights at Bayonne – Sam Domoni jumps best for Fiji.*

Below *England's Jeremy Guscott looks for support against Italy.*

Far right *Swing low . . . English supporters celebrate after the quarter-final win in Paris.*

Below right *Ireland's Phil Matthews hangs on grimly to Australia's fly half Michael Lynagh during the thrilling quarter-final in Dublin.*

Top left *Brian Lima of Western Samoa finds himself held back by Scotland's John Jeffrey.*

Bottom left *Belfast was treated to a fine performance by Japan who beat Zimbabwe 52–8.*

Left *In search of the best view at Otley for the Italy–USA game.*

Below *Star of the tournament David Campese in action against Western Samoa at Pontypool.*

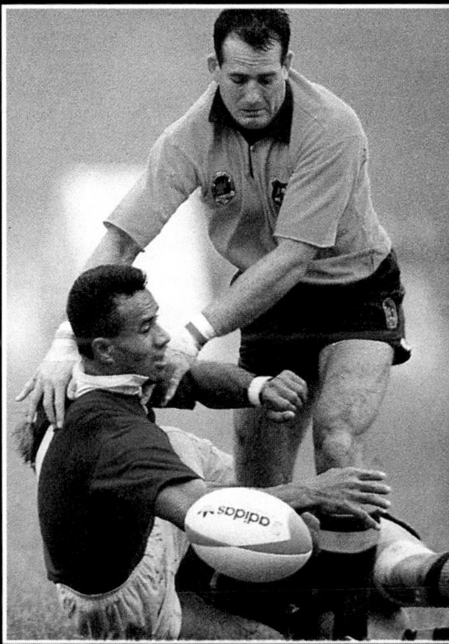

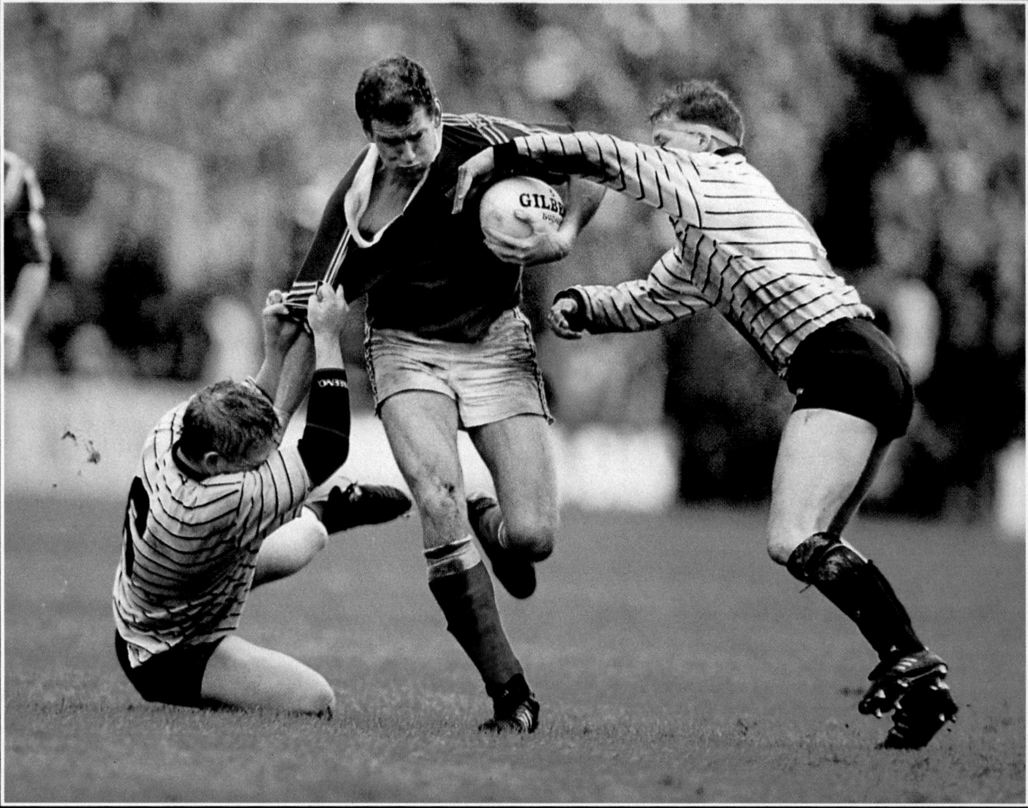

The Five Nations Championship 1992 . . . and another defeat for the French at Murrayfield. Scotland's David McIvor and Andy Nicol bring down Dries Van Heerden.

Wade Dooley scores against Wales to celebrate his 50th appearance for England and seal the Grand Slam. Team-mate Mickey Skinner is first to congratulate him.

Scotland's captain David Sole holds off Stuart Davies at Cardiff Arms Park.

A flying English tackle on Laurent Cabannes at Parc des Princes . . . it can only be Mickey Skinner.

Will Carling bursts past a despairing Welsh tackle as Robert Jones looks on.

A run by Doddie Weir is brought to a halt by Ireland's Mick Galwey. The Scots maintained their recent good record at Lansdowne Road with a win by 18–10.

RANFURLY SHIELD

Though the Ranfurly Shield was presented in 1902, the concept had been born a year earlier with the announcement that the Earl of Ranfurly, the then Governor of New Zealand, had donated a Shield for competition amongst the provincial teams. The NZRFU were asked to accept the Shield and organise their own competition. The Shield was originally meant to be a Cup! Auckland, designated as having the best record in 1902, were first awarded the Shield. The holder accepts challenges from other provinces.

LONGEST TENURE

Auckland	1985–91	48 challenges resisted
Auckland	1960–63	25
Canterbury	1982–85	25
Hawke's Bay	1922–27	24
Auckland	1905–13	23
Canterbury	1953–56	23
Hawke's Bay	1966–69	21

SHORTEST TENURE

Wellington	1973	7 days
Auckland	1972	10
North Auckland	1960	11
Wairarapa	1950	14
South Canterbury	1950	14
Auckland	1952	14

North Auckland resisted one challenge, the other unions were beaten by the first challenger.

BIGGEST WINNING MARGIN

97 points

Auckland 97 Thames Valley 0 in 1986.

INDIVIDUAL PERFORMANCES

Most matches	48	GW Whetton, Auckland
Most points	746	GJ Fox, Auckland
Most tries	46	TJ Wright, Auckland

NATIONAL CHAMPIONSHIP

In 1975 the NZRFU organised a National Championship for the provincial teams. The First Division was selected on the best 11 team records from 1970–5.

Year	Champions	Promoted	Relegated
1976	Bay of Plenty	Taranaki	N Auckland
1977	Canterbury	N Auckland	Marlborough
		S Canterbury	Bay of Plenty
1978	Wellington	Bay of Plenty	Hawke's Bay
1979	Counties	Hawke's Bay	Taranaki
1980	Manawatu	Waikato	S Canterbury
1981	Wellington	Wairarapa Bush	Southland
1982	Auckland	–	–
1983	Canterbury	–	–
1984	Auckland	Southland	Hawke's Bay
1985	Auckland	Taranaki	Waikato
1986	Wellington	Waikato	Southland
1987	Auckland	–	–
1988	Auckland	Hawke's Bay	Manawatu
1989	Auckland	–	–
1990	Auckland	Southland	Hawke's Bay
1991	Otago	King Country	Counties

See overleaf for full tables 1983–91

INTERNATIONAL RECORDS

Most capped player

GW Whetton 58 1981–92

In individual positions

Full-back		
DB Clarke	31	1956–64
Wing		
JJ Kirwan	50	1984–92
Centre (includes 2nd five-eight)		
BJ Robertson	34	1972–81
Fly-half		
GJ Fox	37	1985–92
Scrum-half		
SM Going	29	1967–77
Prop		
SC McDowall	46	1985–92
Hooker		
SBT Fitzpatrick	45	1986–92
Lock		
GW Whetton	58	1981–92
Flanker		
KR Tremain	36 (38)[1]	1959–68
IA Kirkpatrick	36 (39)[2]	1967–77
No. 8		
MG Mexted	34	1979–85

[1] Tremain won 2 caps as a No. 8

[2] Kirkpatrick won 3 caps as a No. 8

NATIONAL CHAMPIONSHIP

1983

	P	W	D	L	F	A	Pts
Canterbury	10	10	0	0	295	109	20
Wellington	10	7	1	2	220	115	15
Auckland	10	6	1	3	164	104	13
Bay of Plenty	10	5	0	5	207	190	10
Counties	10	4	2	4	173	170	10
Waikato	10	5	0	5	161	205	10
Otago	10	4	2	4	124	172	10
Manawatu	10	4	0	6	176	197	8
North Auckland	10	3	0	7	134	160	6
Wairarapa Bush	10	2	1	7	96	206	5
Hawke's Bay	10	1	1	8	101	225	3

1984

	P	W	D	L	F	A	Pts
Auckland	10	9	0	1	434	78	18
Canterbury	10	8	1	1	214	128	17
Otago	10	7	0	3	195	150	14
Wellington	10	7	0	3	288	171	14
Counties	10	5	0	5	183	168	10
Waikato	10	5	0	5	236	231	10
Manawatu	10	4	1	5	112	203	9
North Auckland	10	3	0	7	100	237	6
Wararapa Bush	10	3	0	7	119	227	6
Bay of Plenty	10	2	0	8	110	237	4
Hawke's Bay	10	1	0	9	134	300	2

1986

	P	W	D	L	F	A	Pts
Wellington	10	10	0	0	274	131	40
Auckland	10	9	0	1	308	85	36
Canterbury	10	7	1	2	282	153	31
Otago	10	6	0	4	199	187	25
Bay of Plenty	10	5	0	5	179	214	22
Counties	10	4	0	6	147	234	16
Taranaki	10	3	0	7	189	205	15
North Auckland	10	3	0	7	147	176	13
Wairarapa Bush	10	3	0	7	123	241	13
Manawatu	10	2	1	7	176	225	12
Southland	10	2	0	8	166	339	8

1987

	P	W	D	L	F	A	Pts
Auckland	10	10	0	0	375	90	40
Wellington	10	9	0	1	286	163	36
Otago	10	6	0	4	176	150	27
Bay of Plenty	10	6	0	4	257	228	26
Canterbury	10	5	0	5	201	183	22
Waikato	10	4	1	5	201	227	19
Counties	10	4	0	6	186	244	19
North Auckland	10	4	0	6	180	206	18
Manawatu	10	3	0	7	211	273	14
Taranaki	10	2	0	8	128	302	9

1988

	P	W	D	L	F	A	Pts
Auckland	10	10	0	0	321	114	40
Wellington	10	8	0	2	304	161	34
Otago	10	8	0	2	316	154	32
North Harbour	10	5	1	4	227	187	24
North Auckland	10	5	0	5	237	202	22
Canterbury	10	5	0	5	180	197	22
Counties	10	4	1	5	160	208	19
Waikato	10	4	0	6	174	248	18
Taranaki	10	3	0	7	173	268	14
Bay of Plenty	10	1	0	9	182	282	6
Manawatu	10	1	0	9	84	337	5

1989

	P	W	D	L	F	A	Pts
Auckland	10	9	1	0	348	87	38
Canterbury	10	8	1	1	287	168	34
North Harbour	10	7	1	2	272	164	31
Waikato	10	7	0	3	335	124	29
Otago	10	4	1	5	242	161	21
Bay of Plenty	10	4	1	5	198	231	18
Wellington	10	4	0	6	169	245	17
North Auckland	10	3	1	6	185	255	15
Counties	10	3	0	7	139	319	13
Taranaki	10	2	0	8	156	372	9
Hawke's Bay	10	1	0	9	140	345	4

1990

	P	W	D	L	F	A	Pts
Auckland	10	10	0	0	364	127	40
Waikato	10	8	0	2	364	126	32
Otago	10	8	0	2	245	154	32
Canterbury	10	6	0	4	207	205	25
Wellington	10	5	1	4	205	160	23
North Harbour	10	5	0	5	213	187	22
Bay of Plenty	10	3	2	5	181	214	16
Counties	10	3	1	6	118	205	14
North Auckland	10	2	0	8	142	198	13
Taranaki	10	3	0	7	167	325	12
Southland	10	0	0	10	89	394	0

1991

	P	W	D	L	F	A	Pts
Otago	10	9	0	1	298	119	37
Auckland	10	9	0	1	318	130	36
North Harbour	10	7	0	3	256	138	28
Canterbury	10	6	1	3	252	241	26
Waikato	10	5	0	5	244	248	20
Wellington	10	4	0	6	183	184	18
North Auckland	10	4	0	6	211	218	18
Hawke's Bay	10	3	1	6	170	254	15
Bay of Plenty	10	3	0	7	183	256	14
Taranaki	10	3	0	7	152	249	13
Counties	10	1	0	9	112	302	4

SCOTLAND

FOUNDATION: 1873
Honours: 1991 World Cup fourth
Grand Slam: 1925, 1984, 1990
International Championship: 13 (outright)
Triple Crown: 10
Most points: 420 AG Hastings, 301 AR Irvine (both inc. 28 for British Isles), 210 PW Dods
Most tries: 24 IS Smith, 15 I Tukalo, 14 AG Stanger
Largest victories: Points 60–21 v Zimbabwe 1987 Margin 49–3 v Argentina 1990
Heaviest defeat: 0–44 v South Africa 1951
Clubs: 276
Players: 25 000
Population: 5 125 000
Main stadium: Murrayfield, Edinburgh (cap: 54 250)
Colours: Blue jerseys, white shorts
Headquarters: Scottish Rugby Union
Murrayfield
Edinburgh 12

MILESTONES

1857 Football reported as being played at Glasgow University.
1858 Edinburgh Academicals play a match against a military team. After their first AGM, they print their own set of rules.
1865 West of Scotland formed.
1868 Edinburgh Academicals print their own Green Book of Rules for use by the existing Scottish clubs.
1871 The first international is played at Raeburn Place, Edinburgh, on Monday 27 March 1871 between Scotland and England. The match is won by Scotland by a goal and a try to a try on a ground acquired by the Edinburgh Academy as a cricket ground in 1854.
1873 Scottish Rugby Football Union formed to organise the game in schools and clubs.
1883 First Melrose sevens tournament under auspices of Ned Haig, the local butcher.
1884 The 'game of dispute' with England which ended with a breakdown in fixtures owing to disagreement of what constituted the scoring of tries.
1885 Ireland match abandoned because of appalling conditions.
1887 GC Lindsay scores five tries against Wales – still an international record.
1924 Title changed to Scottish Rugby Union.
1925 Murrayfield opened with a record crowd for the visit of England. Scotland's first Grand Slam.
1959 Undersoil heating introduced to Murrayfield.
1973 League football started in Scotland – the first of the home nations to play league football on a competitive basis.
1984 Scotland's second Grand Slam.
1990 Scotland's third Grand Slam.

The Melrose Sevens tournament, first held in 1883.

INTERNATIONAL RECORDS

Most capped player

JM Renwick	52	1972–84
CT Deans	52	1978–87

In individual positions

Full-back		
AR Irvine	47 (51)[1]	1972–82
Wing		
I Tukalo	37	1985–92
Centre		
JM Renwick	51 (52)[2]	1972–84
Fly-half		
JY Rutherford	42	1979–87
Scrum-half		
RJ Laidlaw	47	1980–88
Prop		
AB Carmichael	50	1967–78
Hooker		
CT Deans	52	1978–87
Lock		
AJ Tomes	48	1976–87
Flanker		
J Jeffrey	40	1984–91
No. 8		
D White	29 (41)[3]	1982–92

[1] Irvine played four matches as a winger
[2] Renwick played once, as a replacement, on the wing [3] White played five games as flanker and seven as lock

Gavin Hastings, Scotland's record points scorer, touches down against Fiji in 1989.

NATIONAL LEAGUE

Scotland were the first of the home nations to adopt a national league structure. The unofficial league was last competed for in 1972–3. The competition was known as the SRU Championship until 1985, when Schweppes took over the sponsorship for one season. McEwan's, the Scottish brewers, took over the sponsorship in 1986.

Division 1

1973–74	P	W	D	L	F	A	Pts
Hawick	11	9	1	1	214	92	19
West of Scotland	11	9	1	1	178	73	19
Gala	10	6	0	4	175	94	12
Glasgow High	11	6	0	5	176	170	12
Edin. Wanderers	11	5	1	5	107	101	11
Melrose	11	5	1	5	120	146	11
Boroughmuir	11	5	0	6	142	114	10
Jordanhill	11	5	0	6	89	105	10
Watsonians	11	4	1	6	125	154	9
Heriot's F.P.	11	4	1	6	139	169	9
Langholm	11	3	2	6	137	192	8
Glasgow Acads	10	0	0	10	52	244	0

1974–75	P	W	D	L	F	A	Pts
Hawick	11	10	0	1	273	77	20
Gala	11	9	0	2	184	102	18
Boroughmuir	11	8	0	3	140	130	16
Heriot's F.P.	11	5	1	5	143	124	11
Watsonians	11	5	1	5	134	136	11
Jordanhill	11	5	0	6	117	116	10
West of Scotland	11	4	1	6	122	119	9
Melrose	11	4	1	6	89	127	9
Kelso	11	4	1	6	121	168	9
Edin. Wanderers	11	4	1	6	117	185	9
Glasgow High	11	4	0	7	97	133	8
Dunfermline	11	1	0	10	72	212	2

1975–76	P	W	D	L	F	A	Pts
Hawick	11	11	0	0	311	86	22
Gala	11	10	0	1	218	123	20
West of Scotland	11	7	1	3	183	96	15
Boroughmuir	11	6	0	5	140	111	12
Langholm	11	6	0	5	145	130	12
Jordanhill	11	5	1	5	185	140	11
Watsonians	11	5	0	6	137	146	10
Kilmarnock	11	4	1	6	115	162	9
Edin. Wanderers	11	4	0	7	121	200	8
Heriot's F.P.	11	3	0	8	113	289	6
Melrose	11	2	0	9	116	203	4
Kelso	11	1	1	9	105	203	3

1976–77	P	W	D	L	F	A	Pts
Hawick*	11	9	0	2	301	115	18
Gala*	11	9	0	2	270	84	18
West of Scotland	11	9	0	2	190	80	18
Kilmarnock	11	7	0	4	197	171	14
Boroughmuir	11	6	1	4	156	121	13
Heriot's F.P.	11	5	2	4	172	143	12
Jordanhill	11	5	0	6	131	126	10
Highlands	11	4	1	6	114	143	9

	P	W	D	L	F	A	Pts
Watsonians	11	3	2	6	148	159	8
Langholm	11	3	0	8	65	232	6
Edin. Wanderers	11	0	0	11	93	293	0

* In a play-off at Melrose Hawick defeated Gala by 15–3.

1977–78	P	W	D	L	F	A	Pts
Hawick	11	10	1	0	324	68	21
Boroughmuir	11	9	1	1	241	95	19
Kilmarnock	11	8	0	3	163	122	16
Heriot's F.P.	11	6	0	5	154	147	12
Langholm	10	5	0	5	118	181	10
West of Scotland	10	4	1	5	123	103	9
Jordanhill	11	3	2	6	104	140	8
Gala	10	4	0	6	139	177	8
Stewart's/Melville	10	4	0	6	127	178	8
Watsonians	11	3	1	7	74	162	7
Melrose	11	3	0	8	123	180	6
Highland	11	2	0	9	86	223	4

1978–79	P	W	D	L	F	A	Pts
Heriot's F.P.	11	10	0	1	246	82	20
Gala	11	8	0	3	150	106	16
Stewart's/Melville	10	7	0	3	144	78	14
Hawick	10	6	0	4	184	115	12
West of Scotland	10	5	1	4	116	92	11
Boroughmuir	11	5	1	5	120	106	11
Kelso	11	5	0	6	139	173	10
Kilmarnock	10	4	1	5	131	129	9
Watsonians	11	4	1	6	97	162	9
Jordanhill	11	3	0	8	133	153	6
Langholm	11	2	1	8	97	215	5
Haddington	11	2	1	8	79	225	5

1979–80	P	W	D	L	F	A	Pts
Gala	11	9	1	1	256	58	19
Heriot's F.P.	11	9	0	2	222	118	18
Hawick	10	7	0	3	223	101	14
Stewart's/Melville	11	6	0	5	140	137	12
Boroughmuir	11	5	1	5	136	171	11
Watsonians	10	3	3	4	92	148	9
Melrose	11	4	1	6	117	206	9
West of Scotland	11	4	0	7	142	149	8
Kelso	11	4	0	7	137	177	8
Kilmarnock	11	4	0	7	99	160	8
Selkirk	11	3	1	7	137	162	7
Jordanhill	11	3	1	7	72	186	7

1980–81	P	W	D	L	F	A	Pts
Gala	11	11	0	0	237	55	22
Heriot's F.P.	11	10	0	1	269	103	20
Hawick	11	6	1	4	246	117	13
West of Scotland	11	6	1	4	167	116	13
Boroughmuir	11	6	1	4	131	142	13
Gordonians	11	5	1	5	156	165	11
Stewart's/Melville	11	4	2	5	121	122	10
Watsonians	11	5	0	6	79	148	10
Kelso	11	4	1	6	153	169	9
Melrose	11	3	1	7	93	155	7
Kilmarnock	11	1	2	8	77	190	4
Langholm	11	0	0	11	39	286	0

1981–82	P	W	D	L	F	A	Pts
Hawick	11	10	0	1	289	115	20
Heriot's F.P.	11	9	1	1	216	117	19
Gala	11	8	0	3	245	102	16
Kelso	11	8	0	3	203	130	16
Boroughmuir	11	6	0	5	154	154	12
Stewart's/Melville	11	5	0	6	210	192	10
Selkirk	11	4	1	6	154	189	9
West of Scotland	11	4	0	7	177	152	8
Watsonians	11	4	0	7	159	176	8
Jed-Forest	11	3	0	8	81	243	6
Melrose	11	2	0	9	96	235	4
Gordonians	11	2	0	9	94	273	4

1982–83	P	W	D	L	F	A	Pts
Gala	13	12	0	1	491	116	24
Hawick	12	11	0	1	355	88	22
Heriot's F.P.	13	10	0	3	259	150	20
Kelso	13	9	0	4	261	138	18
Boroughmuir	13	9	0	4	210	106	18
Stewart's/Melville	12	7	0	5	223	159	14
Selkirk	12	7	0	5	178	156	14
Watsonians	12	7	0	5	189	169	14
West of Scotland	12	5	0	7	193	203	10
Melrose	13	3	2	8	136	201	8
Kilmarnock	13	3	0	10	114	337	6
Jed-Forest	12	2	1	9	113	211	5
Royal High	13	1	1	11	86	339	3
Gordonians	13	0	0	13	57	492	0

1983–84	P	W	D	L	F	A	Pts
Hawick	13	13	0	0	477	53	26
Gala	13	12	0	1	299	75	24
Stewart's/Melville	13	9	0	4	327	151	18
Kelso	13	9	0	4	266	161	18
Heriot's F.P.	12	8	1	3	258	145	17
Watsonians	13	8	0	5	203	190	16
Boroughmuir	12	7	0	5	215	205	14
Selkirk	13	5	0	8	215	222	10
West of Scotland	13	4	0	9	194	303	8
Jed-Forest	13	3	1	9	142	216	7
Melrose	13	3	1	9	118	243	7
Ayr	12	3	1	8	87	310	7
Kilmarnock	13	2	2	9	155	286	6
Haddington	12	0	0	12	64	460	0

1984–85	P	W	D	L	F	A	Pts
Hawick	13	12	0	1	412	132	24
Kelso	12	10	0	2	374	96	20
Heriot's F.P.	12	9	0	3	217	140	18
Boroughmuir	12	8	0	4	214	150	16
Stewart's/Melville	13	7	0	6	220	176	14
Gala	12	7	0	5	226	213	14
Edinburgh Acads	13	7	0	6	147	183	14
Melrose	13	5	1	7	162	204	11
Selkirk	12	5	1	6	125	188	11
Jed-Forest	13	4	1	8	150	204	9
Watsonians	12	4	0	8	138	241	8
West of Scotland	13	3	0	10	139	232	6
Ayr	13	3	0	10	102	225	6
Glasgow Acads	13	2	1	10	149	391	5

The Milne brothers, all front row men capped by Scotland. Left to right: Iain, Kenny and David.

1985–86 Schweppes National League

	P	W	D	L	F	A	Pts
Hawick	13	12	0	1	241	117	24
Kelso	12	10	0	2	266	94	20
Stewart's/Melville	12	9	0	3	289	103	18
Watsonians	13	8	0	5	214	145	16
Heriot's F.P.	13	8	0	5	201	161	16
Gala	12	7	0	5	202	153	14
West of Scotland	12	7	0	5	199	192	14
Boroughmuir	13	7	0	6	143	163	14
Jed-Forest	13	5	0	8	132	218	10
Melrose	13	4	0	9	149	170	8
Edinburgh Acads	13	4	0	9	115	206	8
Selkirk	13	4	0	9	118	208	8
Preston Lodge	13	3	0	10	90	258	6
Kilmarnock	13	1	0	12	123	294	2

1986–87 McEwan's National League

	P	W	D	L	F	A	Pts
Hawick	13	12	0	1	366	148	24
Kelso	13	12	0	1	297	129	24
Watsonians	13	8	1	4	261	151	17
Stewart's/Melville	13	7	0	6	210	184	14
Selkirk	13	7	0	6	215	236	14
West of Scotland	13	6	1	6	204	205	13
Boroughmuir	13	6	0	7	205	189	12
Melrose	13	5	2	6	166	185	12
Glasgow Acads	13	5	0	8	159	272	10
Heriot's F.P.	13	4	1	8	189	199	9
Edinburgh Acads	12	4	1	7	137	204	9
Ayr	13	4	1	8	122	227	9
Gala	13	4	0	9	150	264	8
Jed-Forest	12	2	1	9	109	197	5

1987–88	P	W	D	L	F	A	Pts
Kelso	13	12	0	1	343	108	24
Hawick	13	12	0	1	317	113	24
Melrose	13	10	0	3	273	140	20
Boroughmuir	13	7	2	4	206	152	16
Heriot's F.P.	13	6	0	7	188	220	12
Watsonians	13	6	0	7	137	239	12
Ayr	13	5	1	7	178	178	11
West of Scotland	13	5	1	7	189	214	11
Stewart's/Melville	13	5	1	7	203	249	11
Glasgow Acads	13	5	1	7	156	219	11
Selkirk	13	5	0	8	161	190	10
Edinburgh Acads	13	4	1	8	136	208	9
Musselburgh	13	3	1	9	124	250	7
Kilmarnock	13	2	0	11	139	270	4

1988–89	P	W	D	L	F	A	Pts
Kelso	13	10	0	3	357	111	20
Boroughmuir	13	9	2	2	314	145	20
Hawick	13	10	0	3	280	161	20
Edinburgh Acads	13	8	2	3	242	127	18
Heriot's F.P.	13	9	0	4	301	196	18
Jed-Forest	13	8	1	4	270	164	17
Selkirk	13	7	1	5	175	153	15

	P	W	D	L	F	A	Pts
West of Scotland	13	5	1	7	164	263	11
Stewart's/Melville	13	5	1	7	168	278	11
Melrose	12	5	0	7	208	162	10
Ayr	13	4	1	8	202	271	9
Glasgow High/ K'side	13	3	1	9	144	258	7
Glasgow Acads	12	2	0	10	112	225	4
Watsonians	13	0	0	13	97	520	0

1989–90	P	W	D	L	F	A	Pts
Melrose	12	10	1	1	247	107	21
Heriot's F.P.	13	10	0	3	276	132	20
Jed-Forest	13	10	0	3	203	149	20
Edinburgh Acads	13	9	0	4	212	145	18
Stirling County	13	7	1	5	207	216	15
Boroughmuir	13	7	0	6	240	150	14
Glasgow High/ K'side	13	6	1	6	181	195	13
Gala	13	5	2	6	187	223	12
Hawick	13	5	1	7	187	173	11
Selkirk	13	5	0	8	235	268	10
Kelso	13	4	1	8	195	221	9
Stewart's/Melville	12	4	1	7	140	225	9
Ayr	13	3	0	10	139	281	6
West of Scotland	13	1	0	12	126	308	2

1990–91	P	W	D	L	F	A	Pts
Boroughmuir	13	11	1	1	285	124	23
Heriot's F.P.	13	11	0	2	276	144	22
Jed-Forest	13	10	0	3	268	166	20
Gala	13	9	1	3	271	167	19
Melrose	13	9	0	4	195	155	18
Edinburgh Acads	13	8	1	4	270	139	17
Stirling County	13	6	2	5	191	191	14
Hawick	13	6	0	7	207	191	12
Selkirk	13	5	0	8	184	276	10
Currie	13	3	1	9	200	268	7
Stewart's/Melville	13	3	0	10	166	236	6
Glasgow High/ K'side	13	3	0	10	170	264	6
Kelso	13	3	0	10	209	312	6
Edin. Wanderers	13	1	0	12	144	403	2

1991–92	P	W	D	L	F	A	Pts
Melrose	13	11	1	1	263	142	23
Edinburgh Acads	13	10	1	2	266	130	21
Heriot's F.P.	13	7	1	5	198	218	15
Boroughmuir	12	6	1	5	210	179	13
Gala	13	6	0	7	237	202	12
Selkirk	12	6	0	6	228	210	12
Watsonians	13	5	2	6	202	185	12
Currie	13	6	0	7	231	227	12
Jed-Forest	13	6	0	7	174	173	12
Stirling County	13	6	0	7	145	207	12
Hawick	13	4	2	7	176	193	10
Glasgow High/ K'side	13	4	2	7	206	245	10
Stewart's/Melville	13	5	0	8	164	261	10
West of Scotland	13	3	0	10	163	291	6

SOUTH AFRICA

FOUNDATION: 1889
Most points: 268 HE Botha, 130 PJ Visagie
Most tries: 15 D Gerber, 12 G Germishuys, RA Mordt
Largest victories: Points 50–18 v South America 1982 – Margin 44–0 v Scotland 1951
Heaviest defeat: 9–28 v British Isles 1974
Clubs: 1004
Players: 78 000
Population: 26 129 000
Main stadia: Ellis Park, Johannesburg (cap: 95 000), Loftus Versveld, Pretoria (72 500), Newlands, Cape Town (51 000), Kings Park, Durban (49 500), Free State Stadium, Bloemfontein (41 000), Boet Erasmus, Port Elizabeth (40 000).
Stadia at Wanderers (Johannesburg), Springs, Potchefstroom, East London, Stellenbosch, Welkom and Kimberley all hold in excess of 20 000.
Colours: Green jerseys, old gold collars, white shorts.
Headquarters: South African Rugby Board
PO Box 99
Newlands 7725

The way forward – mixed rugby in South Africa.

INTERNATIONAL RECORDS

Most capped player

FCH du Preez	38	1960–71
JH Ellis	38	1965–76

In individual positions

Full-back		
LG Wilson	27	1960–65
Wing		
JP Engelbrecht	33	1960–69
Centre		
JL Gainsford	33	1960–67
Fly-half		
PJ Visagie	25	1967–71
Scrum-half		
DJ de Villiers	25	1962–70
Prop		
JFK Marais	35	1963–74
Hooker		
GF Malan	18	1958–65
Lock		
FCH du Preez	31 (38)[1]	1960–71
Flanker		
JH Ellis	38	1965–76
No. 8		
DJ Hopwood	22	1960–65

[1] Du Preez won 7 caps as a flanker

MILESTONES

1861 A game of football first played at the Diocesan College (Bishops) in Rondebosch, Cape Town.
1862 First recorded match in the Cape – Civilians v Military. A Van der Bijl, who captained Merchiston School in the first ever inter school match in Scotland in 1858, played in this game.
1875 First club is founded – Hamilton Football Club. The Villagers also claim 1875 as their year of formation. Swellendam (1865) has so far been unproven as the first club.
1883 Western Province Rugby Football Union founded to organise the growth and development of the game in clubs and schools in the Cape.
1889 South African Rugby Football Board founded in Kimberley.
1891 First tourists to South Africa – from the British Isles who win all their 19 matches under captain Bill MacLagan, conceding just one try on tour.
1892 First Currie Cup tournament, held in Kimberley, and won by Western Province.
1896 Formation of the SA Coloured Rugby Board in Kimberley. First South African victory in an international, by 5–0 in the fourth and last international of the British tour under John Hammond. South Africa wore green, their national colours.
1906 First overseas tour – Paul Roos captains the team to Britain. First coining of nickname 'Springboks', and first overseas win (v Ireland at Dublin).
1912 Brothers Freddie, Dick and John Luyt become the first and only three brothers to play in the same international.
1924 First official British Lions tour – visits South Africa.
1926 South Africa (with Australia and New Zealand) has separate representation on International Board.
1931 Legendary player and administrator Danie Craven plays his first international.
1938 Craven completes remarkable record of having played for the Springboks at scrum half, fly half, centre, full back and no. 8! Northern Transvaal RU formed as separate entity.
1951 South Africa beat Scotland 44–0 at Murrayfield to set what was to stand for a long time as a world record for the biggest win in major rugby internationals.
1953 Harry Newton Walker becomes first Springbok son of a Springbok.
1955 First 100 000 crowd at a rugby match to see South Africa v British Isles (22–23) at Ellis Park, Johannesburg.
1965 First Springbok team to fail to win on tour – to Ireland and Scotland.
1984 Last senior tour to South Africa by major nation until 1992 – by England who lose both Tests heavily.
1986 New Zealand Cavaliers tour.
1990 New Constitution in South Africa opens way for return to international sport.

CURRIE CUP

The Premier event in the country, the Cup was donated by Sir Donald Currie, founder of the Currie Shipping Line, to WE McLagan, captain of the first British tourists to South Africa in 1891, and was intended for presentation to the team that played best against the tourists. Griqualand West won that honour, and subsequently presented the Cup to the South African Rugby Board, who in turn utilised it as the trophy for Inter Union competition. The Inter Union competition had started in 1889, two years before Currie's gift.

Winners 1889–1936

1889	Western Province
1892	Western Province
1894	Western Province
1895	Western Province
1897	Western Province
1898	Western Province
1899	Griqualand West
1904	Western Province
1906	Western Province
1908	Western Province
1911	Griqualand West
1914	Western Province
1920	Western Province
1922	Transvaal
1925	Western Province
1927	Western Province
1929	Western Province
1932	Western Province and Border
1936	Western Province

Finals 1939–56

1939	Transvaal 17, Western Province 6
1946	Northern Transvaal 11, Western Province 9
1947	Western Province 16, Transvaal 12
1950	Transvaal 22, Western Province 11
1952	Transvaal 11, Boland 9
1954	Western Province 11, Northern Transvaal 8
1956	Northern Transvaal 9, Natal 8

Winners 1959–66

1959 Western Province
1964 Western Province
1966 Western Province

Finals 1968–91

1968 Northern Transvaal 16, Transvaal 3
1969 Northern Transvaal 28, Western Province 13
1970 Griqualand West 11, Northern Transvaal 9
1971 Northern Transvaal 13, Transvaal 14
1972 Transvaal 25, Eastern Transvaal 19
1973 Northern Transvaal 30, Orange Free State 22
1974 Northern Transvaal 17, Transvaal 15
1975 Northern Transvaal 12, Orange Free State 6
1976 Orange Free State 33, Western Province 16
1977 Northern Transvaal 27, Orange Free State 12
1978 Northern Transvaal 13, Orange Free State 6
1979 Northern Transvaal 15, Western Province 15
1980 Northern Transvaal 39, Western Province 9
1981 Northern Transvaal 23, Orange Free State 6
1982 Western Province 24, Northern Transvaal 7
1983 Western Province 9, Northern Transvaal 3
1984 Western Province 19, Natal 9
1985 Western Province 22, Northern Transvaal 15
1986 Western Province 22, Transvaal 9
1987 Northern Transvaal 24, Transvaal 18
1988 Northern Transvaal 19, Western Province 18
1989 Western Province 16, Northern Transvaal 16
1990 Natal 18, Northern Transvaal 12
1991 Northern Transvaal 27, Transvaal 15

Number of times won

Western Province	27 (1 tied with Border, 1 tied with Northern Transvaal)
Northern Transvaal	17 (1 tied with Western Province)
Transvaal	5
Griqualand West	3
Orange Free State	1
Natal	1
Border	1 (tied with Western Province)

LION CUP

Named after the first sponsors. Lion is a beer produced by South African Breweries. The Cup is organised on a knockout basis, with the smaller Unions taking part at the start, later to be joined by the more powerful Unions. First held in 1983.

Lion Cup Finals

1983 Transvaal 12, Orange Free State 24
1984 Western Province 30, Orange Free State 22
1985 Orange Free State 10, Northern Transvaal 12
1986 Transvaal 22, Orange Free State 12
1987 Transvaal 24, North Transvaal 18
1988 Northern Transvaal 12, Western Province 24
1989 Western Province 21, Northern Transvaal 16
1990 Northern Transvaal 25, Western Province 12
1991 Northern Transvaal 62, Natal 6

Northern Transvaal, the 1991 Currie Cup champions, with the trophy.

TOYOTA CUP

Early season competition, usually held at Durban in April, between the champion clubs of each major province from the previous season. Sponsored by Toyota since its inception, the competition is run on a knockout basis over a long weekend.

Championship Finals

1975 Stellenbosch Univ. 28, Durban Collegians 20
1976 Pretoria Univ. 19, Stellenbosch Univ. 0
1977 Stellenbosch Univ. 12, Pretoria Harlequins 10
1978 Stellenbosch Univ. 15, Pretoria Univ. 9
1979 Stellenbosch Univ. 27, Pretoria Univ. 11
1980 Villagers (Cape Town) 14, Stellenbosch Univ. 3
1981 Stellenbosch Univ. 32, Pretoria Police 9
1982 Stellenbosch Univ. 25, Rand Afrikaans Univ. 6
1983 Pretoria Harlequins 29, Pretoria Univ. 12
1984 Stellenbosch Univ. 16, Pretoria Univ. 15
1985 Despatch (nr. Port Eliz.) 28, Pretoria Univ. 6
1986 Shimlas (OFS Univ.) 14, Pretoria Univ. 6
1987 Western Province 26, Despatch 8
1988 Despatch 13, Pretoria Univ. 12
1989 Roodepoort 29, Goudstad TTC 22
1990 Pretoria Univ. 22, Despatch 20
1991 Old Greys, Bloemfontein 36, Despatch 6
1992 Rand Afrikaan Univ. 40, Pretoria Harlequins 22

THE UNIONS

After some years away from the international scene, South Africa have recently returned, and will begin playing international rugby again from 1992.

The current structure of their rugby is as follows:

Union	Founded	No. of clubs	No. of teams	Most teams	Oldest club
Western Province	1883	32	272	Stellenbosch (6)	Hamiltons (1875)
Griqualand West	1886	24	43	Defence (5)	Pirates (1884)
Eastern Province	1888	23	96	Despatch (9)	Olympics (1881)
Transvaal	1889	25	114	RAU, Wits, Goudstad Police (6)	
Natal	1890	40	114	Durban Collegians (7)	Berea Rovers (1906)
Border	1891	17	36		Buffaloes (1877)
Orange Free State	1895	22	105	University (49)	University (1912)
South Western Districts	1899	28	64	Defence (8)	George (1882)
North Eastern Cape	1903	44	70		Cradock Rovers (1882)
Western Transvaal	1920	13	97	University (31)	Potchefstroom Town (1885)
Northern Transvaal	1938	23	312	University (60)	Pretoria (1888)
Boland	1939	43	85		Malmesbury (1881)
North Western Cape	1967	19	36		Upington Town (1908)
Eastern Transvaal	1947	18	66	Police (7)	Boksburg (1894), though the claim is debatable and it may well be Heidelberg.
Far North	1968	19	51		Pietersburg (1902)
Northern Free State	1968	18	56		Wanderers (1917)
Eastern Free State	1968	18	38		Fickburgs (1895)
South Eastern Transvaal	1968	18	64		Ermelo (1891)
Stellaland	1975	28	57		Mafikeng (1903)
Northern Natal	1973	10	26		Newcastle (1890)
Vaal Triangle	1984	10	37	Iscor (6)	Heilbron or Koppies
Low Veld	1985	17	34		Barberton (1904)

WALES

FOUNDATION: 1880
Honours: 1987 World Cup third
Grand Slam: 1908, 1909, 1911, 1950, 1952, 1971, 1976, 1978
International Championship: 21 (outright – record)
Triple Crown: 17 (outright – record)
Most Points: 301 PH Thorburn, 166 P Bennett
Most Tries: 20 TGR Davies, GO Edwards
Largest victories: Points 49–14 v France 1910
Margin 46–0 v USA 1987
Heaviest defeat: 6–63 v Australia 1991
Clubs: 178
Players: 40 000
Population: 3 105 000
Main stadium: Cardiff Arms Park (cap: 54 000)
Colours: Red shirts, green collars, white shorts
Headquarters: Welsh Rugby Union
PO Box 22
Cardiff CF1 1JL

Right *Paul Thorburn, record points scorer for Wales, who retired from international rugby in 1991.*

MILESTONES

1827 Lampeter College founded – several subsequent entries in local newspapers refer to Town v Gown matches, making Lampeter probably the birthplace of Welsh rugby. Reports that Lampeter played Llandeilo and Llandovery over the years.
1871 Neath RFC founded – the first major club in Wales.
1875 South Wales Union formed.
1880 Welsh Rugby Union formed (the last of the four home nations) with original members being Lampeter, Llandeilo, Llandovery, Brecon, Swansea, Cardiff, Newport, Llanelli, Merthyr, Pontypool and Bangor.
1881 First Wales international – lost to England at Blackheath by seven goals, six tries and a dropped goal (69–0 in modern values).
1886 Wales introduced the four man threequarter line after Cardiff and Newport had tried the experiment – first believed to have been introduced at Llandovery College.
1887 South Wales Challenge Cup introduced.
1891–5 Newport lose just seven of 123 matches.
1893 Some 12 years after their first international, Wales win the International Championship.
1894 Four threequarter line-up universally adopted.
1900–11 First golden age of Welsh rugby with just seven defeats in 11 years.
1905 Wales beat New Zealand 3–0 in controversial circumstances.
1947 Neath win first unofficial Welsh club Championship.
1953 Wales beat New Zealand for the last time in an international to date.
1971 The British Lions, with 14 Welshmen, under captain John Dawes, coach Carwyn James and a record seven London Welshmen, are hub of first series win in New Zealand by the Lions.
1972 Neath beat Llanelli 15–9 in the final to win the inaugural Welsh Rugby Union Challenge Cup.
1975 Charlie Faulkner, Bobby Windsor and Graham Price, the Pontypool front row, play together for Wales for the first time – in Paris against France.
1978 Wales complete their second Grand Slam in three years.
1990 Welsh leagues introduced on a competitive basis for the first time.
1991 Worst period in Welsh rugby history includes a record 63–6 loss in an international to Australia, a 71–8 loss to New South Wales, an International Championship whitewash by record margins and a loss in the World Cup to Western Samoa (pop: 167 000).

Despair on the Welsh sidelines during the defeat against Western Samoa at Cardiff Arms Park in the 1991 World Cup.

WELSH CUP

The Welsh Cup, sponsored by Schweppes, began in the 1971–2 season. Until the arrival in 1990 of the National League, it quickly established itself as the major domestic tournament, as the 'league' between major clubs was unofficial.

1971–2
Semi-finals: Neath 16, Cardiff 9
Llanelli 13, Aberavon 7
Final: NEATH 15, LLANELLI 9
NEATH: W Davies; K Collier, G Ball, D Jenkins, T Poole; M Davies (capt), D Parker; W Williams, N Rees, G Shaw, B Thomas, B Davies, W Lauder, D Morris, W Thomas.
Scorers – T: Parker *C:* Poole *PG:* Poole (3)
LLANELLI: R Davies; A Hill, B Thomas, RWR Gravell, R Mathias; P Bennett (capt), S Williams; A Crocker, R Thomas, D Thomas, R Fouracre, DL Quinnell, A James, H Jenkins, M Trueman.
Scorers – T: Penalty try *C:* Hill *PG:* Hill
Referee: M Joseph

1972–3
Semi-finals: Llanelli 6, Neath 3 (at Swansea)
Cardiff 12, Swansea 8 (at Aberavon)
Final: LLANELLI 30, CARDIFF 7
LLANELLI: R Davies; A Hill, RTE Bergiers, RWR Gravell, JJ Williams; P Bennett, S Williams; A Crocker, ER Thomas, C Charles, D Thomas (capt), DL Quinnell, T David, H Jenkins, G Jenkins.
Scorers – T: Gravell, JJ Williams, Jenkins *C:* Bennett (3) *PG:* Bennett (4)
CARDIFF: L Davies; W Lewis, N Williams, A Finlayson, P Lyn Jones; K James, GO Edwards; R Beard, G Davies, G Wallace (capt), I Robinson, L Baxter, R Lane, C Smith, M John.
Scorers – T: Finlayson *DG:* Edwards
Referee: J Kelleher

1973–4
Semi-finals: Llanelli 16, Pontypool 14 (at Aberavon)
Aberavon 9, Cardiff 4 (at Bridgend)

Final: LLANELLI 12, ABERAVON 10
LLANELLI: C Griffiths; A Hill, D Nicholas, RWR Gravell, J Walters; B Thomas, S Williams; A Crocker, R Thomas (capt), C Charles, DB Llewellyn, WD Thomas, DL Quinnell, H Jenkins, G Jenkins.
Scorers – PG: Hill (4)
ABERAVON: K Davies; S Roper, M Swain, I Hall, A Rees; J Bevan, RC Shell; C Williams, M Howells (capt), J Owen, R Davies, AJ Martin, WT Mainwaring, K Evans, O Alexander.
Scorers – T: Roper *PG:* Martin (2)
Referee: R Lewis

1974–5
Semi-finals: Llanelli 35, Bridgend 6 (at Swansea)
Aberavon 10, Pontypridd 9 (at Cardiff)
Final: LLANELLI 15, ABERAVON 6
LLANELLI: K Coslett; A Hill, RTE Bergiers, RWR Gravell, JJ Williams; P Bennett (capt), S Williams; A Crocker, ER Thomas, DB Llewellyn, A James, R Powell, P May, H Jenkins, TP David.
Scorers – T: Hill, Bennett, David *PG:* David
ABERAVON: K Davies; S Roper, J Thomas, G Rees, D Condon; A Rees, RC Shell; C Williams, M Howells (capt), J Owen, O Alexander, AJ Martin, WT Mainwaring, P Clarke, R Davies.
Scorers – PG: G Rees (2)
Referee: S Lewis

1975–6
Semi-finals: Llanelli 10, Ebbw Vale 4 (at Swansea)
Swansea 22, Pontypool 14 (at Cardiff)
Final: LLANELLI 16, SWANSEA 4
LLANELLI: C Griffiths; JJ Williams, RTE Bergiers, RWR Gravell, D Nicholas; P Bennett (capt), S Williams; C Thomas, ER Thomas, A Crocker, RJ Hyndman, D.L Quinnell, P May, H Jenkins, A James.
Scorers – T: JJ Williams *PG:* Bennett (4)
SWANSEA: WR Blyth; G Jones, J Rees, R Davies, R Woodward; DS Richards, A Meredith; PD Llewellyn, J Herdman, N Webb (capt), M Keyworth, GAD Wheel, BG Clegg, P Davies, TP Evans
Scorers – T: Richards
Referee: D Lloyd

1976–7
Semi-finals: Cardiff 15, Aberavon 6 (at Swansea)
Newport 7, Ebbw Vale 3 (at Cardiff)
Final: NEWPORT 16, CARDIFF 15
NEWPORT: L Davies; K Davies, N Brown, C Webber, J Cranton; D Rogers, A Billinghurst; R Morgan, D Ford, C Smart (capt), R Barrell, I Barnard, D Waters, J Squire, KW Pole.
Scorers – T: K Davies *PG:* L Davies, Webber
CARDIFF: J Davies; TGR Davies (capt), AA Finlayson, M Murphy, C Camilleri; P Evans, GO Edwards; FM Knill, AJ Phillips, BG Nelmes, T Worgan, IR Robinson, C Smith, R Lane, R Dudley-Jones.
Scorers – T: Evans, Dudley-Jones *C:* J Davies (2) *PG:* J Davies
Referee: CGP Thomas

1977–8
Semi-finals: Newport 10, Aberavon 6 (at Cardiff)
Swansea 18, Cardiff 13 (at Aberavon)
Final: SWANSEA 13, NEWPORT 9
SWANSEA: WR Blyth, H Rees, AD Meredith (capt), G Jenkins, A Donovan; DS Richards, H Davies; H Hopkins, J Herdman, PD Llewellyn, TP Evans, GAD Wheel, BG Clegg, R Moriarty, M Keyworth
Scorers – T: Herdman *DG:* Richards Jenkins *PG:* Blyth
NEWPORT: C Webber; K Davies, DH Burcher (capt), N Brown, D Bale; DL Evans, DB Williams; C Smart, S Jones, R Morgan, B Lease, J Watkins, A Mogridge, J Squire, G Evans.
Scorers – PG: Webber (3)
Referee: C Norling

1978–9
Semi-finals: Bridgend 18, Llanelli 13 (at Swansea)
Pontypridd 6, Aberavon 3 (at Bridgend)
Final: BRIDGEND 18, PONTYPRIDD 12
BRIDGEND: JPR Williams (capt); I Davies, SP Fenwick, L Thomas, V Jenkins; I Lewis, G Williams; I Stephens, G Davies, M James, Gareth Williams, L Davies, R Evans, D Brain, G Jones.
Replacement: C Williams (for Fenwick after 47 mins).
Scorers – T: Fenwick *C:* Fenwick *PG:* Fenwick (3), Lewis
PONTYPRIDD: I Walsh; C Bolderson, C Riley, J Poole, S Flynn; S Lewis, R Morgan; R Lott, M Alexander, W Evans, M Shellard, D Shellard, R Penberthy, C Seldon, TP David (capt)
Scorers – T: David *C:* Bolderson *PG:* Riley, Bolderson
Referee: K Rowlands

1979–80
Semi-finals: Bridgend 18, Llanelli 10 (at Swansea)
Swansea 23, Newport 13 (at Cardiff)
Final: BRIDGEND 15, SWANSEA 9
BRIDGEND: JPR Williams; C Williams, SP Fenwick, L Thomas, F Owen; G Pearce, G Williams, M James (capt), G Davies, I Stephens, Gareth Williams, J Morgan, W Hower, S Ellis, G Jones.
Scorers – T: Owen *C:* Fenwick *PG:* Fenwick (3)
SWANSEA: WR Blyth; AH Swift, A Meredith, G Jenkins, M Wyatt; M Dacey, DB Williams; PD Llewellyn, J Herdman, H Hopkins, G Roberts, GAD Wheel (capt), BG Clegg, T Cheeseman, M Keyworth.
Scorers – PG: Blyth (3)
Referee: Corrie Thomas

1980–1
Semi-finals: Bridgend 22, Llanelli 15 (at Swansea)
Cardiff 18, Swansea 7 (at Bridgend)
Final: CARDIFF 14, BRIDGEND 6
CARDIFF: G Davies; D Preece, DH Burcher, N Hutchings, S Evans; WG Davies, TD Holmes; I Eidman, AJ Phillips, J Whitefoot, R Lakin, A Mogridge, K Edwards, JP Scott (capt), B Lease.
Scorers – T: Lakin, Hutchings *PG:* WG Davies (2)
BRIDGEND: JPR Williams; F Owen, SP Fenwick, R James, C Barber; GP Pearce, G Williams; M James (capt), K Townley, I Stephens, G Jones, W Howe, J Morgan, L Davies, GP Williams.
Scorers – PG: Fenwick
Referee: A Richards

1981–2
Semi-finals: Cardiff 21, Newbridge 11 (at Newport)
Bridgend 9, Aberavon 6 (at Swansea)
Final: CARDIFF 12, BRIDGEND 12
Cardiff won on 'most tries' rule
CARDIFF: P Rees; S Evans, D Barry, PCT Daniels, D Preece; WG Davies, TD Holmes; I Eidman, AJ Phillips, J Whitefoot, O Golding, RL Norster, K Edwards, JP Scott (capt), JR Lewis.
Scorers – T: Eidman *C:* Barry *PG:* Barry (2)
BRIDGEND: H Davies; M Titley, P Daniel, C Williams, F Owen; G Pearce, G Williams (capt); M James, G Davies, I Stephens, G Jones, R Evans, W Howe, S Ellis, GP Williams.
Scorers – PG: Pearce (3) *DG:* Pearce
Referee: C Norling

1982–3
Semi-finals: Pontypool 16, Bridgend 3 (at Aberavon)
Swansea 19, Newbridge 6 (at Cardiff)
Final: PONTYPOOL 18, SWANSEA 6
PONTYPOOL: P Lewis; G Davies, L Faulkner, L Jones, B Taylor; M Goldsworthy, D Bishop; RW Windsor, S Jones, G Price, C Huish, M Jones, SJ Perkins, J Squire (capt), M Brown.
Replacement: M Crowley (for Windsor after 10 mins).
Scorers – T: Taylor *C:* Lewis *PG:* Lewis (4)
SWANSEA: WR Blyth; P Gallagher, AH Swift, G Jenkins, A Emyr; M Dacey, H Davies; C Williams, S Davies, G John, M Davies (capt), RD Moriarty, B Clegg, G Roberts, M Ruddock.
Scorers – PG: Blyth (2)
Referee: W Jones

1983–4
Semi-finals: Cardiff 26, Llanelli 6 (at Swansea)
Neath 12, Aberavon 3 (at Bridgend)
Final: CARDIFF 24, NEATH 19
CARDIFF: P Rees; G Cordle, AJ Donovan, M Ring, AM Hadley; WG Davies, TD Holmes; J Whitefoot, AJ Phillips, I Eidman, RL Norster, O Golding, R Lakin, JP Scott (capt), K Edwards.
Replacement: N Humphreys (for Hadley after 48 mins).
Scorers – T: Golding, Cordle *C:* Davies (2) *PG:* Davies (4)
NEATH: N Harris; HE Rees (capt), D Jacob, K Jones, C Bridgwater; J Davies, Gareth Jones; B Williams, M Richards, P Langford, G Jones, S Dando, H Richards, D Morgan, L Jones.
Scorers – T: Jacob (2), Gareth Jones *C:* Harris (2) *PG:* Harris
*Referee:*C Norling

1984–5
Semi-finals: Cardiff 24, Pontypool 3 (at Newport)
Llanelli 24, Bridgend 10 (at Swansea)
Final: LLANELLI 15, CARDIFF 14
LLANELLI: M Gravelle; PI Lewis, N Davies, P Morgan, I Evans; G Pearce, J Griffiths; A Buchanan, D Fox, L Delaney, P May (capt), R Cornelius, A Davies, PT Davies, DF Pickering.
Scorers – T: Griffiths *C:* Pearce *PG:* Pearce (2)
CARDIFF: P Rees; G Cordle, AJ Donovan, D Evans, AM Hadley; WG Davies, TD Holmes (capt); J Whitefoot, AJ Phillips, I Eidman, K Edwards, RL Norster, O Golding, JP Scott, GJ Roberts.
Scorers – T: Phillips, Cordle *PG:* Davies (2)
Referee: WD Bevan

1985–86
Semi-finals: Cardiff 17, Bridgend 9 (at Swansea)
Newport 15, Aberavon 6 (at Cardiff)
Final: CARDIFF 28, NEWPORT 21
CARDIFF: M Rayer; G Cordle, AJ Donovan, M Ring, AM Hadley; WG Davies, N O'Brien; J Whitefoot, AJ Phillips (capt), I Eidman, K Edwards, RL Norster, O Golding, JP Scott, GJ Roberts.
Scorers – T: Hadley (3), O'Brien *C:* Davies (3) *PG:* Davies (2)
NEWPORT: R Knight; M Batten, D Pitt, P Daniel, J White; P Turner, N Callard; J Rawlins, MJ Watkins (capt), R Morgan, J Widdecombe, A Perry, R Collins, DR Waters, R Powell.
Scorers – T: Pitt, Turner, Collins *C:* Turner (3) *PG:* Turner
Referee: K Rowlands

1986–7
Semi-finals: Cardiff 16, Neath 6 (at Swansea)
Swansea 20, Newbridge 3 (at Cardiff)
Final: CARDIFF 16, SWANSEA 16 (after extra time)
CARDIFF: M Rayer; G Cordle, A Donovan, M Ring, AM Hadley; G John, C Hutchings; J Whitefoot, A Phillips (capt), I Eidman, H Stone, RL Norster, R Lakin, G Roberts, J Scott.
Replacements: T Crothers (for Roberts after 90 mins), R Cardus (for Ring after 97 mins).
SWANSEA: M Wyatt; M Titley, R Hopkins, M Dacey, A Emyr; A Clement, R Jones; K Colclough, P Hitchings, D Young, M Colclough, R Moriarty (capt), P Moriarty, R Webster, J Thomas.
Replacement: J Williams (for M Colclough after 51 mins)
Scorers – T: Hopkins *C:* Wyatt *PG:* Wyatt (2) *DG:* Clement
Referee: W Jones

1987–8
Semi-finals: Llanelli 38, Aberavon 0 (at Swansea)
Neath 20, Pontypool 9 (at Cardiff)
Final: LLANELLI 28, NEATH 13
LLANELLI: S Bowling; IC Evans, N Davies, S Davies, C Davies; J Davies, J Griffiths; A Buchanan, D Fox, L Delaney, PS May, R Cornelius, G Jones, PT Davies (capt) M Perego.
Scorers – T: Evans, Delaney, Jones *C:* C Davies (2) *PG:* J Davies (4)
NEATH: PH Thorburn (capt); A Edmunds, S Powell, C Laity, G Davies; A Davies, C Bridges; S Dando, KH Phillips, J Pugh, A Kembery, B Clegg, P Pugh, R Phillips, DF Pickering.
Replacements: A Booth for Bridges (58 mins), M Jones for Clegg (72 mins)
Scorers – T: A Davies *PG:* Thorburn (3)
Referee: WD Bevan

1988–9
Semi-finals: Llanelli 26, Newbridge 24 (at Cardiff)
Neath 19, Cardiff 12 (at Swansea)
Final: NEATH 14, LLANELLI 13
NEATH: PH Thorburn; C Higgs, C Laity, A Bateman, A Edmunds; P Williams, C Bridges; B Williams, KH Phillips (capt), J Pugh, H Richards, G Llewelyn, P Pugh, M Jones, DF Pickering.
Scorers – T: Jones, B Williams, P Williams *C:* Thorburn
LLANELLI: S Bowling; IC Evans, NG Davies, D Setaro, C Davies; C Stephens, J Griffith; A Buchanan, E James, L Delaney, PS May, R Cornelius, G Jones, PT Davies (capt), I Jones
Replacement: E Lewis for G Jones (80 min)

Scorers – T: Evans *PG:* Stephens (2) *DG:* Stephens
Referee: LJ Peard

1989–90
Semi-finals: Neath 24, Swansea 16 (at Cardiff)
Bridgend 12, Aberavon 6 (at Llanelli)
Final: NEATH 16, BRIDGEND 10
NEATH: PH Thorburn; J Ball, C Laity, AG Bateman, A Edmunds; P Williams, C Bridges; BR Williams, KH Phillips (capt), JD Pugh, GO Llewellyn, A Kembery, R Phillips, MA Jones, MS Morris.
Replacement: D Joseph for Pugh
Scorers – T: Morris, Bridges *C:* Thorburn *PG:* Thorburn *DG:* Ball
BRIDGEND: A Parry; GMC Webbe, J Aspee (capt), L Evans, R Diplock; A Williams, K Ellis; D Austin, WH Hall, P Edwards, P Kawnlok, N Spender, S Bryant, O Williams, M Budd
Scorers – T: Ellis *DG:* Williams (2)
Referee: C Norling

1990–91
Semi-finals: Pontypool 28, Swansea 10 (at Cardiff)
Llanelli 22, Neath 10 (at Cardiff)
Final: LLANELLI 24, PONTYPOOL 9
LLANELLI: I Jones; IC Evans, NG Evans, S Davies, S Bowling; C Stephens, R Moon; R Evens, D Fox, L Delaney, PT Davies (capt), A Copsey, EE Lewis, J Williams, L Jones.
Scorers – T: Lewis, IC Evans, Stephens, S Davies, I Jones *C:* Stephens (2)
PONTYPOOL: A Parry; S White, R Lewis, S McGauchie, S Hanson; D Phillips, C Jonathan, A Dibble, G Jenkins, L Mustoe, N Jones, R Goodey, C Huish (capt), D Oswald, V Davies.
Scorers – T: Davies *C:* Parry *PG:* Parry
Referee: WD Bevan

1991–2
Semi-finals: Swansea 23, Newport 9 (aet) (at Cardiff)
Llanelli 27, Pontypridd 6 (at Cardiff)
Final: LLANELLI 16, SWANSEA 7
LLANELLI: I Jones; I Evans, N Davies, S Davies, W Proctor; C Stephens, R Moon; R Evans, D Fox, L Delaney, P Davies (capt), A Copsey, E Lewis, L Jones, S Quinnell
Scorers – T: I Evans, Moon *C:* Stephens *PG:* Stephens *DG:* Moon
SWANSEA: A Clement; M Titley, K Hopkins (capt), S Gibbs, S Davies; A Williams, R Jones; I Buckett, G Jenkins, J Colclough, P Arnold, R Moriarty, A Reynolds, R Webster, S Davies
Scorers – T: A Williams *PG:* A Williams
Referee: LJ Peard

NATIONAL LEAGUE

Wales were one of the last countries – junior and senior – in the world to organise an official National League. Previous 'leagues' had been based on results run by various sponsors, rather than having a set fixture list.

Heineken League Premier Division
1990–91

	P	W	D	L	F	A	Pts
Neath	18	14	0	4	353	218	28
Llanelli	18	12	1	5	409	292	25
Bridgend	18	10	2	6	288	275	22
Cardiff	18	10	1	7	396	261	21
Pontypridd	18	9	2	7	353	270	20
Pontypool	18	9	1	8	402	293	19
Newbridge	18	9	0	9	363	261	18
Swansea	18	9	0	9	353	309	18
Glamorgan Wands	18	3	0	15	192	496	6
Abertillery	18	1	1	16	146	580	3

1991–2

	P	W	D	L	F	A	Pts
Swansea	18	13	1	4	393	205	27
Llanelli	18	11	1	6	381	233	23
Pontypridd	18	11	0	7	289	245	22
Neath	18	9	2	7	309	236	20
Newbridge	18	10	0	8	259	271	20
Bridgend	18	10	0	8	246	270	20
Pontypool	18	7	4	7	282	275	18
Newport	18	7	2	9	240	237	16
Cardiff	18	5	1	12	240	306	11
Maesteg	18	1	1	16	169	530	3

NATIONAL CLUB CHAMPIONS

1946–47	Neath	1961–62	Newport	1976–77	Llanelli
1947–48	Cardiff	1962–63	Pontypridd	1977–78	Pontypridd
1948–49	Cardiff	1963–64	Bridgend	1979–80	Swansea
1949–50	Maesteg	1964–65	Newbridge	1980–81	Bridgend
1950–51	Newport	1965–66	Bridgend	1981–82	Cardiff
1951–52	Ebbw Vale	1966–67	Neath	1982–83	Swansea
1952–53	Cardiff	1967–68	Llanelli	1983–84	Pontypool
1953–54	Ebbw Vale	1968–69	Newport	1984–85	Pontypool
1954–55	Cardiff	1969–70	Bridgend	1985–86	Pontypool
1955–56	Newport	1970–71	Bridgend	1986–87	Neath
1956–57	Ebbw Vale	1971–72	London Welsh	1987–88	Pontypool
1957–58	Cardiff	1972–73	Pontypool	1988–89	Neath
1958–59	Pontypool	1973–74	Llanelli	1989–90	Neath
1959–60	Ebbw Vale	1974–75	Pontypool	1990–91	Llanelli
1960–61	Aberavon	1975–76	Pontypridd	1991–92	Swansea

Welsh hopes for the future lie with Scott Gibbs (above with ball), Player of the Year in his first full season.

LEADING SCORERS IN PREMIER DIVISION OF NATIONAL LEAGUE 1990–92

	Pts
Neil Jenkins (Pontypridd)	300
Aled Williams (Bridgend/Swansea)	252
Paul Thorburn (Neath)	250
Colin Stephens (Llanelli)	231

	Tries
Glen Webbe (Bridgend)	18
Iuean Evans (Llanelli)	18
Alun Harries (Newbridge)	17
Bleddyn Taylor (Swansea)	15

PLAYERS OF THE YEAR

1969	Gareth Edwards
1970	Ray Hopkins
1971	Barry John
1972	JPR Williams
1973	Tommy David
1974	Terry Cobner
1975	Mervyn Davies
1976	Mervyn Davies
1977	Phil Bennett
1978	Terry Cobner
1979	Terry Holmes
1980	David Richards
1981	Clive Burgess
1982	Gwyn Evans
1983	Terry Holmes
1984	Mark Titley
1985	Mark Ring
1986	Jonathan Davies
1987	Stuart Evans
1988	Rob Norster
1989	Phil Davies
1990	Arthur Emyr
1991	Scott Gibbs
1992	Emyr Lewis

INTERNATIONAL RECORDS

Most capped player		
JPR Williams	55	1969–81
In individual positions		
Wing		
KJ Jones	44	1947–57
Centre		
SP Fenwick	30	1975–81
Fly-half		
CI Morgan	29	1951–58
Scrum-half		
GO Edwards	53	1967–78
Prop		
G Price	41	1975–83
Hooker		
BV Meredith	34	1954–62
Lock		
AJ Martin	34	1973–81
RL Norster	34	1982–89
Flanker		
WD Morris	32 (34)[1]	1967–74
No 8		
TM Davies	38	1969–76

[1] Morris won his first two caps as no. 8

OTHER NATIONS

The belief that rugby is a game for the major nations is now thankfully buried. One of the more relevant statistics from the results of the 1991 World Cup in comparison with the 1987 competition was the closing of the gap in scorelines between the senior countries and the remainder. Canada and Western Samoa eliminated seeded countries from the 1991 World Cup.

It now seems that most of these emerging nations have beaten one of the senior partners, admittedly at home. And the increasing exposure to fixtures with the International Board countries can only benefit the development of the game in a world sense.

This chapter deals with those other countries who have in the past qualified or been invited to World Cups. It also includes Namibia, who in 1991 beat World Cup countries Ireland, Italy and Zimbabwe. But perhaps the best compliment to these emerging nations is to suggest that they no longer need the word 'emerging' to describe their capabilities.

ARGENTINA

FOUNDATION: 1899
Honours: 1987 and 1991 World Cup first round
Most points: 530 H Porta (Argentina and South America)
Largest victory: 118–0 v Paraguay 1978
Heaviest defeat: 9–60 v New Zealand 1989
Clubs: 188
Players: 16 500
Population: 26 393 000
Main stadium: Velez Sarsfield FC, Buenos Aires (cap: 47 500)
Colours: Light blue and white hooped jerseys, white shorts
Headquarters: Union Argentina de Rugby
JA Pacheco de Melo 2120
Cod Pos 1126 Capital
Buenos Aires

Argentina is yet another country where the roots of the game have been planted for well over 100 years. British influence was again responsible for the early development, though in common with most other sports around the globe, the pupils are now quite capable of embarrassing the teachers, especially in their own back yard. There is not one rugby nation that regards a provincial match at Tucuman, or an international at the Velez Sarsfield stadium as an easy matter.

Other sports had been established in Argentina before rugby, especially their passion for football, but first mention of rugby appeared at the Buenos Aires Cricket Club, another overseas bastion of Olde England, before the turn of the century. In 1873, rugby was played at the club as a winter pastime by the cricketers. A match was organised at the club between members of the 'Banks' and the 'City'.

Rugby first received a full mention in the newspapers of the time on 18th May 1874, when two British gentlemen, Mr Trench and Mr Hogg, selected teams to do battle. Some descendants of Mr Hogg were still playing representative rugby for Argentina in the 1950s.

Argentina's first official club was the Buenos Aires club, founded in 1886. Buenos Aires played Rosario that year in the first inter-city match. As with so many nations, the game grew amongst the exile population at such a pace that matters needed to be placed on a more organised footing. The Argentine Rugby Union was founded in 1899 with four clubs – Buenos Aires RFC, Belgrano Athletic Club, Lomas Athletic Club and Rosario Athletic Club – all of whom still exist. That same year Lomas won the first championship, following a trend of competitive rugby at the turn of the century which was more advanced in developing nations than the established countries.

By 1904, the Argentinians themselves paraded their first home-based XV, from the School of Engineering (Facultad de Ingenieria) and a year later the locals had embarrassed a British exile side with a 21–5 victory in the first of an annual fixture between locally born players and those born in Britain.

Three British teams, sanctioned by the RFU, toured Argentina before World War II, in 1910, 1927 and 1936. The National Stadium was completed in 1936, and by the outbreak of hostilities, rugby was second in public appeal only to football.

From a solid league base in the 1950s and 1960s, Argentina began to make strides towards

Argentina had a very disappointing World Cup in 1991 including this loss to Western Samoa. Timo Tagaloa scores.

world class. South Africa also provided tours, coaches and influence. In 1965, on a tour to South Africa, the nickname of the Pumas was coined – wrongly in fact. Though the motif on the jersey was a jaguar, a Rhodesian journalist suggested it was a puma in his article. The name stuck. To add to the wound, Rhodesia also won the match 17–12.

By the end of the 1960s, Argentina were a world force in their home environment. The list of victims began with Wales in 1968 – the future basis of the Welsh 1971 Grand Slam XV lost the first Test 9–5 and drew the second 9–9. A year later Scotland were thrashed 20–3 in the first Test. Next on the list were Australia, who lost 24–13 in 1979, then France – who had also done much to promote the game. France were beaten in 1985 and 1986 and again in 1988, while New Zealand escaped with a 21–21 draw in 1985. England began the 1990s by losing the second Test in Buenos Aires 15–13.

Away from home, the Pumas were less effective but no less dangerous. South Africa were added to the list of victims in 1982 with a 21–12 defeat by South America (15 Pumas) at Bloemfontein. Wales got away with a 20–19 win in 1976, England drew 13–13 at Twickenham in 1978, and Ireland 13–13 in 1980 – results that the home nations could camouflage with the suffix 'XV' and by not awarding caps. The common factor throughout this period of success was Hugo Porta, the Banco Nacion fly half, who at one time held the world record with nearly 400 points in international rugby against IRB nations, but who had with him a group of the most able lieutenants in Sansot, Travaglini, Ure, Allen, Milano and Branca.

The wind of change blew through the domestic scene as well. Since the 1960s, the game had been taken with more seriousness and enthusiasm in the provinces. By 1985 Tucuman had become the first team from outside Buenos Aires to win the Provincial Championship.

For years the Pumas were the leaders of those desperate to break down the walls that surrounded the 'Big Eight' rugby nations. Yet when the opportunity arose to parade their talents on the world stage at the World Cups, the cupboard was almost bare. Argentina shared the same problems as Romania – both Unions suffered from a lack of finance and both suffered from domestic government policies. But Argentina base their future in young players – indeed, the game is for the more professional classes – and will base their future in the young 1991 World Cup squad, and trust that defections to countries such as Italy are halted.

ARGENTINA v ENGLAND

14 Oct 1978
Twickenham
ENGLAND 13
T: Gifford, Squires *C:* Bushell
DG: Horton
ARGENTINA 13
T: Camp, Passaglia *C:* Porta *PG:* Porta

30 May 1981
Buenos Aires
ARGENTINA 19
T: Camp (2) *C:* Porta *PG:* Porta
DG: Porta, Landejo
ENGLAND 19
T: Woodward (2), H Davies *C:* Hare (2)
PG: Hare

6 Jun 1981
Buenos Aires
ARGENTINA 6
T: Travaglini *C:* Porta
ENGLAND 12
T: H Davies *C:* Hare *PG:* Hare (2)

28 Jul 1990
Buenos Aires
ARGENTINA 12
PG: Vidou (4)
ENGLAND 25
T: Ryan, Oti *C:* Liley *PG:* Liley (3)

4 Aug 1990
Buenos Aires
ARGENTINA 15
PG: Vidou (5)
ENGLAND 13
T: Hodgkinson, Heslop *C:* Hodgkinson
PG: Hodgkinson

3 Nov 1990
Twickenham
ENGLAND 51
T: Underwood (3), Guscott (2), Hill, Hall
C: Hodgkinson (7) *PG:* Hodgkinson (3)
ARGENTINA 0

ARGENTINA v SCOTLAND

13 Sep 1969
Buenos Aires
ARGENTINA 20
T: A Travaglini (2), Walther *C:* Harris-Smith *PG:* Harris-Smith
DG: Harris-Smith (2)
SCOTLAND 3
T: MA Smith

27 Sep 1969
Buenos Aires
ARGENTINA 3
T: Otano
SCOTLAND 6
T: Carmichael *PG:* Blaikie

24 Nov 1973
Murrayfield
SCOTLAND 12
PG: Morgan (3) *DG:* Telfer
ARGENTINA 11
T: A Travaglini, Porta *DG:* Porta

10 Nov 1990
Murrayfield
SCOTLAND 49
T: Stanger (2), K Milne (2), Moore, Armstrong, Gray, G Hastings, Chalmers
C: G Hastings (5) *PG:* G Hastings
ARGENTINA 3
PG: Meson

ARGENTINA v IRELAND

10 Nov 1973
Lansdowne Road, Dublin
IRELAND 21
T: Slattery, Quinn, Grace, McMaster
C: Ensor *DG:* Quinn
ARGENTINA 8
T: Leiros, Porta

27 Oct 1990
Lansdowne Road, Dublin
IRELAND 20
T: Hooks, Kiernan *PG:* Kiernan (4)
ARGENTINA 18
T: Macome *C:* Porta *PG:* Porta (4)

ARGENTINA v WALES

14 Aug 1968
Buenos Aires
ARGENTINA 9
T: A Travaglini *PG:* Harris-Smith (2)
WALES 5
T: Turner *C:* Dawes

28 Aug 1968
Buenos Aires
ARGENTINA 9
PG: Harris-Smith (2) *DG:* Harris-Smith
WALES 9
T: Ferguson *PG:* Ferguson (2)

16 Oct 1976
Cardiff Arms Park
WALES 20
T: TGR Davies, Edwards *PG:* Bennett (4)
ARGENTINA 19
T: Gauweloose, Beccar-Varela *C:* Porta
PG: Porta, Beccar-Varela (2)

ARGENTINA v FRANCE

1949
Buenos Aires
ARGENTINA 0
FRANCE 5
T: Caron *C:* J Prat

1949
Buenos Aires
ARGENTINA 3
PG: Rene
FRANCE 12
T: Pomathios (2) *C:* J Prat *DG:* J Prat

1954
Buenos Aires
ARGENTINA 3
PG: Bernacci
FRANCE 30
T: Bienes, A Boniface (2), Roge, Morel
C: Vannier (3) *PG:* Vannier *DG:* Vannier (2)

1960
Buenos Aires
ARGENTINA 3
PG: Devoto
FRANCE 37
T: Domenech (2), De Gregorio, Dizabo, Larrue, Celeya (2), Lacroix *C:* Vannier (5) *PG:* Vannier

1960
Buenos Aires
ARGENTINA 3
PG: Karplus
FRANCE 12
T: G Boniface (2) *PG:* Brethes
DG: Dizabo

1960
Buenos Aires
ARGENTINA 6
PG: Rios (2)
FRANCE 29
T: Lacroix, G Boniface, Dupuy (2), Crancee, Dizabo *C:* Vannier (4)
DG: Vannier

1974
Buenos Aires
ARGENTINA 15
T: Jurado *C:* Porta *PG:* Porta
DG: Porta (3)
FRANCE 20
T: Dourthe, Bertranne, Fouroux
C: Fouroux *PG:* Romeu (2)

1974
Buenos Aires
ARGENTINA 27
T: Walther *C:* Porta *PG:* Porta (7)
FRANCE 31
T: Gourdon (2), Bertranne, Dourthe
C: Romeu (3) *PG:* Romeu (3)

19 Oct 1975
Lyon
FRANCE 29
T: Pecune (2), Skrela, Fouroux, Rives, Droitcourt *C:* Romeu *PG:* Romeu
ARGENTINA 6
PG: Porta (2)

25 Oct 1975
Paris
FRANCE 36
T: Bertranne, Skrela, Droitcourt, Romeu, Astre *C:* Romeu (2) *PG:* Romeu (4)
ARGENTINA 21
T: Gauweloose *C:* Porta *PG:* Porta (5)

25 Jun 1977
Buenos Aires
ARGENTINA 3
PG: Porta
FRANCE 26
T: Bustaffa, Bertranne *PG:* Romeu (4), Aguirre *DG:* Romeu

2 Jul 1977
Buenos Aires
ARGENTINA 18
PG: Porta (6)
FRANCE 18
PG: Aguirre (6)

14 Nov 1982
Toulouse
FRANCE 25
T: Sella (2), Esteve, Blanco *PG:* Blanco, Camberabero *DG:* Camberabero
ARGENTINA 12
T: G Travaglini *C:* Porta *PG:* Porta (2)

20 Nov 1982
Paris
FRANCE 13
T: Begu, Blanco *C:* Camberabero
PG: Camberabero
ARGENTINA 6
PG: Porta (2)

22 Jun 1985
Buenos Aires
ARGENTINA 24
T: Ure, Turnes *C:* Porta (2) *PG:* Porta (3) *DG:* Porta
FRANCE 16
T: Blanco, Bonneval *C:* Lescarboura
PG: Lescarboura (2)

29 Jun 1985
Buenos Aires
ARGENTINA 15
T: Cuesta-Silva *C:* Porta *PG:* Porta (3)
FRANCE 23
T: Cordorniou, Erbani, Berbizier, Blanco
C: Lescarboura (2) *PG:* Lescarboura

31 May 1986
Buenos Aires
ARGENTINA 15
T: Ure *C:* Porta *PG:* Porta (3)
FRANCE 13
T: Bonneval *PG:* Laporte (3)

7 Jun 1986
Buenos Aires
ARGENTINA 9
PG: Porta (3)
FRANCE 22
T: Lescarboura, Sella, Dubroca
C: Lescarboura (2) *PG:* Lescarboura (2)

18 Jun 1988
Buenos Aires
ARGENTINA 15
T: Angelillo *C:* Baetti *PG:* Baetti (2)
DG: Turnes
FRANCE 18
T: Dintrans *C:* Berot *PG:* Berot (4)

25 Jun 1988
Buenos Aires
ARGENTINA 18
PG: Baetti (6)
FRANCE 6
PG: Berot (2)

5 Nov 1988
Beaujoire Stadium, Nantes
FRANCE 29
T: Blanco (2), Cecillon, Lagisquet, Rodriguez *C:* Berot (3) *PG:* Berot
ARGENTINA 9
PG: Turnes (3)

11 Nov 1988
Stade Grimomporez-Jooris, Lille
FRANCE 28
T: Sanz, Cecillon, Andrieu, Sella
C: Berot (3) *PG:* Berot (2)
ARGENTINA 18
PG: Turnes (5) *DG:* Madero

ARGENTINA v AUSTRALIA

27 Oct 1979
Buenos Aires
ARGENTINA 24
T: Madero (2) *C:* Porta *PG:* Porta
DG: Porta (3)
AUSTRALIA 13
T: Crowe *PG:* P McLean (2)
DG: Melrose

3 Nov 1979
Buenos Aires
ARGENTINA 12
T: Petersen *C:* Porta *PG:* Porta
DG: Porta
AUSTRALIA 17
T: Moon (2), Batch *C:* P McLean
PG: McLean

31 Jul 1983
Brisbane
AUSTRALIA 3
DG: Campese
ARGENTINA 18
T: Miguens, Petersen *C:* Porta (2)
PG: Porta *DG:* Porta

8 Aug 1983
Sydney
AUSTRALIA 29
T: Moon, (2), Roche, Campese, penalty try *C:* Campese (3) *PG:* Campese
ARGENTINA 13
T: Milano *PG:* Porta (2) *DG:* Porta

6 Jul 1986
Brisbane
AUSTRALIA 39
T: Papworth (2), Grigg, Campese
C: Lynagh (4) *PG:* Lynagh (5)
ARGENTINA 19
T: Cuesta-Silva, J Lanza, Turnes
C: Porta, Madero *PG:* Porta

12 Jul 1986
Sydney
AUSTRALIA 26
T: Campese (2), Tuynman *C:* Lynagh
PG: Lynagh (4)
ARGENTINA 0

31 Oct 1987
Buenos Aires
ARGENTINA 19
T: Cuesta Silva *PG:* Porta (4) *DG:* Porta
AUSTRALIA 19
T: Williams, Cutler, Lynagh *C:* Lynagh (2) *PG:* Lynagh

7 Nov 1987
Buenos Aires
ARGENTINA 27
T: Mendy *C:* Porta *PG:* Porta (5)
AUSTRALIA 19
T: Williams (2) *C:* Lynagh *PG:* Lynagh (3)

ARGENTINA v NEW ZEALAND

30 Oct 1976
Buenos Aires
ARGENTINA 9
PG: Beccar-Varela (2) *DG:* Porta
NEW ZEALAND 21
T: S Wilson, Sloane *C:* Rowlands (2) *PG:* Rowlands (3)

6 Nov 1976
Buenos Aires
ARGENTINA 6
PG: Sansot, Porta
NEW ZEALAND 26
T: Rollerson, Cron, MB Taylor, NM Taylor *C:* Rowlands (2) *PG:* Rowlands (2)

8 Sep 1979
Dunedin
NEW ZEALAND 18
PG: R Wilson (5) *DG:* Dunn
ARGENTINA 9
PG: Porta *DG:* Porta (2)

15 Sep 1979
Wellington
NEW ZEALAND 15
T: Cunningham, Loveridge *C:* R Wilson (2) *PG:* R Wilson
ARGENTINA 6
PG: Porta (2)

27 Oct 1985
Buenos Aires
ARGENTINA 20
T: J Lanza, Cuesta-Silva *PG:* Porta (3) *DG:* Porta
NEW ZEALAND 33
T: Kirwan (2), Crowley, Hobbs *C:* Crowley *PG:* Crowley (4) *DG:* Crowley

3 Nov 1985
Buenos Aires
ARGENTINA 21
PG: Porta (4) *DG:* Porta (3)
NEW ZEALAND 21
T: Kirwan (2), Mexted, Green *C:* Crowley *PG:* Crowley

15 Jul 1989
Carisbrook, Dunedin
NEW ZEALAND 60
T: Gallagher (3), Kirwan (2), Wright (2), Jones (2), penalty try *C:* Fox (7) *PG:* Fox (2)
ARGENTINA 9
T: Turnes *C:* Baetti *PG:* Baetti

29 Jul 1989
Athletic Park, Wellington
NEW ZEALAND 49
T: Wright (2), Deans (2), Gallagher, Kirwan, A Whetton *C:* Fox (6) *PG:* Fox (3)
ARGENTINA 12
T: Dengra *C:* Baetti *PG:* Turnes (2)

6 Jul 1991
Buenos Aires
ARGENTINA 14
T: Garreton, Carreras *PG:* Vidou (2)
NEW ZEALAND 28
T: Earl, Wright *C:* Fox *PG:* Fox (5) *DG:* Crowley

13 Jul 1991
Buenos Aires
ARGENTINA 6
PG: del Castillo (2)
NEW ZEALAND 36
T: Brooke, M Jones, Kirwan, Wright *C:* Fox (4) *PG:* Fox (4)

SOUTH AMERICA v SOUTH AFRICA

26 Apr 1980
Johannesburg
SOUTH AFRICA 24
T: T du Plessis, Mordt, Germishuys *C:* Botha (3) *PG:* Botha *DG:* Botha
SOUTH AMERICA 9
T: Travaglini *C:* Porta *PG:* Porta

3 May 1980
Durban
SOUTH AFRICA 18
T: M du Plessis *C:* Botha *PG:* Botha *DG:* Botha (3)
SOUTH AMERICA 9
PG: Piccardo (3)

18 Oct 1980
Montevideo
SOUTH AMERICA 13
T: Cubelli, Madero *C:* Porta *DG:* Landejo
SOUTH AFRICA 22
T: Stofberg, Gerber, Berger *C:* Botha (2) *PG:* Botha *DG:* Botha

26 Oct 1980
Santiago
SOUTH AMERICA 16
T: Campo, Iachetti *C:* Porta *PG:* Porta *DG:* Porta
SOUTH AFRICA 30
T: Mordt (2), Germishuys (2), Gerber, M du Plessis *C:* Botha (3)

27 Mar 1982
Pretoria
SOUTH AFRICA 50
T: Gerber (3), Mordt (2), Oosthuizen, C du Plessis, W du Plessis *C:* Botha (6) *PG:* Heunis *DG:* Botha
SOUTH AMERICA 18
T: Puccio *C:* Porta *PG:* Porta (4)

3 Apr 1982
Bloemfontein
SOUTH AFRICA 12
T: Gerber *C:* Botha *PG:* Botha (2)
SOUTH AMERICA 21
T: Porta *C:* Porta *PG:* Porta (4) *DG:* Porta

20 Oct 1984
Pretoria
SOUTH AFRICA 32
T: Louw, Gerber, Serfontein, Heunis, Mallet *C:* Tobias (2), Gerber *PG:* Tobias (2)
SOUTH AMERICA 15
T: Palma, de Vedia *C:* Porta (2) *PG:* Porta

27 Oct 1984
Cape Town
SOUTH AFRICA 22
T: C du Plessis, Ferreira, Mordt, Gerber *PG:* Tobias (2)
SOUTH AMERICA 13
T: Sansot *PG:* Porta (3)

DOMESTIC RUGBY STRUCTURE

Buenos Aires club league, provincial leagues and a provincial tournament.
The Buenos Aires Rugby Championship is divided into three divisions each with 12 clubs. Lower divisions contain weaker clubs in a pyramid system. A play-off system has also been in operation recently.

THE ARGENTINE PROVINCIAL CHAMPIONSHIP

Dominated by Buenos Aires, and more latterly by Tucuman, the competition is open to all affiliated Unions. Affiliated Unions and clubs in 1992 were:

Austral	North East
Bahia Blanca	Rio Negro
Buenos Aires	Rosario
Chebut	Salta
Corboda	San Juan
Cuyo	Santa Fe
Jujena	Tandil
Mar del Plata	Tucuman

CHAMPIONS
Prior to 1985 Buenos Aires
1985 Tucuman
1986 Buenos Aires
1987–91 Tucuman

BUENOS AIRES CLUB CHAMPIONS

Club	Wins	Years
Lomas	2	1899, 1913
Buenos Aires	10	1900, 1901, 1902, 1903, 1904, 1908, 1909, 1915, 1958, 1959
Rosario Athletic	3	1905, 1906, 1935
Belgrano	6	1907, 1910, 1914, 1963, 1966, 1967*
Gymnasia y Escrima	3	1911, 1912, 1932
Atletico San Isidro	29	1917, 1918, 1920, 1921, 1922, 1923, 1924, 1925, 1926, 1927, 1928, 1929, 1930, 1943, 1949*, 1954, 1955, 1956, 1957, 1961, 1962, 1964, 1967*, 1974, 1974, 1976, 1981, 1982, 1985
Universitario	12	1931, 1942, 1944, 1945, 1947, 1949*, 1950*, 1951, 1952, 1968*, 1969, 1970*
San Isidro Club	14	1941, 1948, 1968*, 1970*, 1971, 1972, 1973, 1977, 1978, 1979, 1980, 1983, 1984, 1986*
Pucara	2	1946, 1950*
Obrias Sanitarias	1	1953
Banco Nacion	2	1986*, 1988
Alumni	3	1989, 1990, 1991

* Championship shared

CANADA

FOUNDATION: 1929 (reformed 1965)
Honours: 1991 World Cup quarter finalists, 1987 World Cup first round
Most points: 263 M Wyatt
Most tries: 12 S McTavish
Largest victory: 49–26 v Japan 1991
Margin: 37–4 v Tonga 1987
Heaviest defeat: 3–59 v Australia 1985
Clubs: 220
Players: 11 670
Population: 23 499 000
Main stadium: Burnaby, Vancouver (cap: 15 000)
Colours: Red jerseys, white shorts
Headquarters: Canadian Rugby Union
National Sport & Recreation Centre
1600 Prom. James Naismith Drive
Ontario K1B 5N4

When a respected British rugby magazine asked journalists to list their probable list of giant killers for the 1991 World Cup, ninety per cent of them selected Canada as the nation most likely to cause an upset. The fact that Canada then found a route to the quarter finals via wins over seeded Fiji and Romania and made a glorious exit in a fine performance against New Zealand revealed that Rugby scribes can sometimes get it right.

But closer inspection of why there is such a favoured impression reveals a country whose coaching methods are sound, whose grass roots extend firmly into the school curricula, and whose national sides and administrators aim in a positive direction towards sensible promotion of the game and improving standards on the field.

British Columbia was the first significant centre of Canadian rugby-playing operations, being the stop-off point for several New Zealand and Australian touring sides to Britain and vice versa. The British Columbia Rugby Union was founded in 1889 when sides from the British Armed Forces would play local clubs.

That it took the Canadian Rugby Union until 1929 to form itself into a governing body can be explained by the East–West split. Such were the distances involved that the twain rarely met. It was, as today, a case of British Columbia versus the Rest. Barely 10 years later, after war was declared, the Union folded; just one tour had been undertaken to Japan in 1932, when the Canadians won the five provincial matches but lost both internationals 9–8 and 38–5. It was to be another 30 years and 10 months before Canada took the field again – in the more than creditable 3–3 draw with the Barbarians at Gosforth in 1962.

The Canadian Rugby Union was revived in 1965, with aid from the government. Money was spent on coaching and the organisation of the Inter Provincial Rugby Championship which had previously been won by British Columbia in 1958 and 1959, but had not been played since.

The statistics surrounding the Inter Provincial Rugby Championship indicate where current strengths lie, and how far the game has spread throughout the country. Up to 1991 there had been 26 Championships – British Columbia have won 22, Ontario 4, the rest nothing. Only twice have BC not made the final – in 1972 and 1973. Ontario have had 17 runners-up places to add to their four wins. The only other provinces to reach the final have been Alberta (2), Quebec (4) and Newfoundland, whose one appearance was in 1974. Since 1975, Quebec (in 1978) are the only team to have prevented a BC–Ontario final.

The Canadian Rugby Union's research has now unearthed the first games played in each province. The list reads – 1865 Quebec, 1870 Nova Scotia, 1872, Ontario, 1884 Prince Edward Island, New Brunswick, 1889 British Columbia, 1891 Alberta, Manitoba, 1893 Saskatchewan. Newfoundland remains a mystery, but all entries in the list go back to the last century.

Canada entered the Rugby world record books on 25 May 1991. Captain and full back Mark Wyatt erased the previous record of Simon Hodgkinson and Hugo Porta, by kicking eight penalties against the Scotland XV, Canada's first win over one of the home countries. The venue provided further evidence that rugby is now truly a world game – St John (not St John's) in New Brunswick.

Gord McKinnon scores for Canada against Japan in their 49–26 win in 1991.

CANADA v ENGLAND

1964
Vancouver
CANADA 0
ENGLAND XV 29

29 Jun 1982
Vancouver
CANADA 6
PG: Shiefler (2)
ENGLAND 43
T: Swift (2), Scott, SJ Smith, Carleton (2), Cusworth *C:* Hare (3) *PG:* Hare (3)

15 Oct 1983
Twickenham
ENGLAND 27
T: Youngs, Winterbottom, Penalty try *C:* Hare (3) *PG:* Hare (3)
CANADA 0

CANADA v IRELAND

2 Sep 1989
Victoria
CANADA 21
PG: Wyatt (7)
IRELAND 24
T: Dunlea, Sexton *C:* Kiernan (2) *PG:* Kiernan (4)

Canada's finest hour – waving farewell to the French crowd after their heroic deeds at the 1991 World Cup which saw them reach the quarter-finals.

CANADA v WALES

2 Oct 1971
Cardiff Arms Park
WALES 56
T: Mathias (3), David (2), K Hughes (2), Morris, Tovey, B Llewellyn *C:* R Williams (5) *PG:* R Williams *DG:* R Williams
CANADA 10
T: McTavish (2) *C:* Burnham

9 Jun 1973
Toronto
CANADA 20
T: Wyndham (2), Docherty *C:* Deacy *PG:* Deacy (2)
WALES 58
T: David (2), K Hughes (2), JD Bevan, JJ Williams, Bennett, B Llewellyn, Taylor *C:* Bennett (7), Taylor *PG:* Bennett (2)

CANADA v SCOTLAND

25 May 1991
St John, NB
CANADA 24
PG: Wyatt (8)
SCOTLAND XV 19
T: Reid, Stanger *C:* Dods *PG:* Dods (3)

CANADA v FRANCE

30 Sep 1978
Calgary
CANADA 9
T: Peace *C:* Wiley *PG:* Wiley
FRANCE 24
T: Bilbao, Belascian, Noves, Rives *C:* Aguirre *PG:* Aguirre, Vivies

29 Sep 1979
Charlety, Paris
FRANCE 34
T: Gallion, Blanco, Belascain, Gourdon *C:* Caussade (3) *PG:* Caussade (3) *DG:* Caussade
CANADA 15
T: Greig *C:* Taylor *PG:* Taylor (2) *DG:* Bibby

CANADA v NEW ZEALAND

11 Oct 1980
Vancouver
CANADA 10
T: Bibby *PG:* Shiefler
NEW ZEALAND 43
T: M Shaw (3), Mourie, Haden, Osborne, S Wilson, Fraser *C:* Rollerson (4) *PG:* Rollerson

CANADA v AUSTRALIA

15 Jun 1985
Sydney
AUSTRALIA 59
T: Burke (2), Lane (2), Grigg (2), Calcraft, Farr-Jones, Kassulke *C:* Lynagh (7) *PG:* Lynagh (3)
CANADA 3
DG: Wyatt

23 Jun 1985
Brisbane
AUSTRALIA 43
T: Burke (3), Grigg, Cutler, Tuynman, Farr-Jones *C:* Lynagh (3) *PG:* Lynagh (2) *DG:* Lynagh
CANADA 15
T: Tucker *C:* Wyatt *PG:* Wyatt (3)

CANADA v UNITED STATES

1977
Vancouver
CANADA 17
T: Bower, Greig, de Goede *C:* Gonis
PG: Hindson
UNITED STATES 6
PG: Jablonski (2)

1978
Towson
UNITED STATES 12
T: Klein *C:* Jablonski *PG:* Jablonski (2)
CANADA 7
T: McTavish *PG:* Gonis

1979
Toronto
CANADA 19
T: McTavish *PG:* Wiley (4), Billingsley
UNITED STATES 12
PG: Jablonski (4)

1980
Saranac Lake
UNITED STATES 0
CANADA 16
T: McTavish (2) *C:* Shiefler *PG:* Shiefler
DG: Shiefler

1981
Calgary
CANADA 6
PG: Shiefler (2)
UNITED STATES 3
PG: Cooke

1982
Albany
UNITED STATES 3
PG: Halliday
CANADA 3
PG: Wyatt

Dan Jackart reveals a natty line of patriotic hairstyling.

1983
Vancouver
CANADA 15
T: Billingsley *C:* Wyatt *PG:* Wyatt (2), Shiefler
UNITED STATES 9
T: Helu *C:* Nelson *PG:* Nelson

1984
Chicago
UNITED STATES 21
T: Hartman *C:* Nelson *PG:* Nelson (5)
CANADA 13
T: Wyatt *PG:* Wyatt (3)

1985
Vancouver
CANADA 21
PG: Wyatt (6) *DG:* Wyatt
UNITED STATES 10
T: Caulder *PG:* Inns (2)

1986
Tucson
UNITED STATES 16
T: Crivellone, W Everett, Jefferson
C: Inns (2)
CANADA 27
T: Ennis, Lecky *C:* Wyatt (2) *PG:* Wyatt (3) *DG:* Wyatt, Rees

1987
Vancouver
CANADA 33
T: Gray (3), Ennis, de Goede, Evans
C: Rees (3)
UNITED STATES 9
T: Helo *C:* Nelson *PG:* Nelson

1988
UNITED STATES 28
T: O'Brien, Williams, Johnson, Lambert
C: O'Brien (3) *PG:* Williams, O'Brien
CANADA 16
T: Palmer, Vanden-Brink *C:* Tynan
PG: Wyatt *DG:* Wyatt

1989
CANADA 21
T: Brown *C:* Wyatt *PG:* Wyatt (5)
UNITED STATES 3
PG: O'Brien

1990
UNITED STATES 14
T: Dally, Lewis *PG:* Williams, deJong
CANADA 12
T: Ennis *C:* Wyatt *PG:* Wyatt *DG:* Ross

1991
CANADA 34
T: Ennis (2), Palmer (2) *C:* Wyatt (3)
PG: Wyatt (4)
UNITED STATES 15
T: Nelson *C:* O'Brien *PG:* Judge (3)

1992
CANADA 32
T: Rees, Tynan, Gray, Palmer *C:* Rees (2) *PG:* Rees (4)
UNITED STATES 9
PG: Gale (2) *DG:* Gale (2)

VICTORIES OVER MAJOR TOURING TEAMS

British Columbia
1912 Australia W 15–0
1958 Australia W 11–8

Vancouver
1912 Australia W 6–3

Victoria
1912 Australia W 13–11

DOMESTIC RUGBY STRUCTURE

The Inter Provincial Championship is the major event. At club level, each province organises its own league and cup competitions.

Provincial Unions and number of players (1991)

British Columbia	3500
Alberta	1700
Saskatchewan	500
Manitoba	650
Ontario	3500
Quebec	650
New Brunswick	500
Nova Scotia	450
Prince Edward Island	40
Newfoundland	180

THE CARLING BOWL – CANADIAN INTER PROVINCIAL CHAMPIONSHIP TROPHY

Finals	Winners		Runners-up		Venue
1958	BC	18	Western Canada (Que/Ont)	9	Toronto
1959	BC	24	Eastern Canada	3	Vancouver
1960–5	*Not played*				
1966	BC	51	Ontario	3	Vancouver
1967	BC	27	Quebec	6	Montreal
1968	BC	13	Quebec	3	Vancouver
1969	BC	21	Quebec	9	Toronto
1970	BC	26	Ontario	6	Vancouver
1971	Ontario	27	BC	17	Toronto
1972	Ontario	7	Alberta	3	Victoria
1973	Ontario	17	Alberta	7	Ottawa
1974	BC	49	Newfoundland	3	Vancouver
1975	BC	43	Ontario	6	Halifax
1976	BC	35	Ontario	6	Victoria
1977	BC	7	Ontario	3	Toronto
1978	BC	41	Quebec	3	Calgary
1979	BC	36	Ontario	7	Ottawa
1980	BC	48	Ontario	7	Vancouver
1981	BC	9	Ontario	3	Ottawa
1982	Ontario	21	BC	9	Edmonton
1983	BC	25	Ontario	9	Victoria
1984	BC	16	Ontario	9	Montreal
1985	BC	31	Ontario	11	Calgary
1986	BC	29	Ontario	12	Toronto
1987	BC	27	Ontario	0	Vancouver
1988	BC	22	Ontario	13	Edmonton
1989	BC	55	Ontario	7	Victoria
1990	BC	48	Ontario	9	Ottawa
1991	BC	35	Newfoundland	3	Victoria

FIJI

FOUNDATION: 1913
Honours: 1987 World Cup quarter finalists, 1991 World Cup first round
Hong Kong Sevens: 1977, 1978, 1980, 1984, 1990, 1991, 1992
Biggest victories: 113–3 v New Caledonia 1969, 113–13 v Solomon Islands 1969
Heaviest defeat: 13–74 v New Zealand 1987
Clubs: 600 teams in 80 sub-unions
Players: 12 250
Population: 706 000
Main stadium: National Stadium, Suva (cap: 18 000)
Colours: White jerseys, black shorts
Headquarters: Fiji Rugby Union
PO Box 1234
Suva

The key figure in Fijian rugby history was a plumber who fixed the taps and pipes to a Suva hotel back in 1913. It was his organisation during the short period that he was in Fiji, that structured the game, introduced rugby to the natives, and left the legacy of the flamboyant style of play that is uniquely Fijian.

That plumber was a certain Paddy Sheehan. Paddy was a mighty forward for the Southern club Dunedin in New Zealand. He captained Otago for several seasons in Ranfurly Shield games. Sheehan was one of a group of New Zealanders who arrived in Suva to build the Grand Pacific Hotel.

Sheehan immediately saw a need for organising the casual rugby that had sprung up in the country. There were inter-village matches, matches between Suva and the ships in harbour and some clubs even existed. So the persuasive Sheehan promptly invited all players to his half-built hotel, and laid down the rugby law.

The first meeting in 1913 (the exact date is not chronicled) started with Paddy forming his own Pacific club. By the end of the very first day, there were three more clubs – the Cadets Club (bankers), the United Services Club (drawn from Cable and Wireless workers) and the Imperial Club, a team of Suva commercial men. These four clubs formed the Fiji Rugby Union, Paddy Sheehan was elected chairman, and another New Zealander, Otto Strachy, from Timaru, Otago, became Treasurer.

The earliest recorded match was believed, though no one is entirely certain, to have been played at Ba in 1884 between the Europeans and the native Constabulary, who were trained by a Major Thornton. In those Victorian days, when cannibalism was still in vogue, football and cricket were the preferred pastimes.

Fijian archives, both at the Fijian Rugby Union and from old newspapers, are sketchy as to what happened between 1884 and 1913. A club competition result between the Constabulary and the Civil Service appeared on the sports page of the Fiji Times in 1904. A year later Ratu Jone Tabaiwalu arrived from school in Whangerei with a proud possession – his own ball. The natives showed immediate interest in a game they had begun to call Veicaqe-vaka-Peritana (football British style). In 1911, the Davies Rugby Club, the first on the island, had regular fixtures with the warships in Suva harbour.

Having started organised rugby in the country, Sheehan and his group returned to New Zealand. Sheehan became a stalwart of the Marist and North Shore clubs in Auckland, and a member of the Auckland Rugby Union committee. The locals took up his groundwork. The Escott Shield was donated by the then Governor of Fiji, Sir Ernest Bickham Sweet-Escott, for competition between the Suva clubs, and is still the major club trophy today. In 1914, the 'native competition' had its baptism with clubs from Taipou, Tariere, Hill and the Police.

From that firm base, Fijian rugby is virtually the same today. There are 80 sub-unions, to which all the smaller town and village clubs are affiliated. Yet from a total population of some 700 000, some 52% are Indians, brought in as labour for the sugar plantations, who still prefer to play soccer.

Fiji's first international match was a catalogue of events that rides high in any book of sporting comedies. The Fijians played Western Samoa as a stop over match on their way to a more important encounter with Tonga. The tourists all paid their own fares. The match was played at 7.00 am to enable the Samoans to go to work after the match. Fiji won 6–0 in the stadium at Apia, but conceded that they had greater opposition in the form of a large tree in the centre of the pitch than from the willing opponents.

Two years later, the Tongans visited Fiji for the first time, shortly after the island's first tourists, the 1926 Auckland University College club. For the Tonga match, the Fijians wore their familiar white shirt, blue

Mesake Resari in spectacular action for Fiji at the 1992 Hong Kong Sevens. The Fijians are undisputed masters at the game.

shorts and palm tree badge for the first time.

1938 was another landmark in Fijian rugby history. In honour of the visit of the New Zealand Maori team, the locals wore boots for the first time. Most were discarded well before the end of the match. The game was drawn 3–3.

A year later Fiji Schools Rugby Union was founded. Though games had been played since 1914, and a competition had been in full swing since 1928, the need to develop local talent was paramount. Immediately after the war, the Farebrother-Sullivan Trophy was first contested between the sub-unions, named after two leading administrators.

In the 1990s, one does not really know what to expect from the Fijians. Their 1991 season was a typical case. On one hand, the Fijian seven won the Hong Kong Sevens in their usual world beating manner; and Fiji B beat England 27–13 at Lautoka. Their World Cup exploits though were a disaster, as they were the only seeds not to win a match.

Their frustration when met with the more demanding needs of disciplined rugby has often shown another side of their temperament with two sendings off at Twickenham in 1989 as a result of not being able to display their fluent open game. Conversely, the Fijian seven has displayed all their finest characteristics – marvellous handling and ball skills, athleticism of the highest order in both forwards and backs, pace and stamina. If the Fijians can harness their aggression into greater discipline and ball winning capabilities, anything is possible. The last time that Fiji beat a major side was the 1977 victory against the British Lions 25–21 at Suva.

FIJI v ENGLAND

28 Aug 1973
Suva
FIJI 13
T: Kurisaru, Latilevu *C:* Ratudina, Batisbasaga
ENGLAND 13
T: Evans, Squires *C:* Jorden
PG: Jorden

29 May 1979
Suva
FIJI 7
T: Nayate *PG:* Musunamasi
ENGLAND 19
T: Cardus, Beaumont, Squires *C:* H Davies *PG:* H Davies

16 Oct 1982
Twickenham
ENGLAND 60
T: Trick (3), Swift (3), Gadd (2), Scott, SJ Smith, Cusworth, Dodge, Colclough
C: Hare (6)
FIJI 19
T: Tamata, Politini, Namoro *C:* Sevaro (2) *PG:* Sevaro

17 Jun 1988
Suva
FIJI 12
PG: Koroduadua (3) *DG:* Koroduadua
ENGLAND 25
T: Underwood (2), Barley *C:* Barnes (2)
PG: Barnes (3)

4 Nov 1989
Twickenham
ENGLAND 58
T: Underwood (5), Skinner, Bailey, Linnett, Ackford, Guscott
C: Hodgkinson (5), Andrew
PG: Hodgkinson (2)
FIJI 23
T: Eranavula, Teleni, Rasari, Suvai
C: Koroduadua (2) *PG:* Koroduadua

20 Jul 1991
National Stadium, Suva
FIJI 12
T: Seru *C:* Serevi *PG:* Serevi
DG: Serevi
ENGLAND 28
T: Probyn, Underwood, Andrew
C: Webb (2) *PG:* Webb (2) *DG:* Andrew (2)

FIJI v IRELAND

8 Jun 1976
Suva
FIJI 0
IRELAND 8
T: Grace, Clegg

19 Oct 1985
Lansdowne Road, Dublin
IRELAND 16
T: Bradley *PG:* Kiernan (4)
FIJI 15
T: Laulau, Tuvula *C:* Damu (2)
PG: Damu

FIJI v WALES

26 Sep 1964
Cardiff Arms Park
WALES 28
T: Bebb (2), D Thomas (2), Pask, Weaver, Prothero *C:* T Price (2)
PG: Watkins
FIJI 22
T: Walisoliso (3), Soqosoqo, Mucunabitu, Robe *C:* Nawase (2)

25 Jun 1969
Suva
FIJI 11
T: Turagoka, Sikivou *C:* Raitilava
PG: Raitilava
WALES 31
T: D Hughes (3), Taylor (2), Richards
C: Jarrett (5) *DG:* JPR Williams

9 Nov 1985
Cardiff Arms Park
WALES 40
T: PT Davies (2), Titley, Holmes, Hadley, Pickering, James *C:* Thorburn (3)
PG: Thorburn (2)
FIJI 3
PG: Damu

31 May 1986
Suva
FIJI 15
T: Niuqila, Tuvula *C:* Kubu (2)
PG: Lovokuru
WALES 22
T: J Davies, Bowen *C:* Bowen
PG: Dacey (3) *DG:* J Davies

FIJI v SCOTLAND

25 Sep 1982
Murrayfield
SCOTLAND 32
T: Dods (2), Johnston, F Calder, Beattie *C:* Dods (3) *PG:* Dods *DG:* Rutherford
FIJI 12
T: Nadruka *C:* Sevaro *PG:* Sevaro (2)

28 Oct 1989
Murrayfield
SCOTLAND 38
T: Stanger (2), Milne, Gray, G Hastings, Tukalo *C:* G Hastings (4) *PG:* G Hastings (2)
FIJI 17
T: Lovo, Rasari *PG:* Koroduadua, Serevi (2)

FIJI v NEW ZEALAND

14 Jun 1974
Suva
FIJI 13
T: Latilevu, Cavuitati *C:* Naituyaga *PG:* Naituyaga
NEW ZEALAND 14
T: Batty, Williams, Hurst *C:* Karam

23 Jul 1980
Suva
FIJI 6
T: Kunikoro *C:* Gavidi
NEW ZEALAND 30
T: Fraser (3), Allen, B Robertson *C:* Codlin (2) *PG:* Codlin (2)

13 Sep 1980
Auckland
NEW ZEALAND 33
T: Osborne (2), KJ Taylor (2), Wylie, Woodman *C:* Valli (3) *PG:* Valli
FIJI 0

FIJI v AUSTRALIA

26 Jul 1952
Sydney
AUSTRALIA 15
T: Jones, Stapleton, Johnson, Solomon *PG:* Baker
FIJI 9
T: Valewai, Ranavue *PG:* Ranavue

9 Aug 1952
Sydney
AUSTRALIA 15
T: Stapleton, Cox, Shehadie, Windon *DG:* Solomon
FIJI 17
T: Salabogi, Ralagi *C:* Vatabua, Ranavue *PG:* Vatabua, Ranavue

5 Jun 1954
Brisbane
AUSTRALIA 22
T: Cameron, Jones, Phipps, Cross, Tate *C:* Barker, Tooth *PG:* Barker
FIJI 19
T: Naborisi, Cavalevu, Domoni, Boruglevu *C:* Vatabua (2) *PG:* Vatabua

26 Jun 1954
Sydney
AUSTRALIA 16
T: Cross, Shehadie *C:* Barker (2) *PG:* Barker (2)
FIJI 18
T: Seruvatu, Sankuru *PG:* Ranavue (3), Nawalu

10 Jun 1961
Brisbane
AUSTRALIA 24
T: Lisle, R Thornett, Magrath, Cleary, Phelps, Catchpole *C:* Dowe (3)
FIJI 6
PG: Bose (2)

17 Jun 1961
Sydney
AUSTRALIA 20
T: Cleary (2), Ellwood, Reid *C:* Dowse *PG:* Dowse (2)
FIJI 14
T: Nabou, Rasou, Lovodua *C:* Bose *PG:* Tawase

1 Jul 1961
Melbourne
AUSTRALIA 3
T: Lisle
FIJI 3
T: Levula

19 Sep 1927
Suva
FIJI 19
T: Varo (2) *C:* Batisbasaga *PG:* Batisbasaga (3)
AUSTRALIA 21
T: Thompson, Sullivan, Burnett, Stumbles *C:* Thompson *DG:* Fairfax

12 Jun 1976
Sydney
AUSTRALIA 22
T: Batch (2), Ryan, Pearse *PG:* P McLean (2)
FIJI 6
T: Tuiese *C:* Naituyaga

19 Jun 1976
Brisbane
AUSTRALIA 21
T: Ryan (2) *C:* P McLean (2) *PG:* P McLean (2) *DG:* P McLean
FIJI 9
PG: Raitilava (3)

26 Jun 1976
Sydney
AUSTRALIA 27
T: Batch, Pearse, Ryan *PG:* P McLean (5)
FIJI 17
T: Nasave, Matalau, Viriviri *C:* Nasave *PG:* Nasave

24 May 1980
Suva
FIJI 9
PG: Vinetaki, Waiseke *DG:* Radrodo
AUSTRALIA 22
T: Martin, Moon *C:* P McLean *PG:* P McLean *DG:* P McLean

Aug 1983
Suva
FIJI 3
PG: Turuva
AUSTRALIA 16
T: Campese *PG:* Lynagh (4)

10 Aug 1985
Brisbane
AUSTRALIA 52
T: Farr-Jones (2), Reynolds, Cutler, Lawton, Papworth, Grigg *C:* Knox (3) *PG:* Knox (3) *DG:* Knox (2), Campese
FIJI 28
T: Nawalu, Niuqila, Cama, Talawadua *C:* Koroduadua (3) *PG:* Koroduadua (2)

17 Aug 1985
Sydney
AUSTRALIA 31
T: Campese (2), Grigg, McIntyre, Cutler *C:* Knox *PG:* Knox (3)
FIJI 9
PG: Koroduadua (2) *DG:* Koroduadua

OTHER MAJOR VICTORIES

24 Oct 1970
Gosforth
BARBARIANS 9
T: Duckham, JS Spencer *PG:* JPR Williams
FIJI 29
T: Batisabaga, Nasave, Visei, Qoro, Racike, Tuese, Ravouvou
C: Batisabaga (4)

16 Aug 1977
Suva
FIJI 24
T: Narasia (2), Racike (2), Kuinikoro
C: Racike *DG:* Tikoisuva
BRITISH LIONS 21
T: Bennett, Beaumont, Burcher
C: Bennett (3) *PG:* Bennett

Fiji won the 1969 South Pacific Games Championship in Port Moresby, Papua New Guinea, breaking several 'world records'. Owing to the then quality of the opposition, the records do not appear in most official lists. The Fijians scored 457 points in eight days, and their full results were:

16 Aug	Wallis and Futuna	W	84–8
18 Aug	Papua New Guinea	W	79–0
21 Aug	Solomon Islands	W	113–13
22 Aug	New Caledonia	W	113–3
23 Aug	Papua New Guinea	W	88–3

The Fijians were gracious enough to admit that the victories did them no good at all, and doubted whether the opposition would have gleaned much value from such heavy defeats.

DOMESTIC RUGBY STRUCTURE

Each major Union has its own inter club competitions.
The major Unions play for the Farebrother–Sullivan Trophy which is held on Ranfurly Shield lines, with the holders accepting challenges. Suva have held the Trophy over a period of 24 years to 1992 and have done so continuously since September 1988 when they beat Nadi 15–4; Nadroga over a period of 13 years, Nadi 12, and both Lautoka (1965) and Northern Districts (1951) for one year. Similar to the Ranfurly Shield in New Zealand, the holders may accept several challenges per season.

ITALY

FOUNDATION: 1928
Honours: 1987 and 1991 World Cup first round
Leading scorer: 483 S Bettarello
Largest victories: 49–9 v Czechoslovakia 1975
45–0 v Belgium 1937
Heaviest defeats: 6–70 v New Zealand 1987
0–69 v Romania 1977
Clubs: 265
Players: 15 200
Population: 56 799 000
Main stadium: FIR Stadium, Rome (cap: 27 000)
Colours: Blue jerseys, white shorts
Headquarters: Federazione Italiana Rugby
Via L. Franchetti 2
00194 Rome

There are claims that the first rugby ever played was by Roman legions, who played harpastum, a form of handball. Somehow even the Italians are happy to concede the true origins of the game. Their relationship with the modern era is relatively recent, and owes much to the obvious geographical ties with neighbours France.

The first mention of rugby in Italy was in 1910, and, as matters have a habit of moving quite quickly in Italian organisation and enthusiasm, there were 10 clubs in the country by 1927, dotted mainly along the Lombardy plain but reaching south as far as Rome. In 1928 the clubs organised the Federazione Italiana Rugby (FIR); the following year Ambrosiana Milano won the first championship and Italy had lost in their first international match – by 9–0 to Spain at Barcelona.

The exclusion of France from the Five Nations Championship in 1931 benefited countries like Italy. The French, anxious to maintain a fixture list, looked away from Britain and Ireland towards the emerging nations of Europe. Italy, along with France, Romania and the then powerful Germany, were in the forefront of the foundation in 1934 of FIRA, the Federation Internationale de Rugby Amateur, which not only saved international rugby for the French, but became an association that France have supported with conviction ever since.

Italian rugby had, via the FIRA Championship, a ready-made international outlet. Countries such as France 'A', Romania, and, later on, the Soviet Union, gave Italy a strong fixture list from the early 1950s. While Italy have never beaten France, they rightly claim parity in results with Romania.

In modern times there are three distinct patterns in Italian rugby about which more is now being said. The first is that of sponsorship of the clubs by major conglomerates, ostensibly to help with travel costs and to provide improved facilities for the rugby fraternity. The semi-finalists in the 1990–1 championship were Mediolanum of Milan, Benetton of Treviso, Petrarca of Padova and Cagnoni of Rovigo. Other clubs carry delightful prefixes such as Iranium Loom, Pasta Jolly, Scavolini and Delicius. Crowds are sparse in many cases,

The Cattania Stadium in the shadow of Mount Etna, host for the Sicily Sevens and the preliminary rounds of the 1993 World Sevens.

the top league games will attract 5000 people but many have to find their way the length and breadth of the country on average gates of 250. Thus sponsorship is the key to successful finances.

Italy has also been able to entice quality overseas players to bolster the home-produced talent. The quality comes from the southern hemisphere countries who play in Italy in their off season. Of the current international stars, David Campese seems almost to prefer being listed as from the Milan club than Randwick, Australia. He enlisted the new star of Australian rugby, Willie Ofahengaue to help defend the league title in 1991–2. Australia's Michael Lynagh and the Western Samoan captain Peter Fatialofa followed the path after the 1991 World Cup. The New Zealand wings from the 1987 World Cup triumph, John Kirwan and Craig Green, have spent time in Italy – indeed Green never returned down under – and Kieran Crowley used to play for Parma. The South Africans have found Italy a 'safe haven' away from political issues. Naas Botha has been playing with Rovigo for several seasons, while most of the Springbok pack have had spells in the Serie A. Botha's heir apparent, Joel Stransky, the Natal fly half from their 1990 Currie Cup win, plays for L'Aquila. Looking at the coaching staff, Mark Ella has led Milan to the 1991 championship.

But there have been problems in recruitment. Argentina woke one day to find most of its international personnel enjoying life in Italy. Diego

Dominquez and Gustavo Milano have already played international rugby for Italy, but the likes of Turnes, Gomeza, Dengra, Ansaldi and Di Nisio have picked up bans from the ARU.

But the third issue is probably the most exciting in the future of Italian rugby. Their youth policy, laid down many years ago by the likes of Carwyn James and Pierre Villepreux, is now starting to bear fruit. A glance through the recent youth and junior scores since 1987 includes results like:

Scotland Youth 6 **Italy Youth 26**
France U18 7 **Italy U18 10**
Italy Youth 17 England Youth 15
Italy U16 7 England U16 6
Italy U19 21 Scotland U19 18
England Youth 21 **Italy Youth 22**

Italy have also won the prestigious U19 and U16 FIRA tournaments in the last three seasons, beating France and Argentina to claim the trophies. The 1991 B international finished narrowly in England's favour by 12–9. It suggests that if the gap between junior and senior rugby can be adequately bridged, then Italian rugby is in good hands, and that an international rugby weekend in Rome is not a wild pipedream. A World Cup result of New Zealand 31 Italy 21 in 1991, compared with a 70–6 scoreline four years earlier, whilst not suggesting that statistics can prove anything, certainly indicates a rapidly closing gap between the major and emerging nations.

DOMESTIC RUGBY STRUCTURE

Regional feeder leagues through to national leagues (Serie A and B). There are two Series A divisions with the top four in each entering a knockout competition to find the champion club.

ITALIAN CHAMPIONS

(Sponsors names not included i.e. Mediolanum Milan, the 1991 champions, have not always been sponsored by the same firm)

1929, 1930, 1931, 1932, 1933, 1934 Milan
1935 Rome
1936, 1937, 1938, 1939, 1940, 1941, 1942, 1943 Milan
1944, 1945 *Not played*
1946 Milan
1947 Turin
1948, 1949 Rome
1950 Parma
1951, 1952, 1953, 1954 Rovigo
1955 Parma
1956 Treviso
1957 Parma
1958, 1959, 1960, 1961 Padua
1962, 1963, 1964 Rovigo
1965, 1966 Naples
1967 L'Aquila
1968 Padua
1969 L'Aquila
1970, 1971, 1972, 1973, 1974 Padua
1975 Brescia
1976 Rovigo
1977 Padua
1978 Treviso
1979 Rovigo
1980 Padua
1981, 1982 L'Aquila
1983 Treviso
1984, 1985, 1986, 1987 Padua
1988 Rovigo
1989 Treviso
1990 Rovigo
1991 Milan
1992 Treviso

ITALY v ENGLAND

1 May 1990
Rovigo
ITALY 15
T: Cuttita *C:* Troiani *PG:* Troiani (3)
ENGLAND 33
T: Oti, Buckton, Back, Andrew
C: Hodgkinson (4) *PG:* Hodgkinson (2)
DG: Andrew

ITALY v IRELAND

31 Dec 1988
Lansdowne Road, Dublin
IRELAND 31
T: Crossan (2), Matthews (2), Aherne
C: Cunningham *PG:* Danaher (2) *DG:* Dean
ITALY 15
T: Drunello *C:* Troiani *PG:* Troiani (3)

ITALY v NEW ZEALAND

28 Nov 1979
Rovigo
ITALY 12
T: N Francescato *C:* Bettarello
PG: Bettarello (2)
NEW ZEALAND 18
T: Mexted, Fraser *C:* Hewson (2)
PG: Hewson, R Wilson

ITALY v AUSTRALIA

4 Nov 1975
Milan
ITALY 15
T: Manni *C:* Ponzi *PG:* Ponzi (3)
AUSTRALIA 16
T: Crowe, Loane, Batch *C:* P McLean (2)

1 Jun 1986
Brisbane
AUSTRALIA 39
T: Campese (2), Tuynman, McIntyre, Moon, Burke *C:* Lynagh (6)
PG: Lynagh
ITALY 18
T: Barba, Gaetaniello *C:* Bettarello, Troiani *PG:* Bettarello (2)

3 Dec 1988
Rome
ITALY 6
PG: Bettarello (2)
AUSTRALIA 55
T: Campese (3), Niuqila (3), Leeds, Gourley, Lynagh *C:* Lynagh (8)
PG: : Lynagh

JAPAN

FOUNDATION: 1926
Honours: 1987 and 1991 World Cup first round
Asian Champions 1969, 1970, 1972, 1974, 1976, 1980, 1984
Largest victory: 108–0 v Sri Lanka 1980
Heaviest defeat: 4–106 v New Zealand XV 1987
Clubs: 1650
Players: 52 000
(There are also 40 000 students in 957 affiliated colleges and universities)
Population: 143 000 000
Main stadium: National Stadium, Tokyo (cap: 60 000)
Colours: Red and white hooped shirts, white shorts
Headquarters: Japan Rugby Football Union
c/o Shansin Enterprises Co
Ichibancho Central Building
22-1 Chiyoda-Ku
Tokyo 102

Many followers are aware that Rugby is played in Japan, but few may appreciate that the game has been in existence in the Far East for well over 100 years. The give-away is a photo of a match in progress at Yokohama in 1874. While the crowd are Japanese, the players are unmistakably British.

The British were responsible for taking the sport to Japan. For 25 years after the date of the photo, the history of the game is hazy, but in 1899, two gentlemen – one British, one local – introduced the game officially at Keio University. The Briton was Professor EB Clark, who had played college rugby at

Eiji Kutsiki leads the charge for Japan in their impressive 52–8 demolition of Zimbabwe at the 1991 World Cup.

Cambridge University, and was a member of staff at Keio, while Ginnosuke Tanaka, the local, was on hand to help the professor with language problems and the explanation of such tactics that existed at the time.

Keio University were involved in Japan's first official match against Yokohama Country and Athletic Club, a club formed by British residents of the city, in 1900. It was to become an annual affair. Keio's next incursion onto the fixture list was a game against a similar club at Kobe, the KRAC. Until 1911, these clubs were the only known participants, until joined by Kyoto School, and importantly, Doshisha University.

That rugby had serious intentions was illustrated after World War I, when the Prince of Wales attended a match between the KRAC (Kobe Regatta and Athletic Club) and Kyoto's High School XV. The year was 1923, and given later significance by the organisation of the first University match, between Doshisha and Waseda. The strength of the game was to come from the University clubs.

Like so many emerging nations, the need for organisation and structure became paramount, so in 1926, the clubs formed the Japanese Rugby Union.

A year later, the President of the Japanese Rugby Union elect, Mr Kayama, was on a year's course in London. He played for both Harlequins and Richmond, returning with considerable acumen as to how to run administrative affairs. He appreciated the need for schools and universities to be involved, and such was his groundwork that the universities are still the basis of success within the country. The National Schools XV has toured the world extensively.

Development in the early year's before World War II was hindered by circumstances which still prevail today. In a rugby sense Japan is on the geographical road to nowhere. Its immediate hinterland is not a rugby hotbed. The touring sides are not best placed for stopovers from Australia and New Zealand in the way that Fiji, Canada and the USA are.

However, prior to World War II, the Japanese had done their best to overcome the geographical problems. The university teams had reciprocal tours to Canada, New Zealand and Australia. Keio, Waseda and Meiji Universities were watched by crowds in excess of 20000.

Japan's involvement in World War II cost rugby dearly in two significant ways. The military had commandeered most of the pitches, and, after peace was declared, it quickly became evident what disrepair the country was in – both in terms of interest in sport and facilities. The second point was that as Japan recovered its poise and began to build for the future, professional sports began to take hold – notably baseball (under American influence), with many prewar rugby players being lost to other sports.

But such was its resilience that by the 1950s, Japan was back on its feet both politically and in sport. In 1952 Oxford University toured the country, a year later Cambridge University followed suit. In 1956, both the Australian Universities and New Zealand U23 sides toured the country.

But perhaps the most significant year in the re-establishment was 1968. The All Japan side beat the Junior All Blacks to record a victory of national importance. Japan won the first Asian Championship in 1969, the first of five successive wins.

In world terms there are still difficulties which will take time to overcome. The grass roots of the game has always been in the universities, and only recently have the major corporations taken to the sport – Toshiba, Mitsubishi, Toyota and Nippon Steel. Their arrival has helped in part to ease the problem of pitches. Rugby grounds have always been multi-purpose, sharing with at least five other sports – and it is not unusual for five different sports to be played on the same pitch on the same afternoon. Yokohama RFC, for example, take their turn on the same pitch as soccer, baseball and women's hockey. Athletics training rounds off the day. Industry has helped provide sponsorship and better facilities. As if the difficulties of finding adequate facilities are not hard enough, land in Tokyo costs £2 million per acre!

Given their lack of physical stature, which precludes certain styles of play and makes other tactics necessary, given their geographical isolation and given their enormous facility problems, the Japanese have coped with certain hardships in the true spirit of the game.

There is, however, one consistent world record which the Japanese rightly claim – that of the highest attendance for a club match. They cringe every time the Cup final crowds at Twickenham and Cardiff announce new world records of 54500. The club final in Japan (usually between the club champion and the university champion) is always watched by 55000. The Japanese Rugby Union reported a crowd of 66000 for the 1990 final – the world record.

JAPAN v ENGLAND

24 Sep 1971 *Osaka*
JAPAN 19
T: Mizutani, Murata *C:* Yamaguchi
PG: Yamaguchi (3)
ENGLAND 27
T: Cowman (2), Webb, Glover, Janion
C: Cowman, Rossborough
PG: Cowman

28 Sep 1971 *Tokyo*
JAPAN 3
PG: Yamaguchi
ENGLAND 6
PG: Rossborough (2)

13 May 1979 *Osaka*
JAPAN 19
T: Kobayashi, Mori *C:* Matsuo
PG: Matsuo (2) *DG:* Matsuo
ENGLAND 21
T: Wheeler, Squires *C:* Hare (2)
PG: Hare (3)

20 May 1979 *Tokyo*
JAPAN 18
T: Matsuo (3), Minawakawa *C:* Matsuo
ENGLAND 38
T: Dodge (2), Carleton (2), Pomphrey (2) *C:* H Davies (4) *PG:* H Davies (2)

11 Oct 1986 *Twickenham*
ENGLAND 39
T: Underwood, Hall, Bailey, Richards, Rees, Salmon *C:* Rose (6) *PG:* Rose
JAPAN 12
T: Konishi *C:* Matsuo *PG:* Matsuo (2)

JAPAN v SCOTLAND

25 Sep 1976 *Murrayfield*
SCOTLAND 34
T: Gammell (2), McGeechan, Ashton, Lawson, Irvine, Fisher *C:* Irvine (3)
JAPAN 9
T: Fujiwara *C:* Tanaka *PG:* Tanaka

18 Sep 1977 *Tokyo*
JAPAN 9
T: Ujino *C:* Tanaka *PG:* Matsuo
ENGLAND 74
T: Gammell (4), Laidlaw (2), Cranston, Dickson, Moffat, McGuinness, Wilson
C: Mair (9) *PG:* Mair (4)

27 Sep 1986 *Murrayfield*
SCOTLAND 33
T: Tukalo (4), Duncan, Campbell
C: Dods (3) *PG:* Dods
JAPAN 18
T: Onuki, Chida, Katsuki *PG:* Matsuo
DG: Matsuo

28 May 1989 *Tokyo*
JAPAN 28
T: Yamamoto, Nofomuli, Kutusliki, Yoshida, Hayashi *C:* Yamamoto
PG: Yamamoto (2)
SCOTLAND 24
T: Hay *C:* Oliver *PG:* Oliver (5)
DG: Wyllie

JAPAN v WALES

6 Oct 1973 *Cardiff Arms Park*
WALES 62
T: Bennett (2), K Hughes (2), JJ Williams, Bergiers, Shell, Taylor, JPR Williams, TGR Davies, Windsor
C: Bennett (9)
JAPAN 14
T: Itoh (2) *PG:* Yamamoto (2)

21 Sep 1975 *Osaka*
JAPAN 12
PG: Ueyama (4)
WALES 56
T: JJ Williams (2), TGR Davies (2), Gravell (2), TP Evans (2), Shell, JD Bevan *C:* Fenwick (5) *PG:* Fenwick (2)

24 Sep 1975 *Tokyo*
JAPAN 6
PG: Ueyama (2)
WALES 82
T: JPR Williams (3), Bennett (2), TGR Davies (2), Price (2), JJ Williams (2), TM Davies, Gravell, Faulkner *C:* Bennett (10) *PG:* Bennett (2)

22 Oct 1983 *Cardiff Arms Park*
WALES 29
T: Hadley, Brown, Dacey, Bowen, Giles
C: Wyatt (3) *PG:* Wyatt
JAPAN 24
T: Konishi, Tanifuji, Chida, Fujita
C: Kobayashi *PG:* Kobayashi (2)

JAPAN v FRANCE

27 Oct 1973 *Bordeaux*
FRANCE 30
T: Delaigue, Barrau, Bertranne, Saisset, Skrela *C:* Cabrol (3)
JAPAN 18
T: Ohigashi, Shimazaki, Sakata
PG: Ueyama, Shimazaki

23 Sep 1979 *Tokyo*
JAPAN 16
T: Ujino, Sakamoto, Fujiwara
C: Ueyama, Minawakara
FRANCE 55
T: Noves (3), Paparemborde, Maleig, Beguerie, Cholley, Bastiat, Bilbao
C: Aguirre (8) *PG:* Aguirre

19 Oct 1985 *Dax*
FRANCE 50
T: Lafond (4), Fabre, Cassagne, Codorniou, Rodriguez, Detrez, Dubroca
C: D Camberabero (5)
JAPAN 0

26 Oct 1985 *Nantes*
FRANCE 52
T: D Camberabero (2), Lafond (2), Charvet (2), Dintrans (2), Fabre, Rodriguez *C:* D Camberabero (6)
JAPAN 0

JAPAN v AUSTRALIA

2 Aug 1975 *Sydney*
AUSTRALIA 37
T: P McLean (2), Robertson (2), Osborne, Wright *C:* P McLean (5)
PG: P McLean
JAPAN 7
T: Aruga *PG:* Ueyama

17 Aug 1975 *Brisbane*
AUSTRALIA 50
T: Ryan (3), G Shaw (2), A Shaw, Hauser, Price *C:* P McLean (6) *PG:* P McLean (2)
JAPAN 25
T: Fujiwara (2), Aruga, Yoshida, Ishizuka
C: Tanaka *PG:* Ueyama

JAPAN v IRELAND

26 May 1985 *Osaka*
JAPAN 13
T: Ishiyama, Konishi *C:* Honjo *PG:* Honjo
IRELAND 48
T: Ringland (3), Matthews (2), Kiernan, McNeill, Fitzgerald
C: Kiernan (5) *PG:* Kiernan (2)

2 Jun 1985 *Tokyo*
JAPAN 15
T: Onuki, Murai *C:* Kobayashi (2) *PG:* Kobayashi
IRELAND 33
T: Kiernan (2), Mullin, Anderson *C:* Kiernan (4) *PG:* Kiernan (3)

NAMIBIA

FOUNDATION: 1916 as Damaraland; 1952 as South West Africa; 1990 as Namibia
Honours: Ranked no. 3, as South West Africa, in South Africa in 1988
Largest victory: 86–9 v Portugal 1990
Clubs: 28
Players: 2500
Population: 5 000 000
Main stadium: National Stadium, Windhoek (formerly South West Stadium) (cap: 15 000)
Colours: Light blue shirts, dark blue shorts
Headquarters: Namibia Rugby Union
PO Box 138
Windhoek 9000

To the often asked question as to why Namibia were not included in the 1991 World Cup final stages after beating qualifiers Italy (twice), Zimbabwe (four times), and Ireland (twice) immediately prior to the event, the answer is very straightforward; Namibia had not gained its independence when the draw was made.

Rugby's youngest nation has two histories – the most recent being the brief and successful period since independence in 1989, with the earlier history as South West Africa, then part of South Africa.

As South West Africa the province had been a part of the Currie Cup and its feeder tournaments since 1952. Prior to that the side had functioned as Damaraland since its inception in 1916.

In the South African rankings, SWA had established a niche through the 1950s until the mid 1980s at around the 12–14th most powerful province. There were highlights, notably the capping of three of their number as full Springboks, of whom the most famous, Jan Ellis, is still the most capped of all South Africans with 28 international appearances. JJN Swart (1955 v British Lions) and WJ Fourie (2 caps v 1959 French XV) were the others.

However from the period 1985–89, SWA made a vast improvement, their ranking reaching no. 7 for three seasons and peaking at no. 3 in 1988, behind only Northern Transvaal and Western Province, and ahead of such bastions of rugby as Transvaal, Orange Free State, Eastern Province and Natal.

So it may be said that Namibia have inherited a side that is probably the best in the history of the former South West Africa. Andre Stoop, the full back, and Gerhard Mans, wing, were regulars in Springbok trial sides at the time of independence, with at least four others being members of representative sides such as the Barbarians, Gazelles and Quaggas.

It might also be suggested that Namibian domination may wane with the retirement of the current crop of players, which is precisely what concerns the Namibian Rugby Union. The integration of black society into rugby in Zimbabwe and Kenya has proved infectious and enthusiastic, but has yet to progress in terms of ability at national level. By 1995 Namibia will be challenging for Zimbabwe's African World Cup qualification spot, and it will be intriguing to see whether the initial standards are maintained.

DOMESTIC RUGBY STRUCTURE

Club league based around the capital Windhoek. The major clubs are Windhoek RFC, Police, Wanderers and United in the capital, with Tsumeb, Grootfontein and Walvis Bay being the pick of the provincial clubs.

Clubs:
Gobabis
Grootfontein
Harlequins
Karasburg
Katimo Malilo
Keetmanshoop Police
Mariental
Namib Park
Neudam
Okahandja
Oshakati
Outjo
Prisons (Windhoek)
Rehoboth
Rundu
Swakopmund
Swans
Teachers' College
Tsumeb
United
Walvis Bay
Wanderers
Windhoek
Windhoek Police
Number of teams: 50
Oldest club: United (1916)

CLUB CHAMPIONS SINCE INDEPENDENCE

1990 Police RFC
1991 TransNamib RFC

NAMIBIA v IRELAND

20 Jul 1991
Windhoek
NAMIBIA 15
T: Stoop *C:* Coetzee *PG:* Coetzee (2)
DG: Coetzee
IRELAND 6
T: Penalty try *C:* Mullin

27 Jul 1991
Windhoek
NAMIBIA 26
T: Stoop, Maritz, Mans, Barnard, Coetzee *C:* Coetzee (3)
IRELAND 15
T: Staples, Cunningham *C:* Staples *DG:* Curtis

NAMIBIA v WALES

2 Jun 1990
Windhoek
NAMIBIA 9
T: Mans *C:* McCulley *PG:* McCulley
WALES 18
T: Thorburn, Bridges *C:* Thorburn (2) *PG:* Thorburn (2)

9 Jun 1990
Windhoek
NAMIBIA 30
T: Swartz (2), Mans *C:*Coetzee (2), McCulley *PG:* McCulley (2), Coetzee *DG:* Coetzee
WALES 34
T: Emyr (2), Williams, Penalty try *C:* Thorburn (3) *PG:* Thorburn (3) *DG:*Clement

NAMIBIA v FRANCE

23 Jun 1990
Windhoek
NAMIBIA 15
PG: Coetzee (2), Olivier (2) *DG:* Olivier
FRANCE 24
T: Berty *C:* Montlaur *PG:* Montlaur (6)

30 Jun 1990
Windhoek
NAMIBIA 21
T: Swart *C:* McCulley *PG:* McCulley (5)
FRANCE 25
T: Roux, Sauboua, Bonneval *C:* Montlaur (2) *PG:* Montlaur *DG:* Montlaur (2)

13 Nov 1990
Arras
FRANCE 33
T: Jaubert, G Camberabero, Lecomte, Blond *C:* Bianchi (4) *PG:* Bianchi (3)
NAMIBIA 0

ROMANIA

FOUNDATION: 1913
Honours: 1987 and 1991 World Cup first round
FIRA Champions: 1975, 1977, 1981, 1983, 1990 (tie)
Largest victory: 100–0 v Bulgaria 1977
Heaviest defeat: 0–60 v Ireland 1986
Clubs: 98 senior clubs in 40 Districts (1992)
Players: 2000 senior men (plus 5000 at schools and universities)
Population: 22 355 000
Main stadia: 23 August Stadium, Bucharest (cap: 90 000), Giulesti Stadium, Bucharest (cap: 17 500)
Colours: Yellow jerseys, blue shorts
Headquarters: Federatia Romana de Rugbi
Str Vasile conta No 16
Bucharest CO 70 139

Of all the European rugby playing countries outside the Five Nations Championship, Romania are the most successful. Their victories against France (seven wins in Bucharest between 1960–82 and a win at Auch in 1990), Scotland (at the time, the Grand Slam winners) and Wales (both home and away), as well as a draw in Ireland, have led to repeated calls for their promotion into a Six Nations Championship.

But the recent form of Romania is that of the curate's egg – historic wins followed by spectacular defeats.

Romanian rugby dates back to the turn of the century when students returning from London and, especially, Paris, brought basic knowledge of the game to Bucharest. Under their impulse the Romanian Rugby Federation was founded in 1913, and within a year the Romanian Tennis Club of Bucharest were crowned as first champions. All the early clubs were centred in the capital with Stadial Roman, PTT, Sportulul Studentesc, Educatia Fizica, and Viforul Dacia all appearing on the champions roll of honour. The Romanians are proud that the championship has been held every year except 1917–18 when the southern part of the country was under German occupation.

Since 1945, other clubs have known dominance. Steaua Bucharest (the Army team), the current champions Dynamo Bucharest (formerly the Police side), and Grivita Rosie (Railways) have been to the fore. Importantly the game has spread to other centres; Universitea Timisoara were the first provincial champions in 1972, the Farul club from the Black Sea resort of Constanta have won the domestic title four times since 1975, while the Stiinti club (mining) from Baia Mare were successful in 1989–90.

Internationally, the contact with France has been of great significance. The countries first met in 1919 and have been regular opponents since. When France were expelled from the Five Nations championship in 1931, they arranged matches with other European nations. In 1934 the Federation Internationale de Rugby Amateur (FIRA) was founded in Paris, to promote the interests of the emerging nations. Romania have become one of the leading lights in the FIRA Championship where Italy, the Soviet Union, Spain, Romania and France form the key nations in the 'European' league. And when Rugby was part of the Olympic movement until 1924, Romania were high on the list of participants.

The political events of Christmas 1989 shattered the world of Romanian rugby with the deaths of six players, former players and administrators. The problems of the country in many ways highlighted the difficulties that the sport had in attempting to progress. Romanian successes seem now to have been greater for the problems that had to be overcome.

Following the December Revolution, it was imperative that Romanian rugby should find its feet as soon as possible. The early signs were encouraging. The brotherhood of rugby raised over £500000 at Twickenham's first Sunday game in April 1990 with the Home Nations beating the Rest of Europe 43–18. Then on May 24 at Auch, Romania's first international since the troubles resulted in an unspectacular, but historic first win on French soil by 12–6.

ROMANIA v ENGLAND

13 May 1989
Bucharest
ROMANIA 3
T: Ignat
ENGLAND 58
T: Oti (4), Guscott (3), Probyn, Richards *C:* Hodgkinson (8) *PG:* Hodgkinson *DG:* Andrew

ROMANIA v IRELAND

18 Oct 1980
Lansdowne Road, Dublin
IRELAND 13
T: FP Quinn *PG:* Campbell (3)
ROMANIA 13
T: Parachiv *PG:* Constantin (3)

1 Nov 1986
Lansdowne Road, Dublin
IRELAND 60
T: Crossan (3), Mullin (2), Dean (2), Anderson, Bradley, McNeill *C:* Kiernan (7) *PG:* Kiernan (2)
ROMANIA 0

ROMANIA v SCOTLAND

26 Sep 1981
Murrayfield
SCOTLAND 12
PG: Irvine (4)
ROMANIA 6
PG: Constantin (2)

12 May 1984
Stadium August 23rd, Bucharest
ROMANIA 28
T: Dimitru, Parachiv, Radulescu *C:* Alexandru (2) *PG:* Alexandru (3) *DG:* Alexandru
SCOTLAND 22
T: Leslie, Dods *C:* Dods *PG:* Dods (3) *DG:* Robertson

30 Mar 1986
Stadium August 23rd, Bucharest
ROMANIA 18
PG: Ignat (5) *DG:* Ignat
SCOTLAND 33
T: Jeffrey, S Hastings, Deans *C:* G Hastings (3) *PG:* G Hastings (5)

9 Dec 1989
Murrayfield
SCOTLAND 32
T: Stanger (3), White, Sole *C:* G Hastings (3) *PG:* G Hastings (2)
ROMANIA 0

31 Aug 1991
Bucharest
ROMANIA 18
T: Ciorascu, Sasu *C:* Iou (2) *PG:* Iou (2)
SCOTLAND 12
T: Tukalo *C:* Dods *PG:* Dods (2)

ROMANIA v WALES

6 Oct 1979
Cardiff Arms Park
WALES 13
T: Griffiths *PG:* Fenwick *DG:* G Davies (2)
ROMANIA 12
T: Ionescu *C:* Bucos *PG:* Constantin (2)

12 Nov 1983
Bucharest
ROMANIA 24
T: Caraguea, Muriaur, Aldea, Lungu *C:* Alexandru *PG:* Alexandru (2)
WALES 6
PG: G Evans (2)

10 Dec 1988
Cardiff Arms Park
WALES 9
T: Devereux *C:* Thorburn *PG:* Thorburn
ROMANIA 15
T: Ion *C:* Ignat *PG:* Ignat (3)

ROMANIA v NEW ZEALAND

24 Oct 1981
Bucharest
ROMANIA 6
PG: Constantin *DG:* Alexandru
NEW ZEALAND 14
T: Salmon, Dalton *PG:* Hewson *DG:* Hewson

ROMANIA v FRANCE

1919	Paris	France 48, Romania 5
1924	Paris	France 59, Romania 3
1936	Berlin	France 26, Romania 5
1937	Paris	France 27, Romania 11
1938	Bucharest	Romania 8, France 11
1957	Bucharest	Romania 15, France 18
1960	Bucharest	Romania 11, France 5
1961	Bayonne	France 5, Romania 5
1962	Bucharest	Romania 3, France 0
1963	Toulouse	France 6, Romania 6
1964	Bucharest	Romania 6, France 9
1965	Lyon	France 8, Romania 3
1966	Bucharest	Romania 3, France 9
1967	Nantes	France 11, Romania 3
1968	Bucharest	Romania 15, France 14
1969	Tarbes	France 14, Romania 9
1970	Bucharest	Romania 3, France 14
1971	Beziers	France 31, Romania 12
1972	Constanta	Romania 6, France 15
1973	Valencia	France 7, Romania 6
1974	Bucharest	Romania 15, France 10
1975	Bordeaux	France 36, Romania 12
1976	Bucharest	Romania 15, France 12
1977	Clermont-Ferrand	France 9, Romania 6
1978	Bucharest	Romania 6, France 9
1979	Montauban	France 30, Romania 12
1980	Bucharest	Romania 15, France 0
1981	Narbonne	France 17, Romania 9
1982	Bucharest	Romania 13, France 9
1983	Toulouse	France 26, Romania 15
1984	Bucharest	Romania 3, France 18
1985	Lille	France 25, Romania 13
1986	Bucharest	Romania 3, France 20
1987	Agen	France 49, Romania 3
1988	Bucharest	Romania 12, France 16
1990	Auch	France 6, Romania 12
1991	Bucharest	Romania 21, France 33
1992	Le Havre	France 25, Romania 6

DOMESTIC RUGBY STRUCTURE

The national championship consists of a premier division of two groups of six teams with the winners and runners-up meeting in semi-finals and then a final.

National Club Champions

1914, 1915, 1916 Tennis Club Roman Bucharest
1919 Stadiul Roman Bucharest
1920 Educatia Physica Bucharest
1921, 1922, 1923 Tennis Club Roman Bucharest
1924 Stadiul Roman Bucharest
1925 Sportul Studentesc Bucharest
1926 Stadiul Roman Bucharest
1927 Tennis Club Roman Bucharest
1928 Stadiul Roman Bucharest
1929 Sportul Studentesc Bucharest
1930, 1931 Stadiul Roman Bucharest
1932 Sportul Studentesc Bucharest
1933, 1934 PTT Bucharest
1935, 1936, 1937 Sportul Studentesc Bucharest
1938 Tennis Club Roman Bucharest
1939 Sportul Studentesc Bucharest
1940 Tennis Club Roman Bucharest
1941 Viforul Dacia Bucharest
1942 Tennis Club Roman Bucharest
1943, 1944, 1945 Viforul Dacia Bucharest
1946 Sportul Studentesc Bucharest
1947 Stadiul Roman Bucharest
1948 CFR Bucharest
1949 CCA Bucharest
1950 CFR Bucharest
1951, 1952 Dinamo Bucharest
1953, 1954 CCA Bucharest
1955 Lokomotiva Grivitza Rosie
1956 Dinamo Bucharest
1957 Lokomotiva Grivitza Rosie
1958, 1959, 1960 CFR Grivitza Rosie Bucharest
1961 Steaua Bucharest
1962 Grivitza Rosie Bucharest
1963, 1964 Steaua Bucharest
1965 Dinamo Bucharest
1966, 1967 Grivitza Rosie Bucharest
1968, 1969 Dinamo Bucharest
1970 Grivitza Rosie Bucharest
1971 Steaua Bucharest
1972 Universitea Timisoara
1973, 1974 Steaua Bucharest
1975, 1976 Farul Constanta
1977 Steaua Bucharest
1978 Farul Constanta
1979, 1980, 1981 Steaua Bucharest
1982 Dinamo Bucharest
1983, 1984, 1985 Steaua Bucharest
1986 Farul Constanta
1987, 1988, 1989 Steaua Bucharest
1990 Stiinta Baia Mare
1991 Dinamo Bucharest
1992 Dinamo Bucharest

TONGA

FOUNDATION: 1924
Honours: 1987 World Cup first round
South Pacific Championship: 1983, 1986
Largest victory: 31–13 v Western Samoa 1986
(Tonga beat Solomon Islands 92–3 in 1979 South Pacific Games)
Heaviest defeat: 8–44 v Scotland 1974
Clubs: 70
Players: 2457
Population: 110 000
Main stadium: Teufaiva Park, Nuku'Alofa (cap: 15 000)
Colours: Green jerseys, white shorts
Headquarters: Tonga Rugby Football Union
PO Box 369
Nuku'Alofa

Tonga were the one country who were at the 1987 World Cup but failed to qualify for the 1991 competition. That Western Samoa – who were to do so well – and Japan went through in the Asian/Pacific qualifiers is of no consolation to Tonga. Their belief is that they too were capable of causing ripples. In the qualifiers Tonga were beaten just 12–3 by the Samoans, but disappointed in a 28–16 defeat by Japan which was to cost them World Cup entry. However, like Samoa, the Tongans are spread throughout the leading New Zealand and Australian sides, and with more use than before of their availability, another power could emerge for 1995.

The game was first played in Tonga in 1990, based around the Tupau and Tonga Colleges, who had benefited from having Australian teachers. A gradual mixture of students going to, and returning from, Australia and New Zealand, and teachers from Britain, Australia and New Zealand working on contracts, enabled a solid base to be constructed. Henry Selwood, an Australian physical education teacher from Tonga College, was a leading coach and administrator – he had a good working relationship with Newington College, one of Australia's leading schools. The Tongan RU was founded in 1923, with organised rugby and the first international following a year later.

Fiji were the first international visitors to Nuku'Alofa in 1924, playing three internationals, Tonga winning the first 9–6, Fiji the second 14–3, with honours even in the decider at 0–0. The fixture remains the highlight of the season, supported by the addition of Western Samoa into the three nations Pacific Championship in 1981.

Tours, both in and out, widened the horizons. In 1954, fittingly, Australia became the first to tour with an invitation team. In 1969 Tonga toured New Zealand and in 1973, to celebrate 50 years of the Tongan Rugby Union, a tour to Australia was arranged. Here one of rugby's great upsets took place: Tonga won the 2nd Test in Brisbane 16–11 after losing the first 30–12.

In 1974 Tonga visited Britain and, after an opening win against East Wales, lost the next nine, including the internationals against Scotland (44–8) and Wales (26–7). Since then tours have tended to be Pacific based.

After winning the South Pacific Championship in 1986, Tonga were invited to the 1987 World Cup, losing to Wales (29–16), Ireland (32–9) and, finally, Canada (37–4) when several players were unhappy at having to play on a Sunday. Sunday is a day of rest in Tonga.

Qualification for the 1995 World Cup will be helpful – if not crucial – to the Tongan cause. With the arrival of Western Samoa as a world force, Tonga may have to hope for an extra place in 1995. The standards in the South Pacific may now warrant that.

DOMESTIC RUGBY STRUCTURE

The club championship is centred around the capital Nuku'Alofa. Feeder leagues to this championship are in operation as are cup competitions.

NATIONAL CHAMPIONS SINCE 1977

In 1986 there were seven competitions for the Shield – A1 (championship), A2, B1, B3, C1, C2, C3 divisions; the same divisions also applied for the Cup competition:

	Shield	Cup
1977	Hihifo and Kolomotu'a	
1978	Hihifo	
1979	Hihifo and Kolomotu'a	
1980	Polisi	
1981	Hihifo	
1982	Tavatu'utolu	
1983	Hihifo	
1984	Hihifo	Kolomotu'a
1985	Hihifo	Hihifo
1986	Polisi	Polisi and Hihifo
1987	Polisi	Polisi
1988	Polisi	Hihifo
1989	Hihifo	Kilomotu'a
1990	Hihifo	Polisi
1991	Polisi	Polisi

TONGA v ENGLAND

1 Jun 1979
Nuku'Alofa
TONGA 17
T: Finau, Valu (2) *C:* Ma'ake
PG: Ma'ake
ENGLAND 37
T: Slemen (2), Allchurch, Scott, Carleton
C: H Davies (4) *PG:* H Davies (3)

TONGA v SCOTLAND

28 Sep 1974
Murrayfield
SCOTLAND 44
T: Steele (4), Dick, Lauder, MacLauchlan *C:* Irvine (5) *PG:* Irvine (2)
TONGA 8
T: Fifita, 'Iskeli

TONGA v WALES

19 Oct 1974
Cardiff Arms Park
WALES 26
T: Finlayson (2), Fenwick, JD Bevan, Cobner *PG:* Martin (2)
TONGA 7
T: Talilotu *PG:* Valita

10 Jun 1986
Nuku'Alofa
TONGA 7
T: Fifita *PG:* Lovo
WALES 15
T: P Moriarty *C:* Dacey *PG:* Bowen (2), Dacey

TONGA v AUSTRALIA

23 Jun 1973
Sydney
AUSTRALIA 30
T: Stephens (2), Richardson, Cole, Hipwell, Penalty try *C:* McGill (2), Richardson
TONGA 12
T: Tupi, Latu *C:* Ma'ake (2)

30 Jul 1973
Brisbane
AUSTRALIA 11
T: Cole, Tindall *PG:* McGill
TONGA 16
T: Vave, Latu, Kavapulu, Mafi

USA

FOUNDATION: 1975
Honours: 1987 and 1991 World Cup first round
Largest victory: 60–6 v Uruguay 1989
Heaviest defeats: 0–59 v England 1982
9–67 v Australia 1990
Most points: 89 C O'Brien
Most tries: 5 G Hein, G Higgins
Clubs: 1349
Players: 45 000
Population: 225 000 000
Main stadia: Various
Colours: Red jerseys, white shorts
Headquarters: USA RFU
830 North Tejon, Suite 104B
Colorado Springs
Colorado 80903

One of the more popular quiz questions is 'Who are the reigning Olympic rugby champions?'. It is one of those answers that is either known or ends with fruitless guessing through all the countries of the world. The USA are the current Olympic champions having won the last tournament in 1924 in Paris beating France 17–3 in the final. To make statistics even more revealing, the Americans in fact retained the gold medal in 1924, having secured a win in Antwerp four years earlier.

The United States Rugby Football Union was founded in 1975 which makes the Olympic success all the more difficult to understand. The fact is that, in the early days, there were just pockets of rugby interest in a vast country, which took until 1975 to organise under one roof. The Olympic team came from Stanford University, California, with, in all probability, the rest of the USA knowing absolutely nothing about them.

It is known that rugby, or football as it was then, was played at Harvard, Yale and Princetown in the 1840s. In 1862 Harvard and Yale banned the sport as being too dangerous and without any recourse to basic rules. In 1911, with the advent of the forward pass, the USA was on its way to producing its own game, American Football.

California was the only real centre of rugby in the early 1900s with the New Zealand tourists stopping off en route for home after the successful tour to Britain. To confuse issues, the All Blacks played British Columbia (Canada) at Berkeley and San Francisco. In 1913 New Zealand played 13 matches in California, winning all 13.

The Olympic matches in many ways epitomise the humour and camaraderie that makes rugby unique. In 1920, no one is certain who won the gold medal; the Olympic authorities concede that the Antwerp celebration is the only Games from which no records have been accurately kept. Who won the gold medal depends on whose view is believed.

The Antwerp Games were run not by the Belgians, but by the French from Paris. The offices of the founder of the Olympic movement, Baron de Coubertin, organised the event. The French claim a win by 14–5 at Stade Colombes on 10 October. The Americans say that the match did not count – they claim an 8–0 win in Antwerp some three months earlier. The French (naturally) claim that the good Baron, keeping up the Olympic ideal, sent a posse of players to Antwerp to play the USA, but ended up playing American Football because there was no other opposition! Both Olympic bodies claim the gold.

In 1924, there was no doubting American supremacy. In one of sport's great upsets they beat France 17–3 at Colombes just five months after France had beaten Scotland 12–10. The American preparation included a 1920 re-union at Stanford University, a train journey across America, a boat to Plymouth and a match against Devonport Services, then a train to London where they were beaten by both Harlequins and Blackheath. After a few further hours in London, the Americans caught the Boat Train to Paris, where, within 24 hours, they were playing for the gold medal.

From those heady days, rugby in the United States seemed in terminal decline. Most of the problems were geographical, with distances making too much demand on finances and time. It is to the enormous credit of the organisers of recent times that these crippling difficulties are on their way to being solved.

Throughout the 1950s and 1960s, the game had functioned within different Unions with the Mid-West, the Pacific and the East Coast Unions being in the vanguard of discussions towards unity. At the 1968 congress the three unions failed to agree a blueprint for a national union. But under the aegis of the Mid-West Union in Chicago, the committees persevered with ideas and correspondence until the 1975 meeting when a draft was drawn up for a national union. A year later the first international of the present era

The United States take on Thailand at the Hong Kong Sevens tournament.

was staged at Anaheim, California, with Australia winning 24–13.

The first international 'success' came in 1986 with the plate competition in the Hong Kong Sevens, a win repeated in 1988. These small indents at least gave the team a taste of trophies, gongs and medals, albeit at a low level. Contacts each season with Canada in the Can-Am international plus tours to and from the major countries are raising standards appreciably.

In 1991 that standard quiz question on Olympic rugby gold medallists had a new slant. It became a two-part question with the addition of 'Who are the reigning Women's Rugby World Champions?' The USA won the inaugural World Cup at Cardiff Arms Park on 14 April 1991, beating England 19–6 in the final.

NATIONAL CLUB CHAMPIONSHIP FINALS

1983 Old Blues 23, Dallas Harlequins 0
1984 Dallas Harlequins 31, Los Angeles 12
1985 Milwaukee 10, Denver Barbarians 4
1986 Old Blues 20, Old Blue 0
1987 Old Blues 28, Pittsburgh 10
1988 OMBAC 29, Milwaukee 12
1989 OMBAC 19, Philadelphia Whitemarsh 9
1990 Denver Barbarians 15, Chicago Blaze 9
1991 OMBAC 12, Washington 9
1992 Old Blues 32, Chicago Lions 9

UNITED STATES v ENGLAND

15 Oct 1977
Twickenham
ENGLAND 37
T: Wyatt (4), Scott, Carleton *C:* Hare (3) *PG:* Hare
UNITED STATES 11
T: Kelso, Duncanson *PG:* Halliday

19 Jun 1982
Hartford
UNITED STATES 0
ENGLAND 59
T: SJ Smith (2), Swift (2), Scott (2), Carleton, Rendall, Wheeler *C:* Hare (7) *PG:* Hare (2) *DG:* Cusworth

UNITED STATES v SCOTLAND

18 May 1991
Hartford
UNITED STATES 12
PG: Dejong (4)
SCOTLAND 41
T: Reid (2), Stanger (2), MacDonald *C:* Dods (3) *PG:* Dods (5)

UNITED STATES v IRELAND

9 Sep 1989
New York
UNITED STATES 7
T: Siano *PG:* Williams
IRELAND 32
T: Dunlea, Mannion, Crossan, Bradley *C:* Kiernan (2) *PG:* Kiernan (3) *DG:* Smith

UNITED STATES v WALES

7 Nov 1987
Cardiff Arms Park
WALES 46
T: Bowen (2), Clement (2), Webbe, Young, Moriarty, Norster *C:* Thorburn (4) *PG:* Thorburn (2)
UNITED STATES 0

UNITED STATES v FRANCE

13 Jul 1991
Denver
UNITED STATES 9
PG: O'Brien (3)
FRANCE 41
T: Blanco (2), Lafond, Saint-Andre, Champ, Courtiols, Cecillon, Mesnel *C:* Camberabero (3) *PG:* Camberabero

20 Jul 1991
Colorado Springs
UNITED STATES 3
PG: O'Brien
FRANCE 10
T: Mesnel, Blanco *C:* Camberabero
Match abandoned after 42 mins

UNITED STATES v SOUTH AFRICA

1981
Glenville
UNITED STATES 7
T: Walton *PG:* Smith
SOUTH AFRICA 38
T: Mordt (3), Geldenhuys, Germishuys (2), Beck, Berger *C:* Botha (3)

UNITED STATES v AUSTRALIA

16 Nov 1912
Berkeley
UNITED STATES 8
T: Harrigan *C:* Erb *PG:* Erb
AUSTRALIA 12
T: Meibusch (2), Carroll *PG:* Prentice

31 Jan 1976
Anaheim
UNITED STATES 12
PG: Oxman (4)
AUSTRALIA 24
T: Ryan, Price, Pearse *C:* Hindmarsh (3) *PG:* Hindmarsh (2)

9 Jul 1983
Sydney
AUSTRALIA 49
T: Campese (4), Slack (2), Ross, Roche, Hanley *C:* Gould (4), Campese *DG:* M Ella
UNITED STATES 3
PG: Meyerseick

8 Jul 1990
Ballymore, Brisbane
AUSTRALIA 67
T: Lynagh (2), Williams (2), Daly, McKenzie, Kearns, Gavin, Farr-Jones, Slattery, Campese, Little *C:* Lynagh (8) *DG:* Campese
UNITED STATES 9
T: Leversee *C:* O'Brien *PG:* O'Brien

UNITED STATES v NEW ZEALAND

15 Nov 1913
Berkeley
UNITED STATES 3
PG: Peart
NEW ZEALAND 51
T: Roberts (3), McKenzie (2), Gray (2), Murray (2), McDonald (2), Wylie, McGregor *C:* Graham (4), McDonald, Mitchinson

1980
San Diego
UNITED STATES 6
PG: Cooke (2)
NEW ZEALAND 53
T: Woodman (3), Osborne (2), Wilson, Allen, Old *C:* Codlin (6) *PG:* Codlin (3)

WESTERN SAMOA

FOUNDATION: 1927
Honours: 1991 World Cup quarter-finalists
South Pacific Champions: 1982, 1985, 1990, 1991
Largest victory: 74–7 v South Korea 1990
Heaviest defeat: 22–49 v Ireland 1988
Clubs: 91
Players: 4400 (inc. 'overseas' players)
Population: 167 000
Main stadium: National Stadium, Apia (cap: 12 000)
Colours: Blue shirts, white shorts
Headquarters: Western Samoa RFU
PO Box 3940
Apia

Before the 1991 World Cup, as Michael Caine might have remarked, not a lot of people knew anything about Samoan rugby. That was quite true as the early days are characterised by a lack of information with the most important dates not having been fully recorded. But all that is different now. What has emerged in the modern era is that the flow of talent, especially to New Zealand, places Manu Samoa, as it is called, as probably the greatest single producer, per capita, of players in the rugby world. The population of the island is some 170 000, while the size of the country is such that eight Western Samoa's can fit into Wales.

Western Samoa inflicted such damage at the World Cup that the repercussions will be felt for many, many years. The Samoans beat Wales, lost narrowly to the eventual winners, Australia, by just 9–3, then thrashed Argentina before bowing to Scottish home advantage in the quarter-finals. Yet closer scrutiny of the context of their squad revealed that 24 of the 26 had played top provincial and club rugby in New Zealand and Australia in 1991, while all 15 who beat Wales had played in New Zealand at some stage in 1991, many of them for the top sides such as Auckland, Canterbury and Wellington.

Western Samoa's first known contact with other countries was the much chronicled game against Fiji, who stopped over

The great upset – Sila Vaifale takes line-out possession against Wales at Cardiff during the Samoans' 16–13 victory.

The brothers Bachop represent different countries in the Southern Hemisphere. Graeme (left) plays for New Zealand and Stephen (below) for Western Samoa.

on the island on their way to Tonga in 1924. This was the famous game played at 7.00 am to allow the Samoans to go to work afterwards, and was played in a park with a large tree on halfway. A glance at an atlas, though, will show Western Samoa some 300 miles north east of Fiji, while Tonga appears to be the same distance, but south east, of Fiji! However, as a consequence, the Western Samoan Rugby Union was founded in 1927 to foster the game, but there appears to have been little contact with the outside world before World War II. The proximity to New Zealand, and to a lesser degree, Australia, meant that players who had gone to those countries in search of work, were able to pass on sound knowledge of technical and administrative skills.

The Samoans first tour was to Fiji in 1956, a year after Fiji had again visited Samoa. They managed a couple of wins in eight games against the major Fijian sub-unions. In 1963, Western Samoa entered the South Pacific Championships with little success; eight years later they won the Championship, though Fiji and Tonga were not represented. It was at least a start.

Western Samoa's emergence as a rugby nation was confirmed in 1976, when they made a tour to New Zealand. It was not an auspicious tour in terms of results, with just one win, by 24–10 against Buller. Most of their seven defeats, though, were by respectable margins, including 6–19 and 8–24 to the New Zealand Maoris.

Around this era, the New Zealand winger Bryan Williams was parading his talents around the world stage. Though born in Auckland, he was of Samoan extraction. His performance was to encourage many fellow Polynesians.

With the economic situation on the Polynesian islands becoming critical from the 1970s, New Zealand and Australia appeared as the 'new world' to those young men looking for job opportunities. New Zealand rugby clubs were inundated with Samoans in the way that most English clubs used to contain legions of Welsh. The national side benefited from the availability of these 'overseas' players and Fiji and Tonga became victims; there was genuine feeling that having beaten both countries, the Samoans should have been considered for the 1987 World Cup.

In 1986, Wales were the first major country to tour Western Samoa. Some thought that the awarding of caps was premature, but Wales were beating England a decade earlier by a greater margin than their 32–14 win. That afternoon the Samoans fielded an M Jones in the back row – not another exiled Welshman, but Michael Jones, the world's outstanding flanker before his cruel 1989 injury, and now happily restored to Kiwi colours.

Samoan preparation for the World Cup was very thorough. They toured Wales and Ireland in 1988, followed by France and England in 1989. In 1990 and 1991 they made tours to New Zealand. And of course they competed in the South Pacific Championship which is held every season. Western Samoa sauntered through the World Cup zone programme, including a 37–11 win against Japan. Their 1989 European tour also took in the Soviet Union and Romania.

One of rugby's more interesting aspects of the 1990s will be to determine how the Samoans fare after their 1991 World Cup exploits. The New Zealand, and, to a lesser degree, the Australian connection will be a source of development as ever. But cynics who suggest that the side is composed of New Zealanders who have not quite made the grade with the All Blacks, may care to reflect that five Western Samoans – Joe Stanley, John Schuster, Va'aiga Tuigamala, Olo Brown and Graeme Bachop – were 1990–1 All Blacks.

DOMESTIC RUGBY STRUCTURE

There is a club competition, Senior A grade being the top division. The Morris Headstrom Shield is the major Cup competition, with the Vailima Beer trophy for the winner of the playoffs.

Recent Club Champions

1990 Vaiala

1991 Marist St Joseph's

The other major club sides are Vaimoso, SCOPA, Apia and Moataa.

WESTERN SAMOA v IRELAND

29 Oct 1988
Lansdowne Road, Dublin
IRELAND 49
T: Crosson (3), Kiernan, Matthews, Mullin, Francis, McBride, Sexton
C: Kiernan (4) *PG:* Kiernan (2)
DG: Sexton
WESTERN SAMOA 22
T: Young (2), Koko, Ahkuoi *C:* Aiolupo (2), Crichton

WESTERN SAMOA v WALES

1986
Suva
WESTERN SAMOA 14
T: Tafua, Palamo *PG:* Ailupo (2)
WALES 32
T: Titley (2), R Moriarty, Bowen
C: Dacey (2) *PG:* Dacey (3) *DG:* J Davies

12 Nov 1988
Cardiff Arms Park
WALES 24
T: N Davies (2), J Davies, C Davies
C: Thorburn (4)
WESTERN SAMOA 6
T: Lemamea *C:* Aiolupo

ZIMBABWE

FOUNDATION: 1895 (as Rhodesian RU)
Honours: 1987 and 1991 World Cup first round
1991 African Qualifying zone winners.
Largest victory: 111–12 v Nigeria 1987
Heaviest defeat: 12–70 v France 1987
Clubs: 35
Players: 1000
Population: 7 000 000
Main stadia: National Stadium, Harare (cap: 30 000), Bulawayo (cap: 17 500)
Colours: Olive green and white hooped jerseys, white shorts
Headquarters: Zimbabwe Rugby Union
PO Box 1129
Harare

The proudest moment in Zimbabwean rugby was at the Hartsfield Stadium, Bulawayo on 27 July 1949. Zimbabwe (then Rhodesia) met the All Blacks and beat them 10–8 to record their finest victory. Both sides scored two tries each, both had their chances to win, but none would deny the Rhodesians their finest hour. Led by their new Springboks, the centre Ryk van Schoor and lock Salty du Rand, the locals celebrated for days.

Three days later, on 30 July, the second instalment took place at the Glamis Stadium, Salisbury, now Harare. This time the All Blacks got away with a 3–3 draw, and headed for South Africa wondering what they had let themselves in for. The All Blacks spoke highly of the Rhodesian rugby.

There have been many changes over the years in Zimbabwean rugby. When in the Currie Cup as Rhodesia, the game was based around professional workers of white stock, but with independence has come the introduction to the black population.

The game started in 1890 in Rhodesia with the arrival of the Pioneer Column from the Cape. Salisbury was several days ox-trek from South Africa and Johannesburg was four years old. The first recorded game on Rhodesian soil was on the sandy bed of the Shashi River, hard by the Botswana border, between members of the Pioneer column, who played during stops on the trek to Salisbury.

Overcoming travel problems was a major factor and a formidable challenge to the expansion of the game. Zimbabwe is 500 miles by 500 miles in extent. The communications were poor – the first railway line arrived in Salisbury in 1901, the same year as the first inter-provincial match between Salisbury and Bulawayo. For that match, the Bulawayo players were involved in a three week 600 miles stage-coach journey to the capital. They were rewarded with a 16–0 win. Even before that first inter provincial game, a national side was selected to participate in a Currie Cup tour of South Africa. The players were away for over six months, but had the consolation of victories against Orange Free State and Eastern Province.

Between 1900 and 1945, rugby struggled to find itself a niche in the community. Certainly the game spread its roots through that part of the African continent. Contact with South Africa became more frequent, but the highlights were just five trips from touring teams en route to South Africa. The Lions won 24–11 in 1910, 16–3 in 1924 and in 1938 by 45–11 and 25–11; the All Blacks won 44–8 in 1928 and the 1933 Wallabies were successful 24–5.

The golden age of rugby arrived after World War II. The burgeoning copper mines in Zambia (which for rugby purposes was also Rhodesia), the tobacco farms and the arrival of professional colonials from Britain and South Africa gave the sport a tremendous boost. The win and draw against the All Blacks was followed by an 8–8 draw against the Wallabies at Kitwe (Zambia) in 1953, and narrow losses to that fine 1955 Lions side by just 16–12, and by only 13–9 to the All Blacks. Rhodesia played in the top echelon of South Africa's Currie Cup and regularly beat Western Province, Northern Transvaal and the likes. Seven players were invited to the 1951 Springbok trials. In 1960 Des Van Jaarsveld achieved the ultimate honour, captaining South Africa against Scotland.

The 1960s, though, proved to be lean years. The break-up of the Federation of Rhodesia and Nyasaland caused a reduction in the flow of players. Zimbabwe would have to develop their own talent. By the 1970s, the team was back on course – the country was beating the Currie Cup sides regularly, and several players were progressing to the very top. Ray Mordt, David Smith and Ian Robertson playing for South Africa. Mordt and Smith caused Bill Beaumont's 1980 Lions no end of trouble.

Zimbabwe's independence brought further changes. Mordt and Co. headed for the Transvaal to continue their careers. Gone, temporarily, was the South African connection; Zimbabwe looked to their future via the new emerging rugby nations – Spain,

Richard Tsimba (with ball), an integral part of Zimbabwe's rugby future, in action against France in the 1987 World Cup.

Portugal, USSR, Romania – and the World Cup. Ravages of war and poor finances had brought the number of clubs down to 27.

But the 1990s have brought another remarkable change. The Zimbabwean Rugby Union has taken the game to the schools, and back to the grass roots. Already the interest has been extraordinary. The number of senior clubs has swelled to 42, with over 1000 senior players. But the statistics for the schools are staggering. There are over 170 schools playing rugby, some have as many as 21 teams in a school, while most have between 8–10 teams. Ten thousand schoolchildren are actively involved. Fruits of this policy were not seen in the 1991 World Cup but with the wind of change blowing over Southern Africa again, the contacts with the South will be re-established.

Back in 1949, five of the team that beat the All Blacks were farmers from the little village of Inyarza, just off the Harare–Umtali road; Du Rand and Van Schoor became Springboks. A few years later their little club was part of the African bush, posts and all. The ZRU have ensured that will not happen again.

With sights on the 1995 World Cup, there has been an immediate threat to Zimbabwe's hold as African representatives. South Africa will return, but will be seeded. Namibia, though, may join Zimbabwe in the qualifying groups. Zimbabwe need the exposure of world competition, and have suggested that readmittance to the Currie Cup may be a way forward.

DOMESTIC RUGBY STRUCTURE

National Division (8 clubs) centred around the two major cities of Harare and Bulawayo; regional feeder leagues.

Inter City League

1980	Old Harareans/Salisbury Sports Club (shared)
1981	Salisbury Sports Club
1982	Harare Sports Club
1983	Old Harareans
1984	Harare Sports Club
1985	No competition
1986	Old Georgians
1987	Old Hararians
1988	Harare Sports Club
1989	Harare Sports Club
1990	Harare Sports Club
1991	Old Hararians

ZIMBABWE v SCOTLAND XV

21 May 1988
Bulawayo
ZIMBABWE 10
T: Kuhn *PG:* Grobler (2)
SCOTLAND 31
T: Oliver (3), Duncan, Butcher *C:* Dods (4) *PG:* Dods

28 May 1988
Harare Police Ground
ZIMBABWE 7
T: Kamba *PG:* Grobler
SCOTLAND 34
T: Dods, Moore, Parker, Rafferty *C:* Dods (3) *PG:* Dods (3) *DG:* Chalmers

MINOR NATIONS

After the major nations and the World Cup participants come the other rugby playing countries of the world. Like many rugby clubs who maintain that the 2nd and 3rd XVs are the corner-stone of the game, so it is with the smaller nations.

These smaller countries cover a wide spectrum. At the top of the tree are those countries which made it through to the final qualifying stages of the World Cup only to be beaten by those who did eventually reach the last 16. Holland and Spain in Europe, South Korea, along with Morocco, Tunisia and Ivory Coast, almost rubbed shoulders with the International Board countries.

Then there are countries where lack of population size cannot disguise the excellence of organisation, structure and enthusiasm. Finally, the most courageous of all – the countries where expatriates, teachers, oil-men and the like, battle against lack of finance, lack of facilities and inhospitable climates. Rugby people who have been known to arrange games on the floor of the Dead Sea, players who have braved sub-zero temperatures in Siberia, and those whose enthusiasm is such that pitches have been created out of the jungle.

If countries have been omitted then it is because some have disbanded, and quietly reformed, or because communications have sometimes let us down. But it just proves that wherever one goes in the world these days, there is always a welcoming club somewhere.

EUROPE

Most of the European countries are members of FIRA and play in the FIRA Championship. A system of promotion and relegation through the Groups is in existence. In 1992 Group A consisted of France, Soviet Union (CIS), Italy, Romania and Spain ; there were two Group B divisions based mainly on geographical regions, which included Morocco, Tunisia (see Africa), Belgium, Germany, Holland, Poland, Czechoslovakia and Bulgaria and a Group C of the small nations – Luxembourg, Andorra and Yugoslavia. Several other countries in Europe are affiliated to FIRA but not all play in the league. In 1992 the Scandinavian countries played a summer league as an experiment, as another Group C, but Sweden proved too strong in a lop-sided tournament.

BELGIUM

Honours: FIRA Championship Group B
No of senior clubs: 59
Players: 3400
Foundation: 1931
Stadium: FBR Ground, Brussels

Founder members of FIRA, the Belgians have benefited recently from the EEC developments in Brussels, but though bordering France and close to Britain, neither country has a rugby hotbed in the proximity. The Belgian league began in 1959, the Cup in 1968 and the University Championship in 1971.

CLUB CHAMPIONS

ASUB Brussels 12, Anderlecht 6 , SCAB Brussels 3 , Coq Mosan 3, Boitsfort 2 , Brussels British 1, Avia Kituro 1 BUC Brussels 1

GERMANY

Honours: FIRA Championship Group A 1981, 1982
No of senior clubs: 75
No of players: 5800
Foundation: 1900

The standard of rugby in Germany may have been higher in world terms before World War II than since. In 1846 Heidelberg Turnverien was allegedly founded, making it one of the earliest clubs in world rugby. The German Federation was founded in 1900, the year that Frankfurt won the silver medal at the Olympic Games against France – losing 17–27. At the turn of the century there were 10 clubs.

In 1927 Germany played their first international, a 30–5 loss to France, but three weeks later had reversed that result 17–16 at Frankfurt against a French side that had beaten England 3–0 two months earlier. When France were ejected from the International Championship, Germany played them on a regular basis. Since the war, international performances have been low key, but in 1990, Germany were beaten in the World Cup qualifiers by Holland only 12–6. In 1991, with the fusion of the two Germanys, it was confirmed that 14 clubs flourished in the old East Germany, centred around Berlin, Potsdam and Brandenburg.

The German club championship began in 1909, the Cup in 1962. The major rugby centres are Hanover, Berlin and Heidelberg, and the list of winners below indicates the early formation of some of the top clubs.

LEADING CHAMPIONSHIP WINNERS

Victoria Linden 17, 1878 Hannover 8, Neuenheim, Odin Hannover, and Heidelberg RK 1872 all 6, SC Frankfurt 1880 and 1897 Linden both 4.

LEADING CUP WINNERS

1878 Hannover 9, Germania List and Victoria Linden 4, Neuenheim 3

The German defence is stretched against the United States in Hong Kong.

HOLLAND

Honours: FIRA Championship Group A 1975
No of clubs: 104
Players: 5000
Foundation: 1932
Stadium: Geementilijk Sportpark, Hilversum (cap: 23 000)

In 1879 Pim Mulder arrived from London with the first rugby ball. By 1913 Northern Wanderers had experimented with rugby and in 1918 Delft (DRSC) became the first club. Delft beat Amersfoort in 1919 in the first interclub match by 3–0. The first national cup was won by Groningen University in 1929, the first international was played at The Hague in 1930, against Belgium (0-6), while in 1934 Holland became founder members of FIRA.

Holland are now part of the home nations youth and B XV fixture lists, with regular contacts with the British international set up. In 1972, the first international sevens tournament was held in Amsterdam and in 1980, Holland secured perhaps their best victory, by 15–13 against Japan.

The Netherlands in action at Hong Kong.

POLAND

Honours: FIRA Championship Group A every season from 1973 to 1981 except 1974, then 1983 and 1989
No of clubs: 21
No of players: 3200
Foundation: 1956
Stadium: Polski Zwiazek Rugby, Warsaw

Polish rugby had just begun to surface before World War II with the military and mining communities running four clubs at Warsaw and in Silesia. Miners returning from the French coalfields were particularly influential in starting the game.

The Polish Rugby Union was founded in 1956 to control and structure 15 clubs into a league format, and the first international was a 9–8 win against East Germany at Lodz in 1958.

Poland had been regular members of the FIRA Group A until the late 1980s, but just failed to reach the final qualifying pool of the European section for the 1991 World Cup after defeats by Holland (27–33) and Spain (9–23) and a win over Belgium (25-23) in Madrid. The Poland XV which played France in 1990–1 consisted of 14 players of Polish extraction who were playing Division 2 club football in France, an indication of the widening scope for future selections.

PORTUGAL

Honours: FIRA Championship Group A 1985
No of clubs: 42
No of players: 3500
Foundation: 1957
Stadium: Estadio Universitario, Lisbon (cap: 12 500)

British influence at the Lisbon Cricket Club was responsible for the introduction of the game in 1908, when the hosts played Carcevelos. The famous soccer clubs, Benfica and Sporting Lisbon, opened rugby football clubs in 1921, while Porto and Lisbon formed their own Unions. The club championship began in 1927, and was extended in 1933. Though Portugal were founder members of FIRA in 1934, their Union was not formed until 1957.

Currently the game is structured from the first two divisions of the national league down to regional leagues. In recent times, Portugal has become a haven for winter training for the home nations, while the Lisbon Sevens is a popular and extending festival. Portugal hope that mixing with overseas internationals will improve their own standing.

SOVIET UNION (CIS)

Honours: FIRA Championship Group A 1978 to date; runners up Group A every season 1984–91 – some shared with Romania and Italy
No of clubs: 148
No of players: 25 000
Foundation: 1966
Stadium: National Stadium, Moscow (cap: 30 000), Kutaisi (cap: 20 000)

Quite what will happen to Soviet rugby after the monumental changes of the early 1990s, is not clear. But what *is* clear is that had there been just a little more organisation, a little more finance, a little more coaching and better communication with the rest of the world, then their emergence as one of the stronger rugby nations might not have

Above *Igor Mironov, the Soviet captain.*

Left *Mironov celebrates victory for the Soviet Union at the 1990 Sicily Sevens.*

been far removed. The split into separate nations may well mean that just when impetus was needed, the whole rugby concept could move into reverse.

Soviet rugby is a modern phenomenon. Certainly there were matches in 1933 between Moscow Physical Education College and Dynamo Moscow, and an inter city match in which Moscow beat Minsk 6–0. Dynamo then won the first club championship in 1934. But it was the 1957 Festival of Youth which promoted the game in the schools and clubs and made sports clubs keen to open rugby sections, despite a somewhat torrid final between Llanelli and the Romanian club Grivitza Rosie.

The Rugby Federation was founded in 1966 to organise club matches on a league structure – lack of finance to accommodate vast travel distances was a major problem for the clubs, some of whom had been meeting on a regular basis since 1936. However, the national team began its fixtures in 1975 with a 28-0 win against Czechoslovakia and by 1978 the Soviets had moved into FIRA Group A.

Inspired by Igor Mironov, the captain and utility threequarter, and Alexei Tikhonov, the lock, both of whom were honoured by the Barbarians, the Soviets defeated France A, Italy and Romania on several occasions. They also beat the USA. But tours to the major nations, England (1989), Australia (1990), and New Zealand (1991) may have revealed the reaching of the watershed.

The future difficulties of the new CIS are found in the list of club champions, which reveal how widespread the rugby centres are. Moscow provided champions from the Slava, VVA (Gagarin) and Dynamo clubs; Aviator Kiev is now in the Ukraine; Tblisi in Georgia, as are the recent champions Kutaisi, while Krasnoyarsk is in deepest Siberia. Six of the team

VICTORIES OVER WORLD CUP COUNTRIES SINCE 1978

Date	Venue	Result
18 Nov 1978	Rome	Italy 9, Soviet Union 11
28 Oct 1979	Moscow	Soviet Union 9, Italy 0
2 Nov 1980	Rovigo	Italy 3, Soviet Union 4
1 Nov 1982	Merignac	France 6, Soviet Union 12
30 Oct 1983	Kiev	Soviet Union 16, Italy 7
31 May 1985	Kiev	Soviet Union 14, Romania 6
1985/86	Moscow	Soviet Union 15, Italy 13
1986	Belges	France 9, Soviet Union 15
1986	Genoa	Italy 14, Soviet Union 16
7 Nov 1987	Kishinev	Soviet Union 12, Italy 9
22 May 1988	Kutaisi	Soviet Union 17, France 10
23 Oct 1988	Alma-Ata	Soviet Union 23, Romania 9
6 Nov 1988	Treviso	Italy 12, Soviet Union 18
5 Oct 1989	Moscow	Soviet Union 15, Italy 12

The match they said would never happen – the USSR against the USA in 1990.

which faced England in 1991 came from Alma-Ata, the reigning champions – Alma-Ata is in Kazakhstan. Add to these centres the venues of recent internationals in Kishinev (Moldova) and Minsk (Belorussia) and some indication of the difficulties can be gained. In 1992 there were no plans for a league, while internationals in the FIRA Championship were being postponed.

SPAIN

Honours: FIRA Championship Group A 1973–79, 1980, 1984, 1987–89, 1991 to date
Final European 1991 World Cup qualifying pool
No of clubs: 236
No of players: 14 300
Foundation: 1923

Granted a crystal ball to predict where the next breakthrough to international status may occur, many observers would vote for Spain. Their Union is well run and well administered; clubs are progressing and increasing in numbers, there is a proximity to the rugby hotbed of the south of France, sponsorship is available, and television coverage of the International Championship is widely featured.

The Spanish Rugby Federation was founded in 1923, and – as Catalonia, the area around Barcelona – were founder members of FIRA in 1934. The national cup knockout tournament has taken place since 1941, and a national league has been in operation since 1953.

The growth of the game is mirrored in the Spanish Union statistics – up to 1945 there were 12 senior clubs and 500 players, by 1966 the figure was up to 20 clubs and 1000 players, and by 1980 the number had mushroomed to 147 clubs and 11 109 players.

In the 1991 World Cup qualifiers, Spain finished third in the final European Zone behind Italy and Romania, and ahead of Holland. Two countries qualified for the World Cup, Spain missed out by one place – it was that close.

OTHER NATIONS

FIRA AFFILIATED

	Formed	Clubs	Players
Andorra	1963	2	285
Austria	1981	5	200
Bulgaria	1967	14	1200
Czechoslovakia	1926	21	2987
Denmark	1950	25	1710
Finland	1985	4	150
Gibraltar*	1971	4	500
Hungary	1989	8	500
Israel	1971	7	400
Luxembourg	1973	2	230
Malta*	–	1	30
Norway	1985	2	110
Sweden	1931	51	3500
Switzerland	1971	25	1000
Yugoslavia	1954	17	2900

* Not full members of FIRA

The first 1991 World Cup preliminary tournament featured Sweden, Denmark, Switzerland, and Israel. Sweden, the winners, moved into the next round when they were beaten by Holland 24–3. The tournament took place in and around Tours in France, with a host of junior clubs in the region hosting the event.

Sweden, the largest of the competing nations have a three division league, based on promotion and relegation. The first division is a national league, with regional feeder leagues based around Gothenburg, Stockholm and the South. Sweden's best player of recent vintage is Kari Tapper, a no. 8 who has played for Aberavon and was honoured as a Barbarian.

Denmark runs a first division of six clubs, and regional leagues in Jutland, Fyn and Zeeland. **Switzerland**, unhappy with several large FIRA Championship defeats, have staked their future in the youth set up. Their proximity to France meant an early introduction to the game and interestingly, their two leading soccer clubs Grasshoppers of Zurich and Servette of Geneva were once rugby clubs!

Geneva, Lausanne, Neuchatel and Zurich were the base of a resurgence by the British and French in the 1930s, while the Swiss Rugby Union was restarted in both 1968 and 1971. There are three national divisions with promotion and relegation.

Israel have a small eight club national league, formed mainly by South Africans, with the strength being at Jerusalem University, Tel Aviv University and Netanya.

The former Iron Curtain countries are well represented, and were well structured as part of multi-sports clubs and national leagues.

Czechoslovakia's introduction was via British students in Vienna playing at Bratislava. They were a founder member of FIRA and have a national league of 10 clubs with two regional second divisions – one in Moravia and one in Prague. Their first serious game was in the year of the foundation of their Union in 1926 between Prague and Brno. Children's writer Ondreij Sekora, the Enid Blyton of Czechoslovakia(!) translated the rules from French.

Rugby in **Yugoslavia** may not recover from the traumas of 1991–2 Like the Soviet Union, the game was well spread around the country with Nada Split, Dynamo Zagreb, and RFC Zagreb from Croatia having won the national league (started in 1958) with Pancevo and several Belgrade clubs winning the honour for Serbia. The largest club, Celik Zenica, with 110 playing members, is in Bosnia. The national league starts in regions, with the winners going to a final pool.

Right the way down the scale, the FIRA organisation is sound. **Luxembourg**, who have clubs in the city and the EEC community, and **Andorra** are examples. Both play in the regional Lorraine and Catalan leagues of neighbouring France and Spain respectively. And if the lack of depth is apparent because of lack of population, even the smallest countries are soundly structured and run. In some cases their own leagues started well before the home nations!

AFRICA

Rugby in Africa, away from South African influence in the south of the continent and French influence in the north, is going through a transitional period. Much of the English and French colonies are now independent and much of the way of life (which included rugby) has passed on.

But that is not to say that there has been too great a decline in standards or enthusiasm. Those that have remained on the continent have worked ceaselessly to impart their knowledge and skills to the native population, and in the case of countries like Zimbabwe, the former colonial and Currie Cup regime has been augmented by 170 000 black schoolchildren playing the game.

Certainly there have been problems. Lack of finance, lack of facilities, vast travel distances, and the fact that many locals prefer soccer, have conspired to block the path of progress. But FIRA, who are a worldwide body, and not just European, have – since 1986 – organized CARA, the Confederation de Afrique Rugby Amateur, to discuss these problems, and to promote the sport. Rugby's entry into the African Games is certain. In 1991, there were 15 members of CARA.

For the purposes of grading African Nations, the top group outside South Africa, Namibia and Zimbabwe would include the remaining three World Cup qualifying group countries, Morocco, Tunisia and the Ivory Coast, plus Kenya. Information from some of the other countries is difficult to come by with constant changes in personnel and politics.

IVORY COAST

Honours: 1991 World Cup African Qualifying group
No of clubs: 15
No of players: 2700
Foundation: 1973

The former French colony formed its Union in 1973, an idea first mooted in 1970, and is now a member of both FIRA and CARA. The first international was against Senegal in 1984, the second in the World Cup qualifiers! This strange circumstance is largely explained by the fact that 17 players were registered with leading French clubs (Biarritz, Tulle, Cognac, Cahors, and Condom), 11 of whom played in the World Cup.

The major clubs today are in the capital Abijdian, where the University and the national Electricity Board and Port Authority are to the fore; provincial clubs at Yabusuko and Bouake also prosper.

Though the Ivory Coast lost all three World Cup games, to Zimbabwe (22-9), Tunisia (12-7) and Morocco (11-4), the points deficit was just 20-45. The unruly discipline that caused the Morocco game to be abandoned after 70 minutes was a cause for concern though.

Success on another field could prove a problem to the Ivory Coast. The soccer team won the 1992 African Championship for the first time ever, turning eyes towards the round ball. But the future of rugby lies in the hands of players such as Djakaria Sanojo, who plays top class French club rugby with Serge Blanco at Biarritz, and was chosen for the 1990 French tour to Namibia.

KENYA

No of clubs: 12
No of players: 1000
Foundation: 1921 (East African RU 1953)
Stadium: East African RFU ground, Nairobi (cap; 8000)

A country with a proud rugby history, which today stills boasts some 12 clubs playing in league and cup competitions. Yet developments have mirrored much of the 'wind of change' that has blown through Africa.

In the immediate post World War II years, Kenya (through Nairobi) was the stop-off point for tourists to and from South Africa to Europe. Major teams used to play there on the way through – the British Lions of 1955 and 1962, the 1958 Barbarians, South Africa in 1961, and the 1964 Welsh tourists to South Africa. There was a large colonial presence in farms, teaching, industry and commerce.

The first recorded match between Officials and Settlers took place at Mombasa in 1909, the local sports club being the focal point for visiting Royal Naval personnel. By 1923, the game had spread to the Rift Valley (Nakuru), the high plateau (Eldoret and Kitale) and to Nairobi. In 1921 the Kenya Rugby Union was founded, in 1925 the Nairobi District Championship was first held, and in 1930 the Naval ship HMS Enterprise donated a cup of the same name for club competition, which is still today the backbone of club rugby.

In 1953, the East Africa Rugby Union was founded to include Tanzania and Uganda and tours from Universities in Stellenbosch and Cape Town as well as Oxford and Cambridge flowed. But with the granting of independence and the arrival of non-stop flights to South Africa, the heady days passed.

In the 1990s, the old 'colonial' clubs still prosper, Kenya Harlequins, Nondescripts and Impala. They have been joined by sides such as Mwamba and Watembezi Pacesetters. Banks and Universities field regular sides. But in the provinces, only Nakuru and the Mombasa Sports Club survive consistently. The Enterprise Cup is still the showpiece, while the Kenya Festival and sevens tournaments still feature in a full fixture list.

MOROCCO

Honours: 1991 World Cup qualifying pool
FIRA Championship Group A 1973, 1976, 1979, 1982, 1983
No of clubs: 14
No of players: 2015
Foundation: 1956

The French introduced the game to Morocco in 1924, but it remained almost an exclusive French enclave until 1935, when two local players joined the Casablanca Rugby Club.

The Union was founded in independence year, 1956, and was a founder member of the first FIRA Championship in 1973. Morocco have made several appearances in Group A.

The strength of the national XV depends on who is available from the French clubs. The case of their most famous player, Abdelatif Benazzi, is typical. Benazzi played for Morocco in group B of the FIRA Championship as a youngster (not in the World Cup) but his talents took him to the top French club Agen, and into the National XV. There are several other players with leading Division 1 clubs in France, but availability and eligibility are major issues.

Currently the league has eight clubs in the Northern group and seven in the Southern group – with a final each season.

TUNISIA

Honours: 1991 World Cup qualifying Pool – runners up
FIRA Championship Group A 1984, 1985
No of clubs: 32
No of players: 3000
Foundation: 1972

Again the French connection, with the game started by locals and expatriate Frenchmen, was instrumental in the development of the game. Tunisian rugby enjoyed spectacular success in the years from 1979 to 1985, but a case of too much development too quickly has subsequently been diagnosed.

In 1979, at the Mediterranean Games, the gulf between the top and the emerging nations was graphically illustrated when France, easing down, beat Tunisia 104–3 at Split. Tunisia joined FIRA's Group C, and, with the help of players in the French league, moved from Group C to Group A by 1984. In 1986 they deservedly beat Romania 17–15 at Tunis.

However, reliance on French based players meant that the basic infrastructure was not in place. The game has now been reorganised into a league system, and the youth, school and student factions have been catered for.

In 1992, the first division had 15 clubs, with 20 in the second division. In the World Cup qualifiers, Tunisia beat Morocco 16–12 and the Ivory Coast 12–7, losing only to the eventual qualifiers Zimbabwe 24–13, this after leading 13–12 at half time.

Tunisia in action against Papua New Guinea at Hong Kong.

OTHER NATIONS

Quite what has happened to rugby in some of the African countries is now difficult to discern. Many of the colonial expatriates have left and progress – even stabilisation – has been difficult in countries which are headline news sadly because of factors such as bankruptcy and even famine.

In the immediate post World War II era, **Zambia**, then Northern Rhodesia, possessed several clubs. The copper mining belt around Kitwe and Ndola was a rugby stronghold; in 1953 Rhodesia held the Wallabies 8–8, in 1955 the British Lions beat Rhodesia 27–14, in 1960 the All Blacks scraped home against Rhodesia 13–9 at Kitwe, and the 1963 Wallabies beat Rhodesia 22–11, all of these matches taking place at Kitwe, which also hosted Currie Cup and other tour matches.

The Diggers RFC at Kitwe were a local legend ; Roan Antelope at Luanysha not only had a fine side but were in The Guinness Book of Records for the tallest rugby posts in the world! There were other fine clubs at Ndola, Broken Hill, Mufilara, and Nchanga. In the capital Lusaka, the local RFC and Sports Club provided several fine players.

Rugby reached Zambia in 1900, and their participation with a combined Southern and Northern Rhodesia is chronicled under Zimbabwe. The clubs still survive, but the country struggles with bankruptcy, and although there are bound to be several enthusiasts keeping the game afloat, the glory days of an 8–8 draw with the Wallabies are, perhaps, for the scrapbooks.

There are other countries where similar stories unfold. **Tanzania** and **Uganda** were part of the East African Union in 1953, and rugby flourished in both countries. Nowadays there are clubs in the capitals, but the Dar-es- Salaam Gymkhana RFC and Kampala RFC make sporadic appearances in the Kenya tournaments, often only at sevens meetings.

Tanzania at one stage in the 1950s and 1960s had 20 clubs centred around Arusha in the north, Dar on the coast and Iringa and Dodoma in the central region. The Tanzanian RFU was founded in 1953 but ceased in 1959, beaten by politics, administration costs, and transport problems. In 1970 five clubs existed at Dar, Arusha, Moshi Mufindi and Dordonda.

A similar story surrounds rugby in Uganda. In the East African RU days there were clubs at Kampala, Mount Elgon, Nile RFC of Jinja, Entebbe and at Police and Colleges. Rugby began in 1923 when Uganda Railways played the Chief Secretary's XV. Gradual improvement on the domestic front enabled Kampala to become the first club to take the Enterprise Cup out of Kenya in 1956. An inter provincial East African tournament saw Kampala as the winners in the same year.

Research for the Guinness Book of Rugby Facts and Feats (1981) provided two marvellous rugby anecdotes. In 1935, Uganda played Kenya at Entebbe – both teams turned out in white. A lady spectator promptly turned out a large bottle of dye, and with the aid of water buckets, proceeded to dye the jerseys of the home side. Uganda – their shirts barely dry – played in black from there on.

In the 1950s, there was but one black member of the Nile RFC of Jinja. A large, strapping winger and athlete, the young Idi Amin, who had shown not a little skill at Sandhurst, was the official reserve to face the 1955 British Lions when they played East Africa. Sadly his actions would help crush the game he enjoyed.

The same story of demise, for the same reasons could well be applied to West Africa, for **Ghana** and **Nigeria** both had a sound structure during 'colonial' days, and both now have seemingly allowed matters to drift. Reports of three clubs and 150 players in Ghana in the 1980s cannot be substantiated, and in Nigeria, where the game was becoming established, very little is now known.

What is known in Nigeria is that there were clubs at Lagos, who had clubs in the colonial sports clubs, the oil companies and students, Kaduna, Kano, Zaria and Jos. London Welsh visited Lagos and Kano on their 1981 tour. Since then a cloak of silence has fallen over the country. It seems extraordinary considering that Andrew Harriman, the Harlequins and England winger, and the Bath and England B players Victor Ubogu, Steve Omojoh and Adedayo

OTHER AFRICAN NATIONS

	Clubs	Players
Botswana	3	150
Cameroon	2	100
Ghana	2	100
Madagascar (Malagasay)	10	450
Malawi	3	150
Nigeria	4	150
Senegal	8	175
Swaziland	4	220
Tanzania	1	20
Uganda	1	20
Zambia	8	350
Mauritius	2	50
Reunion	13	500
Seychelles	2	60

Adebayo – top players with the top English clubs – were all born in Nigeria. Chris Oti, the England wing, is also of Nigerian descent.

Some of the smaller former British countries, **Swaziland**, **Botswana** and **Malawi** still play the game. Malawi still has the Blantyre Sports Club, while Lilonwe, Limbe and Thyolo all have connections. Again, the movement away from South African and British influence and the distances to what was Rhodesia (for tours in and out) have taken their toll, but the Grenager Trophy, Milward Trophy and Leslie Sevens, the domestic competitions, are still on the agenda. Malawi's problem is that it appears from a rugby standpoint to have become geographically isolated.

Botswana and Swaziland's capitals, Gabarone and Mbabane, are so close to the South African border that games can easily be organised with South African clubs. That this will happen in the future on a more regular basis is in no doubt. Facilities are available but politics have so far hindered development.

The former French colonies report similar problems. There were clubs in the **Cameroon** capital of Douala. But **Mauritius**, **Seychelles** and **Senegal** were full members of FIRA, who confirm their basic statistics. The entry for **Malagasay** reveals 60 clubs, but FIRA doubt this – nearer 10 and 450 players (if that) would appear to be the better figure for one of the world's more remote countries. France also confirm that rugby prospers of the island of **La Reunion** with four clubs in the capital St Denis, and visits to and from the neighbours Mauritius and Seychelles.

What the future holds for Africa is difficult to judge. The southern part of the continent should come alive with tours and provide some of the highest standard of rugby in the world. The other countries, with political problems, bankruptcy, lack of local interest and huge tracts of the African bush to encounter, may find themselves isolated. For those players, coaches and especially administrators, who are still managing to keep the game very much alive in difficult circumstances, the world's rugby fraternity will hope that the efforts prove successful.

Andrew Harriman, one of Nigeria's talented exiles, playing for Harlequins in the Pilkington Cup Final.

THE PACIFIC

Following the success of Western Samoa, the world-beating sevens performances of Fiji and the known ability in Tonga, the obvious question for the major rugby nations is whether the Pacific islands are likely to throw up any more nasty surprises.

The short answer is probably not, but on the remaining islands that play the game the standard is high and further links with Australia and New Zealand have been established. These islands are even smaller than Fiji, Tonga and Samoa, and, like the others, struggle to find employment for their youth, hence the drift to the larger centres in the region.

The **Solomon Islands** are members of FIRA, and are in the record books for the wrong reason – their 113–13 loss to Fiji in the 1969 South Pacific Games. Like Western Samoa, whose number of clubs might be misconstrued for number of teams, the Solomons have a large playing strength. The French Rugby federation confirm the figures for their former colonies, Tahiti, New Caledonia, and Wallis and Futuna, with whom they still have contacts.

The **Cook Islands** are the current regional champions from the South Pacific Games, which the big three do not contest. In 1985 they beat New Caledonia in the final and have remained strong ever since. In 1980, the Cook Islands actually beat Italy on the Italians' return from a hard tour in New Zealand. At Rarotonga, the locals won 15–6. Their only previous headline was in 1976, when they toured New Zealand, losing all six but proving no walkovers.

Hawaii, in a rugby sense, can legimately count itself as a separate Union. Although one of the 52 United States of America, for rugby purposes Hawaii are independent. The 1992 US National Directory lists 11 clubs on the islands and two colleges. The Hawaii Harlequins and Hawaii Barbarians are perhaps the best known, if only because they specialize in the organisation of spectacular sevens and Golden Oldie events.

The first senior club was the Harlequins in 1964, founded, so local legend has it, by an Irishman, Jack Keenan, who started a rugby side because of his ignorance of the local American football rules! Hawaii is now sensibly marketing its touring values as a meeting place between the Canadian and US clubs (British Columbia providing most of the 1991 World Cup quarter-final team paraded by Canada) and Australian and New Zealand sides ; the other Pacific islands have also benefited. Stop-overs are becoming more common: France stayed in 1979 and 1981 in Tahiti, playing the locals in unofficial acclimatisation matches – in 1979 France won 92–12, with Luc Averous scoring seven of their 20 tries.

SOUTH PACIFIC TRIANGULAR TOURNAMENT

Year	Winners
1982	Western Samoa
1983	Tonga
1984	Fiji
1985	Western Samoa
1986	Tonga
1987	Fiji
1988	Fiji
1989	–
1990	Western Samoa
1991	Western Samoa

RUGBY-PLAYING PACIFIC ISLANDS

	Clubs	Players
Cook Islands	3	170
Hawaii	11	690
New Caledonia	8	400
Solomon Islands	2	100
Tahiti	4	220
Wallis and Futuna	2	60

THE FAR EAST

Junior rugby in the Far East begins with two nations, Hong Kong and South Korea. Hong Kong is now justifiably world famous for its Hong Kong Sevens, the world's premier event, but deserves as much credit for its plate competition which enables the lesser countries , having faced the heavy guns, to participate at their own standard. To many in Singapore, Malaysia, Thailand, the Middle East and others, the pinnacle of their rugby careers is to compete in Hong Kong.

South Korea are not only recent Asian Champions on a number of occasions, which gains them a commendation on merit, but were within a vote or two of getting rugby included in the Olympics. The Koreans backed rugby for the 1988 Games with great skill and enthusiasm, citing first, the obvious boost to the sport and second, that as rugby was part of their Sports Council (as with many emerging nations), then participation in the Olympics would release future funds from the Council towards the future of the game. The world of rugby knows little of how close the Koreans were to putting rugby back on the Olympic programme.

There are mentions of rugby played in **Hong Kong** as early as 1886 and its geographical position, the harbour and more recently the airport have ensured that full use is made of the various touring stopovers.Hong Kong has acted as a link between Europe and Australasia, but is now involved in two major new developments besides the Hong Kong Sevens – the amazing growth of mini-rugby in the colony, and the first, tentative, steps to introducing the game to China where, under the old regimes, rugby was banned as it was classed as a contact sport. Hong Kong can be proud of its contribution.

Ian Calder makes ground for Hong Kong against Japan.

South Korea has 14 teams in its national league – 10 University sides, the Army, Navy and Air Force and the Korean Electricity and Power clubs. If the game's growth is at all stunted it may be because for many players beyond their mid-twenties there are not the senior, mature clubs, to join. The fact that Korea beat Japan before and after the 1987 World Cup indicates that a possible invitation to that tournament might have been in order.

Of the other nations, all have British connections. **Singapore**, that other worthy stopover of bygone days, also has a proud history.The HMS Malaysia Cup stems from a 1922 visit by the ship of the same name, originally competed for by both Singapore and Malaysia. The splendid Singapore Cricket Club hosts many tournaments, the annual sevens (like Hong Kong) has a fine following, and a relatively new venture, 10-a-side rugby, may well have had its first airing in Singapore. This is another variation which has proved popular locally and with the Australian and New Zealand connections.

Malaysia still contests the Malaysia Cup (also Singapore),

EASTERN RUGBY-PLAYING NATIONS

	Founded	Clubs	Players
Brunei	1975	7	550
Hong Kong	1953	10	850
Indonesia	1978	6	400
Malaysia		11	750
Papua New Guinea		16	1100
Sarawak		2	80
Singapore		18	800
South Korea	1945	14	1000
Taiwan		14	1250
Thailand	1938	22	1600

South Korea distinguished themselves at the 1992 Hong Kong Sevens as their tough tackling put out the Barbarians.

and is proving an increasingly popular venue for club tours, while Brunei, Indonesia and Sarawak have a similar existence – all were formed by expatriates, all have had to hue their pitches out of inhospitable terrain, and all are managing to survive in some style. Thailand, originally via another splendid remnant of colonialism, the Royal Bangkok Sports Club, were one of the founder members of the Asian Union in 1968, their own Union having been formed as early as 1938. The strength of the game in the country is still with the Armed Forces and Universities, but the country takes credit for the popular schools festival for Asian countries which started in 1976.

Two interesting countries in terms of the future are Taiwan and Papua New Guinea. There is a known explosion of rugby enthusiasm in Taiwan, sides are even going to New Zealand to learn and play. Their Asian Championship record is improving, as contacts widen. Current FIRA estimates are that there are now 60 clubs at all levels.

Papua New Guinea's success in beating Great Britain's Rugby League side 20–18 in May 1990 has obviously posed questions as to whether the 'Kumuls' run Union clubs. To date there are 16 clubs mainly centred around the capital Port Moresby. Waliya, University, Defence and the Barbarians are the main clubs, but evidence of a Union stronghold is not yet clear. But the raw ability, fostered by aid from neighbouring Australia, is certainly there.

MIDDLE EAST

Above and below *The Dubai Rugby Sevens.*

The Gulf War, and its aftermath, raised suggestions that rugby, never an easy sport to play in the desert, may have foundered. However, reports quickly came through that Kuwait would continue to run a side as normal, while there were frequent pictures of troops playing rugby in the desert.

The Middle East has, as its backbone, the Gulf League with the usual participants being Dahrain, Dubai, Oman, Sharjah, Kuwait, Abu Dhabi, and Qatar. The Dubai Sevens is internationally known, and while some British, New Zealand and Australian expatriates find some difficulty with the local licensing hours and laws, the rugby scene is part of the way of life in the Middle East. The Hong Kong Sevens used to accept entries from various countries in the Gulf, but a Gulf States side is now selected.

INDIA

In the geographical divide between the Gulf and the East are two other countries – India and Sri Lanka. In rugby terms India will always have a special place in the evolution of the game. They joined the RFU in 1874, claiming to be the oldest overseas Union. The first game had taken place two years earlier, Christmas Day 1872, when under the aegis of Old Rugbeians stationed in India, players from the four Home nations played a 20-a-side game. The Calcutta Football Club was formed a month later, with 137 members enrolled – partly encouraged by the use of a free bar. When this courtesy ceased, membership mysteriously fell away.

Having no internal opposition, the British proceeded to organise group games themselves – Wales v Scotland, Army v Navy, Bankers v Calcutta Club and so on. The withdrawal of the troops from India in 1876, though, had a devastating effect. The Calcutta Club

Sri Lanka attempt to slow Welsh progress at the Dubai Sevens.

and the Football Club struggled for survival – polo and tennis had become alternatives. The club would close its rugby section.

At this stage, one of the club's founders, GAJ Rothney, suggested that the available money be put to a worthwhile cause, not something that would be forgotten. He wrote to the Rugby Football Union, who accepted his offer of a 'Calcutta Cup', in memory of the Club. The RFU blandly replied that 'The Committee accept with very great pleasure your generous offer of the Cup as an International Challenge Cup that will be played for annually between England and Scotland – the Cup remaining the property of the RFU'.

The Cup was accepted in February 1878, the first Calcutta Cup match took place in 1879 at Raeburn Place, Edinburgh, finishing all square at a goal each. Contrary to general belief the Calcutta Cup was not made of silver, but of melted down rupees that had been drawn from the Calcutta Club's bank. The original design was 18 inches (457mm) high with three snakes as handles and an elephant on the lid. When the Calcutta Club was reformed in 1884, they did not wish it returned.

Unsurprisingly, the various tournaments in India are some of the oldest in the world game. In 1890 a Calcutta Tournament was started with clubs from all over the country and Ceylon (Sri Lanka).

The All India Tournament began in 1924 (by 1926 the RFU had reciprocated with a trophy of their own), the India Sevens started in 1956, and the Calcutta Cup tournament in 1978. These days India has 7000 players and 150 clubs – surprisingly large figures.

If **Sri Lanka** cannot claim a similar place in history as its larger neighbour, its roots are from a similar era. The Ceylon Rugby Union was founded in 1878, and in earlier days when British servicemen were active on the island, the game flourished in Colombo and Kandy. Stop-overs were made by the 1950 Lions (6–44) and by England in 1971 (11–40 and 6–34). Physical size is a handicap to the locals, but it must be noted that when the 1990 Asian Championships were staged in Sri Lanka, over 30 000 watched the final between Japan and South Korea.

CENTRAL AMERICA & THE CARIBBEAN

British and French colonial interest in the West Indies helped foster the game in these parts, but in recent years the West Indies have become one of the world's major touring centres – rightly so, with a combination of climate and hospitality to match anywhere.

The Caribbean has become a centre for offshoots of the real thing – Golden Oldies events, Sevens tournaments and Festivals for touring teams. Bermuda, the Bahamas, Jamaica, the Cayman Islands, Trinidad and Barbados are particularly popular with the Rugby Travel Agencies from Britain, France, and, increasingly, the USA.

That is not to say that the traditional game is neglected – far from it. The Caribbean Championship is the fulcrum of the 15-a-side game, having first been contested in 1966. The tournament has been won by virtually every competing nation.

The first inter island match took place in 1926 between Trinidad and Guyana (which is of course on the mainland!), with fixtures snowballing since then.

CENTRAL AMERICA & CARIBBEAN NATIONS

	Founded	Clubs	Players
Bahamas	1962	8	400
Barbados	1964	4	275
Bermuda	1964	6	500
Cayman Islands	1972	4	150
Guadeloupe	1976	6	400
Guyana		6	120
Jamaica	1959	8	350
Martinique	1976	12	565
Mexico	1972	10	850
St Lucia		1	40
Trinidad and Tobago	1927	9	475
Virgin Islands (UK)		1	30
Virgin islands (USA)		3	90

THE AMERICAS

Rugby now has a strong presence on the American continent with Canada's excellent quarter final placing in the 1991 World Cup, the development of the game in the United States, and Argentina's powerful home record. However, there are many other countries, perhaps not maybe as strong in playing terms, where the sport is flourishing.

Argentina play in the South American Championship against Chile, Brazil, Uruguay and Paraguay, and though totally dominated by the Pumas, the other countries are quietly establishing themselves.

Of the four, **Chile** is currently the most advanced, based loosely on the fact that they tend not to lose to the Pumas by as large a margin as the others. Their representation on the 1980 and 1982 tours by South America was greater than any except Argentina. Chile had five players on the two tours by South America to South Africa. The strength of the game is centred around the capital Santiago, and Valparaiso. Proximity to the strong Tucuman province of Argentina is an advantage.

Uruguay has British 'colonial' connections with the Montevideo Cricket Club organising games as long ago as 1880. The next date on the calendar is 1919 when the Cricket Club played rugby against the famous Belgrano Athletic club from Buenos Aires.

The Cricket Club formed their rugby section in 1929, while rugby was made compulsory in 1937 at the British School. The first four clubs were the Montevideo Club, the Old Boys of the British School, the Colonia RFC and Carrasco Polo Club RFC. By 1975 there were 14 clubs, the total in 1992 was 18 in three divisions centred around Montevideo. The Championship had begun in 1951.

Brazil's base is around the two cities of Sao Paulo and Rio de Janeiro, both of whom run their own leagues. Winners meet in the Championship final. The first inter city match was in 1924 when Sao Paulo beat Santos 24–0, and Rio then promptly beat Sao Paulo 23–3. The players were all British or of British stock, later augmented by Argentine and French links.

The Brazilian Union was founded in 1963, as in so many other countries, to organise the game on a league and Cup basis. The national league began in 1964, with the winners of the 'Torneio Aberto' coming from Sao Paulo each season until 1979. The national sevens have been in operation since 1977, while regional leagues have also been implemented since 1977.

Paraguay complete the group of countries competing in the South American Championship. Theirs is the youngest Union in the region, being founded in 1968, and until 1977 the country was always at the foot of the Championship table. Since then, Paraguay have picked off Brazil, Uruguay and Chile, but are still far away from Argentina.

Other known nations to be playing the game include **Ecuador**, **Peru** and **Venezuela**. However only the Lima Bulldogs (Peru), Quito RFC (Ecuador), and Simon Bolivar University (Venezuela) are known outside their own spheres, which raises questions of how the clubs manage to survive if long haul travel is necessary and whether there are other clubs in the capital cities against whom the known clubs can display their talents. As with all South American countries, soccer is king, and finances for travel and basic structure are not an easy commodity. As with Africa, the enthusiasts deserve nothing but the greatest credit for working and playing in difficult circumstances. It is ironic that Venezuela, not in the mainstream of rugby matters, should be the birthplace of the most capped of all rugby internationals, Serge Blanco of France – even though he did leave when he was two years of age!

SOUTH AMERICAN RUGBY NATIONS

	Founded	Clubs	Players
Brazil	1972	12	1000
Chile	1948	90	6000
Ecuador	–	1	25
Paraguay	1968	8	1500
Peru	–	1	30
Uruguay	1951	11	1100
Venezuela	–	1	30

Chile, Paraguay and Uruguay are members of FIRA

Just one nation may have been forgotten – for like Hawaii, the US state of **Alaska** is, for rugby purposes, an independent country as it once was politically. There are eight clubs in Alaska: five senior clubs (three in Anchorage and two in Fairbanks) a military club called the Fairbanks Wild Hares, and two Masters clubs, one each at Fairbanks and Anchorage. Fittingly it means that rugby – the world game – is played from Alaska in the cold north to Zimbabwe in the sunny south – with a mere 104 countries in between . . .

OTHER CHAMPIONSHIPS

THE FIRA CHAMPIONSHIP

FIRA (Federation Internationale de Rugby Amateur) has been running its own championship since 1954. Though FIRA has members from all over the world, the FIRA Championship is limited currently to European countries. Not that other nations did not want to join the leagues, but the geographical and finacial implications of, say, USA and Argentina playing in a first division with France, Italy and Romania would be too great to surmount at present. An attendance of under 10 000 would not create revenue and time differences and non-availability of players would hamper progress.

The FIRA Championship before 1973 was a hotchpotch. There was a lack of a proper fixture list and newspapers tended to invent tables when another country had fixtures with France and Romania in the same season . The structuring of the Championship into divisions based on ability, and consequent credibility, took place from 1973.

FINAL TABLES 1973–1991

GROUP A

1973–1974

1. France	12 pts
2. Romania	10 pts
3. Spain	8 pts
4. Poland	6 pts
5. Morocco	4 pts

1974–75

1. Romania	11 pts
2. France	10 pts
3. Italy	9 pts
4. Spain	6 pts
5. Czechoslovakia	4 pts

1975–76

1. France	15 pts
2. Italy	13 pts
3. Romania	11 pts
4. Poland	10 pts
5. Spain	6 pts
6. Holland	6 pts

1976–77

1. Romania	15 pts
2. France	13 pts
3. Italy	9 pts
4. Spain	9 pts
5. Poland	7 pts
6. Morocco	7 pts

1977–78

1. France	15 pts
2. Romania	12 pts
3. Spain	12 pts
4. Poland	8 pts
5. Italy	7 pts
6. Czechoslovakia	5 pts

1978–79

1. France	15 pts
2. Romania	13 pts
3. USSR	11 pts
4. Italy	9 pts
5. Poland	7 pts
6. Spain	5 pts

1979–80

1. France	15 pts
2. Romania	11 pts
3. Italy	11 pts
4. USSR	11 pts
5. Poland	7 pts
6. Morocco	5 pts

1980–81

1. Romania	15 pts
2. France	13 pts
3. USSR	11 pts
4. Italy	9 pts
5. Poland	7 pts
6. Spain	5 pts

1981–82

1. France	11 pts
2. Italy	9 pts
3. Romania	8 pts
4, USSR	6 pts
5. West Germany	6 pts

1982–83

1. Romania	15 pts
2. Italy	12 pts
3. USSR	11 pts
4. France	10 pts
5. Morocco	7 pts
6. West Germany	5 pts

1983–84

1. France	15 pts
2. Romania	11 pts
3. Italy	11 pts
4. USSR	11 pts
5. Poland	6 pts
6. Morocco	4 pts

1984–85

1. France	15 pts
2. USSR	11 pts
3. Italy	11 pts
4. Romania	11 pts
5. Spain	7 pts
6. Tunisia	5 pts

1985–86 & 1986–87

Teams played each other in 1985–6, then played the reverse fixtures in 1986–7; ie home against a country one season, away the following season.

1. France	28 pts
2. USSR	24 pts
3. Romania	22 pts
4. Italy	20 pts
5. Tunisia	16 pts
6. Portugal	10 pts

1987–88 & 1988–89

1. France	22 pts
2. USSR	20 pts
3. Romania	18 pts
4. Italy	12 pts
5. Spain	8 pts

1989–90

One season only due to World Cup qualification matches

1. France	10 pts
2. USSR	10 pts
3. Romania	10 pts
4. Italy	6 pts
5. Poland	4 pts

1990–91

This was intended to include 1991–2, but the uncertainty surrounding the participation of the USSR (CIS) has meant a reorganisation of fixtures

1. France	12 pts
2. Italy	10 pts
3. Romania	8 pts
4. USSR	6 pts
5. Spain	4 pts

THE ASIAN CHAMPIONSHIP

The tournament was first staged in Tokyo in 1969 and has been held every two years since. Dominated by Japan in the early tournaments, recent Championships have seen the emergence of other nations, notably South Korea . The various venues indicate the spread of the game in Asia, and the number of countries capable of staging an event with several competing nations.

RESULTS

Year	Winner	Runner-up	Score	Venue
1969	Japan	Korea	23–5	Tokyo
1970	Japan	Thailand	42–11	Bangkok
1972	Japan	Hong Kong	16–0	Hong Kong
1974	Japan	Sri Lanka	44–6	Colombo
1976	Japan	Korea	–	Tokyo
1978	Japan	Korea	16–4	Kuala Lumpur
1980	Japan	Korea	21–12	Taiwan
1982	Korea	Japan	12–9	Singapore
1984	Japan	Korea	20–13	Tokyo
1986	Korea	Japan	24–22	Bangkok
1988	Korea	Japan	17–13	Hong Kong
1990	Korea	Japan	13–9	Colombo

HONG KONG SEVENS

Within a matter of a few years Hong Kong has become a byword for the best sevens event in the world. Best not only in terms of ability, but best in terms of planning, organisation, and for spreading interest among countries of lesser ability. Strong teams were camouflaged under various pseudonyms in the early days, but the Hong Kong Sevens are now a truly international event with the 'World Champions' tag usually bestowed on the winners

Hong Kong, winners of their own sevens Plate competition in 1992.

Mesake Resari in determined mood for Fiji in the 1992 final against New Zealand.

HONG KONG SEVENS WINNERS

Year	Cup	Plate	Bowl
1976	Cantabrians	Hong Kong	
1977	Fiji	Tonga	
1978	Fiji	Bahrain	
1979	Australia	Papua New Guinea	
1980	Fiji	Japan	
1981	Barbarians	Tonga	
1982	Australia	Korea	
1983	Australia	Korea	
1984	Fiji	Australia	Sri Lanka
1985	Austalia	Tonga	Hong Kong
1986	New Zealand	American Eagles	Papua New Guinea
1987	New Zealand	French Barbarians	Hong Kong
1988	Australia	American Eagles	Kwang-Hua Taipei
1989	New Zealand	Tonga	Netherlands
1990	Fiji	Hong Kong	West Germany
1991	Fiji	Argentina	Korea
1992	Fiji	Hong Kong	Romania

OLYMPIC RUGBY

Introduced by Baron Pierre de Coubertin (who refereed the first ever French championship final), rugby was on the Olympic programme at Paris in 1900, London in 1908, Antwerp in 1920, and Paris again in 1924. In 1928 the International Olympic Committee turned down the request to stage rugby at the Amsterdam Games. Three factors were believed to be behind this: the IOC wanted more emphasis on individual sports; women's athletics had swollen the number of competitors; and the sport did not receive the backing that it should have from the British entries. Both the Soviet Union in 1980 and South Korea in 1988 made attempts to have rugby readmitted, and it should be pointed out that South Korea came desperately close to achieving their aim.

OLYMPIC RESULTS

1900 Paris

Three teams entered – France, Germany and Britain. France won the gold, winning 27–17 against Germany, who were awarded the silver medal. Britain lost 27–8 to France in the only other match, and were awarded the bronze.

1908 London

Two teams entered – Britain, the hosts, and Australia. Just one match was played, a straight final, won by Australia 32–3.

1912 Stockholm

Not held.

1920 Antwerp

Two teams entered – USA and France. The USA caused a shock by winning the only match 8–0 to take the gold medal.

1924 Paris

Three teams entered – France, USA and Romania. Each country played two games. Both France and USA beat Romania, who were awarded the bronze medal. France won 59–3, scoring 13 tries including four by the fine Stade Francais winger Adolphe Jaureguy. The USA then defeated Romania 39–0. The final was played at the Colombes Stadium, Paris on 18 May 1924 and the USA took the gold with a 17–3 victory before 30000. The Americans, from Stanford University, scored five tries (Farrish (2), Patrick, Rogers and Manelli), with a conversion from Doe. Gallau scored the lone French try. The match finished in uproar, when Gideon Nelson, one of the reserves, was flattened by a walking stick. The American anthem was jeered, and rugby ceased at the Olympics.

1991 WOMEN'S WORLD CUP

Claire Godwin, 5ft 6in wing forward from Florida, pounced for two tries to swing the Cup Final in the favour of the USA and they went on to defeat England 19–6 at Cardiff RFC on April 14, 1991 in the inaugural Women's World Cup.

With more flair and ideas behind the scrum, the female Eagles were in control throughout before a crowd of some 3000 spectators. Scrum half Patty Connell also crossed for a try and Chris Harju converted two and put over a penalty goal. England's penalty try was converted by Gill Burns.

The USA went on to complete a women's 'double' with their win in the inaugural FIFA Women's Football World Cup.

The Women's Rugby World Cup trophy.

RESULTS

Pool 1
NZ 24, Canada 8
Wales 9, Canada 9
NZ 24, Wales 6
Pool 2
France 62, Japan 0
France 37, Sweden 0
Sweden 20, Japan 0
Pool 3
USA 7, Netherlands 0
Netherlands 28, USSR 0
USA 46, USSR 0
Pool 4
England 12, Spain 0
England 25, Italy 9
Spain 13, Italy 7
Semi-finals
USA 7, NZ 0
England 13, France 0
Final
USA 19, England 6

Spectacular action from Pool 1 as Wales take on New Zealand.

THE INTERNATIONAL GROUNDS

In the modern era, international rugby venues are amongst the finest sporting arenas in the world. But it has not always been thus – in earlier days internationals were not always played under such conditions. Some had beer barrels to stand on as part of the grandstand, one took just 62 days to construct, some were turned into potato fields, there have been fires in car parks. One ground was so small that the crowd kept the balls as an act of protest. Even Twickenham today is rumoured not to have floodlights because of a deal with local residents.

The stadia listed below have all hosted major international matches between International Rugby Board countries – not including World Cup matches.

SCOTLAND

MAIN STADIUM: MURRAYFIELD

First international: 21 March 1925

The youngest of the Five Nations Championships grounds. Murrayfield staged its first international in 1925 when Scotland beat England 14–11 before 70 000, ruining England's Grand Slam hopes. It was formerly the grounds of the Edinburgh Polo Club at Murray's Field.

It seems strange that the country which hosted the first ever rugby international in 1871 at Raeburn Place, Edinburgh, on the cricket field of the Edinburgh Academicals Club, should wait a further 54 years before finding a permanent home. Murrayfield took over from the outdated Inverleith as the home of Scottish rugby with the announcement of the purchase in 1922. In 1959 undersoil heating was installed at the world's most northerly major stadium and in 1992 a further £37 million development was begun.

Capacity: 52 886

Raeburn Place, Edinburgh

First international: 27 March 1871

The first international rugby match was played at Raeburn Place between England and Scotland, won by Scotland by one try and a goal to one try, and watched by a crowd of 4000. The decision to stage a rugby match on the ground met with some disapproval, and the pitch was only 55 yards wide which did not suit the visitors' speedy backs.

The ground hosted internationals until 1895, and today is the headquarters of the Edinburgh Academicals Club.

Hamilton Crescent, Glasgow

First international: 3 March 1873

During the discussions leading up to the first international rugby match, Hamilton Crescent had been shortlisted as a possible venue. But at this time Hamilton Crescent lay some distance outside Glasgow at Partick on the then outskirts of the city. It was the home of West of Scotland RFC and staged four internationals.

Old Hampden Park, Glasgow

First international: 14 March 1896

Old Hampden Park was secured by the Scottish Union in 1896 after the Academical Cricket Club decided not to lease Raeburn Place. The ground was then being used by Queen's Park FC. It staged the 1896 international between Scotland and England, and later became the home of Third Lanark FC, changing its name to Cathkin Park.

Powderhall, Edinburgh

First international: 20 Feb 1897

Home of the Powderhall Sports Club, and venue for the famous Powderhall Sprint,the ground was used for the Ireland and England games of 1897 and 1898 respectively.

Inverleith, Edinburgh

First international: 18 Feb 1899

Inverleith hosted Scotland's international matches between

1899 and 1925 – it was the first ground to be acquired by any of the home unions. The first international there saw Ireland's first win on Scottish soil (9–3) while the second became the most postponed ever as poor weather prevented the game being played on no less than on four occasions. Eventually Scotland beat Wales 21-10. By 1925 the ground, which could accomodate no more than 30 000 spectators, had become too small and was replaced by Murrayfield.

Hampden Park, Glasgow
First international: 17 Nov 1906
Hosted one international against South Africa which the Springboks won 6–0 . The attendance was 32 000 at the home of Queens Park FC and the Scoltand national football team.

ENGLAND

MAIN STADIUM: TWICKENHAM
First international: 15 Jan 1910
Fed up with a nomadic existence which meant having to play internationals at the Oval, Crystal Palace, Richmond, Blackheath and several provincial centres, the Twickenham ground was discovered in 1907 for the Rugby Union by Billy Williams, who was a first-class cricketer, Harlequins fullback, and referee. The land cost £5,572 12s 6d.

The first match on the ground was held on 2 October 1909 when Harlequins beat Richmond 14–10. England beat Wales 11–6 on 15 January 1910 in the first international at the stadium. During the First World War, the stadium became a grazing ground for horses and sheep. As part of the Second World War 'Dig for Victory' campaign, the East car park became an allotment, the West car park a coal dump, the RFU offices were used by the Ministry of Defence and the stands became garages for lorries and fire engines.

The weather vane, depicting Hermes passing a rugby ball, was designed by a Mr Kenny Dalgleish. Harlequins, the home club, have won the English Cup there on two occasions, in 1988 and 1991.
Capacity: 56 208

Kennington Oval, London
The Kennington Oval hosted the first England versus Scotland match on English soil. It resulted in England posting their first win in international rugby, winning by a dropped goal (then worth 4 points) to a try (then worth 3 points). The ground also staged football internationals and is still the home of Surrey County Cricket Club and the traditional final Test match of the summer. The Oval staged England's first international at football, cricket and rugby union.

Whalley Range, Manchester
First international: 28 Feb 1880
The ground staged England's first game on a Saturday.

Blackheath
First international: 19 Feb 1881
Blackheath, one of the oldest clubs in England, founded in 1858, hosted internationals on two adjacent grounds. From 1881–84 the ground was called Mr Richardson's Field, where Wales played their first disastrous international. The current ground, the Rectory Field, staged several internationals from 1884 when England beat Scotland by one goal to one try.

Cardigan Fields, Leeds
First international: 5 Jan 1884
The England v Wales match – the first international in Yorkshire – was staged at St John's Ground.

Birkenhead Park
First international: 12 March 1887
Until the World Cups, the Birkenhead Park RFC had staged the first neutral international, 100 years earlier. Ireland met Wales at the club so that no further expense should be incurred by the hard-up Irish, who could not have afforded to travel to Cardiff or Swansea. In 1894, Wales played England at the club.

Crown Flatt, Dewsbury
First international: 15 Feb 1890
Still the home of the Dewsbury Rugby League club, the England v Wales match took place at the quaintly named Crown Flatt; Wales won 1–0. One of the Welsh players, WH Stadden, eventually joined Dewsbury RLFC.

Athletic Ground, Richmond
First international: 7 March 1891
Richmond Athletic Ground is the home of Richmond RFC, formed in 1861, a club that has played a leading role in the establishment of the game. Their founder, Edwin Ash, was also responsible for the formation of the Rugby Union and was its first secretary. The club moved to the Athletic Ground in 1899 and has remained there ever since, after being based at Richmond Green from 1861–72 and in Old Deer Park from 1872–

99. It hosted its first international match in 1891, when Scotland beat England 9–3. On the five occasions England played Scotland at the ground, Scotland always won.

Headingley, Leeds
First international: 4 March 1893
England played Scotland at Headingley,home of the present Leeds Rugby League club and next door to the Test match cricket ground at Headingley.

Meanwood Road, Leeds
First international: 1 Feb 1896
England lost to Ireland 10–4 in the only international staged here.

Crystal Palace, London
First international: 2 Dec 1905
England played New Zealand in the first international staged at the old Crystal Palace (not the current home of Crystal Palace FC – the ground was in the Exhibition centre at Crystal Palace). The FA Cup final was staged at the ground from 1895–1914. The official capacity should have been 40 000 but over double that figure usually attended.

Fallowfield, Manchester
First international: 13 March 1897
England played Scotland in the only international staged at the Manchester Athletic Club ground at Fallowfield.

Kingsholm, Gloucester
First international: 6 Jan 1900
Gloucester is one of the great names in English rugby – a rugby city if ever there was one. The club has produced internationals virtually from the start, as well as administrators to the rank of President of the RFU, referees and committee men of far-reaching vision. Kingsholm staged its only international on 6 Jan 1900 when Wales beat England 13–3.

The Gloucester Club was founded in 1873, and in the intervening years its teams have been held in high regard by all their opponents. Proximity to Bristol, Bath, the Midlands and Wales has ensured a strong fixture list. Gloucester have won the English Cup on two occasions: in 1972 when they were the first winners, and in 1978. In 1982 they and Moseley shared the Cup.
Capacity: 11 992

Welford Road, Leicester
First international: 8 Feb 1902
One of England's largest rugby grounds, this is the home of the Leicester Tigers, the dominant force in English club rugby from 1979–81 when they won the Cup three years in succession. The club was founded in 1880 and numbers amongst its internationals the former England full-back Dusty Hare, who, with 7337 points, is the world record holder for points scored in first class rugby.

Welford Road staged its first international on 8 Feb 1902 when England beat Ireland 6–3. It went on to stage another three internationals in the early part of the century,when the game was taken to the provinces.
Capacity: 15 463

Ashton Gate, Bristol
First international: 18 Jan 1908
England played Wales at Ashton Gate, home then and now of Bristol City FC, Wales winning 28–18 in the fog in front of 25 000. The previous season Bristol City had been runners-up in the First Division.

WALES

MAJOR STADIUM: CARDIFF ARMS PARK
First international: 12 April 1884
Thankfully restored to its proper title in the 1980s after a spell as the 'National Stadium', the name of the Arms Park dates from 1845 when Cardiff Cricket Club formed one of the first cricket clubs in the country on a field at the back of the Cardiff Arms Coaching Inn. In 1876 Cardiff Rugby and Cricket clubs joined forces to alternate summer and winter facilities on the same ground.

Cardiff Arms Park became the sole Welsh international ground in 1954, after all four major clubs, Cardiff, Swansea, Llanelli and Newport, had staged internationals. The redevelopment of the National Stadium was mooted in the 1960s, the first part completed in 1970 and the entire project finished in 1984. The first move was by next door neighbours Glamorgan County Cricket Club to nearby Sophia Gardens, which allowed space for Cardiff RFC to be accommodated in a 15 000 capacity stadium beside the main ground.

The total cost of the new stadium was £9 million, with 36 000 seats. The 1958 Empire Games were held at the venue, and nowadays the Welsh national soccer team play important home matches at the stadium. Cardiff RFC have won the Welsh Cup on five occasions – 1981, 1982, 1984, 1986 and 1987.
Capacity: 52,554

St Helen's, Swansea
First international: 16 Dec 1882
Swansea staged the first international in Wales. The ground is owned by the Swansea City Council and accommodates Glamorgan County Cricket Club in the summer months. The rugby section is enclosed, with only the dead ball line being part of the cricket ground. As the ground is owned by the Council, not the club, the Wales Rugby League XIII have also been allowed to play there. The ground, close to Mumbles Bay, was the scene of Gary Sobers' 36 runs off a Malcolm Nash over in 1968.

Rodney Parade, Newport
First international: 12 Jan 1884
Home of Newport RFC, who at the turn of the century were arguably the top club in the United Kingdom.

Stradey Park, Llanelli
First international: 8 Jan 1887
Famous home of Llanelli RFC, the ground was first used in 1879 by the club. Their famous scarlet jerseys were adopted in 1884. Australia have lost there to Llanelli on three occasions: in 1908, 1967 and 1984. The 1908 win coined the song 'Who beat the Wallabies'. The 1975 match finished 28–28. Llanelli also beat New Zealand in 1972, and have twice lost by just a single point to South Africa.

Wales have played three internationals at Stradey Park, drawing 0–0 with England in 1887 and beating Ireland twice, 6–4 in 1891 and 2–0 in 1893. Llanelli have won the Welsh Cup on a record seven occasions.
Capacity: 14 161

IRELAND

MAIN STADIUM: LANSDOWNE ROAD, DUBLIN
First international: 11 Mar 1878
Lansdowne Road has hosted internationals since 1878, which makes it the oldest major ground of the modern era. Lansdowne Road was the venue for Ireland's third game, after Rathmines and Ormeau, and, bar occasional sorties, has remained first choice since.

Lansdowne Road was the inspiration of Henry William Dunlop, a graduate at Trinity College, Dublin. He bought seven acres of land between the River Dodder and the Lansdowne Road railway station which he turned into a multi-sports centre. A rugby club (Lansdowne) was started in the centre of a cinder athletics track, to be joined in 1880 by Wanderers. Dunlop was paid £5 by the IRFU for the first international, and the two clubs and the national side have remained in harmony since – to be joined in recent years by Jack Charlton's successful football team. In the 1985–6 season Lansdowne Road became the first ground to notch up 150 internationals.
Capacity: 51 442

Rathmines, Dublin
First international: 13 Dec 1875
Home of the Leinster Cricket Club, Rathmines staged the first home international against England, the IRFU renting the ground for £10. The gate receipts were £22 9s.

Ormeau, Belfast
First international: 19 Feb 1877
Ormeau was the North of Ireland Cricket Club's ground, where a rugby section was formed in the autumn of 1868, much to the dissatisfaction of the cricketers. NIFC have always been one of the leading clubs.

Ballynafeigh, Belfast
First international: 21 Feb 1891
The home of Ulster Cricket Club, the ground was considered unsuitable in 1894.

Balmoral, Belfast
First international: 19 Feb 1898
The Balmoral Showgrounds were the home of the Ulster Rugby Union.

Limerick
First international: 18 March 1898
Just one international has been played at the Limerick Club,when Wales won 11–3.

Mardyke, Cork
First international: 11 Feb 1905
This was the former site of the Cork Exhibition at the turn of the century, but when the Exhibition closed in 1903, the Cork County RFC and the Cork Constitution RFC became joint tenants . Ireland met England in the first international at Mardyke and secured a famous 17–3 victory. For this – and subsequent internationals at the venue – the local brewers Beamish & Crawford & JJ Murphy lent several hundred brewers' barrels, tied together with hairy twine, for spectators to stand on. The barrels ran both lengths of the pitch!

Ravenhill, Belfast
First international: 9 Feb 1924
Ravenhill took 62 days to construct – and many Irish will unkindly tell you that it shows! The ground was mooted after the Anglo–Irish treaty of 1922, so that Belfast and Dublin should share top matches Home of the Ulster RFU, Ravenhill did stage several internationals in tandem with Lansdowne Road until 1954 and is now home to the Ulster challenges for the Inter Provincial Championship and other representative matches. The first international was staged in Belfast in 1877, but at the NIFC ground at Ormeau.
Capacity: 11 500

AUSTRALIA

Sydney Cricket Ground
First international: 15 Aug 1903
The famous Test cricket arena was Australia's first and most used international rugby venue until 1987. New Zealand won the first international at the ground by 22–3, but the SCG had already staged the first New South Wales v Queensland match in 1882 and hosted a British side in 1899.

Woollongabba, Brisbane
First international: 3 Aug 1907
Another Test match cricket ground, the 'Gabba' was rented by the Queensland Rugby Union, and was also known as the Brisbane Cricket Ground. The poor attendance of 4500 against New Zealand in 1951 is one of the lowest in rugby history.

Sydney Sports Ground
First international: 18 July 1914
The SSG staged two internationals against New Zealand just before the First World War and then hosted the 1959 British Lions, and 1963 England XVs. Now home of Rugby League internationals.

Exhibition Ground, Brisbane
First international: 20 July 1929
Another ground rented by the then hard-up Queensland Rugby Union from the Royal National Association. Crowds were in the region of 17 000 for most major internationals.

Concord Oval, Sydney – the city's 1987 World Cup venue.

Lang Park, Brisbane
First international: 26 June 1965
This ground was rented by the QRU from their Rugby League counterparts while Ballymore was being discussed and built. Australia scored a fine 12-8 win against the Springboks here and Australia played the 1966 Lions at Lang Park.

Ballymore Oval, Brisbane
First international: 22 June 1968
Home of the Queensland RFU since 1967, the stadium has done much to give the Queensland RFU a home base for playing and administration. The ground is a traditional rugby venue with the McLean stand named after Australia's most famous rugby family.

It stands in 19 acres, with Queensland playing New South Wales in 1967 in the first major match at the venue.

Concord Oval, Sydney
First international: 21 June 1986
Now called Waratah Park, the Oval was named after the suburb in West Sydney where it was constructed by the New South Wales RU to give the Union some identity away from the Sydney Cricket Ground. It hosted Sydney's matches in the 1987 World Cup.

Sydney Football Stadium
The SFS, next to the SCG – Sydney Cricket Ground – became the venue for major matches from 1990. There are now three stadia side by side in the city, though strangely none holds much more than 50 000 which is raising wry comments in the city. The plan is for major internationals (including football) to be staged at the SFS, with Waratah Park taking the New South Wales representative games.

SOUTH AFRICA

Crusader Ground, Port Elizabeth
First international: 30 July 1891
The former home of the Eastern Province RFU until the move to the Boet Erasmus Stadium in the city in 1960, the Crusader club was in St George's Park which has staged Test cricket. The ground hosted the first ever international in South Africa, apparently because Herbert Castens, the first ever South African captain, hailed from Port Elizabeth, while his father was President of the Eastern Province Rugby Union. South Africa's first international was against the touring British XV.

Griqualand West Stadium, Kimberley
First international: 28 Aug 1891
Often known as the De Beers stadium after the mining conglomerate in the town, Kimberley staged South Africa's second international. The ground at the time was home to the Eclectic Cricket Club. South Africa lost 3–0 to the British XV.

Newlands, Cape Town
First international: 5 Sept 1891
Probably the best siting of any rugby ground in the world, Newlands nestles under Table Mountain in the Newlands district of Cape Town. It is the home of the Western Province RFU and the administrative offices of the South African Rugby Board. The ground has a capacity of 52 000 and is 800 metres from Newlands cricket ground.

Wanderers Ground, Johannesburg
First international: 22 Aug 1896
Also the home of the Transvaal Cricket Union, the Wanderers stadium hosted internationals in the 1980s while the main Transvaal Rugby stadium at Ellis Park was being refurbished. The ground is part of the famous Wanderers Club, just about the largest sports club in the world, with outstanding facilities. The Wanderers club was founded in 1887 and was one of the founder members of the Transvaal Rugby Union in 1889.

Boet Erasmus Stadium, Port Elizabeth
First international: 27 Aug 1960
Boet Erasmus was the former Lord Mayor of Port Elizabeth under whose aegis the stadium was built. Internationals have been staged here since 1960, when it replaced the Crusader Ground. In the first international at the new stadium, a mile from St George's Park, South Africa beat New Zealand before a crowd of 60 000.

Free State Stadium, Bloemfontein
First international: 2 Sept 1933
Home of the Orange Free State RFU, close to the city centre and on the edge of a large park, it is an open complex, with the stadium having grown in size as the Orange Free State RU (founded 1895) expanded.

Loftus Versveld Stadium, Pretoria
First international: 3 Sept 1955
An open bowl accomodating over 65 000 spectators,the stadium was completed in 1938 and named after Loftus Versveld, a former Springbok and administrator, who played against the 1891 British tourists and whose brother Hansie scored the only point of the tour against the British team.

It has been the home of the Northern Transvaal RU since that Union broke away from the Transvaal Union in 1937, setting up Pretoria as a rugby centre. Loftus Versveld founded Pretoria RFC in 1899. The original ground had been around since 1908, the first international was against the British Isles in 1955, and the stadium was restyled in 1976.

Kingsmead, Durban
First international: 16 Aug 1924
Home of Natal cricket and a ground which has staged Test cricket matches, Kingsmead became too small for international rugby (cap: 30,000) so King's Park was constructed a mile away. Kingsmead's first international was the visit of the 1924 British Isles XV.

Kings Park, Durban
First international: 23 May 1964
A £3 million refit to the stadium was completed in time for Natal to win the 1990 Currie Cup – their first win in the Cup – and to lay plans for further development. The stadium was designed to hold 48 500 in 1985 but now accommodates over 51 000. King's Park was completed in 1957 for the Natal RU with 33 000 places.

Pam Brink Stadium, Springs
First international: 21 July 1964
Just one interntional was played at this stadium, the South Africa v France match in 1964. The ground is the home of the Eastern Transvaal RU and was officially opened when the locals beat the All Blacks 8–6 in 1949. The international was a fiasco: the ground was too small, far too many were let in (25 000) and as a consequence, no one could see the match properly. To compound matters, the balls

were kept by the crowd as an act of protest, France won 8–6 and there was a fire in the car park afterwards!

Ellis Park, Johannesburg
First international: 21 July 1928
Formerly a mine dump and brickworks, Ellis Park, named after a local administrator, was opened in 1928 after the original Wanderers Club ground, the former home of the Transvaal RU, was wanted for rail yards. The ground is in Dornfontein, close to the business centre, and has since been restyled on several occasions. Always claiming to have accomodated 95 000, there are now 104 000 seats after the 1982 overhaul and it will be the largest international stadium in the world as soon as South Africa begins playing internationals at the venue.

FRANCE

MAIN STADIUM: PARC DES PRINCES, PARIS
First international: 1 Jan 1906
An impressive all-seater stadium, the Parc des Princes hosts French international rugby matches, French international soccer matches, the French soccer and rugby Cup Finals and is home for the leading first division soccer club Paris St Germain. It is also too small!

The Parc has had two careers as a venue for French rugby internationals. The old Parc hosted the first French rugby international match when New Zealand beat France 38–8 in 1906 before 8000, but it was not a successful venue as it was too small and antiquated. It never staged a home French win before the First World War. After 1919, French rugby moved to Colombes, homes of Racing Club. But the need for an international multi-sport stadium saw the restoration of the Parc (which had lain dormant since 1920) to a 48 500 capacity stadium. France played Scotland on 12 January 1973 in the first international in the new stadium, but it is significant that several French soccer stadia (built for the 1984 European Championships and possible future World Cups) are now bigger than the Parc.
Capacity: 49711

Stade Colombes, Paris
First international: 1 Jan 1908
The former home ground for the French national rugby XV, the Stade Colombes was rebuilt for the 1924 Olympics, scene of the triumphs of Harold Abrahams and Eric Liddell portrayed in the film *Chariots of Fire*. Since the refurbishment of the Parc des Princes, the Stade Colombes has not featured internationally, but in 1992 plans were at an advanced stage to refit the stadium. The famous Racing Club de France, the 1990 French club champions, play at the stadium.

Stade Bouscat, Bordeaux
First international: 11 Jan 1913
The first international ground outside Paris, this is the home of Stade Bordelais, the leading club team in the country at the time of the internationals.

Stade Pershing, Paris
First international: 1 Jan 1924
It staged a one-off international between France and Scotland when the Stade Colombes was underwater following flooding from the River Seine. Pershing was the closest ground available.

Stade des Ponts Jumeaux, Toulouse
First international: 18 Jan 1925
Home of Stade Toulousain at the time, but too small for major internationals.

Stade Yves du Manoir, Paris
The Stade Colombes was renamed as the above for some years after the death in 1928 of the French fly-half Yves du Manoir, at the age of 23. He gained eight caps from 1925–27 and was established as the new national hero before being killed in an early plane crash. Du Manoir played for Racing Club at Colombes,and a memorial is erected to him outside the front gates.

Stade de Toulouse
First international: 20 Nov 1971
The main municipal stadium in Toulouse, it stages home fixtures for Toulouse FC in the French First Division and the major rugby matches. The capacity is 35 000.

Stade Marcel Michelen, Clermont Ferrand
First international: 13 Nov 1983
One international has been played at the Montferrand club ground, a 15–15 draw between France and Australia. Recent French internationals Philippe Saint-Andre and Philippe Marocco play for the club.

The French national side line up at Nantes in 1990.

Stade Beaujoire, Nantes
First international: 15 Nov 1986
The Stade Beaujoire has a place in French rugby history – the first major international at the stadium saw the defeat of the 1986 New Zealand tourists by France. The ground is also the home of the French First Division club FC Nantes and was redeveloped to meet the requirements for staging the 1984 European Football Championships. The capacity of 54 500 exceeds that of the Parc des Princes.

Stade de Meinau, Strasbourg
First international: 4 Nov 1989
Another predominantly football stadium – like Nantes – in a non-rugby stronghold, the ground is also the home of French Division 1 club Racing Strasbourg. The ground was also used for the 1984 European Football Championship. France played Australia at the venue in 1989.

Stade Grimpooris, Lille
First international: 11 Nov 1989
Also known as the Stade du Nord, this is a new complex on the outskirts of the northern industrial city of Lille. The stadium was completed in 1976 and is also the home of the First Division football club Lille OSC. In the summer it hosts one of the major Mobil Grand Prix athletics meetings and staged the Ben Johnson–Carl Lewis rematch in 1991. The stadium also hosted the quarter-final of the 1991 World Cup between New Zealand and Canada.
Capacity: 30 397

NEW ZEALAND

Athletic Park, Wellington
First international: 13 Aug 1904
The home of the Wellington RU, where rugby has been played since 1879, and used for provincial matches from 1899. The ground staged New Zealand's first home match, against the 1904 British tourists. The imposing Millard stand was added in 1961.

Tahuna Park, Dunedin
First international: 2 Sept 1905
A one-off international against Australia,when the match was scheduled for the Caledonian Ground. New Zealand won 14–3, the gate was 3000 and receipts £85.

Carisbrook, Dunedin
First international: 6 June 1908
Home of the Otago RU, the ground was first used in 1908 for New Zealand's 32–6 against the Anglo-Welsh XV, and was also the scene of the infamous win by New Zealand by six penalties to four tries over the 1959 British Isles XV.

Potter's Park, Auckland
First international: 25 July 1908
In Alexandra Park, Potter's Park, also known as Potter's Paddock, was also used for an Anglo-Welsh match. The crowd was 12 000 for the sole international.

Lancaster Park, Christchurch
First international: 20 Sept 1913
Home of the Canterbury RU, and used as a Test match cricket ground in the summer where Sir Richard Hadlee caused such chaos against visiting teams, Lancaster Park has also hosted the 1982 Davis Cup final and was the venue for some of Peter Snell's middle-distance world records. In World War I it was, like Twickenham, a potato patch; it was revamped in 1982.

Eden Park, Auckland
First international: 27 Aug 1921
First used for a 9–5 win over New Zealand by South Africa, Eden Park is the home of the successful Auckland RU and is also a Test match cricket ground, where the semi-final of the 1992 World Cup was staged. Before the First World War, the ground was a shallow lake. Eden Park hosted the final of the 1987 Rugby World Cup.

Epsom Showgrounds, Auckand
First international: 20 Sept 1958
New Zealand beat Australia 17–8 at the Showgrounds thanks to a try by Colin Meads and 14 points from Don Clarke in an international staged at the ground because the No 1 grandstand at nearby Eden Park had not been completed. The attendance was 25 000.

Eden Park, Auckland, scene of the 1987 World Cup Final.

WORLD CUP GROUNDS

The following stadia have all hosted a World Cup match or matches:

1987

Concord Oval, Sydney, Australia
Ballymore Oval, Brisbane, Australia
McLean Park, Napier, Australia
Athletic Park, Wellington, New Zealand
Showgrounds Oval, Palmerston North, New Zealand
Carisbrook, Dunedin, New Zealand
Rugby Park, Invercargill, New Zealand
Eden Park, Auckland, New Zealand
Rugby Park, Hamilton, New Zealand
Lancaster Park, Christchurch, New Zealand
Rotorua International Stadium, Rotorua, New Zealand

1991

Cross Green, Otley, England
Cardiff Arms Park, Cardiff, Wales
Kingsholm, Gloucester, England
Pontypool Park, Pontypool, Wales
Lansdowne Road, Dublin, Eire
Sardis Road, Pontypridd, Wales
Stradey Park, Llanelli, Wales
Ravenhill, Belfast, Northern Ireland
Twickenham, Middlesex, England
Welford Road, Leicester, England
Parc Municipal, Brive, France
Murrayfield, Edinburgh, Scotland
Stade Armandie, Agen, France
Stade du Nord, Lille, France
Parc des Princes, Paris, France
Stade Municipal, Toulouse, France
Les Diguieres, Grenoble, France
Stade de la Mediterranee, Beziers, France
Stade Saint Leon, Bayonne, France

RUGBY'S ROLL OF DISHONOUR

France's double sending-off against England in 1992 has kept them comfortably ahead in the international table of shame, hoisting their total to seven banished players of the 25 sent off in rugby international history. Over 50 years passed before the first dismissal and another 42 before the next, in 1925 and 1967. Both were New Zealanders.

The readiness of referees to dismiss players in recent years is illustrated by the fact that 17 of the sending-offs have come inside the last five years. Fiji and Wales have lost four players to referee's decisions, while Scotland and South Africa are the only major countries to retain an immaculate disciplinary record.

THE GUILTY MEN

C Brownlie	NZ	v Eng	1925
C Meads	NZ	v Scot	1967
M Burton	Eng	v Aus	1975
J Sovau	Fiji	v Aus	1976
G Wheel	Wales	v Ire	1977
W Duggan	Ire	v Wales	1977
P Ringer	Wales	v Eng	1980
J-P Garuet	Fra	v Ire	1984
H Richards	Wales	v NZ, World Cup	1987
D Codey	Aus	v Wales, World Cup	1987
M Taga	Fiji	v Eng	1988
A Lorieux	Fra	v Arg	1988
T Vonolagi	Fiji	v Eng	1989
N Nadruku	Fiji	v Eng	1989
K Mosley	Wales	v Fra	1990
A Carminati	Fra	v Scot	1990
A Stoop	Namibia	v Wales	1990
A Benazzi	Fra	v Aus	1990
P Gallart	Fra	v Aus	1990
F Mendez	Arg	v Eng	1990
C Cojocariu	Rom	v Fra	1991
M Keenan	W Samoa	v Arg, World Cup	1991
P Sporleder	Arg	v W Samoa, World Cup	1991
G Lascube	Fra	v Eng	1992
V Moscato	Fra	v Eng	1992

O Roumat (France) was also sent off when playing for World XV v New Zealand in 1992

Right *You're off! John Gadd of Gloucester is the guilty man in England's domestic Cup final.*

GLOSSARY OF TERMS

Below are the common terms used in the game of rugby union. It is worth noting that the rules and laws of the game are always being altered and the ones mentioned below are current but subject to change.

ADVANTAGE
The referee does not whistle for an infringement during play which is followed by an advantage gained by the team that did not make the infringement. The referee is the sole judge of whether an advantage has been gained.

FOULS
Players may not: strike, hack, kick or trip an opponent; make a dangerous tackle (high tackle) or tackle with a stiff arm; wilfully charge, obstruct or grab an opponent who does not have the ball, except in a ruck or a maul.

Obstruction or deliberate time-wasting are penalised by a penalty kick or a penalty try.

A deliberate knock-on or forward throw is punished by a penalty kick at the place of the infringement.

MAUL
A maul occurs in free play when one or more players close around a player who is carrying the ball. It is allowed to continue until the ball is on the ground, the ball or player carrying it emerges from the maul, or when a scrummage is ordered. A 'rolling maul' is a series of mauls. Here the player with the ball can emerge from the maul and 'peel off' to form another maul, and so on.

MARK
A player makes a mark when, being stationary with both feet on the ground in or behind his own 22-metre area, he cleanly catches the ball direct from a kick, knock-on or throw-forward by one of his opponents and at the same time he exclaims 'Mark!'. If the player is adjudged to have made a mark a free kick is awarded, which must be taken by the same player.

LINE-OUT
If the ball or player carrying it touches or crosses the touchline, the ball is 'in touch' and must be restarted by a 'line-out'. The players then line up to receive the ball and must stay in the line at least one metre from the next player in their team and half a metre from an opponent, until the ball touches the ground or another player. The thrower is from the team that did not touch the ball last. He throws the ball between the two lines of players who jump and attempt to catch it or palm it down towards their respective scrum-halves.

OFFSIDE
A player is offside if he is in front of the ball when a team-mate is playing it. A penalty is then awarded. However, he may be made onside if a team-mate carries the ball past him or kicks the ball past him and pursues it. If the player's position is unavoidable and he retires immediately and without interfering with an opponent, no penalty will be given. If the player who is offside cannot avoid contact he is 'accidentally offside' and a scrummage is formed.

A player is also offside if he is found to be in front of the rear of his team's scrummage whilst the ball is in play. A scrum half

POSITIONS (ON THE FIELD)

Fullbacks and hookers are instantly recognised around the world because the name of their position is the same. Yet for other positions on the field there is considerable variation of names from country to country. The following shows some of the variations and similarities:

Fullback	Used everywhere.
Wing	Sometimes winger or wing three-quarter, with either 'left' or 'right' added.
Outside centre	Centre three-quarter (NZ)
Inside centre	Second five-eighths (NZ)
Fly-half	GB, SA. Also outside half. First five-eighths (NZ). Sometimes stand-off (GB, Aus).
Halfback	Scrum half (GB)
No.8	Sometimes lock (Aus) or back-rower (GB), once eighth man (NZ).
Flanker	Breakaway (Aus), sometimes side-row. Wing forward (GB), not often heard these days.
Loose forwards	Sometimes loosies (NZ), also back row (GB).
Locks	Sometimes second row (GB, Aus).
Props	Sometimes front row (Aus).
Hooker	Used everywhere.
Reserves	Emergencies (NZ), sometimes replacements.
Referee	Used everywhere, usually shortened to 'ref' or even 'sir'!

can also be penalised if he attempts to retrieve the ball before it has left the opponent's side of the scrummage.

PENALTIES
Penalties can be awarded for a number of infringements. The referee can award either a penalty kick or a penalty try.

RUCK
A ruck occurs in free play when one or more players close around the ball when it is on the ground between them. The players must be on their feet and must bind with at least one arm around a team-mate.

SCORING
A **try** (5 points) is scored by grounding the ball in the opponent's goal area. The player must be touching the ball as it is grounded. A penalty try may be given if a foul prevents a try.

A **conversion** (2 points), a place kick or drop kick at goal, follows a try. It is taken on a line through where the try was scored. After a penalty try it is taken as if the try was scored between the posts.

A **dropped goal** (3 points) is scored during play when the ball is dropped from the hands and kicked over the crossbar and between the posts on the half volley.

A **penalty goal** (3 points) is scored from a penalty kick awarded for an infringement. The ball is placed at the spot where the infringement occured and kicked over the crossbar and between the posts.

SCRUMMAGE
Players are formed into a scrummage, usually by their own forwards, at or near the place of the infringement. The team not responsible for the stoppage puts the ball in. If there is doubt as to who is responsible, the ball is put in by the team moving forward or by the attacking team.

There must be at least three players in each front row. The front rows interlock, leaving a clear tunnel between them. Other forwards bind with at least one arm onto a team-mate. Other players remain behind the line of the rear of their pack.

The scrum-half stands midway between the two front rows, and then aims to make the ball hit the ground just beyond the width of the near prop's shoulders. If the ball runs straight through the scrummage it must be put in again.

The two hookers must strike for possession. They must not raise their feet but deflect the ball back through their pack.

POSTSCRIPT

From Stephen Jones, Rugby correspondent, The Sunday Times

On the eve of the Rugby World Cup final, two strangers approached members of the organising committee in a London hotel. It was at a time when the fever pitch of excitement which the tournament caused throughout the country and throughout the sporting world was at its height.

The men were a delegation. They were representing rugby in Latvia, the Baltic country then proudly and recently returned to independence from the crumbling edifice that was the USSR. They wanted to join one of sports biggest families. They wanted to warm their toes at the hearth of rugby union.

They were warmly welcomed, given two seats for the World Cup final itself and were therefore present to see Australia become champions. A few weeks after the tournament ended, five more countries were admitted to the burgeoning International Rugby Board at the Board's November meeting – they were Andorra, Chile, Hungary, Luxembourg – and Latvia. Other countries of the old USSR are expected to follow suit; later in the same season, it was announced that the first official rugby match had taken place on Mainland China, where a team from Hong Kong had played against a team at Beijing University.

The World Cup and especially the long process of its qualifying competitions dotted around the world, illustrated the global nature of the game, as did the arrival of Latvia and the fact that the IRB now has over 50 members. But this is only a part of it – rugby is now played in well over 100 countries and the vast proportion of those countries have a properly-constituted governing union.

The point is this – one of the great strides in rugby over the last 10 years and especially in the last five years, is that the old order has recognised that it is not alone; that rugby is global, and that all the other nations where the game is played want to join the club, need sympathetic guidance, funds, technical help. They want a say.

For too long, giants of the game (the Four Home Unions plus France, South Africa, Australia and New Zealand) were exclusive, almost frightened. With the exception of France's work with FIRA (European rugby), and of odd contacts made by the English and Welsh Unions, the blinkers remained. Romania, Argentina and Fiji were colourful newcomers, but were somehow looked upon as citizens of a lower class.

Now, the old nations as a collective, as the IRB, have bravely voted themselves out as the game's sole controllers, have recognised aspirations. To their credit, they announced that receipts from the World Cup, once expenses had been deducted, would be devoted to the worldwide expansion and fostering of the game. They have created a happy problem for themselves – qualifying for future world cups will be a painfully difficult and expensive logistic problem. It is an absolute priority, however, that every nation wishing to compete will be allowed to do so and as far as humanly possible, will be helped to find the means to prepare properly. Latvia may find it difficult to win the World Cup, but at least they will be allowed to try and will become further infected with the game's essential goodness.

It is a high time for anyone, individual or country, to join the game. The current era is probably the best rugby has ever enjoyed in terms of worldwide appeal and interest. The World Cup has given the game a massive and broad-based appeal and brought along a whole new constituency. In Britain, the fact that club leagues are now established had revolutionised the game, cleared away much of the dead wood, forced people to think in commercial terms, attracted new spectators and, with the RFU at Twickenham in the lead, attracted the sort of commercial support that could only have been dreamt of 20 years ago and, to give some indication of

Former British Lion Tony O'Reilly of Ireland, now a successful businessman as chairman of the Heinz Corporation.

The future of the game – a young Scottish international.

the pace of change, five years ago. The demand for tickets for major internationals and even for the major club matches is out of all proportion to the numbers that can be accommodated. The queue of companies wishing to sponsor the game, or even to obtain some outlet in the sport, is endless.

There are more and more big games, big deals, big crowds, big players. It is no exaggeration to say that the last five years in rugby have been a profound revolution, that the game will never be the same or anything like it.

Yet it is not a smooth ride. In fact, the game is seated uncertainly on the back of a wild tiger. And it is quite obvious which is the most significant aspect of the current era, the most significant point in any discussion of the way the game is developing. It is that rugby's own success is causing problems, and that the game must resolve them before it can look forward to the fruits of the new era.

The vast increases in big occasions and crowds, in tension and expectation, have put the burden of this new era squarely on the shoulders of the players. Certainly, rugby has become far more austere and conscious of the bottom line in its commercial dealings at all levels and especially at the major clubs, but the men really needing help and understanding are the guys out on the field.

The commitment demanded of the leading players, both in the national squads and with their club teams, is staggering. In most cases and in the cause of self-betterment and the good of the team, that commitment is given without question. But emphatically, that is no reason to take the players for granted. It is also no time at all for old players and observers of yesteryear to complain about any benefits accruing to the modern player compared to what they see as the privations of their time. Rugby has changed dramatically and the old standards of old cannot be applied.

Boot money . . . an issue for rugby to confront in the 1990s.

The pressure on players, obviously, is pressure upon the principle of the game's amateurism. The pressure simply had to be released. Accordingly, the IRB announced at the end of the 1980s that players were to be allowed to take the proceeds of certain commercial activities provided that they were from activities not directly related to the game. This, in itself, was a sweeping move because it was less than a year before this announcement that the RFU, for one, completely ruled out any earnings for the players whatsoever.

But this is where the great need for care and helmsmanship comes in. That IRB announcement was to prove so woolly in practice, so open to different interpretation, that it caused more problems than if the old laws had remained. Some clarification had been forthcoming and some of the groups of players from the various national squads have launched relatively small schemes to market themselves. In my opinion, however, the IRB have to face the fact that sooner rather than later, they will have to sweep away all restrictions and allow any and all ancillary activity. They must put up the barrier to pay-for-play and win incentives and so on. For the sake of clarity, everything else must be allowable.

The question is no longer whether the erosion of strict amateurism is a good thing is no longer relevant, harsh though it may be for many to accept – and in their favour, it has to be said that much of the essential greatness and nobility of the sport has sprung from that amateurism, much of the ambience and forgiving nature of the pursuit has stemmed from the self-denial of amateurism. Unfortunately, change has become imperative. the old principle has simply been overtaken.

The quicker the game accepts that, the quicker it will set in place last laws and principles to serve the game in the same wonderful way as the old principles served rugby as it used to be. If that sort of structure can be put in place, and if every administrative body continues to regard the players as their principal asset and treats them accordingly, then the sport is in safe hands.

It is the duty of every single person involved in the game to maintain the old ambience, the old, glories, in the new commercial age and to prove that rugby need not go the way of the other sports in false competition and drugs, or the individual sportsman as spoilt brat, perhaps avoiding fair competition simply to maintain commercial value. Rugby demands no shirking, demands that all challenges are met. It would also be true to the game's essential egalitarianism if earnings were diverted chiefly to a team pool when it is the efforts of that team which has given an individual a special marketability.

It may all sound at odds with the old days and even with the immediate history. Yet there will always be a stratum to satisfy anyone – from the mini rugby players (and what a responsibility is borne by the people who run the tots' game), up through the ranks of coarse and club rugby to the top levels. There must always be a place for the poor player, the armchair viewer, for the high and ambitious achiever. Latvia must find their niche, and the All Blacks theirs. If everyone is comfortable with their role and their sporting life, then the potential of rugby is limitless.

In the first Guinness Book, the closing paragraphs discussed the feasibility of a Rugby World Cup, with qualifying groups and knock out stages, some few years before the inaugural 1987 World Cup took place.

The World Cup can be said to have completed the jigsaw, and that there are precious few avenues to explore. Yet the following article appeared via Reuters news agency, which may suggest that rugby continues to expand:

Rugby is in its infancy in China, but the pioneers of the game behind the bamboo curtain are predicting a bright future following a first taste of international competition there. It ended in a heavy defeat for a team from the Beijing Agricultural University, beaten 32–0 in front of thousands of spectators on March 16th 1992.

The victorious Hong Kong side featured seasoned players from the British territory, Chinese as well as expatriate, and the size of their win came as no surprise. But officials from both sides are hailing it as historic.

'After what has happened today, I would think that China can field a national team in five years,' said professor Cao Xihuang, the driving force behind rugby in China.

The head of the Beijing Agricultural University's physical education department added that the Beijing schools rugby union would be formed in April. 'After that we will try to push to establish an all-China Rugby Union,' said professor Cao, who pioneered rugby at the college two years ago.

Popular sports like table tennis, basketball and soccer are as yet under no threat from rugby, but the new game is already making inroads. There are nine college teams in Beijing and the game has a foothold in China's biggest city, Shanghai, where one team has been established. Hong Kong Rugby Football Union's technical director George Simpkin echoed the optimism of Professor Cao.

'If rugby really takes off in China, and the commitment is similar to that shown by these players today, then the Chinese will rapidly become a force,' Simpkin said. 'Then the rest of the world had better watch out.'

Simpkin said he would be writing to the International Rugby Football Board (IRFB) and the Federation Internationale de Rugby Amateur (FIRA) urging them to set up development programmes in China.

INDEX

Page references in italics denote illustrations.